The
Greatest
Survival Stories
Ever Told

Books by Lamar Underwood

On Dangerous Ground

Books Edited by Lamar Underwood

The Greatest Fishing Stories Ever Told
The Greatest Hunting Stories Ever Told
The Greatest War Stories Ever Told
The Greatest Survival Stories Ever Told
Lamar Underwood's Bass Almanac
Man Eaters
The Quotable Soldier

The Greatest Survival Stories Ever Told

EDITED AND WITH AN INTRODUCTION BY
LAMAR UNDERWOOD

THE LYONS PRESS
Guilford, Connecticut
An imprint of The Globe Pequot Press

Dedicated to my brother, ANDY UNDERWOOD,
who shares my fascination with
the wild, dangerous places of the world
and the literature they have inspired

The Lyons Press is an imprint of The Globe Pequot Press.

Printed in the United States of America
10 9 8 7 6 5 4 3 2 1

ISBN 1–58574–238–4
Design by Compset, Inc.

The Library of Congress Cataloging-in-Publication Data is available on file.

. . . made weak by time and fate,
but strong in will
to strive, to seek, to find,
and not to yield
—Alfred, Lord Tennyson
Ulysses

Acknowledgments

Many people are involved in the process of publishing a book, and this one is no exception. In particular, I would like to express my deep gratitude to all the contributors and to the following individuals who made this collection possible: Tony Lyons, who originally came up with the idea and trusted me to bring it off; Mark Weinstein, the Lyons Press editor who shepherded the book from original conception to printed page; Fred Courtright, for working with the various contributors and their publishers and agents to arrange permissions for reprinting the material; and to my wife Debbie, for the pages and pages of material she copied for the final manuscript.

Contents

Introduction

It was Woody Allen, I believe, who said he preferred radio to television as a young man because "the pictures were better."

That's quite a tribute to radio's power to stimulate the imagination, especially coming from a film buff like Woody. I happen to share some of the same feeling, especially when it comes to my years in Alaska as a high school student in the early fifties. Television was not available in the Fairbanks area then, and the radio was a key source of news, information, and entertainment. One program that had me glued to the set whenever it aired was a rousing little adventure called *Escape*. It began with a somber, teasing narration that went something like this:

"Tired of the everyday grind? Want to get away from it all? Ever dream of a life of romantic adventure? We offer you *ESCAPE!*" Then another voice would add, "*ESCAPE!* Designed to free you from the four walls of today for a half hour of high adventure!" Finally, the narration would switch to the second person and go for the clincher, setting up that evening's particular story to come with something like this:

"You are in the Yukon, on the trail with your malamute, on a day you were warned not to travel through the wilderness, for the temperature is somewhere in the vicinity of 75 degrees below zero Fahrenheit. You do not realize you are on the razor edge of disaster. You press on. Noon comes, a little snack. Now it's early afternoon, the sun will only be around for a couple of more hours. And then the hammer falls! Presenting tonight Jack London's classic story, 'To Build a Fire.'"

That opening hooked me—every time! I never turned the set off, disenchanted with the promo. I can't recall "To Build a Fire" being on—I merely cited it as an example of how the show was done—but I do distinctly remember such classics as Evelyn Waugh's "The Man Who Liked Dickens" and Somerset Maugham's "The Outstation" being presented.

As you might imagine, life for a teenager living in Alaska was never boring. But I turned to the radio the same way I had already learned to turn to books: to share others' lives; to live, in my mind, the adventures of others. To be a hero in the face of extreme and desperate circumstances, even though I suspected I could never be a real hero if a real test ever came along. (And, thank God, it never has!)

Reading has always been the bedrock foundation my life has rested upon. I have been fortunate to build a career, editing, around this activity that is essentially as natural and important to me as breathing. And while I enjoy reading everything from poetry to biography to a good love story, the books and stories that have me most eager to turn the pages are set in the great outdoors. They are survival stories. They take place in locations that excite my interest, and they are about men and women I admire for their fortitude.

In this book, my goal has been to make available to others, in one place, the greatest survival stories I have ever been privileged to read. Some of the accounts are from events as real as the newspaper headlines which heralded their passing. Others are pure tales of fiction, no less gripping and often, as most good fiction is, based on events of real life. Several of the stories are excerpts from complete works which I hope the reader will eventually consider. Books like *A First-Rate Tragedy, Alive, Cooper's Creek, South,* and others. They were all written with great love and skill, and they deserve as wide an audience as possible.

For someone such as myself, it has been very gratifying in recent years to see many survival books soar onto the bestseller charts. Jon Krakauer's *Into Thin Air,* Sebastian Junger's *The Perfect Storm,* and Nathaniel Philbrick's *In the Heart of the Sea* are but three examples. It has become obvious, friend, that you and I are far, far from being alone in enjoying books like these.

Recently, the *Survivor* television show has created a boom of interest in the subject that goes beyond vicarious thrills. People have become fascinated by the real "nuts and bolts" of survival, the "rope and tools," if you will, that can keep you alive in the most dire situations. Survivor equipment lists and how-to books have always been popular, and now *Survivor* is heating up even more interest. Actually, even though this is not a "how-to" book, the survival stories chosen for this anthology contain more than a few nuggets of survival wisdom and lore. In reading the tales of those who survived, and those who "went under" as the mountain men were fond of saying, one finds countless examples of what works out there—and what doesn't.

In the reading and countless re-readings of these stories, I have been curiously struck by the impression that survival tales may end in tragedy or heroism, but they almost always begin with fate, foul-ups, and plain old bad luck. Jon Krakauer, in his wonderful book *Eiger Dreams,* references a Vilhjalmur

Stefansson quote from *My Life With the Eskimo:* "Having an adventure shows that someone is incompetent, that something has gone wrong. An adventure is interesting enough in retrospect, especially to the person who didn't have it; at the time it happens it usually constitutes an exceedingly disagreeable experience."

Many adventures begin with the suddenness and randomness of a bolt of lightning. A storm descends, a boat overturns, a plane crashes, a grizzly attacks out of nowhere, a wilderness traveler becomes lost. Others—the classics of exploration, conquering the blank spaces on the old maps—begin slowly as carefully planned expeditions so skillfully manned and well supplied that seemingly nothing can stop them. Still others, the mountain-climbing tales, for instance, reveal the bold ironmen who challenge the extreme faces of danger, all of them fully expecting to emerge unscathed and victorious because of their skill and fortitude.

Hopefully, in my personal quests for a little adventure, the word "survival" will never be a part of the experience. A wilderness canoe trip is an adventure, to me. So is backpacking and fishing in the high mountains. So is flying into remote lakes and rivers in Alaska or Canada. Great adventures—all of them. And I think I know what it takes and can do what it takes to go on enjoying them. By taking care of my butt!

In the meantime, though, especially when the house is quiet and there's a little fire in the fireplace, and the reading lamp is set just right, I'm ready to take on anything!

—Lamar Underwood
March, 2001

Leiningen Versus the Ants

BY CARL STEPHENSON

From its incredible opening sentence to its last, "Leiningen Versus the Ants" qualifies as one of the most engaging adventure short stories of all time. If you've never read it, I envy you. If you have, then I'm sure you're like me and return to it every now and then to relive an enjoyable experience.

This tale was originally published by legendary editor and publisher Arnold Gingrich in *Esquire* magazine in 1938. It's probably safe to say that a hundred years from now it will still be finding new appreciative readers. Film buffs may be interested to know that "Leiningen" made it to the screen as *The Naked Jungle,* staring Charlton Heston, Eleanor Parker, and William Conrad.

★   ★   ★   ★   ★

"Unless they alter their course and there's no reason why they should, they'll reach your plantation in two days at the latest."

Leiningen sucked placidly at a cigar about the size of a corn cob and for a few seconds gazed without answering at the agitated District Commissioner. Then he took the cigar from his lips, and leaned slightly forward. With his bristling grey hair, bulky nose, and lucid eyes, he had the look of an aging and shabby eagle.

"Decent of you," he murmured, "paddling all this way just to give me the tip. But you're pulling my leg of course when you say I must do a bunk. Why, even a herd of saurians couldn't drive me from this plantation of mine."

The Brazilian official threw up lean and lanky arms and clawed the air with wildly distended fingers. "Leiningen!" he shouted. "You're insane! They're not creatures you can fight—they're an elemental—an 'act of God!' Ten miles long, two miles wide—ants, nothing but ants! And every single one of them a fiend from hell; before you can spit three times they'll eat a full-grown buffalo

1

to the bones. I tell you if you don't clear out at once there'll be nothing left of you but a skeleton picked as clean as your own plantation."

Leiningen grinned. "Act of God, my eye! Anyway, I'm not an old woman; I'm not going to run for it just because an elemental's on the way. And don't think I'm the kind of fathead who tries to fend off lightning with his fists, either. I use my intelligence, old man. With me, the brain isn't a second blindgut; I know what it's there for. When I began this model farm and plantation three years ago, I took into account all that could conceivably happen to it. And now I'm ready for anything and everything—including your ants."

The Brazilian rose heavily to his feet. "I've done my best," he gasped. "Your obstinacy endangers not only yourself, but the lives of your four hundred workers. You don't know these ants!"

Leiningen accompanied him down to the river, where the Government launch was moored. The vessel cast off. As it moved downstream, the exclamation mark neared the rail and began waving its arms frantically. Long after the launch had disappeared round the bend, Leiningen thought he could still hear that dimming, imploring voice, "You don't know them, I tell you! *You don't know them!*"

But the reported enemy was by no means unfamiliar to the planter. Before he started to work on his settlement, he had lived long enough in the country to see for himself the fearful devastations sometimes wrought by these ravenous insects in their campaigns for food. But since then he had planned measures of defence accordingly, and these, he was convinced, were in every way adequate to withstand the approaching peril.

Moreover, during his three years as a planter, Leiningen had met and defeated drought, flood, plague and all other "acts of God" which had come against him—unlike his fellow-settlers in the district, who had made little or no resistance. This unbroken success he attributed solely to the observance of his lifelong motto: *The human brain needs only to become fully aware of its powers to conquer even the elements.* Dullards reeled senselessly and aimlessly into the abyss; cranks, however brilliant, lost their heads when circumstances suddenly altered or accelerated and ran into stone walls, sluggards drifted with the current until they were caught in whirlpools and dragged under. But such disasters, Leiningen contented, merely strengthened his argument that intelligence, directed aright, invariably makes man the master of his fate.

Yes, Leiningen had always known how to grapple with life. Even here, in this Brazilian wilderness, his brain had triumphed over every difficulty and danger it had so far encountered. First he had vanquished primal forces by cunning and organization, then he had enlisted the resources of modern science to increase miraculously the yield of his plantation. And now he was sure he would prove more than a match for the "irresistible" ants.

That same evening, however, Leiningen assembled his workers. He had no intention of waiting till the news reached their ears from other sources. Most of them had been born in the district; the cry "The ants are coming!" was to them an imperative signal for instant, panic-stricken flight, a spring for life itself. But so great was the Indians' trust in Leiningen, in Leiningen's word, and in Leiningen's wisdom, that they received his curt tidings, and his orders for the imminent struggle, with the calmness with which they were given. They waited, unafraid, alert, as if for the beginning of a new game or hunt which he had just described to them. The ants were indeed mighty, but not so mighty as the boss. Let them come!

They came at noon the second day. Their approach was announced by the wild unrest of the horses, scarcely controllable now either in stall or under rider, scenting from afar a vapor instinct with horror.

It was announced by a stampede of animals, timid and savage, hurtling past each other; jaguars and pumas flashing by nimble stags of the pampas, bulky tapirs, no longer hunters, themselves hunted, outpacing fleet kinkajous, maddened herds of cattle, heads lowered, nostrils snorting, rushing through tribes of loping monkeys, chattering in a dementia of terror; then followed the creeping and springing denizens of bush and steppe, big and little rodents, snakes and lizards.

Pell-mell the rabble swarmed down the hill to the plantation, scattered right and left before the barrier of the water-filled ditch, then sped onwards to the river, where, again hindered, they fled along its bank out of sight.

This water-filled ditch was one of the. defence measures which Leiningen had long since prepared against the advent of the ants. It encompassed three sides of the plantation like a huge horseshoe. Twelve feet across, but not very deep, when dry it could hardly be described as an obstacle to either man or beast. But the ends of the "horseshoe" ran into the river which formed the northern boundary, and fourth side, of the plantation. And at the end nearer the house and outbuildings in the middle of the plantation, Leiningen had constructed a dam by means of which water from the river could be diverted into the ditch.

So now, by opening the dam, he was able to fling an imposing girdle of water, a huge quadrilateral with the river as its base, completely around the plantation, like the moat encircling a medieval city. Unless the ants were clever enough to build rafts, they had no hope of reaching the plantation, Leiningen concluded.

The twelve-foot water ditch seemed to afford in itself all the security needed. But while awaiting the arrival of the ants, Leiningen made a further improvement. The western section of the ditch ran along the edge of a tamarind wood, and the branches of some great trees reached over the water. Leiningen now had them lopped so that ants could not descend from them within the "moat."

The women and children, then the herds of cattle, were escorted by peons on rafts over the river, to remain on the other side in absolute safety until the plunderers had departed. Leiningen gave this instruction, not because he believed the non-combatants were in any danger, but in order to avoid hampering the efficiency of the defenders. "Critical situations first become crises," he explained to his men, "when oxen or women get excited."

Finally, he made a careful inspection of the "inner moat"—a smaller ditch lined with concrete, which extended around the hill on which stood the ranch house, barns, stables and other buildings. Into this concrete ditch emptied the inflow pipes from three great petrol tanks. If by some miracle the ants managed to cross the water and reach the plantation, this "rampart of petrol" would be an absolutely impassable protection for the besieged and their dwellings and stock. Such, at least, was Leiningen's opinion.

He stationed his men at irregular distances along the water ditch, the first line of defence. Then he lay down in his hammock and puffed drowsily away at his pipe until a peon came with the report that the ants had been observed far away in the South.

Leiningen mounted his horse, which at the feel of its master seemed to forget its uneasiness, and rode leisurely in the direction of the threatening offensive. The southern stretch of ditch—the upper side of the quadrilateral—was nearly three miles long; from its center one could survey the entire countryside. This was destined to be the scene of the outbreak of war between Leiningen's brain and twenty square miles of life-destroying ants.

It was a sight one could never forget. Over the range of hills, as far as eye could see, crept a darkening hem, ever longer and broader, until the shadow spread across the slope from east to west, then downwards, downwards, uncannily swift, and all the green herbage of that wide vista was being mown as by a giant sickle, leaving only the vast moving shadow, extending, deepening, and moving rapidly nearer.

When Leiningen's men, behind their barrier of water, perceived the approach of the long-expected foe, they gave vent to their suspense in screams and imprecations. But as the distance began to lessen between the "sons of hell" and the water ditch, they relapsed into silence. Before the advance of that awe-inspiring throng, their belief in the powers of the boss began to steadily dwindle.

Even Leiningen himself, who had ridden up just in time to restore their loss of heart by a display of unshakable calm, even he could not free himself from a qualm of malaise. Yonder were thousands of millions of voracious jaws bearing down upon him and only a suddenly insignificant, narrow ditch lay between him and his men and being gnawed to the bones "before you can spit three times."

Hadn't his brain for once taken on more than it could manage? If the blighters decided to rush the ditch, fill it to the brim with their corpses, there'd still be more than enough to destroy every trace of that cranium of his. The planter's chin jutted; they hadn't got him yet, and he'd see to it they never would. While he could think at all, he'd flout both death and the devil.

The hostile army was approaching in perfect formation; no human battalions, however well-drilled, could ever hope to rival the precision of that advance. Along a front that moved forward as uniformly as a straight line, the ants drew nearer and nearer to the water-ditch. Then, when they learned through their scouts the nature of the obstacle, the two outlying wings of the army detached themselves from the main body and marched down the western and eastern sides of the ditch.

This surrounding maneuver took rather more than an hour to accomplish; no doubt the ants expected that at some point they would find a crossing.

During this outflanking movement by the wings, the army on the center and southern front remained still. The besieged were therefore able to contemplate at their leisure the thumb-long, reddish black, long-legged insects; some of the Indians believed they could see, too, intent on them, the brilliant, cold eyes, and the razor-edged mandibles, of this host of infinity.

It is not easy for the average person to imagine that an animal, not to mention an insect, can *think*. But now both the European brain of Leiningen and the primitive brains of the Indians began to stir with the unpleasant foreboding that inside every single one of that deluge of insects dwelt a thought. And that thought was: Ditch or no ditch, we'll get to your flesh!

Not until four o'clock did the wings reach the "horseshoe" ends of the ditch, only to find these ran into the great river. Through some kind of secret telegraphy, the report must then have flashed very swiftly indeed along the entire enemy line. And Leiningen, riding—no longer casually—along his side of the ditch, noticed by energetic and widespread movements of troops that for some unknown reason the news of the check had its greatest effect on the southern front, where the main army was massed. Perhaps the failure to find a way over the ditch was persuading the ants to withdraw from the plantation in search of spoils more easily attainable.

An immense flood of ants, about a hundred yards in width, was pouring in a glimmering-black cataract down the far slope of the ditch. Many thousands were already drowning in the sluggish creeping flow, but they were followed by troop after troop, who clambered over their sinking comrades, and then themselves served as dying bridges to the reserves hurrying on in their rear.

Shoals of ants were being carried away by the current into the middle of the ditch, where gradually they broke asunder and then, exhausted by their struggles, vanished below the surface. Nevertheless, the wavering, floundering hundred-yard front was remorselessly if slowly advancing towards the besieged on the other bank. Leiningen had been wrong when he supposed the enemy would first have to fill the ditch with their bodies before they could cross; instead, they merely needed to act as stepping-stones, as they swam and sank, to the hordes ever pressing onwards from behind.

Near Leiningen a few mounted herdsmen awaited his orders. He sent one to the weir—the river must be damned more strongly to increase the speed and power of the water coursing through the ditch.

A second peon was dispatched to the outhouses to bring spades and petrol sprinklers. A third rode away to summon to the zone of the offensive all the men, except the observation posts, on the near-by section of the ditch, which were not yet actively threatened.

The ants were getting across far more quickly than Leiningen would have deemed possible. Impelled by the mighty cascade behind them, they struggled nearer and nearer to the inner bank. The momentum of the attack was so great that neither the tardy flow of the stream nor its downward pull could exert its proper force; and into the gap left by every submerging insect, hastened forward a dozen more.

When reinforcements reached Leiningen, the invaders were halfway over. The planter had to admit to himself that it was only by a stroke of luck for him that the ants were attempting the crossing on a relatively short front: had they assaulted simultaneously along the entire length of the ditch, the outlook for the defenders would have been black indeed.

Even as it was, it could hardly be described as rosy, though the planter seemed quite unaware that death in a gruesome form was drawing closer and closer. As the war between his brain and the "act of God" reached its climax, the very shadow of annihilation began to pale to Leiningen, who now felt like a champion in a new Olympic game, a gigantic and thrilling contest, from which he was determined to emerge victor. Such, indeed, was his aura of confidence that the Indians forgot their stupefied fear of the peril only a yard or two away; under the planter's supervision, they began fervidly digging up to the edge of the bank and throwing clods of earth and spadefuls of sand into the midst of the hostile fleet.

The petrol sprinklers, hitherto used to destroy pests and blights on the plantation, were also brought into action. Streams of evil-reeking oil now soared and fell over an enemy already in disorder through the bombardment of earth and sand.

The ants responded to these vigorous and successful measures of defence by further developments of their offensive. Entire clumps of huddling insects began to roll down the opposite bank into the water. At the same time, Leiningen noticed that the ants were now attacking along an ever-widening front. As the numbers both of his men and his petrol sprinklers were severely limited, this rapid extension of the line of battle was becoming an overwhelming danger.

To add to his difficulties, the very clods of earth they flung into that black floating carpet often whirled fragments towards the defenders' side, and here and there dark ribbons were already mounting the inner bank. True, wherever a man saw these they could still be driven back into the water by spadefuls of earth or jets of petrol. But the file of defenders was too sparse and scattered to hold off at all points these landing parties, and though the peons toiled like madmen, their plight became momently more perilous.

One man struck with his spade at an enemy clump, did not draw it back quickly enough from the water; in a trice the wooden haft swarmed with upward scurrying insects. With a curse, he dropped the spade into the ditch; too late, they were already on his body. They lost no time; wherever they encountered bare flesh they bit deeply; a few, bigger than the rest, carried in their hindquarters a sting which injected a burning and paralyzing venom. Screaming, frantic with pain, the peon danced and twirled like a dervish.

Realizing that another such casualty, yes, perhaps this alone, might plunge his men into confusion and destroy their morale, Leiningen roared in a bellow louder than the yells of the victim: "Into the petrol, idiot! Douse your paws in the petrol!" The dervish ceased his pirouette as if transfixed, then tore off his shirt and plunged his arm and the ants hanging to it up to the shoulder in one of the large open pits of petrol. But even then the fierce mandibles did not slacken; another peon had to help him squash and detach each separate insect.

Distracted by the episode, some defenders had turned away from the ditch. And now cries of fury, a thudding of spades, and a wild trampling to and fro, showed that the ants had made full use of the interval, though luckily only a few had managed to get across. The men set to work again desperately with the barrage of earth and sand. Meanwhile an old Indian, who acted as medicine-man to the plantation workers, gave the bitten peon a drink he had prepared some hours before, which, he claimed, possessed the virtue of dissolving and weakening ants' venom.

Leiningen surveyed his position. A dispassionate observer would have estimated the odds against him at a thousand to one. But then such an on-looker would have reckoned only by what he saw—the advance of myriad battalions of ants against the futile efforts of a few defenders—and not by the unseen activity that can go on in a man's brain.

For Leiningen had not erred when he decided he would fight elemental with elemental. The water in the ditch was beginning to rise; the stronger damming of the river was making itself apparent.

Visibly the swiftness and power of the masses of water increased, swirling into quicker and quicker movement its living black surface, dispersing its pattern, carrying away more and more of it on the hastening current.

Victory had been snatched from the very jaws of defeat. With a hysterical shout of joy, the peons feverishly intensified their bombardment of earth clods and sand.

And now the wide cataract down the opposite bank was thinning and ceasing, as if the ants were becoming aware that they could not attain their aim. They were scurrying back up the slope to safety.

All the troops so far hurled into the ditch had been sacrificed in vain. Drowned and floundering insects eddied in thousands along the flow, while Indians running on the bank destroyed every swimmer that reached the side.

Not until the ditch curved towards the east did the scattered ranks assemble again in a coherent mass. And now, exhausted and half-numbed, they were in no condition to ascend the bank. Fusilades of clods drove them round the bend towards the mouth of the ditch and then into the river, wherein they vanished without leaving a trace.

The news ran swiftly along the entire chain of outposts, and soon a long scattered line of laughing men could be seen hastening along the ditch towards the scene of victory.

For once they seemed to have lost all their native reserve, for it was in wild abandon now they celebrated the triumph—as if there were no longer thousands of millions of merciless, cold and hungry eyes watching them from the opposite bank, watching and waiting.

The sun sank behind the rim of the tamarind wood and twilight deepened into night. It was not only hoped but expected that the ants would remain quiet until dawn. But to defeat any forlorn attempt at a crossing, the flow of water through the ditch was powerfully increased by opening the dam still further.

In spite of this impregnable barrier, Leiningen was not yet altogether convinced that the ants would not venture another surprise attack. He ordered his men to camp along the bank overnight. He also detailed parties of them to patrol the ditch in two of his motor cars and ceaselessly to illuminate the surface of the water with headlights and electric torches.

After having taken all the precautions he deemed necessary, the farmer ate his supper with considerable appetite and went to bed. His slumbers were in no wise disturbed by the memory of the waiting, live, twenty square miles.

Dawn found a thoroughly refreshed and active Leiningen riding along the edge of the ditch. The planter saw before him a motionless and unaltering throng of besiegers. He studied the wide belt of water between them and the plantation, and for a moment almost regretted that the fight had ended so soon and so simply. In the comforting, matter-of-fact light of morning, it seemed to him now that the ants hadn't the ghost of a chance to cross the ditch. Even if they plunged headlong into it on all three fronts at once, the force of the now powerful current would inevitably sweep them away. He had got quite a thrill out of the fight—a pity it was already over.

He rode along the eastern and southern sections of the ditch and found everything in order. He reached the western section, opposite the tamarind wood, and here, contrary to the other battle fronts, he found the enemy very busy indeed. The trunks and branches of the trees and the creepers of the lianas, on the far bank of the ditch, fairly swarmed with industrious insects. But instead of eating the leaves there and then, they were merely gnawing through the stalks, so that a thick green shower fell steadily to the ground.

No doubt they were victualing columns sent out to obtain provender for the rest of the army. The discovery did not surprise Leiningen. He did not need to be told that ants are intelligent, that certain species even use others as milch cows, watchdogs and slaves. He was well aware of their power of adaptation, their sense of discipline, their marvelous talent for organization.

His belief that a foray to supply the army was in progress was strengthened when he saw the leaves that fell to the ground being dragged to the troops waiting outside the wood. Then all at once he realized the aim that rain of green was intended to serve.

Each single leaf, pulled or pushed by dozens of toiling insects, was borne straight to the edge of the ditch. Even as Macbeth watched the approach of Birnam Wood in the hands of his enemies, Leiningen saw the tamarind wood move nearer and nearer in the mandibles of the ants. Unlike the fey Scot, however, he did not lose his nerve; no witches had prophesied his doom, and if they had he would have slept just as soundly. All the same, he was forced to admit to himself that the situation was now far more ominous than that of the day before.

He had thought it impossible for the ants to build rafts for themselves—well, here they were, coming in thousands, more than enough to bridge the ditch. Leaves after leaves rustled down the slope into the water, where the current drew them away from the bank and carried them into midstream. And every single leaf carried several ants. This time the farmer did not trust to the alacrity of his messengers. He galloped away, leaning from his saddle and yelling orders as he rushed past outpost after outpost: "Bring petrol pumps to the southwest front! Issue spades to every man along the line facing the wood!" And arrived at the eastern and southern sections, he dispatched every man except the observation posts to the menaced west.

Then, as he rode past the stretch where the ants had failed to cross the day before, he witnessed a brief but impressive scene. Down the slope of the distant hill there came towards him a singular being, writhing rather than running, an animal-like blackened statue with a shapeless head and four quivering feet that knuckled under almost ceaselessly. When the creature reached the far bank of the ditch and collapsed opposite Leiningen, he recognized it as a pampas stag, covered over and over with ants.

It had strayed near the zone of the army. As usual, they had attacked its eyes first. Blinded, it had reeled in the madness of hideous torment straight into the ranks of its persecutors, and now the beast swayed to and fro in its death agony.

With a shot from his rifle Leiningen put it out of its misery. Then he pulled out his watch. He hadn't a second to lose, but for life itself he could not have denied his curiosity the satisfaction of knowing how long the ants would take—for personal reasons, so to speak. After six minutes the white polished bones alone remained. That's how he himself would look before you can— Leiningen spat once, and put spurs to his horse.

The sporting zest with which the excitement of the novel contest had inspired him the day before had now vanished; in its place was a cold and violent purpose. He would send these vermin back to the hell where they belonged, somehow, anyhow. Yes, but how was indeed the question; as things stood at present it looked as if the devils would raze him and his men from the earth instead. He had underestimated the might of the enemy; he really would have to bestir himself if he hoped to outwit them.

The biggest danger now, he decided, was the point where the western section of the ditch curved southwards. And arrived there, he found his worst expectations justified. The very power of the current had huddled the leaves and their crews of ants so close together at the bend that the bridge was almost ready.

True, streams of petrol and clumps of earth still prevented a landing. But the number of floating leaves was increasing ever more swiftly. It could not be long now before a stretch of water a mile in length was decked by a green pontoon over which the ants could rush in millions.

Leiningen galloped to the weir. The damming of the river was controlled by a wheel on its bank. The planter ordered the man at the wheel first to lower the water in the ditch almost to vanishing point, next to wait a moment, then suddenly to let the river in again. This maneuver of lowering and raising the surface, of decreasing then increasing the flow of water through the ditch was to be repeated over and over again until further notice.

This tactic was at first successful. The water in the ditch sank, and with it the film of leaves. The green fleet nearly reached the bed and the troops on the far banks swarmed down the slope to it. Then a violent flow of water at the original depth raced through the ditch, overwhelming leaves and ants, and sweeping them along.

This intermittent rapid flushing prevented just in time the almost completed fording of the ditch. But it also flung here and there squads of the enemy vanguard simultaneously up the inner bank. These seemed to know their duty only too well, and lost no time accomplishing it. The air rang with the curses of bitten Indians. They had removed their shirts and pants to detect the quicker the upwards-hastening insects; when they saw one, they crushed it; and fortunately the onslaught as yet was only by skirmishers.

Again and again, the water sank and rose, carrying leaves and drowned ants away with it. It lowered once more nearly to its bed; but this time the exhausted defenders waited in vain for the flush of destruction. Leiningen sensed disaster; something must have gone wrong with the machinery of the dam. Then a sweating peon tore up to him—

"They're over!"

While the besieged were concentrating upon the defence of the stretch opposite the wood, the seemingly unaffected line beyond the wood had become the theatre of decisive action. Here the defenders' front was sparse and scattered; everyone who could be spared had hurried away to the south.

Just as the man at the weir had lowered the water almost to the bed of the ditch, the ants on a wide front began another attempt at a direct crossing like that of the preceding day. Into the emptied bed poured an irresistible throng. Rushing across the ditch, they attained the inner bank before the slow-witted Indians fully grasped the situation. Their frantic screams dumbfounded the man at the weir. Before he could direct the river anew into the safeguarding bed he saw himself surrounded by raging ants. He ran like the others, ran for his life.

When Leiningen heard this, he knew the plantation was doomed. He wasted no time bemoaning the inevitable. For as long as there was the slightest chance of success, he had stood his ground, and now any further resistance was both useless and dangerous. He fired three revolver shots into the air—the pre-arranged signal for his men to retreat instantly within the "inner moat." Then he rode towards the ranch house.

This was two miles from the point of invasion. There was therefore time enough to prepare the second line of defence against the advent of the ants. Of the three great petrol cisterns near the house, one had already been half emptied by the constant withdrawals needed for the pumps during the fight at the water ditch. The remaining petrol in it was now drawn off through underground pipes into the concrete trench which encircled the ranchhouse and its outbuildings.

And there, drifting in twos and threes, Leiningen's men reached him. Most of them were obviously trying to preserve an air of calm and indifference, belied, however, by their restless glances and knitted brows. One could see their belief in a favorable outcome of the struggle was already considerably shaken.

The planter called his peons around him.

"Well, lads," he began, "we've lost the first round. But we'll smash the beggars yet, don't you worry. Anyone who thinks otherwise can draw his pay here and now and push off. There are rafts enough and to spare on the river and plenty of time still to reach 'em."

Not a man stirred.

Leiningen acknowledged his silent vote of confidence with a laugh that was half a grunt. "That's the stuff, lads. Too bad if you'd missed the rest of the show, eh? Well, the fun won't start till morning. Once the blighters turn tail, there'll be plenty of work for everyone and higher wages all round. And now run along and get something to eat; you've earned it all right."

In the excitement of the fight the greater part of the day had passed without the men once pausing to snatch a bite. Now that the ants were for the time being out of sight, and the "wall of petrol" gave a stronger feeling of security, hungry stomachs began to assert their claims.

The bridges over the concrete ditch were removed. Here and there solitary ants had reached the ditch; they gazed at the petrol meditatively, then scurried back again. Apparently they had little interest at the moment for what lay beyond the evil-reeking barrier; the abundant spoils of the plantation were the main attraction. Soon the trees, shrubs and beds for miles around were hulled with ants zealously gobbling the yield of long weary months of strenuous toil.

As twilight began to fall, a cordon of ants marched around the petrol trench, but as yet made no move towards its brink. Leiningen posted sentries with headlights and electric torches, then withdrew to his office, and began to reckon up his losses. He estimated these as large, but, in comparison with his bank balance, by no means unbearable. He worked out in some detail a scheme of intensive cultivation which would enable him, before very long, to more than compensate himself for the damage now being wrought to his crops. It was with a contented mind that he finally betook himself to bed where he slept deeply until dawn, undisturbed by any thought that next day little more might be left of him than a glistening skeleton.

He rose with the sun and went out on the flat roof of his house. And a scene like one from Dante lay around him; for miles in every direction there was nothing but a black, glittering multitude, a multitude of rested, sated, but none the less voracious ants: yes, look as far as one might, one could see nothing but that rustling black throng, except in the north, where the great river drew a boundary they could not hope to pass. But even the high stone breakwater, along the bank of the river, which Leiningen had built as a defence against inundations, was, like the paths, the shorn trees and shrubs, the ground itself, black with ants.

So their greed was not glutted in razing that vast plantation? Not by a long chalk; they were all the more eager now on a rich and certain booty— four hundred men, numerous horses, and bursting granaries.

At first it seemed that the petrol trench would serve its purpose. The besiegers sensed the peril of swimming it, and made no move to plunge blindly over its brink. Instead they devised a better maneuver; they began to collect shreds of bark, twigs and dried leaves and dropped these into the petrol. Everything green, which could have been similarly used, had long since been eaten. After a time, though, a long procession could be seen bringing from the west the tamarind leaves used as rafts the day before.

Since the petrol, unlike the water in the outer ditch, was perfectly still, the refuse stayed where it was thrown. It was several hours before the ants succeeded in covering an appreciable part of the surface. At length, however, they were ready to proceed to a direct attack.

Their storm troops swarmed down the concrete side, scrambled over the supporting surface of twigs and leaves, and impelled these over the few remaining streaks of open petrol until they reached the other side. Then they began to climb up this to make straight for the helpless garrison.

During the entire offensive, the planter sat peacefully, watching them with interest, but not stirring a muscle. Moreover, he had ordered his men not to disturb in any way whatever the advancing horde. So they squatted listlessly along the bank of the ditch and waited for a sign from the boss.

The petrol was now covered with ants. A few had climbed the inner concrete wall and were scurrying towards the defenders.

"Everyone back from the ditch!" roared Leiningen. The men rushed away, without the slightest idea of his plan. He stooped forward and cautiously dropped into the ditch a stone which split the floating carpet and its living freight, to reveal a gleaming patch of petrol. A match spurted, sank down to the oily surface—Leiningen sprang back; in a flash a towering rampart of fire encompassed the garrison.

This spectacular and instant repulse threw the Indians into ecstasy. They applauded, yelled and stamped, like children at a pantomime. Had it not been for the awe in which they held the boss, they would infallibly have carried him shoulder high.

It was some time before the petrol burned down to the bed of the ditch, and the wall of smoke and flame began to lower. The ants had retreated in a wide circle from the devastation, and innumerable charred fragments along the outer bank showed that the flames had spread from the holocaust in the ditch well into the ranks beyond, where they had wrought havoc far and wide.

Yet the perseverance of the ants was by no means broken; indeed, each setback seemed only to whet it. The concrete cooled, the flicker of the dying flames wavered and vanished, petrol from the second tank poured into the trench—and the ants marched forward anew to the attack.

The foregoing scene repeated itself in every detail, except that on this occasion less time was needed to bridge the ditch, for the petrol was now already filmed by a layer of ash. Once again they withdrew; once again petrol flowed into the ditch. Would the creatures never learn that their self-sacrifice was utterly senseless? It really was senseless, wasn't it? Yes, of course it was senseless—provided the defenders had an *unlimited* supply of petrol.

When Leiningen reached this stage of reasoning, he felt for the first time since the arrival of the ants that his confidence was deserting him. His skin began to creep; he loosened his collar. Once the devils were over the trench there wasn't a chance in hell for him and his men. God, what a prospect, to be eaten alive like that!

For the third time the flames immolated the attacking troops, and burned down to extinction. Yet the ants were coming on again as if nothing had happened. And meanwhile Leiningen had made a discovery that chilled him to the bone—petrol was no longer flowing into the ditch. Something must be blocking the outflow pipe of the third and last cistern—a snake or a dead rat? Whatever it was, the ants could be held off no longer, unless petrol could by some method be led from the cistern into the ditch.

Then Leiningen remembered that in an outhouse near-by were two old disused fire engines. Spry as never before in their lives, the peons dragged them out of the shed, connected their pumps to the cistern, uncoiled and laid the hose. They were just in time to aim a stream of petrol at a column of ants that had already crossed and drive them back down the incline into the ditch. Once more an oily girdle surrounded the garrison, once more it was possible to hold the position—for the moment.

It was obvious, however, that this last resource meant only the postponement of defeat and death. A few of the peons fell on their knees and began to pray; others, shrieking insanely, fired their revolvers at the black, advancing masses, as if they felt their despair was pitiful enough to sway fate itself to mercy.

At length, two of the men's nerves broke: Leiningen saw a naked Indian leap over the north side of the petrol trench, quickly followed by a second. They sprinted with incredible speed towards the river. But their fleetness did not save them; long before they could attain the rafts, the enemy covered their bodies from head to foot.

In the agony of their torment, both sprang blindly into the wide river, where enemies no less sinister awaited them. Wild screams of mortal anguish informed the breathless onlookers that crocodiles and sword-toothed piranhas were no less ravenous than ants, and even nimbler in reaching their prey.

In spite of this bloody warning, more and more men showed they were making up their minds to run the blockade. Anything, even a fight midstream against alligators, seemed better than powerlessly waiting for death to come and slowly consume their living bodies.

Leiningen flogged his brain till it reeled. Was there nothing on earth could sweep this devils' spawn back into the hell from which it came?

Then out of the inferno of his bewilderment rose a terrifying inspiration. Yes, one hope remained, and one alone. It might be possible to dam the great river completely, so that its waters would fill not only the water ditch but overflow into the entire gigantic "saucer" of land in which lay the plantation.

The far bank of the river was too high for the waters to escape that way. The stone breakwater ran between the river and the plantation; its only gaps occurred where the "horseshoe" ends of the water-ditch passed into the river. So its waters would not only be forced to inundate into the plantation, they would also be held there by the breakwater until they rose to its own high level. In half an hour, perhaps even earlier, the plantation and its hostile army of occupation would be flooded.

The ranch house and outbuildings stood upon rising ground. Their foundations were higher than the breakwater, so the flood would not reach them. And any remaining ants trying to ascend the slope could be repulsed by petrol.

It was possible—yes, if one could only get to the dam! A distance of nearly two miles lay between the ranch house and the weir—two miles of ants. Those two peons had managed only a fifth of that distance at the cost of their lives. Was there an Indian daring enough after that to run the gauntlet five times as far? Hardly likely; and if there were, his prospect of getting back was almost nil.

No, there was only one thing for it, he'd have to make the attempt himself; he might just as well be running as sitting still, anyway, when the ants finally got him. Besides, there *was* a bit of a chance. Perhaps the ants weren't so almighty, after all; perhaps he had allowed the mass suggestion of that evil black throng to hypnotize him, just as a snake fascinates and overpowers.

The ants were building their bridges. Leiningen got up on a chair. "Hey, lads, listen to me!" he cried. Slowly and listlessly, from all sides of the trench, the men began to shuffle towards him, the apathy of death already stamped on their faces.

"Listen, lads!" he shouted. "You're frightened of those beggars, but you're a damn sight more frightened of me, and I'm proud of you. There's still a chance to save our lives—by flooding the plantation from the river. Now one of you might manage to get as far as the weir—but he'd never come back. Well, I'm not going to let you try it; if I did I'd be worse than one of those ants. No, I called the tune, and now I'm going to pay the piper.

"The moment I'm over the ditch, set fire to the petrol. That'll allow time for the flood to do the trick. Then all you have to do is to wait here all

snug and quiet till I'm back. Yes, I'm coming back, trust me"—he grinned—
"when I've finished my slimming-cure."

He pulled on high leather boots, drew heavy gauntlets over his hands,
and stuffed the spaces between breeches and boots, gauntlets and arms, shirt
and neck, with rags soaked in petrol. With close-fitting mosquito goggles he
shielded his eyes, knowing too well the ants' dodge of first robbing their victim
of sight. Finally, he plugged his nostrils and ears with cotton-wool, and let the
peons drench his clothes with petrol.

He was about to set off, when the old Indian medicine man came up
to him; he had a wondrous salve, he said, prepared from a species of chafer
whose odor was intolerable to ants. Yes, this odor protected these chafers from
the attacks of even the most murderous ants. The Indian smeared the boss'
boots, his gauntlets, and his face over and over with the extract.

Leiningen then remembered the paralyzing effect of ants' venom, and
the Indian gave him a gourd full of medicine he had administered to the bitten
peon at the water ditch. The planter drank it down without noticing its bitter
taste; his mind was already at the weir.

He started off towards the northwest corner of the trench. With a
bound he was over—and among the ants.

The beleaguered garrison had no opportunity to watch Leiningen's
race against death. The ants were climbing the inner bank again—the lurid
ring of petrol blazed aloft. For the fourth time that day the reflection from the
fire shone on the sweating faces of the imprisoned men, and on the reddish-
black cuirasses of their oppressors. The red and blue, dark-edged flames leaped
vividly now, celebrating what? The funeral pyre of the four hundred, or of the
hosts of destruction?

Leiningen ran. He ran in long, equal strides, with only one thought,
one sensation, in his being—he *must* get through. He dodged all trees and
shrubs; except for the split seconds his soles touched the ground the ants
should have no opportunity to alight on him. That they would get to him
soon, despite the salve on his boots, the petrol in his clothes, he realized only
too well, but he knew even more surely that he must, and that he would, get to
the weir.

Apparently the salve was some use after all; not until he had reached
halfway did he feel ants under his clothes, and a few on his face. Mechanically,
in his stride, he struck at them, scarcely conscious of their bites. He saw he was
drawing appreciably nearer the weir—the distance grew less and less—sank to
five hundred—three—two—one hundred yards.

Then he was at the weir and gripping the ant-hulled wheel. Hardly had he seized it when a horde of infuriated ants flowed over his hands, arms and shoulders. He started the wheel—before it turned once on its axis the swarm covered his face. Leiningen strained like a madman, his lips pressed tight; if he opened them to draw breath. . . .

He turned and turned; slowly the dam lowered until it reached the bed of the river. Already the water was overflowing the ditch. Another minute, and the river was pouring through the near-by gap in the breakwater. The flooding of the plantation had begun.

Leiningen let go the wheel. Now, for the first time, he realized he was coated from head to foot with a layer of ants. In spite of the petrol, his clothes were full of them, several had got to his body or were clinging to his face. Now that he had completed his task, he felt the smart raging over his flesh from the bites of sawing and piercing insects.

Frantic with pain, he almost plunged into the river. To be ripped and slashed to shreds by piranhas? Already he was running the return journey, knocking ants from his gloves and jacket, brushing them from his bloodied face, squashing them to death under his clothes.

One of the creatures bit him just below the rim of his goggles; he managed to tear it away, but the agony of the bite and its etching acid drilled into the eye nerves; he saw now through circles of fire into a milky mist, then he ran for a time almost blinded, knowing that if he once tripped and fell. . . . The old Indian's brew didn't seem much good; it weakened the poison a bit, but didn't get rid of it. His heart pounded as if it would burst; blood roared in his ears; a giant's fist battered his lungs.

Then he could see again, but the burning girdle of petrol appeared infinitely far away; he could not last half that distance. Swift-changing pictures flashed through his head, episodes in his life, while in another part of his brain a cool and impartial onlooker informed this ant-blurred, gasping, exhausted bundle named Leiningen that such a rushing panorama of scenes from one's past is seen only in the moment before death.

A stone in the path . . . too weak to avoid it . . . the planter stumbled and collapsed. He tried to rise . . . he must be pinned under a rock . . . it was impossible . . . the slightest movement was impossible. . . .

Then all at once he saw, starkly clear and huge, and, right before his eyes, furred with ants, towering and swaying in its death agony, the pampas stag. In six minutes—gnawed to the bones. God, he *couldn't* die like that! And something outside him seemed to drag him to his feet. He tottered. He began to stagger forward again.

Through the blazing ring hurtled an apparition which, as soon as it reached the ground on the inner side, fell full length and did not move. Leiningen, at the moment he made that leap through the flames, lost consciousness for the first time in his life. As he lay there, with glazing eyes and lacerated face, he appeared a man returned from the grave. The peons rushed to him, stripped off his clothes, tore away the ants from a body that seemed almost one open wound; in some places the bones were showing. They carried him into the ranch house.

As the curtain of flame lowered, one could see in place of the illimitable host of ants an extensive vista of water. The thwarted river had swept over the plantation, carrying with it the entire army. The water had collected and mounted in the great "saucer," while the ants had in vain attempted to reach the hill on which stood the ranch house. The girdle of flames held them back.

And so imprisoned between water and fire, they had been delivered into the annihilation that was their god. And near the farther mouth of the water-ditch, where the stone mole had its second gap, the ocean swept the lost battalions into the river, to vanish forever.

The ring of fire dwindled as the water mounted to the petrol trench, and quenched the dimming flames. The inundation rose higher and higher: because its outflow was impeded by the timber and underbrush it had carried along with it, its surface required some time to reach the top of the high stone breakwater and discharge over it the rest of the shattered army.

It swelled over ant-stippled shrubs and bushes, until it washed against the foot of the knoll whereon the besieged had taken refuge. For a while an alluvial of ants tried again and again to attain this dry land, only to be repulsed by streams of petrol back into the merciless flood.

Leiningen lay on his bed, his body swathed from head to foot in bandages. With fomentations and salves, they had managed to stop the bleeding, and had dressed his many wounds. Now they thronged around him, one question in every face. Would he recover? "He won't die," said the old man who had bandaged him, "if he doesn't want to."

The planter opened his eyes. "Everything in order?" he asked.

"They're gone," said his nurse. "To hell." He held out to his master a gourd full of a powerful sleeping draught. Leiningen gulped it down.

"I told you I'd come back," he murmured, "even if I am a bit streamlined." He grinned and shut his eyes. He slept.

To Build a Fire

BY JACK LONDON

Cast your mind back over time for a moment, if you will, and try to recall the coldest weather you've ever experienced. Well, it's about to get a lot colder.

Perhaps this is the classic of all survival tales. You can throw all the adjectives you wish at it, and they will all stick: gripping, stirring, surprising . . . the list would be endless.

London wrote this one in 1907, and it is set in the Yukon during the Gold Rush, familiar terrain and time for London.

Jack London (1876–1916) was an extraordinary man, whose life has always reminded me of a shooting star, brilliant, irresistible, suddenly gone. Not only did he write volumes of wonderful prose created from his seafaring and wilderness trail adventures, he was a true champion of the weak and the poor, the abused people of his time. What a man he was! And what a writer!

★   ★   ★   ★   ★

Day had broken cold and gray, exceedingly cold and gray, when the man turned aside from the main Yukon trail and climbed the high earth-bank, where a dim and little-travelled trail led eastward through the fat spruce timberland. It was a steep bank, and he paused for breath at the top, excusing the act to himself by looking at his watch. It was nine o'clock. There was no sun nor hint of sun, though there was not a cloud in the sky. It was a clear day, and yet there seemed an intangible pall over the face of things, a subtle gloom that made the day dark, and that was due to the absence of sun. This fact did not worry the man. He was used to the lack of sun. It had been days since he had seen the sun, and he knew that a few more days must pass before that cheerful orb, due south, would just peep above the skyline and dip immediately from view.

The man flung a look back along the way he had come. The Yukon lay a mile wide and hidden under three feet of ice. On top of this ice were as many feet of snow. It was all pure white, rolling in gentle undulations where the ice jams of the freeze-up had formed. North and south, as far as his eye could see, it was unbroken white, save for a dark hairline that curved and twisted from around the spruce-covered island to the south, and that curved and twisted away into the north, where it disappeared behind another spruce-covered island. This dark hairline was the trail—the main trail—that led south five hundred miles to the Chilcoot Pass, Dyea, and salt water; and that led north seventy miles to Dawson, and still on to the north a thousand miles to Nulato, and finally to St. Michael, on Bering Sea, a thousand miles and half a thousand more.

But all this—this mysterious, far-reaching hairline trail, the absence of sun from the sky, the tremendous cold, and the strangeness and weirdness of it all—made no impression on the man. It was not because he was long used to it. He was a newcomer in the land, a *chechaquo,* and this was his first winter. The trouble with him was that he was without imagination. He was quick and alert in the things of life, but only in things, and not in the significances. Fifty degrees below zero meant eighty-odd degrees of frost. Such fact impressed him as being cold and uncomfortable, and that was all. It did not lead him to meditate upon his frailty as a creature of temperature, and upon man's fraility in general, able only to live within certain narrow limits of heat and cold; and from there on it did not lead him to the conjectural field of immortality and man's place in the universe. Fifty degrees below zero stood for a bite of frost that hurt and that must be guarded against by the use of mittens, ear flaps, warm moccasins, and thick socks. Fifty degrees below zero was to him just precisely fifty degrees below zero. That there should be anything more to it than that was a thought that never entered his head.

As he turned to go, he spat speculatively. There was a sharp, explosive crackle that startled him. He spat again. And again, in the air, before it could fall to the snow, the spittle crackled. He knew that at fifty below spittle crackled on the snow, but this spittle had crackled in the air. Undoubtedly it was colder than fifty below—how much colder he did not know. But the temperature did not matter. He was bound for the old claim on the left fork of Henderson Creek, where the boys were already. They had come over across the divide from the Indian Creek country, while he had come the roundabout way to take a look at the possibilities of getting out logs in the spring from the islands in the Yukon. He would be in to camp by six o'clock; a bit after dark, it was true, but the boys would be there, a fire would be going, and a hot supper would be ready. As for lunch, he pressed his hand against the protruding bundle under his jacket. It was also under his shirt, wrapped up in a handkerchief and lying against the naked skin. It was the only way to keep the biscuits from freezing. He smiled agreeably to himself as he thought of those biscuits, each cut open and sopped in bacon grease, and each enclosing a generous slice of fried bacon.

He plunged in among the big spruce trees. The trail was faint. A foot of snow had fallen since the last sled had passed over, and he was glad he was without a sled, travelling light. In fact, he carried nothing but the lunch wrapped in the handkerchief. He was surprised, however, at the cold. It certainly was cold, he concluded, as he rubbed his numb nose and cheekbones with his mittened hand. He was a warm-whiskered man, but the hair on his face did not protect the high cheek-bones and the eager nose that thrust itself aggressively into the frosty air.

At the man's heels trotted a dog, a big native husky, the proper wolf dog, gray-coated and without any visible or temperamental difference from its brother, the wild wolf. The animal was depressed by the tremendous cold. It knew that it was no time for travelling. Its instinct told it a truer tale than was told to the man by the man's judgment. In reality, it was not merely colder than fifty below zero; it was colder than sixty below, than seventy below. It was seventy-five below zero. Since the freezing point is thirty-two above zero, it meant that one hundred and seven degrees of frost obtained. The dog did not know anything about thermometers. Possibly in its brain there was no sharp consciousness of a condition of very cold such as was in the man's brain. But the brute had its instinct. It experienced a vague but menacing apprehension that subdued it and made it slink along at the man's heels, and that made it question eagerly every unwonted movement of the man as if expecting him to go into camp or to seek shelter somewhere and build a fire. The dog had learned fire, and it wanted fire, or else to burrow under the snow and cuddle its warmth away from the air.

The frozen moisture of its breathing had settled on its fur in a fine powder of frost, and especially were its jowls, muzzle and eyelashes whitened by its crystalled breath. The man's red beard and mustache were likewise frosted, but more solidly, the deposit taking the form of ice and increasing with every warm, moist breath he exhaled. Also, the man was chewing tobacco, and the muzzle of ice held his lips so rigidly that he was unable to clear his chin when he expelled the juice. The result was that a crystal beard of the color and solidity of amber was increasing its length on his chin. If he fell down it would shatter itself, like glass, into brittle fragments. But he did not mind the appendage. It was the penalty all tobacco chewers paid in that country, and he had been out before in two cold snaps. They had not been so cold as this, but by the spirit thermometer at Sixty-Mile he knew that they had been registered at fifty below and at fifty-five.

He held on through the level stretch of woods for several miles, crossed a wide flat of nigger heads, and dropped down a bank to the frozen bed of a small stream. This was Henderson Creek, and he knew he was ten miles from the forks. He looked at his watch. It was ten o'clock. He was making four miles an hour, and he calculated that he would arrive at the forks at half-past twelve. He decided to celebrate that event by eating his lunch there.

The dog dropped in again at his heels, with a tail drooping discouragement, as the man swung along the creek bed. The furrow of the old sled trail was plainly visible, but a dozen inches of snow covered the marks of the last runners. In a month no man had come up or down that silent creek. The man held steadily on. He was not much given to thinking, and just then particularly he had nothing to think about save that he would eat lunch at the forks and that at six o'clock he would be in camp with the boys. There was nobody to talk to; and, had there been, speech would have been impossible because of ice muzzle on his mouth. So he continued monotonously to chew tobacco and to increase the length of his amber beard.

Once in a while the thought reiterated itself that it was very cold and that he had never experienced such cold. As he walked along he rubbed his cheekbones and nose with the back of his mittened hand. He did this automatically, now and again changing hands. But, rub as he would, the instant he stopped his cheekbones went numb, and the following instant the end of his nose went numb. He was sure to frost his cheeks; he knew that, and experienced a pang of regret that he had not devised a nose strap of the sort Bud wore in cold snaps. Such a strap passed across the cheeks, as well, and saved them. But it didn't matter much, after all. What were frosted cheeks? A bit painful, that was all; they were never serious.

Empty as the man's mind was of thoughts, he was keenly observant, and he noticed the changes in the creek, the curves and bends and timber jams, and always he sharply noted where he placed his feet. Once, coming around a bend he shied abruptly, like a startled horse, curved away from the place where he had been walking, and retreated several paces back along the trail. The creek he knew was frozen clear to the bottom—no creek could contain water in that arctic winter—but he knew also that there were springs that bubbled out from the hillsides and ran along under the snow and on top the ice of the creek. He knew that the coldest snaps never froze these springs, and he knew likewise their danger. They were traps. They hid pools of water under the snow that might be three inches deep, or three feet. Sometimes a skin of ice half an inch thick covered them, and in turn was covered by the snow. Sometimes there were alternate layers of water and ice skin, so that when one broke through he kept on breaking through for a while, sometimes wetting himself to the waist.

That was why he had shied in such panic. He had felt the give under his feet and heard the crackle of a snow-hidden ice skin. And to get his feet wet in such a temperature meant trouble and danger. At the very least it meant delay, for he would be forced to stop and build a fire, and under its protection to bare his feet while he dried his socks and moccasins. He stood and studied the creek bed and its banks, and decided that the flow of water came from his right. He reflected awhile, rubbing his nose and cheeks, then skirted to the left, stepping gingerly and testing the footing for each step. Once clear of the danger, he took a fresh chew of tobacco and swung along at his four-mile gait.

In the course of the next two hours he came upon several similar traps. Usually the snow above the hidden pools had a sunken, candied appearance that advertised the danger. Once again, however, he had a close call; and once, suspecting danger, he compelled the dog to go on in front. The dog did not want to go. It hung back until the man shoved it forward, and then it went quickly across the white, unbroken surface. Suddenly it broke through, floundered to one side, and got away to firmer footing. It had wet its forefeet and legs, and almost immediately the water that clung to it turned to ice. It made quick efforts to lick the ice off its legs, then dropped down in the snow and began to bite out the ice that had formed between the toes. This was a matter of instinct. To permit the ice to remain would mean sore feet. It did not know this. It merely obeyed the mysterious prompting that arose from the deep crypts of its being. But the man knew, having achieved a judgment on the subject, and he removed the mitten from his right hand and helped tear out the ice particles. He did not expose his fingers more than a minute, and was astonished at the swift numbness that smote them. It certainly was cold. He pulled on the mitten hastily, and beat the hand savagely across his chest.

At twelve o'clock the day was at its brightest. Yet the sun was too far south on its winter journey to clear the horizon. The bulge of the earth intervened between it and Henderson Creek, where the man walked under a clear sky at noon and cast no shadow. At half-past twelve, to the minute, he arrived at the forks of the creek. He was pleased at the speed he had made. If he kept it up, he would certainly be with the boys by six. He unbuttoned his jacket and shirt and drew forth his lunch. The action consumed no more than a quarter of a minute, yet in that brief moment the numbness laid hold of the exposed fingers. He did not put the mitten on, but, instead, struck the fingers a dozen sharp smashes against his leg. Then he sat down on a snow-covered log to eat. The sting that followed upon the striking of his fingers against his leg ceased so quickly that he was startled. He had had no chance to take a bite of biscuit. He struck the fingers repeatedly and returned them to the mitten, baring the other hand for the purpose of eating. He tried to take a mouthful, but the ice muzzle prevented. He had forgotten to build a fire and thaw out. He chuckled at his foolishness, and as he chuckled he noted the numbness creeping into the exposed fingers. Also, he noted that the stinging which had first come to his toes when he sat down was already passing away. He wondered whether the toes were warm or numb. He moved them inside the moccasins and decided that they were numb.

He pulled the mitten on hurriedly and stood up. He was a bit frightened. He stamped up and down until the stinging returned into the feet. It certainly was cold, was his thought. That man from Sulphur Creek had spoken the truth when telling how cold it sometimes got in the country. And he had laughed at him at the time! That showed one must not be too sure of things. There was no mistake about it, it *was* cold. He strode up and down, stamping his feet and threshing his arms, until reassured by the returning warmth. Then he got out matches and proceeded to make a fire. From the undergrowth, where high water of the previous spring had lodged a supply of seasoned twigs, he got his firewood. Working carefully from a small beginning, he soon had a roaring fire, over which he thawed the ice from his face and in the protection of which he ate his biscuits. For the moment the cold of space was outwitted. The dog took satisfaction in the fire, stretching out close enough for warmth and far enough away to escape being singed.

When the man had finished, he filled his pipe and took his comfortable time over a smoke, then he pulled on his mittens, settled the ear flaps of his cap firmly about his ears, and took the creek trail up the left fork. The dog was disappointed and yearned back towards the fire. This man did not know cold. Possibly all the generations of his ancestry had been ignorant of cold, of real cold, of cold one hundred and seven degrees below freezing point. But the dog knew; all its ancestry knew, and it had inherited the knowledge. And it knew that it was not good to walk abroad in such fearful cold. It was the time to lie snug in a hole in the snow and wait for a curtain of cloud to be drawn across the face of outer space whence this cold came. On the other hand, there was no keen intimacy between the dog and the man. The one was the toil slave of the other, and the only caresses it had ever received were the caresses of the whip lash and of harsh and menacing throat sounds that threatened the whip lash. So the dog made no effort to communicate its apprehension to the man. It was not concerned in the welfare of the man; it was for its own sake that it yearned back toward the fire. But the man whistled, and spoke to it with the sound of whip lashes, and the dog swung in at the man's heels and followed after.

The man took a chew of tobacco and proceeded to start a new amber beard. Also, his moist breath quickly powdered with white his mustache, eyebrows, and lashes. There did not seem to be so many springs on the left fork of the Henderson, and for half an hour the man saw no signs of any. And then it happened. At a place where there were no signs, where the soft, unbroken snow seemed to advertise solidity beneath, the man broke through. It was not deep. He wet himself halfway to the knees before he floundered out to the firm crust.

He was angry, and cursed his luck aloud. He had hoped to get into camp with the boys at six o'clock, and this would delay him an hour, for he would have to build a fire and dry out his footgear. This was imperative at that low temperature—he knew that much; and he turned aside to the bank, which he climbed. On top, tangled in the underbrush about the trunks of several small spruce trees, was a high-water deposit of dry firewood—sticks and twigs, principally, but also larger portions of seasoned branches and fine, dry, last year's grasses. He threw down several large pieces on top of the snow. This served for a foundation and prevented the young flame from drowning itself in the snow it otherwise would melt. The flame he got by touching a match to a small shred of birch bark that he took from his pocket. This burned even more readily than paper. Placing it on the foundation, he fed the young flame with wisps of dry grass and with the tiniest dry twigs.

He worked slowly and carefully, keenly aware of his danger. Gradually, as the flame grew stronger, he increased the size of the twigs with which he fed it. He squatted in the snow, pulling the twigs out from their entanglement in the brush and feeding directly to the flame. He knew there must be no failure. When it is seventy-five below zero, a man must not fail in his first attempt to build a fire—that is, if his feet are wet. If his feet are dry, and he fails, he can run along the trail for half a mile and restore his circulation. But the circulation of wet and freezing feet cannot be restored by running when it is seventy-five below. No matter how fast he runs, the wet feet will freeze the harder.

All this the man knew. The old-timer on Sulphur Creek had told him about it the previous fall, and now he was appreciating the advice. Already all sensation had gone out of his feet. To build the fire he had been forced to remove his mittens, and the fingers had quickly gone numb. His pace of four miles an hour had kept his heart pumping blood to the surface of his body and to all the extremities. But the instant he stopped, the action of the pump eased down. The cold of space smote the unprotected tip of the planet, and he, being on that unprotected tip, received the full force of the blow. The blood of his body recoiled before it. The blood was alive, like the dog, and like the dog it wanted to hide away and cover itself up from the fearful cold. So long as he walked four miles an hour, he pumped the blood, willy–nilly, to the surface; but now it ebbed away and sank down into the recesses of his body. The extremities were the first to feel its absence. His wet feet froze the faster, and his exposed fingers numbed the faster, though they had not yet begun to freeze. Nose and cheeks were already freezing, while the skin of all his body chilled as it lost its blood.

But he was safe. Toes and nose and cheeks would be only touched by the frost, for the fire was beginning to burn with strength. He was feeding it with twigs the size of his finger. In another minute he would be able to feed it with branches the size of his wrist, and then he could remove his wet footgear, and, while it dried, he could keep his naked feet warm by the fire, rubbing them at first, of course, with snow. The fire was a success. He was safe. He remembered the advice of the old–timer on Sulphur Creek, and smiled. The old–timer had been very serious in laying down the law that no man must travel alone in the Klondike after fifty below. Well, here he was; he had had the accident; he was alone; and he had saved himself. Those old–timers were rather womanish, some of them, he thought. All a man had to do was to keep his head, and he was all right. Any man who was a man could travel alone. But it was surprising, the rapidity with which his cheeks and nose were freezing. And he had not thought his fingers could go lifeless in so short a time. Lifeless they were, for he could scarcely make them move together to grip a twig, and they seemed remote from his body and from him. When he touched a twig, he had to look and see whether or not he had hold of it. The wires were pretty well down between him and his finger ends.

All of which counted for little. There was the fire, snapping and crackling and promising life with every dancing flame. He started to untie his moccasins. They were coated with ice; the thick German socks were like sheaths of iron halfway to the knees; and the moccasin strings were like rods of steel all twisted and knotted as by some conflagration. For a moment he tugged with his numb fingers, then, realizing the folly of it, he drew his sheath knife.

But before he could cut the strings, it happened. It was his own fault or, rather, his mistake. He should not have built the fire under the spruce tree. He should have built it in the open. But it had been easier to pull the twigs from the brush and drop them directly on the fire. Now the tree under which he had done this carried a weight of snow on its boughs. No wind had blown for weeks, and each bough was full freighted. Each time he had pulled a twig he had communicated a slight agitation to the tree—an imperceptible agitation, so far as he was concerned, but an agitation sufficient to bring about the disaster. High up in the tree one bough capsized its load of snow. This fell on the boughs beneath, capsizing them. This process continued, spreading out and involving the whole tree. It grew like an avalanche, and it descended upon the man and the fire, and the fire was blotted out! Where it had burned was a mantle of fresh and disordered snow.

The man was shocked. It was as though he had just heard his own sentence of death. For a moment he sat and stared at the spot where the fire had been. Then he grew very calm. Perhaps the old-timer on Sulphur Creek was right. If he had only had a trail mate he would have been in no danger now. The trail mate could have built the fire. Well, it was up to him to build the fire over again, and this second time there must be no failure. Even if he succeeded, he would most likely lose some toes. His feet must be badly frozen by now, and there would be some time before the second fire was ready.

Such were his thoughts, but he did not sit and think them. He was busy all the time they were passing through his mind. He made a new foundation for a fire, this time out in the open, where no treacherous tree could blot it out. Next he gathered dry grasses and tiny twigs from the high-water flotsam. He could not bring his fingers together to pull them out, but he was able to gather them by the handful. In this way he got many rotten twigs and bits of green moss that were undesirable, but it was the best he could do. He worked methodically, even collecting an armful of larger branches to be used later when the fire gathered strength. And all the while the dog sat and watched him, a certain wistfulness in its eyes, for it looked upon him as the fire provider, and the fire was slow in coming.

When all was ready, the man reached in his pocket for a second piece of birch bark. He knew the bark was there, and though he could not feel it with his fingers, he could hear its crisp rustling as he fumbled for it. Try as he would, he could not clutch hold of it. And all the time, in his consciousness, was the knowledge that each instant his feet were freezing. This thought tended to put him in a panic, but he fought against it and kept calm. He pulled on his mittens with his teeth, and threshed his arms back and forth, beating his hands with all his might against his sides. He did this sitting down, and he stood up to do it; and all the while the dog sat in the snow, its wolf brush of a tail curled around warmly over its forefeet, its sharp wolf ears pricked forward intently as it watched the man. And the man, as he beat and threshed with his arms and hands, felt a great surge of envy as he regarded the creature that was warm and secure in its natural covering.

After a time he was aware of the first faraway signals of sensations in his beaten fingers. The faint tingling grew stronger till it evolved into a stinging ache that was excruciating, but which the man hailed with satisfaction. He stripped the mitten from his right hand and fetched forth the birch bark. The exposed fingers were quickly going numb again. Next he brought out his bunch of sulphur matches. But the tremendous cold had already driven the life out of his fingers. In his effort to separate one match from the others, the whole bunch fell into the snow. He tried to pick it out of the snow, but failed. The dead fingers could neither clutch nor touch. He was very careful. He drove the thought of his freezing feet, and nose, and cheeks, out of his mind, devoting his whole soul to the matches. He watched, using the sense of vision in place of that of touch, and when he saw his fingers on each side the bunch, he closed them—that is, he willed to close them, for the wires were down, and the fingers did not obey. He pulled the mitten on the right hand, and beat it fiercely against his knee. Then, with both mittened hands, he scooped the bunch of matches, along with much snow, into his lap. Yet he was no better off.

After some manipulation he managed to get the bunch between the heels of his mittened hands. In this fashion he carried it to his mouth. The ice crackled and snapped when by a violent effort he opened his mouth. He drew the lower jaw in, curled the upper lip out of the way and scraped the bunch with his upper teeth in order to separate a match. He succeeded in getting one, which he dropped on his lap. He was no better off. He could not pick it up. Then he devised a way. He picked it up in his teeth and scratched it on his leg. Twenty times he scratched before he succeeded in lighting it. As it flamed he held it with his teeth to the birch bark. But the burning brimstone went up his nostrils and into his lungs, causing him to cough spasmodically. The match fell into the snow and went out.

The old-timer on Sulphur Creek was right, he thought in the moment of controlled despair that ensued: after fifty below, a man should travel with a partner. He beat his hands, but failed in exciting any sensation. Suddenly he bared both hands, removing the mittens with his teeth. He caught the whole bunch between the heels of his hands. His arm muscles not being frozen enabled him to press the hand heels tightly against the matches. Then he scratched the bunch along his leg. It flared into flame, seventy sulphur matches at once! There was no wind to blow them out. He kept his head to one side to escape the strangling fumes, and held the blazing bunch to the birch bark. As he so held it, he became aware of sensation in his hand. His flesh was burning. He could smell it. Deep down below the surface he could feel it. The sensation developed into pain that grew acute. And still he endured it, holding the flame of the matches clumsily to the bark that would not light readily because his own burning hands were in the way, absorbing most of the flame.

At last, when he could endure no more, he jerked his hands apart. The blazing matches fell sizzling into the snow, but the birch bark was alight. He began laying dry grasses and the tiniest twigs on the flame. He could not pick and choose, for he had to lift the fuel between the heels of his hands. Small pieces of rotten wood and green moss clung to the twigs, and he bit them off as well as he could with his teeth. He cherished the flame carefully and awkwardly. It meant life, and it must not perish. The withdrawal of blood from the surface of his body now made him begin to shiver, and he grew more awkward. A large piece of green moss fell squarely on the little fire. He tried to poke it out with his fingers, but his shivering frame made him poke too far, and he disrupted the nucleus of the little fire, the burning grasses and the tiny twigs separating and scattering. He tried to poke them together again, but in spite of the tenseness of the effort, his shivering got away with him, and the twigs were hopelessly scattered. Each twig gushed a puff of smoke and went out. The fire provider had failed. As he looked apathetically about him, his eyes chanced on the dog, sitting across the ruins of the fire from him, in the snow, making restless, hunching movements, slightly lifting one forefoot and then the other, shifting its weight back and forth on them with wistful eagerness.

The sight of the dog put a wild idea into his head. He remembered the tale of the man, caught in a blizzard, who killed a steer and crawled inside the carcass, and so was saved. He would kill the dog and bury his hands in the warm body until the numbness went out of them. Then he could build another fire. He spoke to the dog, calling it to him; but in his voice was a strange note of fear that frightened the animal, who had never known the man to speak in such a way before. Something was the matter, and its suspicious nature sensed danger—it knew not what danger, but somewhere, somehow, in its brain arose an apprehension of the man. It flattened its ears down at the sound of the man's voice, and its restless, hunching movements and the liftings and shiftings of its forefeet became more pronounced; but it would not come to the man. He got on his hands and knees and crawled toward the dog. This unusual posture again excited suspicion, and the animal sidled mincingly away.

The man sat up in the snow for a moment and struggled for calmness. Then he pulled on his mittens, by means of his teeth, and got upon his feet. He glanced down at first in order to assure himself that he was really standing up, for the absence of sensation in his feet left him unrelated to the earth. His erect position in itself started to drive the webs of suspicion from the dog's mind; and when he spoke peremptorily, with the sound of whip lashes in his voice, the dog rendered its customary allegiance and came to him. As it came within reaching distance, the man lost his control. His arms flashed out to the dog, and he experienced genuine surprise when he discovered that his hands could not clutch, that there was neither bend nor feeling in his fingers. He had forgotten for the moment that they were frozen and that they were freezing more and more. All this happened quickly, and before the animal could get away, he encircled its body with his arms. He sat down in the snow, and in this fashion held the dog, while it snarled and whined and struggled.

But it was all he could do, hold its body encircled in his arms and sit there. He realized that he could not kill the dog. There was no way to do it. With his helpless hands he could neither draw nor hold his sheath knife nor throttle the animal. He released it, and it plunged wildly away, with tail between its legs, and still snarling. It halted forty feet away and surveyed him curiously, with ears sharply pricked forward.

The man looked down at his hands in order to locate them, and found them hanging on the ends of his arms. It struck him as curious that one should have to use his eyes in order to find out where his hands were. He began threshing his arms back and forth, beating the mittened hands against his sides. He did this for five minutes, violently, and his heart pumped enough blood up to the surface to put a stop to his shivering. But no sensation was aroused in his hands. He had an impression that they hung like weights on the ends of his arms, but when he tried to run the impression down, he could not find it.

A certain fear of death, dull and oppressive, came to him. This fear quickly became poignant as he realized that it was no longer a mere matter of freezing his fingers and toes, or of losing his hands and feet, but that it was a matter of life and death with the chances against him. This threw him into a panic, and he turned and ran along the old, dim trail. The dog joined in behind and kept up with him. He ran blindly, without intention, in fear such as he had never known in his life. Slowly, as he plowed and floundered through the snow, he began to see things again—the banks of the creek, the old timber jams, the leafless aspens, and the sky. The running made him feel better. He did not shiver. Maybe, if he ran on, his feet would thaw out; and, anyway, if he ran far enough, he would reach camp and the boys. Without doubt he would lose some fingers and toes and some of his face; but the boys would take care of him, and save the rest of him when he got there. And at the same time there was another thought in his mind that said he would never get to the camp and the boys; that he would soon be stiff and dead. This thought he kept in the background and refused to consider. Sometimes it pushed itself forward and demanded to be heard, but he thrust it back and strove to think of other things.

It struck him as curious that he could run at all on feet so frozen that he could not feel them when they struck the earth and took the weight of his body. He seemed to himself to skim along above the surface, and to have no connection with the earth. Somewhere he had once seen a winged Mercury, and he wondered if Mercury felt as he felt when skimming over the earth.

His theory of running until he reached camp and the boys had one flaw in it: he lacked the endurance. Several times he stumbled, and finally he tottered, crumpled up, and fell. When he tried to rise, he failed. He must sit and rest, he decided, and next time he would merely walk and keep on going. As he sat and regained his breath, he noted that he was feeling quite warm and comfortable. He was not shivering, and it even seemed that a warm glow had come to his chest and trunk. And yet, when he touched his nose or cheeks, there was no sensation. Running would not thaw them out. Nor would it thaw out his hands and feet. Then the thought came to him that the frozen portions of his body must be extending. He tried to keep this thought down, to forget it, to think of something else; he was aware of the panicky feeling that it caused, and he was afraid of the panic. But the thought asserted itself, and persisted, until it produced a vision of his body totally frozen. This was too much, and he made another wild run along the trail. Once he slowed down to a walk, but the thought of the freezing extending itself made him run again.

And all the time the dog ran with him, at his heels. When he fell down a second time, it curled its tail over its forefeet and sat in front of him, facing him, curiously eager and intent. The warmth and security of the animal angered him, and he cursed it till it flattened down its ears appeasingly. This time the shivering came more quickly upon the man. He was losing in his battle with the frost. It was creeping into his body from all sides. The thought of it drove him on, but he ran no more than a hundred feet, when he staggered and pitched headlong. It was his last panic. When he had recovered his breath and control, he sat up and entertained in his mind the conception of meeting death with dignity. However, the conception did not come to him in such terms. His idea of it was that he had been making a fool of himself, running around like a chicken with its head cut off—such was the simile that occurred to him. Well, he was bound to freeze anyway, and he might as well take it decently. With this newfound peace of mind came the first glimmerings of drowsiness. A good idea, he thought, to sleep off to death. It was like taking an anesthetic. Freezing was not so bad as people thought. There were lots worse ways to die.

He pictured the boys finding his body the next day. Suddenly he found himself with them, coming along the trail and looking for himself. And, still with them, he came around a turn in the trail and found himself lying in the snow. He did not belong with himself any more, for even then he was out of himself, standing with the boys and looking at himself in the snow. It certainly was cold, was his thought. When he got back to the States he could tell the folks what real cold was. He drifted on from this to a vision of the old-timer on Sulphur Creek. He could see him quite clearly, warm and comfortable, and smoking a pipe.

"You were right, old hoss; you were right," the man mumbled to the old-timer of Sulphur Creek.

Then the man drowsed off into what seemed to him the most comfortable and satisfying sleep he had ever known. The dog sat facing him and waiting. The brief day drew to a close in a long, slow twilight. There were no signs of a fire to be made, and, besides, never in the dog's experience had it known a man to sit like that in the snow and make no fire. As the twilight drew on, its eager yearning for the fire mastered it, and with a great lifting and shifting of forefeet, it whined softly, then flattened its ears down in anticipation of being chidden by the man. But the man remained silent. Later the dog whined loudly. And still later it crept close to the man and caught the scent of death. This made the animal bristle and back away. A little longer it delayed, howling under the stars that leaped and danced and shone brightly in the cold sky. Then it turned and trotted up the trail in the direction of the camp it knew, where there were other food providers and fire providers.

Cooper's Creek

BY ALAN MOOREHEAD

T he Burke and Wills Expedition, generally dated as August 1860–June 1861, sought to put civilized man's first footprints on one of the largest blank spaces on the map of that era, the Australian Outback. From Melbourne and a few scattered outlying settlements in the south, to the Gulf of Carpentaria, hundreds of miles away, about which very little was known. The "ghastly blank," as it was called, might contain anything the imagination could conjure up—fields of gold, an inland sea, high mountains totally unlike the scorching "miles and miles of bloody all" as the desert outback was sometimes called.

Robert O'Hara Burke, the expedition's leader, was an adventurer and explorer, a man of action suitable to the untamed Australian wilderness. William John Wills was a scientist, dedicated to using his instruments and keen powers of observation and research to unravel the secrets that would be revealed as the party crossed the continent.

Alan Moorehead, an Australian himself, is perhaps most famous for his amazing books on Africa—*Blue Nile, White Nile* and *No Room in the Ark*. To me, however, *Cooper's Creek* will always be his magnum opus, for it is an adventure and survival classic almost without peer. The Burke and Wills Expedition had it all as far as storytelling drama and settings go: heroic men struggling against nature, an amazing landscape, hardships almost unimaginable, and a Greek tragedy ending Shakespeare would have loved.

Cooper's Creek is a location about halfway through the route to the Gulf where the expedition established a permanent camp. Here a party of men, headed by William Brahe, waited as Burke and Wills and a small group of men, using camels, made the final push to the north. They departed Cooper's Creek on December 16, and after great hardship did reach the Gulf on February 10. Then, as Moorehead tells us, "The one thought now in all their minds was how to reach the depot on Cooper's Creek before their rations ran out."

They knew time was running out. What they did not yet know was that their luck was running out as well.

*   *   *   *   *

On Cooper's Creek, meanwhile, the depot was well established. After he had seen off Burke's party on December 16, Brahe had ridden straight back to Depot LXV and had got his men to work cutting timber for a stockade. He pressed on with this work, since the blacks had now begun to gather round the camp, and they were constantly pilfering things. They were not really aggressive—they were like boys robbing an orchard—but on December 26 they got away with six camel bags which had been washed and laid out on the bank of the creek to dry. Sometimes they stalked the camp by night, and the guard on duty had to keep a close lookout when there was no moon. One night Brahe saw a group of them coming stealthily along the creek under the cover of the bank, and they were being directed by another man who was hiding behind the trunk of a large tree. Brahe waited until they were within twenty yards of him, and then he shouted out and fired a shot over their heads. They stood terrified for a moment and then bolted into the night.

Then again early in the New Year a large party came right into the camp by daylight. Brahe grabbed one of the men and shoved him so hard that he fell down. In the afternoon the whole tribe returned, some of the men armed with spears and boomerangs and with their faces and bodies painted—a sign of war. Brahe walked out to meet them, and while they watched he drew a large circle round the camp. He then indicated by signs that if any man crossed the line he would fire. Out of bravado some of the men did cross the line and Brahe shot off his gun into the trees. At this the whole tribe ran off, and although they did not return he could still see from their campfires that they had not gone far off.

So long as Brahe and his men had their fire-arms the depot was safe enough; still, no one could be absolutely sure; other explorers and settlers had been killed in the bush before this, and McDouall Stuart had been strongly attacked in his last journey to the centre. It was a question of constant watchfulness, of handling childish minds that were disposed to be friendly and yet, through fear or misunderstanding, could give way to a sudden convulsive rage. The tribesmen seemed to like the camels and never molested them, but one day they surrounded the horses while they were grazing and appeared to be about to drive them off. Once again Brahe went out with his gun and there was a wild stampede of both animals and men when he pulled the trigger. It was not until after nightfall that they managed to round up the horses and bring them back.

After this the blacks became less troublesome, or rather they seemed to accept the fact of these strangers living among them, and occasionally they would come up to the camp with gifts of fish and nardoo cakes. Brahe thought it wiser to refuse these gifts, but he offered the blacks some of his beads and cast-off clothes and they seemed delighted.

By the New Year the depot was entrenched. The stockade was a solid palisade of saplings driven deep into the ground and covering an area of twenty feet by eighteen. In it Burke's tent was erected and the fire-arms and ammunition were stored. The other tents were set up outside the stockade, close to the cooking fires and the place where the twelve horses and six camels were tied up at night. The provisions were hung in sacks from all the surrounding trees to keep them safe from the rats, and sometimes they killed as many as forty rats a day.

Brahe was not altogether satisfied about the site of the camp; the blacks indicated to him that in the wet weather all this land might be under water, but there was no sign of rain as yet, the nights were often intolerably hot and sultry, and the level of the water in the creek was dropping slightly every day.

Apart from Brahe's account we do not know much about the other members of the little party at this time—Patton, McDonough and the Pathan, Dost Mahomet—except that Dost Mahomet had a mortal fear of the blacks; but they appear to have got along very well together. They worked hard at first building the stockade, and then settled into a routine of daily jobs. Each morning one man went out with the camels and another with the horses, while two men stayed in camp. They never cared to take the animals to grazing grounds that were more than six or seven miles away for fear of the blacks, but there was still good feed close by. Inside the camp the days went by in a regular routine of cooking, washing, mending the equipment, taking observations with the instruments Wills had left behind, shooting rats and ducks, and fishing in the creek. The flies were appalling but they managed to deal with the mosquitoes by lighting fires. Burke had left them with provisions for six months, and until the constant shooting scared them off they had plenty of duck to eat. They had rice and sugar for breakfast, and then at noon their main meal of the day—damper, tea, and, while it lasted, salt pork or beef. In the evening they had tea and biscuits. In short, they had all they wanted to eat, and because of the heat none of them was ever very hungry.

It must have been a life of extraordinary dullness; one suspects that they sat around for hour after hour drinking tea and simply gazing at the campfire; without books, without work, without amusement of any kind, what else was there for them to do? Yet it was not exactly a garrison life, their circumstances were too outlandish for that; the element of danger was always there, the sense of being suspended in the unmapped bush out of space and time. Despite its drabness and its heavy stillness and silence the bush had its moments of spectacle as well. In central Australia fantastic dawns and sunsets break across the sky: colours of such leaping brilliance that all the earth, every bush and tree and the dry ground itself, is illuminated for a few minutes in shades of scarlet, orange, pink and gold. It is doubtful if any of these men were keen students of wild life, but they can hardly have failed to be impressed by the continuous movement along the creek, for the waterholes of the Cooper must be one of the great bird sanctuaries of the world. The pool at the site of Depot LXV, about a quarter of a mile long and a hundred yards across, is a particularly good place; one sits on the bank during the hour before dusk like a spectator in a theatre. As the full fierce blaze of the sun begins to soften at last, the white cockatoos, the corellas, come in by the thousand, screeching hideously, and they settle on one tree after another, never quite able to make up their minds.

On the ground the timid little coots that have been hiding in the reeds all day emerge into the open and come nervously down to the water to drink. The slightest disturbance is enough to make them scuttle back into cover again, and with their black feathers and red beaks they look like frightened chickens as they run. Now everywhere the trees are alive with parrots and cockatoos—the mulgas skimming by in green flocks, the parrot-cockatoos in grey, the Major Mitchells in pink—and it is not possible for the eye to follow all the arrivals and departures, the plovers, the eagles, crows, the harlequin colours of the blue-bonnets, the little waxbills, the ring-necks and the herons. Sometimes there are black swans on the pool, and the pelicans, with their curious undulating flight—a series of upward flaps and a down-glide—descend in line, each bird braking himself for his landing on the water by putting out his webbed feet before him. As the light fades the colour of the pool turns to gold, and this is the moment when the galahs, two by two, come in to drink from the bank, anxiously jerking up their heads to look around between each sip, and the bright pink of their breast feathers is reflected in the gold. With darkness silence and stillness return, but then some idiot corella falls off the rotten twig on which it has perched and the whole white flock wheels screeching into the air again. One can expect this to happen half a dozen times but in the end all is quiet.

These evenings are the reward for the hot day, and it is possible on Cooper's Creek for the traveller to have a sense of great contentment, at any rate for an hour or two. But then an inertia supervenes, and in the case of these men no doubt a dead weight of waiting. Day after day the same thing: never a visitor, never a word from the outside world. In these conditions men lose their volition, the judgement falters, the mind becomes obsessed with imagined grievances and doubts, and there is a powerful inducement to dream and to do nothing.

They were not really so well off as the Carpentaria party, who, despite all their discomforts, had the daily stimulus of movement, the necessity of getting somewhere, and the prospect of seeing over the other side of the next hill. After a while Brahe and his men did not bother to fish or to shoot ducks any more; what was the use? It was easier just to go on with the rations they had. This was dangerous, since they needed fresh food, but the creeping paralysis of a static routine made it each day more difficult to do anything out of the ordinary. Did he keep a diary, Brahe was asked later. No, he said, he did not, what was the point? Nothing happened.

So they sat round their depot, and the myriad insects that crept and crawled and flew about them in the light of the campfire—the horrendous six-inch centipedes with their great nippers, the scorpions, the soft moths, the stick insects, the beetles with huge veined transparent wings and the teeming ants—were, for them, a long way from being an interesting manifestation of nature in a new country; they were simply poisonous bugs that had been sent, like the flies and the rats, to plague them in this dreary wilderness. Cooper's Creek, as Burke had said, was not really a desirable summer residence. And so they waited, because there was nothing else for them to do.

As February drifted into March, Brahe was not greatly disturbed about the failure of Burke to return; after all, he could not reasonably expect him before the three-month period was up, and that would be in the middle of March. But the failure of Wright to appear was absolutely baffling. He had turned back from Torowoto at the end of October with the explicit understanding that he would bring the bulk stores up to the Cooper as soon as possible. But now more than four months had gone by, time enough to have made several journeys to the Cooper, and not so much as a message had arrived from him. What could be happening at Menindie? Why did he not come?

For months the temperature at the depot had remained at a steady 112 degrees in the shade, but on March 24 it suddenly dropped. Now Brahe and his party had thunder and lightning ranging around, the wind blew hard and the nights were very cold. The blacks were still about—they got away with a pack-saddle one night, and it was torn to pieces when Patton retrieved it from a mile down the creek—but the depot's supplies of food were still holding out. The trouble was that they had no dried fruit or vegetables, and early in April Patton began to complain that his gums were sore and that he was not feeling very well. He was the blacksmith of the party, and as the horses needed shoeing he set about the work at once in case his illness gained on him. On April 4 the job was done and Patton collapsed. His legs and arms were swollen and his mouth was now so sore he could not eat. They put him to bed in one of the tents and there he lay. About this time too both Brahe and McDonough began to observe the same symptoms in themselves. They had no idea of what the affliction was—no one appears to have warned them of scurvy—and only the Pathan, Dost Mahomet, was entirely well.

It was now nearly four months since Burke and his party had gone away—a month longer than they had predicted—and Brahe rode out to the hills around the creek to search the horizon: to the south-east for Wright, to the north for Burke. Absolutely nothing broke the stillness of the plain. Brahe kept revolving the problem round and round in his mind: what were they to do? Were they to go on like this forever, never to have news from anywhere, never to have an end of this waiting in a vacuum? Burke's last words were recalled again and again; he could be considered "perished," he had said, if he was not back in three months. No, he did not expect to be picked up by a boat on the Gulf, nor would he make for the settled districts of Queensland if he had any chance of getting back to Cooper's Creek. And yet was it not possible that he *had* been picked up, that he *had* gone to Queensland? Then why no news, why nothing from Menindie? Was it possible that the little party on the Cooper had been altogether forgotten? Were the others, being all safe and sound, simply expecting him to come back to civilization now that the three months had run out? How much longer could he *afford* to stay, with Patton unable to leave his bed and getting feebler every day, and he himself and McDonough also failing in health? Their ankles now became swollen every time they got on a horse. Suppose Burke were dead or stuck fast in the centre, was it not his duty to go back now and get help? After all, the Cooper's Creek party were the only ones who knew anything definite about Burke's plans; they were his last link with the outside world. Yet Burke had specifically said that they were to hang on at Cooper's Creek so long as the rations lasted; and the rations were lasting. They were sick to death of them but there was enough. And the weather was cooler, they had actually had some rain. Should he set a date then, Brahe wondered, should they wait, say, until May?

Each day these questions posed themselves and there was never any answer.

The Return from the Gulf

As soon as they rejoined Gray and King at Camp CXIX on the Gulf of Carpentaria on February 12, Burke and Wills took stock of their situation. They had been fifty-seven days on the outward journey from Cooper's Creek, and in that time they had eaten more than two-thirds of their three months' supply of rations. There remained now only 83 lb. of flour, 3 lb. of pork, 25 lb. of dried meat, 12 lb. of biscuit, 12 lb. of rice—say one month's provisions in all, or just half of what they required.

This could be supplemented, of course, by portulaca, which was now flowering in the wet season, by such birds as they could shoot—mainly ducks, hawks and crows—and by fish; but their experiences in coming up to the Gulf had shown that they could not expect much from this source. On the other hand, they still had five camels and the horse Billy, and there was a reasonable prospect of recapturing Golah, the camel they had left behind. Some at least of these animals could be killed and eaten.

They had roughly 700 miles to go in order to reach the depot on Cooper's Creek, and on the outward journey they had managed between twelve and fifteen miles a day. There seemed to be no reason why they should not repeat this performance; the animals' loads were lighter, they knew the way, and except for Gray, who was complaining of headaches, they were all reasonably fit. The animals, it was true, were in need of rest and would have benefited from three or four weeks' feeding around Camp CXIX, but the shortage of rations made any such delay impossible. Even as it was they would have to live on a greatly reduced diet, and Burke fixed on a basic daily scale of twelve sticks of dried meat and ¼ lb. of flour for each man.

Before they left Camp CXIX they cut the initial B on a circle of fifteen trees, and buried a parcel of books together with a letter saying who they were and what they had done. Then, on February 13, after only one day of rest, they set out. It was still raining.

We know a good deal less about this return journey than we do of the outward one. Burke took no notes at all, and Wills no longer kept any exact record of their line of march or of their progress. In his field-books he mostly contented himself with noting down dates and the names of camps, and one can measure his increasing weariness by the way in which the entries grow more and more scrappy and laconic. They were probably all much more tired than they realized, and the constant rain had turned the ground into a quagmire. It rained and rained and they had no tents; they slept in the wet. When they had had a week of it, Wills made a typical entry in his diary: "Between four and five o'clock a heavy thunderstorm broke over us, having given very little warning of its approach. There had been lightning and thunder towards S.E. and S. ever since noon yesterday. The rain was incessant and very heavy for an hour and a half, which made the ground so boggy that the animals could scarcely walk over it. We nevertheless started at 10 minutes to seven am, and after floundering along for half an hour, halted for breakfast. We then moved on again, but soon found that the travelling was too heavy for the camels, so we camped for the remainder of the day. In the afternoon the sky cleared a little, and the sun soon dried the ground, considering. Shot a pheasant, and much disappointed at finding him all feathers and claws."

And then on the following day: "A fearful thunderstorm in the evening about eight pm, E.S.E., moving gradually round to the S. The flashes of lightning were so vivid and incessant as to keep up a continual light for short intervals, overpowering even the moonlight."

As the four men crawled over the enormous landscape like wet insects they began to long for the dry fresh heat of the desert. It was still hot here in the north, but it was the dull enervating heat of the tropics, and now King as well as Gray began to suffer from headaches and pains in his legs and back. Wills, who was the most vigorous of them all, wrote in his diary: "The evening [February 23] was most oppressively hot and sultry, so much so that the slightest exertion made one feel as if he were in a state of suffocation. The dampness in the atmosphere prevented any evaporation, and gave one a helpless feeling of lassitude that I have never before experienced to such an extent. All the party complained of the same symptoms, and the horses [*sic*] showed distinctly the effect of the evening trip, short as it was."

Even by travelling at night like this they were making nothing like twelve miles a day, and at the beginning of March they were still trudging up the Cloncurry River more or less on their old route. But now they found Golah. "He looks thin," Wills wrote, "and miserable, seems to have fretted a great deal, probably at finding himself left behind, and he has been walking up and down the tracks till he has made a regular pathway. Could find no sign of his having been far off it, although there is splendid feed to which he could have gone. He began to eat as soon as he saw the other camels."

It was too late however. Somehow the heart had gone out of the beast, and they had to abandon him four days later when he absolutely refused to come on, even when his pack and saddle were taken off. Meanwhile there was the incident of the snake: "In crossing a creek by moonlight," Wills wrote,

"Charley rode over a large snake. He did not touch him, and we thought it was a log until he struck it with the stirrup-iron. We then saw that it was an immense snake, larger than any I have ever before seen in a wild state." It had a black head, a pattern of brown and yellow stripes on its back, and measured eight feet four inches in length. It did not appear to have poisonous fangs, and inspired, perhaps, by their having seen the blacks eat snakes, but mainly by their own hunger, they cooked this monster. The next night they started out at 2 a.m., but Burke almost immediately complained of severe dysentery. He felt giddy, and when he got on to his horse he was unable to keep his seat. They were forced then to give up all further progress for the night, and for the next two days Burke dragged himself miserably along.

By the end of the first week of March they had covered barely a hundred miles, but at last there was a first whiff of the dry desert air. Only Gray failed to respond to it. "Mr. Burke," Wills' diary says, "almost recovered, but Charley is again very unwell, and unfit to do anything. He caught cold last night through carelessness in covering himself."

They did not entirely believe in Gray's complaints, they thought he was "gammoning"—trying to get out of his fair share of the work. After all, he was under no more strain than the others, and Burke was absolutely impartial about the rations; at each meal he carefully doled out the food on to four numbered plates which he covered with a towel. The others were then obliged to stand with their backs turned and to call a number, and were each served with the plate of that number. Food now entirely dominated their lives, and so the incident that occurred on March 25 was for them all a shocking and outrageous thing.

Wills describes it thus: "After breakfast took some altitudes, and was about to go back to last camp for some things that had been left, when I found Gray behind a tree, eating skilligolee (or gruel). He explained that he was suffering from dysentery, and had taken the flour without leave. Sent him to report himself to Mr. Burke and went on. Having got King to tell Mr. Burke for him, was called up and received a good thrashing. There is no knowing to what extent he has been robbing us. Many things have been found to run unaccountably short."

King's version of the affair does not quite agree as to "the good thrashing"; he states that Gray merely received "six or seven slaps on the ear," and he goes on to say that, apart from this, he had never known Burke strike a man before. One must recall, of course, that King was devoted to Burke, and that Wills was a disciplined and self-controlled young man; from now on in his notes he refers to Charley as Gray, and clearly he believed that Gray deserved nothing less than a good thrashing. Be all this as it may, Burke was in a towering rage—one understands it very well—and henceforth Gray, who had been in charge of the stores, was put on to other duties.

By now, March 25, they had been forty days on the return journey and were only about half-way back. But they were through the Selwyn Ranges, and in the more bracing air of the centre they made better time. No day went past without their struggling on to another camp, even though the rain continued to fall. Wills' diary becomes a string of *ad hoc* place names: Fig Tree Camp, Sandstone Cave, Scratchley's Creek, Humid Camp, Muddy Camp, Mosquito Camp, Three Hour Camp, Native Dog Camp and Saltbush Camp. There is also more than one "Feasting Camp." We do not know exactly when or in what circumstances each of the animals was killed, but a "Feasting Camp" no doubt was a place where the starving men gorged themselves and then cut up as much meat as they could carry. On March 30 we have an entry: "Boocha's Rest. [Boocha was one of the camels.] Employed all day in cutting up, jerking and eating Boocha. The day turned out as favourable for us as we could have wished, and a considerable portion of the meat was completely jerked before sunset."

Then eleven days later, on April 10, we have: "Remained at Camp LII R. all day to cut up and jerk the meat of the horse Billy, who was so reduced and knocked up for want of food, that there appeared little chance of his reaching the other side of the desert; and as we were running short of food of every description ourselves, we thought it best to secure his flesh at once. We found it healthy and tender, but without the slightest trace of fat in any portion of the body."

Now there is a great deal of meat on a horse, let alone a camel, and in the end only two camels of the original six remained. One would have thought that there was enough meat here to keep four men going for a very long time, and one can only conclude that they were all now growing very weak, and quite unable to carry more than a light pack. And in fact they were beginning to discard every article that was not absolutely essential. On March 20 they had already jettisoned 60 lb. of equipment, hanging it from the branches of a tree so that it could be found if they ever came back; and they began to take turns at riding the two remaining camels. Cyclonic storms either blowing with rain or red dust continued to hold them back, and once they "halted fifteen minutes to send back for Gray, who gammoned he could not walk." And now, on April 10, they faced Sturt's Stony Desert again. Wills says very little of the passage except that they managed to find water on the way—the spring was now well advanced—and they appear to have got through in several days. On April 15, two months out from the Gulf, they were moving slowly down towards Cooper's Creek in driving rain, and they had to pause for a while when Landa, one of the camels, became knocked up and would not go on. Gray by now could no longer ride by himself and had to be strapped to the saddle.

He was not really gammoning. On April 17 we get the simple entry in Wills' diary: "This morning about sunrise, Gray died. He had not spoken a word distinctly since his first attack, which was just as we were about to start." According to King, they found him dead in his bedroll when they went to call him in the morning. They buried him as he was, in his flannel trousers, his short-sleeved shirt and his wideawake hat, and they were so feeble it took them all day to dig a grave three feet deep. When it was done they abandoned the last of their equipment. Wills already had lost nearly all his instruments—some had been broken when a camel had rolled on them, others had been buried—but he still clutched his field-books, the only written record of what they had achieved; and now to mark Charley's grave they placed a rifle above it on a tree and some unwanted camel-pads, intending to come back for them later. They were seventy miles from the depot, and on April 18 they set out again, carrying with them a little dried meat, a couple of spades, the remaining fire-arms and a few camel-pads for bedding. Burke in particular had been generous in giving away his spare shirts to the blacks, and they were all badly in need of new clothes and boots. They were so cold when they laid down to sleep they had to keep a fire going throughout the night.

Friday, April 19, was a bad day; the Cooper's Creek blacks had again caught sight of these incredible bearded white men who dragged themselves along on their aimless journeys as though bewitched by some fetish, and they would not leave them alone. Wills wrote: "Camped again without water on the sandy bed of the creek, having been followed by a lot of natives who were de-sirous of our company; but as we preferred camping alone, we were compelled to move on until rather late, in order to get away from them. The night was very cold. A strong breeze was blowing from the south, which made the fire so irregular that, as on the previous two nights, it was impossible to keep up a fair temperature."

On Saturday, April 20, they trudged on again, Burke riding one camel and Wills and King taking turns with the other, and that night, their sixty-sixth night since leaving the Gulf, they camped within thirty miles of the depot. They made a division of their remaining provisions and ate them all except for the last pound and a half of dried meat. On April 21—it was another Sunday, all the great events on this journey seemed to be occurring on Sunday—they made a superhuman effort. Rising early, they set out to cover in one day the entire thirty miles that divided them from the depot. They paused only to allow King to take pot-shots at hawks and crows, and at nightfall they were still going. In other circumstances they would have long since collapsed, but now they were driven on by dreams of food and rest and companionship, and beyond this they hardly knew what they were doing any more. The moon came up and by its light Burke rode on ahead through the silent scrub. "I think I see their tents ahead," he kept saying, "I think I see them." As he neared the site of the depot he raised his voice in the long-drawn-out bushman's cry: *Coo-ee, Coo-ee,* and he shouted out the names of the men they had left there, Brahe, McDonough, Patton. And then again *Coo-ee.*

There was no answer from the silent bush, no movement anywhere in the moonlight.

It was just 7:30 p.m. when they came into the camp and saw the wooden stockade, the ashes of burnt-out fires, bits of discarded equipment scattered about, and fresh traces of horse and cattle dung, but no sign of men or animals anywhere. They stood for a moment in a confused daze, and Burke said: "I suppose they have shifted to some other part of the creek."

It was hardly likely and they all knew it. No equipment would have been left behind had Brahe merely set up a depot in another place. Then Wills caught sight of a fresh blaze on the coolibah tree and they read the words that had been cut into the wood with a knife:

DIG
3 FT. N.W.
APR.21 1861

"If they had shifted to another part of the creek," Wills said, "they would not have left that."

Burke collapsed on the ground in despair, and Wills and King paced out the distance from the tree to a spot where the earth had been freshly turned over. Digging down two feet they came on a camel box containing rations, and there was a bottle with a message written in pencil inside it. King smashed the bottle and handed the message to Burke. By the bright light of the moon he read aloud:

"Depot, Cooper's Creek, 21 April 1861,
The depot party of the V.E.E. leaves this camp today to return to the Darling.
I intend to go S.E. from Camp LX, to get into our old track near Bulloo. Two
of my companions and myself are quite well; the third—Patton—has been

unable to walk for the last eighteen days, as his leg has been severely hurt when thrown by one of the horses. No person has been up here from the Darling.

We have six camels and twelve horses in good working condition.

William Brahe."

The date of the message was perhaps the most agonizing thing: Brahe and his men had left the depot that same morning. After four months they had missed them by a matter of nine or ten hours, or even less. Even now they were probably encamped no more than twenty miles away. If they had gone a week earlier the situation would have been just the same, but to have been too late by one day—the day that they lost by burying Gray—this was too bitter. Why at least could Brahe's party not have heard King's rifle as he shot at the hawks and crows further down the creek that morning? Why couldn't the blacks have told them that there were white men approaching the camp? And where was Wright? Why hadn't he come up? Why wasn't he here now?

In the last hundred years the scene that night on Cooper's Creek has become something of a legend in Australian history, and it made a strong appeal to the illustrative artists of the day. Even as late as 1907 John Longstaff painted an enormous canvas showing the three haggard men grouped around the fatal tree, Burke in his tattered shirt and trousers staring dully into the distance, Wills slumped on one of the camel packs, with bowed head and his hands on his knees, and King lying prone on the ground. The spade is flung down beside the opened cache, and in the background the two camels have sunk to their knees in utter exhaustion. The silent and unresponsive bush envelops them all. As a study of helpless despair it could hardly be improved upon.

And probably it was like that. Such brief descriptions as have been left behind by the three men make it clear that at first they simply could not bring themselves to believe that Brahe had gone, and that after all this enormous struggle to reach the camp, and the visions they had had of rest and safety, they were now alone.

When they had recovered a little their first instinct, of course, was to consider their chances of being able to follow Brahe while there was still time. Burke put it to Wills and King: were they able to march on through the night? They both answered no, and Burke then said that he also was too exhausted to go on. Then what to do? To eat certainly, and then to rest. And then? Wills and King were all for traveling on in Brahe's wake; after all, something might happen to delay him, and they would then catch him up. Burke was emphatically against this. It would be madness, he thought; in his message Brahe specifically said that his six camels and twelve horses were in good condition. How could they possibly catch them with their own two exhausted camels? There was no water for long stretches on the way to Menindie, and Menindie was over 400 miles away. A much better plan would be to go down Cooper's Creek to Mount Hopeless, where they knew there was a police-station, only 150 miles away, and from there the journey to Adelaide would be through settled districts. Gregory had done the journey from the Cooper to Mount Hopeless in a week; the Committee in Melbourne had recommended that route as a line of communication. In the end both Wills and King were persuaded.

They now broached the rations that Brahe had left behind. They were so weak that King had to crawl on his hands and knees to fill a billy from the creek, but they all felt better after the meal and stretched themselves out on the ground to sleep.

Next day they hung listlessly about the camp gathering their strength, and debating their predicament over and over again. Why had Brahe gone? Why on that very day? Admittedly they had been away longer than they had thought, but he still had provisions—he could have eaten the horses. Why had Wright never come up? Why had they been abandoned? In his bitterness Burke declared that Brahe and his men would be punished; their salaries would go to Wills and King. He would arrange it when they got back.

An inventory of rations in the cache revealed that they had a month's supply, just about enough to get them to Mount Hopeless if all went well. They had left clothes behind at the depot, and now that they needed them so badly it was one more charge against Brahe that he had had the idiocy to take them away with him.

In the circumstances, the letter that Burke now wrote was exceptionally restrained:

"Depot No. 2, Cooper's Creek, Camp no. LXV.
The return party from Carpentaria, consisting of myself, Mr. Wills and King (Gray dead), arrived here last night and found that the depot party had only started on the same day. We proceed on tomorrow slowly down the creek towards Adelaide, by Mount Hopeless, and shall endeavour to follow Gregory's tracks, but we are very weak. The two camels are done up, and we shall not be able to travel farther than four or five miles a day. Gray died on the road from exhaustion and fatigue. We have all suffered much from hunger. The provisions left here will, I think, restore our strength. We have discovered a practicable route to Carpentaria, the chief portion of which lies on the 140th

meridian of east longitude. There is some good country between this and the stony desert. From there to the tropic [Capricorn] the country is dry and stony. Between the tropic and Carpentaria a considerable portion is rangy, but it is well watered and richly grassed.

We reached the shores of Carpentaria on the 11th February 1861. Greatly disappointed at finding the party here gone.

R. O'Hara Burke, Leader.

22 April 1861.
P.S.—The camels cannot travel, and we cannot walk, or we should follow the other party. We shall move very slowly down the creek."

Wills in his diary was more outspoken:

"Sunday 21st April 1861.—Arrived at the depot this evening, just in time to find it deserted. A note left in the plant by Brahe communicates the pleasing information that they have started today for the Darling, their camels and horses all well and in good condition; we and our camels being just done up, and scarcely able to reach the depot have very little chance of overtaking them. Brahe has fortunately left us ample provisions to take us to the bounds of civilization, namely: flour, 50 lb., rice 20 lb., oatmeal 60 lb., sugar 60 lb. and dried meat 15 lb. These provisions, together with a few horseshoes and nails, and some castaway odds and ends, constitute all the articles left, and place us in a very awkward position in respect to clothing.

"Our disappointment at finding the depot deserted may easily be imagined; returning in an exhausted state, after four months of the severest travelling and privation, our legs almost paralysed, so that each of us found it a most trying task only to walk a few yards. Such a leg-bound feeling I never before experienced and hope I never shall again. The exertion required to get up a slight piece of rising ground, even without any load, induces an indescribable sensation of pain and helplessness, and the general lassitude makes one unfit for anything. Poor Gray must have suffered very much, many times, when we thought him shamming. It is most fortunate for us that these symptoms, which so early affected him, did not come on us until we were reduced to an exclusively animal diet of such an inferior description as that offered by the flesh of a worn-out and exhausted horse.

"We were not long in getting out the grub that Brahe had left, and we made a good supper off some oatmeal porridge and sugar. This, together with the excitement of finding ourselves in such a peculiar and unexpected position, had a wonderful effect in removing the stiffness from our legs. Whether it is possible that the vegetables can so have affected us, I know not; but both Mr.

B. and I remarked a most decided relief and a strength in the legs greater than we had had for several days. I am inclined to think that but for the abundance of portulac that we obtained on the journey, we should scarcely have returned to Cooper's Creek at [all]."

So then, with this new supply of food, there was a chance of their getting through to Mount Hopeless, and after only one day's delay they began preparations for getting on the road again. King had broken the bottle that contained Brahe's letter and had put the pieces on top of the stockade, but another bottle was found, and with Burke's letter inside it was buried in the cache. One never knew, there was just a chance that someone might come looking for them. With a rake which he had found leaning against the stockade King smoothed over the ground above the cache, leaving it exactly as it was before. Afterwards he propped the rake against the coolibah tree. There was little, apart from the rations, for them to take away; King cut a large square from a hide that formed the door of the stockade, with the idea no doubt of making boots from it, but a bag of horseshoe nails he rejected and scattered about on the ground. He also hung a few rags and pieces of leather for which they had no use on some nails driven into the stockade. The ashes of their campfires were left as they were.

At a quarter past nine on April 23 they set out in the opposite direction to Brahe's, a bedraggled little group with their weary camels and their tattered clothes, moving slowly back on their tracks down the south bank of the Cooper.

Editor's Postscript: The tragedy at this point—and the unfolding elements of Elizabethan drama were far from over, as you will see if you take the time to read Moorehead's wonderful book. The decision by Burke, Wills, and King to "tidy up" the "Dig Here" site before moving on down the creek was to become disastrous. As things turned out, Brahe and Wright (who had failed in his mission to resupply Brahe and relieve his party on Cooper's Creek) returned to the Creek on May 8, fifteen days after the site had been abandoned by Brahe and the Burke-Wills-King trio arrived only hours later. Now, Brahe and Wright failed to notice that the "Dig" had been disturbed, and they left immediately. When a search party led by Alfred William Howitt later reached the creek on Sept. 13, they found John King, starving and in rags, barely alive and able to stand. Burke and Wills had died in June of malnutrition and other privations, even though the native blacks along the river had assisted them. (The climate is so harsh here, the natives could barely stay alive themselves, and moved frequently.) King survived the ordeal. Wills' diaries filled in the blanks of the story.

Walk Well, My Brother

BY FARLEY MOWAT

Northof the Arctic Circle, death lurks in the land of the little sticks, where the tiny wind-lashed black spruce give way to endless tundra dotted with lakes and crisscrossed by strange brawling rivers. These are the Canadian Barrens, home of the caribou, the "deer," as The People call them, home of multitudinous animals, fish, and birds—not barren at all in times of plenty. But here only the rocks and moss and wind are constants, and for the Ihalmiut, The People [inland Eskimos], all life is lived on the razor edge of danger and starvation.

The man who knows The People best and has brought their lives to the printed page time and time again is Farley Mowat, whose travels and adventures throughout the Arctic have inspired such classics as *People of the Deer* and *Never Cry Wolf.* When it comes to Arctic storytelling, Mowat, in my opinion, is The Man.

"Walk Well, My Brother" is from Mowat's book of stories called *The Snow Walker* and is one of two from that wonderful book we feel privileged to bring to your attention in this collection.

★   ★   ★   ★   ★

When Charlie Lavery first went north just after the war, he was twenty-six years old and case hardened by nearly a hundred bombing missions over Europe. He was very much of the new elite who believed that any challenge, whether by man or nature, could be dealt with by good machines in the hands of skilled men. During the following five years, flying charter jobs in almost every part of the arctic from Hudson Bay to the Alaska border, he had found no reason to alter this belief. But though his familiarity with arctic skies and his ability to drive trackless lines across them had become considerable, he remained a stranger to the land below. The monochromatic wilderness of rock and tundra, snow and ice, existed outside his experience and comprehension, as did the native people whose world this was.

One mid-August day in 1951 he was piloting a war-surplus Anson above the drowned tundra plains south of Queen Maud Gulf, homeward bound to his base at Yellowknife after a flight almost to the limit of the aircraft's range. The twin engines thundered steadily and his alert ears caught no hint of warning from them. When the machine betrayed his trust, it did so with shattering abruptness. Before he could touch the throttles, the starboard engine was dead and the port one coughing in staccato bursts. Then came silence—replaced almost instantly by a rising scream of wind as the plane nosed steeply down toward the shining circlet of a pond.

It was too small a pond and the plane had too little altitude. As Lavery frantically pumped the flap hydraulics, the floats smashed into the rippled water. The Anson careened wickedly for a few yards and came to a crunching stop against the frost-shattered rocks along the shore.

Lavery barely glanced at his woman passenger, who had been thrown into a corner of the cabin by the impact. He scrambled past her, flung open the door and jumped down to find himself standing knee deep in frigid water. Both floats had been so badly holed that they had filled and now rested on the rocky bottom.

The woman crawled to the door and Lavery looked up into an oval, warmly tinted face framed in long black hair. He groped for the few Eskimo words he knew:

"*Tingmeak . . . tokoiyo . . .* smashed to hell! No fly! Understand?"

As she stared back uncomprehending, a spasm of anger shook him. What a fool he'd been to take her aboard at all . . . now she was a bloody albatross around his neck.

Four hours earlier he had landed in a bay on the Gulf coast to set out a cache of aviation gas for a prospecting company. No white men lived in that part of the world and Lavery had considered it a lucky accident to find an Eskimo tent pitched there. The two men who had run out to watch him land had been a godsend, helping to unload the drums, float them to tideline and roll them up the beach well above the storm line.

He had given each of them a handful of chocolate bars in payment for their work and had been about to head back for Yellowknife when the younger Eskimo touched his arm and pointed to the tent. Lavery had no desire to visit that squat skin cone hugging the rocks a hundred yards away and it was not the Eskimo's gentle persistence that prevailed on him—it was the thought that these Huskies might have a few white fox pelts to trade.

There were no fox pelts in the tent. Instead there was a woman lying on some caribou hides. *Nuliak*—wife—was the only word Lavery could understand of the Eskimo's urgent attempt at explanation.

The tent stank of seal oil and it was with revulsion that Lavery looked more closely at the woman. She was young and not bad looking—for a Husky—but her cheeks were flushed a sullen red by fever and a trickle of blood had dried at the corner of her mouth. Her dark eyes were fixed upon him with grave intensity. He shook his head and turned away.

T.B. . . . sooner or later all the Huskies got it . . . bound to the filthy way they lived. It would be no kindness to fly her out to the little hospital at Yellowknife already stuffed with dying Indians. She'd be better off to die at home. . . .

Lavery was halfway back to the Anson before the younger Eskimo caught up with him. In his hands he held two walrus tusks, and the pilot saw they were of exceptional quality.

Ah, what the hell . . . no skin off my ass. I'm deadheading anyhow. . . .

"*Eeema*. Okay, I'll take your *nuliak*. But make it snappy. *Dwoee, dwoee!*"

While Lavery fired up the engines, the men carried the woman, wrapped in caribou-skin robes, and placed her in the cabin. The younger Eskimo pointed at her, shouting her name: Konala. Lavery nodded and waved them away. As he pulled clear of the beach he caught a glimpse of them standing in the slipstream, as immobile as rocks. Then the plane was airborne, swinging around on course for the long haul home.

Barely two hours later he again looked into the eyes of the woman called Konala . . . wishing he had never seen or heard of her.

She smiled tentatively but Lavery ignored her and pushed past into the cabin to begin sorting through the oddments which had accumulated during his years of arctic flying. He found a rusty .22 rifle and half a box of shells, a torn sleeping bag, an axe and four cans of pork and beans. This, together with a small box of matches and a pocket knife in his stylish cotton flying jacket, comprised a survival outfit whose poverty testified to his contempt for the world that normally lay far below his aircraft.

Shoving the gear into a packsack he waded ashore. Slowly Konala followed, carrying her caribou robes and a large sealskin pouch. With mounting irritation Lavery saw that she was able to move without much difficulty. Swinging the lead to get a free plane ride, he thought. He turned on her.

"The party's over, lady! Your smart-assed boy friend's got you into a proper mess—him and his goddamn walrus tusks!"

The words meant nothing to Konala but the tone was clear enough. She walked a few yards off, opened her pouch, took out a fishing line and began carefully unwinding it. Lavery turned his back on her and made his way to a ledge of rock where he sat down to consider the situation.

A thin tongue of fear was flickering in the back of his mind. Just what the hell *was* he going to do? The proper drill would be to stick with the Anson and wait until a search plane found him . . . except he hadn't kept to his flight plan. He had said he intended to fly west down the coast to Bathurst before angling southwest to Yellowknife . . . instead he'd flown a direct course from the cache, to save an hour's fuel. Not so bright maybe, considering his radio was out of kilter. There wasn't a chance in a million they'd look for him this far off-course. Come to that, he didn't even know exactly where he was . . . fifty miles or so north of the Back River lakes would be a good guess. There were so damn few landmarks in this godforsaken country. . . . Well, so he wasn't going to be picked up . . . that left Shanks' mare, as the Limeys would say . . . but which way to go?

He spread out a tattered aeronautical chart on the knees of his neat cotton pants. Yellowknife, four hundred miles to the southwest, was out of the question. . . . The arctic coast couldn't be more than a hundred and fifty miles away but there was nobody there except a scattering of Huskies. . . . How about Baker Lake? He scaled off the airline distance with thumb and forefinger, ignoring the innumerable lakes and rivers across the route. About two hundred miles. He was pretty fit . . . should be able to manage twenty miles a day . . . ten days, and presto.

Movement caught his eye and he looked up. Konala, a child-like figure in her bulky deerskin clothes, had waded out to stand on the submerged tail of a float. Bent almost double, she was swinging a length of line around her head. She let the weighted hook fly so that it sailed through the air to strike the surface a hundred feet from shore.

Well, there was no way she could walk to Baker. She'd have to stay put until he could bring help. His anger surged up again. . . . Fishing, for God's sake! What in Jesus' sweet name did she think she was going to catch in that lousy little pond?

He began to check his gear. Lord, no *compass* . . . and the sun was no use this time of year. He'd never bothered to buy one of the pocket kind . . . no need for it . . . but there was a magnetic compass in the instrument panel of the old crate. . . .

Lavery hurried back to the Anson, found some tools and went to work. He was too preoccupied to notice Konala haul in her line and deftly slip a fine char off the hook. He did not see her take her curved woman's knife and slice two thick fillets from the fish. The first he knew of her success was when she appeared at the open cabin door. She was so small that her head barely reached the opening. With one hand she held a fillet up to him while with the other she pushed raw pink flesh into her mouth, pantomiming to show him how good it was.

"Jesus, no!" He was revolted and waved her away. "Eat it your-self . . . you animal!"

Obediently Konala disappeared from the doorway. Making her way ashore she scraped together a pile of dry lichens then struck a light with flint and steel. The moss smoked and began to glow. She covered it with dwarf willow twigs, then spread pieces of the fish on two flat rocks angled toward the rising flames. When Lavery descended from the plane with the compass in his hand his appetite woke with a rush at the sight and smell of roasting fish. But he did not go near the fire. Instead he retreated to the rocks where he had left his gear and dug out a can of beans. He gashed his thumb trying to open the can with his pocket knife.

Picking up the axe, he pounded the can until it split. Raging against this wasteland that had trapped him, and the fate that had stripped him of his wings, he furiously shovelled the cold mess into his mouth and choked it down.

Konala sat watching him intently. When he had finished she rose to her feet, pointed northward and asked, "*Peehuktuk?* We walk?"

Lavery's resentment exploded. Thrusting his arms through the straps of the packsack, he heaved it and the sleeping back into position then picked up the rifle and pointed with it to the southwest.

"You're goddamn right!" he shouted. "Me—*owunga peehuktuk* that way! *Eeetpeet*—you bloody well stay here!"

Without waiting to see if she had understood, he began to climb the slope of a sandy esker that rose to the south of the pond. Near the crest he paused and looked back. Konala was squatting by the tiny fire seemingly unaware that he was deserting her. He felt a momentary twinge of guilt, but shrugged it off . . . no way she could make it with him to Baker, and she had her deerskins to keep her warm. As for food, well, Huskies could eat anything . . . she'd make out. He turned and his long, ungainly figure passed over the skyline.

With a chill of dismay he looked out across the tundra rolling to a measureless horizon ahead of him—a curving emptiness more intimidating than anything he had seen in the high skies. The tongue of fear began to flicker again but he resolutely shut his mind to it and stumbled forward into that sweep of space, his heavy flight boots slipping on rocks and sucking in the muskeg, the straps of the packsack already cutting into his shoulders through the thin cotton jacket.

There is no way of knowing what Konala was thinking as she saw him go. She might have believed he was going hunting, since that would have been the natural thing for a man to do under the circumstances. But in all likelihood she guessed what he intended—otherwise, how to explain the fact that ten days later and nearly sixty miles to the south of the downed plane, the sick woman trudged wearily across a waste of sodden muskeg to climb a gravel ridge and halt beside the unconscious body of Charlie Lavery?

Squatting beside him she used her curved knife to cut away the useless remnants of his leather boots, then wrapped his torn and bloody feet in compresses of wet sphagnum moss. Slipping off her parka, she spread it over his tattered jacket to protect him from the flies. Her fingers on his emaciated and insect-bitten flesh were tender and sure. Later she built a fire, and when Lavery opened his eyes it was to find himself under a rude skin shelter with a can of fish broth being pressed lightly against his lips.

There was a hiatus in his mind. Anxiously he raised himself to see if the aircraft was still on the pond, but there was no pond and no old Anson . . . only that same stunning expanse of empty plains. With a sickening lurch, memory began to function. The seemingly endless days of his journey flooded back upon him: filled with roaring clouds of mosquitoes and flies; with a mounting, driving hunger; the agony of lacerated feet and the misery of rain-swept hours lying shelterless in a frigid void. He remembered his matches getting soaked when he tried to ford the first of a succession of rivers that forever deflected his course toward the west. He remembered losing the .22 cartridges when the box turned to mush after a rain. Above all, he remembered the unbearable sense of loneliness that grew until he began to panic, throwing away first the useless gun, then the sodden sleeping bag, the axe . . . and finally sent him, in a heart-bursting spasm of desperation, toward a stony ridge that seemed to undulate serpent-like on the otherwise shapeless face of a world that had lost all form and substance.

Konala's face came into focus as she nudged the tin against his lips. She was smiling and Lavery found himself smiling weakly back at this woman who not so long before had roused his contempt and anger.

They camped on the nameless ridge for a week while Lavery recovered some of his strength. At first he could hardly bear to leave the shelter because of the pain in his feet. But Konala seemed always on the move: gathering willow twigs for fires, collecting and cooking food, cutting and sewing a new pair of boots for Lavery from the hides she had brought with her. She appeared tireless, but that was an illusion. Her body was driven to its many tasks only at great cost.

Time had telescoped itself so that Lavery would wake from sleep with shaking hands, hearing the engines of the Anson fail. It would seem to him that the plane had crashed only a few minutes earlier. It would seem that the terrible ordeal of his march south was about to begin again and he would feel a sick return of panic. When this happened, he would desperately fix his thoughts on Konala for she was the one comforting reality in all this alien world.

He thought about her a great deal, but she was an enigma to him. Sick as she was, how had she managed to follow him across those sodden plains and broken rock ridges . . . how had she managed to keep alive in such a country?

After Konala gave him the completed skin boots carefully lined with cotton grass, he began to find answers to some of these questions. He was able to hobble far enough from camp to watch her set sinew snares for gaudy ground squirrels she called *hikik,* scoop suckers from a nearby stream with her bare hands, outrun snow geese that were still flightless after the late-summer moult, and dig succulent lemmings from their peat bog burrows. Watching her, Lavery slowly came to understand that what had seemed to him a lifeless desert was in fact a land generous in its support of those who knew its nature.

Still, the most puzzling question remained unanswered. Why had Konala not stayed in the relative safety of the aircraft or else travelled north to seek her own people? What had impelled her to follow him . . . to rescue a man of another race who had abandoned her?

Toward the end of their stay on the ridge, the sun was beginning to dip well below the horizon at night—a warning that summer was coming to an end. One day Konala again pointed north and, with a grin, she waddled duck-like a few paces in that direction. The joke at the expense of Lavery's splayed and painful feet did not annoy him. He laughed and limped after her to show his willingness to follow wherever she might lead.

When they broke camp, Konala insisted on carrying what was left of Lavery's gear along with her own pouch and the roll of caribou hides which was both shelter and bedding for them. As they trekked northward she broke into song—a high and plaintive chant without much melody which seemed as much part of the land as the fluting of curlews. When Lavery tried to find out what the song was all about, she seemed oddly reticent and all he could gather was that she was expressing kinship for someone or for some thing beyond his ken. He did not understand that she was joining her voice to the voice of the land and to the spirits of the land.

Retracing their path under Konala's tutelage became a journey of discovery. Lavery was forever being surprised at how different the tundra had now become from the dreadful void he had trudged across not long since.

He discovered it was full of birds ranging from tiny longspurs whose muted colouring made them almost invisible, to great saffron-breasted hawks circling high above the bogs and lakes. Konala also drew his attention to the endless diversity of tundra plants, from livid orange lichens to azure flowers whose blooms were so tiny he had to kneel to see them clearly.

Once Konala motioned him to crawl beside her to the crest of an esker. In the valley beyond, a family of white wolves was lazily hunting lemmings in a patch of sedge a hundred feet away. The nearness of the big beasts made Lavery uneasy until Konala boldly stood up and called to the wolves in their own language. They drew together then, facing her in a half circle, and answered with a long, lilting chorus before trotting away in single file.

Late one afternoon they at last caught sight of a splash of brilliant colour in the distance. Lavery's heartbeat quickened and he pushed forward without regard for his injured feet. The yellow-painted Anson *might* have been spotted by a search plane during their absence . . . rescue by his own kind might still be possible. But when the man and woman descended the esker to the shore of the pond, they found the Anson exactly as they had left it. There had been no human visitors.

Bitterly disappointed, Lavery climbed into the cockpit, seated himself behind the controls and slumped into black depression. Konala's intention of travelling northward to rejoin her own people on the coast now loomed as an ordeal whose outcome would probably be death during the first winter storm . . . if they could last that long. Their worn clothing and almost hairless robes were already bare adequate to keep the cold at bay. Food was getting harder to find as the birds left, the small animals began to dig in and the fish ran back to the sea. And what about fuel when the weather really began to turn against them?

Lavery was sullen and silent that evening as they ate their boiled fish, but Konala remained cheerful. She kept repeating the word *tuktu*—caribou— as she vainly tried to make him understand that soon they would have the wherewithal to continue the journey north.

As the night wind began to rise he ignored the skin shelter which Konala had erected and, taking one of the robes, climbed back into the plane and rolled himself up on the icy metal floor. During the next few days he spent most of his time in the Anson, sometimes fiddling with the knobs of the useless radio, but for the most part morosely staring through the Plexiglass windscreen at a landscape which seemed to grow increasingly bleak as the first frosts greyed the tundra flowers and browned the windswept sedges.

Early one morning an unfamiliar sound brought him out of a chilled, nightmarish sleep. It was a muffled, subdued noise as of waves rolling in on a distant shore. For one heart-stopping instant he thought it was the beat of an aircraft engine, then he heard Konala's exultant cry.

"*Tuktoraikayai*—the deer have come!"

From the window of the dead machine Lavery looked out upon a miracle of life. An undulating mass of antlered animals was pouring out of the north. It rolled steadily toward the pond, split, and began enveloping it. The rumble resolved itself into a rattling cadence of hooves on rock and gravel. As the animals swept past, the stench of barnyard grew strong even inside the plane. Although in the days when he had flown high above them Lavery had often seen skeins of migrating caribou laced across the arctic plains like a pattern of beaded threads, he could hardly credit what he now beheld . . . the land inundated under a veritable flood of life. His depression began to dissipate as he felt himself being drawn into and becoming almost a part of that living river.

While he stared, awe-struck and incredulous, Konala went to work. Some days earlier she had armed herself with a spear, its shaft made from a paddle she had found in the Anson and its double-edged blade filed out of a piece of steel broken from the tip of the plane's anchor. With this in hand she was now scurrying about on the edge of the herd. The press was so great that individual deer could not avoid her. A snorting buck leapt high as the spear drove into him just behind the ribs. His dying leap carried him onto the backs of some of his neighbours, and as he slid off and disappeared into the ruck, Konala's blade thrust into another victim. She chose the fattest beasts and those with the best hides.

When the tide of caribou finally thinned, there was much work for Konala's knife. She skinned, scraped and staked out several prime hides destined for the making of clothes and sleeping robes, then turned her attention to a small mountain of meat and began slicing it into paper-thin sheets which she draped over dwarf willow bushes. When dry this would make light, imperishable food fit to sustain a man and woman—one injured and the other sick—who must undertake a long, demanding journey.

Revitalized by the living ambience of the great herd, Lavery came to help her. She glanced up at him and her face was radiant. She cut off a piece of brisket and held it out to him, grinning delightedly when he took it and tore off a piece with his teeth. It was his idea to make a stove out of two empty oil cans upon which the fat which Konala had gathered could be rendered into white cakes that would provide food *and* fuel in the times ahead.

Several days of brisk, clear weather followed. While the meat dried on the bushes, Konala laboured on, cutting and stitching clothing for them both. She worked herself so hard that her cheeks again showed the flame of fever and her rasping cough grew worse. When Lavery tried to make her take things a little easier she became impatient with him. Konala knew what she knew.

Finally on a day in mid–September she decided they were ready. With Lavery limping at her side, she turned her back on the white men's fine machine and set out to find her people.

The skies darkened and cold gales began sweeping gusts of snow across the bogs whose surfaces were already crusting with ice crystals. One day a sleet storm forced them into early camp. Konala had left the little travel tent to gather willows for the fire and Lavery was dozing when he heard her cry of warning through the shrilling of the wind.

There was no mistaking the urgency in her voice. Snatching up the spear he limped from the tent to see Konala running across a narrow valley. Behind her, looming immense and forbidding in the leaden light, was one of the great brown bears of the barrenlands.

Seeing Lavery poised on the slope above her, Konala swerved away, even though this brought her closer to the bear. It took a moment for Lavery to realize that she was attempting to distract the beast, then he raised the spear and flung himself down the slope, shouting and cursing at the top of his lungs.

The bear's interest in the woman shifted to the surprising spectacle Lavery presented. It sat up on its massive haunches and peered doubtfully at him through the veil of sleet.

When he was a scant few yards from the bear, Lavery tripped and fell, rolling helplessly among the rocks to fetch up on his back staring upward into that huge, square face. The bear looked back impassively then snorted, dropped on all fours and shambled off.

The meeting with the bear crystallized the changes which had been taking place in Lavery. Clad in caribou-skin clothing, a dark beard ringing his cheeks, and his hair hanging free to his shoulders, he had acquired a look of litheness and vigour—and of watchfulness. No longer was he an alien in an inimical land. He was a man now in his own right, able to make his way in an elder world.

In Konala's company he knew a unity that he had previously felt only with members of his bombing crew. The weeks they had spent together had eroded the barrier of language and he was beginning to understand much about her that had earlier baffled him. Yet the core of the enigma remained for he had not found the answer to the question that he haunted him since she brought life back to his body on that distant southern ridge.

For some time they had been descending an already frozen and snow-covered river which Konala had given him to understand would lead them to the coast. But with each passing day, Konala had been growing weaker even as Lavery regained his strength. At night, when she supposed him to be asleep, she sometimes moaned softly, and during the day she could walk only for short distances between paroxysms of coughing that left blood stains in the new snow at her feet.

When the first real blizzard struck them, it was Lavery who set up the travel tent and lit the fire of lichens and caribou fat upon which to simmer some dried deer meat. Konala lay under their sleeping robes while he prepared the meal, and when he turned to her he saw how the lines of pain around her mouth had deepened into crevices. He came close and held a tin of warm soup to her dry lips. She drank a mouthful then lay back, her dark eyes glittering too brightly in the meagre firelight. He looked deep into them and read the confirmation of his fear.

Keeping her eyes on his, she took a new pair of skin boots from under the robes and slowly stroked them, feeling the infinitely fine stitching which would keep them waterproof. After a time she reached out and placed them in his lap. Then she spoke, slowly and carefully so he would be sure to understand.

"They are not very good boots but they might carry you to the camps of my people. They might help you return to your own land. . . . Walk well in them . . . my brother."

Later that night the gale rose to a crescendo. The cold drove into the tent and, ignoring the faint flicker of the fire, pierced through the thick caribou robes wrapped about Konala and entered into her.

When the storm had blown itself out, Lavery buried her under a cairn of rocks on the high banks of the nameless river. As he made his way northward in the days that followed, his feet finding their own sure way, he no longer pondered the question which had lain in his mind through so many weeks . . . for he could still hear the answer she had made and would forever hear it: Walk well . . . my brother. . . .

Three Skeleton Key

BY GEORGE G. TOUDOUZE

E arlier in the book, when I introduced Carl Stephenson's memorable "Leiningen Versus the Ants," I cited the story as being one of the gems unearthed by the legendary editor and publisher Arnold Gingrich during the years he was making *Esquire* magazine an American icon.

Here is another tale from Gingrich's early *Esquire* years, the thirties, when he wasn't afraid to publish nonfiction and fiction from unknown writers right alongside the era's literary varsity—writers like Ernest Hemingway, F. Scott Fitzgerald, John Steinbeck, Theodore Dreiser, and Irwin Shaw.

Carl Stephenson and George G. Toudouze were such "unknowns," but their stories have survived to this day.

In Stephenson's tale there was a problem with some ants. This time out, the mischief is being created by some rats.

* * * * *

My most terrifying experience? Well, one does have a few in thirty-five years of service in the Lights, although it's mostly monotonous routine work—keeping the light in order, making out the reports.

When I was a young man, not very long in the service, there was an opening in a lighthouse newly built off the coast of Guiana, on a small rock twenty miles or so from the mainland. The pay was high, so in order to reach the sum I had set out to save before I married, I volunteered for service in the new light.

Three Skeleton Key, the small rock on which the light stood, bore a bad reputation. It earned its name from the story of the three convicts who, escaping from Cayenne in a stolen dugout canoe, were wrecked on the rock during the night, managed to escape the sea but eventually died of hunger and

6 1

thirst. When they were discovered, nothing remained but three heaps of bones, picked clean by the birds. The story was that the three skeletons, gleaming with phosphorescent light, danced over the small rock, screaming. . . .

But there are many such stories and I did not give the warnings of the old-timers at the *Isle de Sein* a second thought. I signed up, boarded ship and in a month I was installed at the light.

Picture a grey, tapering cylinder, welded to the solid black rock by iron rods and concrete, rising from a small island twenty odd miles from land. It lay in the midst of the sea, this island, a small, bare piece of stone, about one hundred fifty feet long, perhaps forty, wide. Small, barely large enough for a man to walk about and stretch his legs at low tide.

This is an advantage one doesn't find in all lights, however, for some of them rise sheer from the waves, with no room for one to move save within the light itself. Still, on our island, one must be careful, for the rocks were treacherously smooth. One misstep and down you would fall into the sea—not that the risk of drowning was so great, but the waters about our island swarmed with huge sharks who kept an eternal patrol around the base of the light.

Still, it was a nice life there. We had enough provisions to last for months, in the event that the sea should become too rough for the supply ship to reach us on schedule. During the day we would work about the light, cleaning the rooms, polishing the metalwork and the lens and reflector of the light itself, and at night we would sit on the gallery and watch our light, a twenty thousand candlepower lantern, swinging its strong, white bar of light over the sea from the top of its hundred twenty foot tower. Some days, when the air would be very clear, we could see the land, a thread-like line to the west. To the east, north and south stretched the ocean. Landsmen, perhaps, would soon have tired of that kind of life, perched on a small island off the coast of South America for eighteen weeks, until one's turn for leave ashore came around. But we liked it there, my two fellow-tenders and myself—so much so that, for twenty-two months on end with the exception of shore leaves, I was greatly satisfied with the life on Three Skeleton Key.

I had just returned from my leave at the end of June, that is to say midwinter in that latitude, and had settled down to the routine with my two fellow-keepers, a Breton by the name of Le Gleo and the head-keeper Itchoua, a Basque some dozen years or so older than either of us.

Eight days went by as usual, then on the ninth night after my return, Itchoua, who was on night duty, called Le Gleo and me, sleeping in our rooms in the middle of the tower, at two in the morning. We rose immediately and, climbing the thirty or so steps that led to the gallery, stood beside our chief.

Itchoua pointed, and following his finger, we saw a big three-master, with all sail set, heading straight for the light. A queer course, for the vessel must have seen us, our light lit her with the glare of day, each time it passed over her.

Now, ships were a rare sight in our waters for our light was a warning of treacherous reefs, barely hidden under the surface and running far out to sea. Consequently we were always given a wide berth, especially by sailing vessels, which cannot maneuver as readily as steamers.

No wonder that we were surprised at seeing this three-master heading dead for us in the gloom of early morning. I had immediately recognized her lines, for she stood out plainly, even at the distance of a mile, when our light shone on her.

She was a beautiful ship of some four thousand tons, a fast sailer that had carried cargoes to every part of the world, plowing the seas unceasingly. By her lines she was identified as Dutch-built, which was understandable as Paramaribo and Dutch Guiana are very close to Cayenne.

Watching her sailing dead for us, a white wave boiling under her bows, Le Gleo cried out:

"What's wrong with her crew? Are they all drunk or insane? Can't they see us?"

Itchoua nodded soberly, looked at us sharply as he remarked: "See us? No doubt—if there *is* a crew aboard!"

"What do you mean chief?" Le Gleo had started, turned to the Basque, "Are you saying that she's the 'Flying Dutchman'?"

His sudden fright had been so evident that the older man laughed:

"No, old man, that's not what I meant. If I say that no one's aboard, I mean she's a derelict."

Then we understood her queer behavior. Itchoua was right. For some reason, believing her doomed, her crew had abandoned her. Then she had righted herself and sailed on, wandering with the wind.

The three of us grew tense as the ship seemed about to crash on one of our numerous reefs, but she suddenly lurched with some change of the wind, the yards swung around and the derelict came clumsily about and sailed dead away from us.

In the light of our lantern she seemed so sound, so strong, that Itchoua exclaimed impatiently:

"But why the devil was she abandoned? Nothing is smashed, no sign of fire—and she doesn't sail as if she were taking water."

Le Gleo waved to the departing ship:

"*Bon voyage!*" He smiled at Itchoua and went on. "She's leaving us, chief, and now we'll never know what—"

"No, she's not!" cried the Basque. "Look! She's turning!"

As if obeying his words, the derelict three-master stopped, came about and headed for us once more. And for the next four hours the vessel played around us—zigzagging, coming out, stopping, then suddenly lurching forward. No doubt some freak of current and wind, of which our island was the center, kept her near us.

Then suddenly, the tropic dawn broke, the sun rose and it was day, and the ship was plainly visible as she sailed past us. Our light extinguished, we returned to the gallery with our glasses and inspected her.

The three of us focused our glasses on her poop, saw standing out sharply, black letters on the white background of a life-ring, the stenciled name:

"*Cornelius-de-Witt, Rotterdam.*"

We had read her lines correctly, she was Dutch. Just then the wind rose and the *Cornelius de Witt* changed course, leaned to port and headed straight for us once more. But this time she was so close that we knew she would not turn in time.

"Thunder!" cried Le Gleo, his Breton soul aching to see a fine ship doomed to smash upon a reef, "she's going to pile up! She's gone!"

I shook my head:

"Yes, and a shame to see that beautiful ship wreck herself. And we're helpless."

There was nothing we could do but watch. A ship sailing with all sail spread, creaming the sea with her forefoot as she runs before the wind, is one of the most beautiful sights in the world—but this time I could feel the tears stinging in my eyes as I saw this fine ship headed for her doom.

All this time our glasses were riveted on her and we suddenly cried out together:

"The rats!"

Now we knew why this ship, in perfect condition, was sailing without her crew aboard. They had been driven out by the rats. Not those poor specimens of rats you see ashore, barely reaching the length of one foot from their trembling noses to the tip of their skinny tails, wretched creatures that dodge and hide at the meer sound of a footfall.

No, these were ships' rats, huge, wise creatures, born on the sea, sailing all over the world on ships, transferring to other, larger ships as they multiply.

There is as much difference between the rats of the land and these maritime rats as between a fishing smack and an armored cruiser.

The rats of the sea are fierce, bold animals. Large, strong and intelligent, clannish and seawise, able to put the best of mariners to shame with their knowledge of the sea, their uncanny ability to foretell the weather.

And they are brave, these rats, and vengeful. If you so much as harm one, his sharp cry will bring hordes of his fellows to swarm over you, tear you and not cease until your flesh has been stripped from the bones.

The ones on this ship, the rats of Holland, are the worst, superior to other rats of the sea as their brethren are to the land rats. There is a well-known tale about these animals.

A Dutch captain, thinking to protect his cargo, brought aboard his ship—not cats—but two terriers, dogs trained in the hunting, fighting and killing of vicious rats. By the time the ship, sailing from Rotterdam, had passed the Ostend light, the dogs were gone and never seen again. In twenty-four hours they had been overwhelmed, killed and eaten by the rats.

At times, when the cargo does not suffice, the rats attack the crew, either driving them from the ship or eating them alive. And studying the *Cornelius de Witt,* I turned sick, for her small boats were all in place. She had not been abandoned.

Over her bridge, on her deck, in the rigging, on every visible spot, the ship was a writhing mass—a starving army coming towards us aboard a vessel gone mad!

Our island was a small spot in that immense stretch of sea. The ship could have grazed us, passed to port or starboard with its ravening cargo—but no, she came for us at full speed, as if she were leading the regatta at a race, and impaled herself on a sharp point of rock.

There was a dull shock as her bottom stove in, then a horrible crackling as the three masts went overboard at once, as if cut down with one blow of some gigantic sickle. A sighing groan came as the water rushed into the ship, then she split in two and sank like a stone.

But the rats did not drown. Not these fellows! As much at home in the sea as any fish, they formed ranks in the water, heads lifted, tails stretched out, paws paddling. And half of them, those from the forepart of the ship, sprang along the masts and onto the rocks in the instant before she sank. Before we had time even to move, nothing remained of the three-master save some pieces of wreckage floating on the surface and an army of rats covering the rocks left bare by the receding tide.

Thousands of heads rose, felt the wind and we were scented, seen! To them we were fresh meat, after possible weeks of starving. There came a scream, composed of innumerable screams, sharper than the howl of a saw attacking a bar of iron, and in the one motion, every rat leaped to attack the tower!

We barely had time to leap back, close the door leading onto the gallery, descend the stairs and shut every window tightly. Luckily the door at the base of the light, which we never could have reached in time, was of bronze set in granite and was tightly closed.

The horrible band, in no measurable time, had swarmed up and over the tower as if it had been a tree, piled on the embrasures of the windows, scraped at the glass with thousands of claws, covered the lighthouse with a furry mantle and reached the top of the tower, filling the gallery and piling atop the lantern.

Their teeth grated as they pressed against the glass of the lantern-room, where they could plainly see us, though they could not reach us. A few millimeters of glass, luckily very strong, separated our faces from their gleaming, beady eyes, their sharp claws and teeth. Their odor filled the tower, poisoned our lungs and rasped our nostrils with a pestilential, nauseating smell. And there we were, sealed alive in our own light, prisoners of a horde of starving rats.

That first night, the tension was so great that we could not sleep. Every moment, we felt that some opening had been made, some window given way, and that our horrible besiegers were pouring through the breach. The rising tide, chasing those of the rats which had stayed on the bare rocks, increased the numbers clinging to the walls, piled on the balcony—so much so that clusters of rats clinging to one another hung from the lantern and the gallery.

With the coming of darkness we lit the light and the turning beam completely maddened the beasts. As the light turned, it successively blinded thousands of rats crowded against the glass, while the darkside of the lantern-room gleamed with thousands of points of light, burning like the eyes of jungle beasts in the night.

All the while we could hear the enraged scraping of claws against the stone and glass, while the chorus of cries was so loud that we had to shout to hear one another. From time to time, some of the rats fought among themselves and a dark cluster would detach itself, falling into the sea like a ripe fruit from a tree. Then we would see phosphorescent streaks as triangular fins slashed the water—sharks, permanent guardians of our rock, feasting on our jailors.

The next day we were calmer, and amused ourselves teasing the rats, placing our faces against the glass which separated us. They could not fathom the invisible barrier which separated them from us and we laughed as we watched them leaping against the heavy glass.

But the day after that, we realized how serious our position was. The air was foul, even the heavy smell of oil within our stronghold could not dominate the fetid odor of the beasts massed around us. And there was no way of admitting fresh air without also admitting the rats.

The morning of the fourth day, at early dawn, I saw the wooden framework of my window, eaten away from the outside, sagging inwards. I called my comrades and the three of us fastened a sheet of tin in the opening, sealing it tightly. When we had completed the task, Itchoua turned to us and said dully:

"Well—the supply boat came thirteen days ago, and she won't be back for twenty-nine." He pointed at the white metal plate sealing the opening through the granite—"If that gives way—" he shrugged—"they can change the name of this place to Six Skeleton Key."

The next six days and seven nights, our only distraction was watching the rats whose holds were insecure, fall a hundred and twenty feet into the maws of the sharks—but they were so many that we could not see any diminution in their numbers.

Thinking to calm ourselves and pass the time, we attempted to count them, but we soon gave up. They moved incessantly, never still. Then we tried identifying them, naming them.

One of them, larger than the others, who seemed to lead them in their rushes against the glass separating us, we named "Nero"; and there were several others whom we had learned to distinguish through various peculiarities.

But the thought of our bones joining those of the convicts was always in the back of our minds. And the gloom of our prison fed these thoughts, for the interior of the light was almost completely dark, as we had to seal every window in the same fashion as mine, and the only space that still admitted daylight was the glassed-in lantern-room at the very top of the tower.

Then Le Gleo became morose and had nightmares in which he would see the three skeletons dancing around him, gleaming coldly, seeking to grasp him. His maniacal, raving descriptions were so vivid that Itchoua and I began seeing them also.

It was a living nightmare, the raging cries of the rats as they swarmed over the light, mad with hunter; the sickening, strangling odor of their bodies—

True, there is a way of signaling from lighthouses. But to reach the mast on which to hang the signal we would have to go out on the gallery where the rats were.

There was only one thing left to do. After debating all of the ninth day, we decided not to light the lantern that night. This is the greatest breach of our service, never committed as long as the tenders of the light are alive; for the light is something sacred, warning ships of danger in the night. Either the light gleams, a quarter hour after sundown, or no one is left alive to light it.

Well, that night, Three Skeleton Light was dark, and all the men were alive. At the risk of causing ships to crash on our reefs, we left it unlit, for we were worn out—going mad!

At two in the morning, while Itchoua was dozing in his room, the sheet of metal sealing his window gave way. The chief had just time enough to leap to his feet and cry for help, the rats swarming over him.

But Le Gleo and I, who had been watching from the lantern-room, got to him immediately, and the three of us battled with the horde of maddened rats which flowed through the gaping window. They bit, we struck them down with our knives—and retreated.

We locked the door of the room on them, but before we had time to bind our wounds, the door was eaten through, and gave way and we retreated up the stairs, fighting off the rats that leaped on us from the knee deep swarm.

I do not remember, to this day, how we ever managed to escape. All I can remember is wading through them up the stairs, striking them off as they swarmed over us; and then we found ourselves, bleeding from innumerable bites, our clothes shredded, sprawled across the trapdoor in the floor of the lantern-room—without food or drink. Luckily, the trapdoor was metal set into the granite with iron bolts.

The rats occupied the entire light beneath us, and on the floor of our retreat lay some twenty of their fellows, who had gotten in with us before the trapdoor closed, and whom we had killed with our knives. Below us, in the tower, we could hear the screams of the rats as they devoured everything edible that they found. Those on the outside squealed in reply, and writhed in a horrible curtain as they stared at us through the glass of the lantern-room.

Itchoua sat up, stared silently at his blood trickling from the wounds on his limbs and body, and running in thin streams on the floor around him. Le Gleo, who was in as bad a state (and so was I, for that matter) stared at the chief and me vacantly, started as his gaze swung to the multitude of rats against the glass, then suddenly began laughing horribly:

"Hee! Hee! The Three Skeletons! Hee! Hee! The Three Skeletons are now *six* skeletons! *Six* skeletons!"

He threw his head back and howled, his eyes glazed, a trickle of saliva running from the corners of his mouth and thinning the blood flowing over his chest. I shouted to him to shut up, but he did not hear me, so I did the only thing I could to quiet him—I swung the back of my hand across his face.

The howling stopped suddenly, his eyes swung around the room, then he bowed his head and began weeping softly, like a child.

Our darkened light had been noticed from the mainland, and as dawn was breaking the patrol was there, to investigate the failure of our light. Looking through my binoculars, I could see the horrified expression on the faces of the officers and crew when, the daylight strengthening, they saw the light completely covered by a seething mass of rats. They thought, as I afterwards found out, that we had been eaten alive.

But the rats had also seen the ship, or had scented the crew. As the ship drew nearer, a solid phalanx left the light, plunged into the water and, swimming out, attempted to board her. They would have succeeded, as the ship was hove to, but the engineer connected his steam to hose on the deck and scalded the head of the attacking column, which slowed them up long enough for the ship to get underway and leave the rats behind.

Then the sharks took part. Belly up, mouths gaping, they arrived in swarms and scooped up the rats, sweeping through them like a sickle through wheat. That was one day that sharks really served a useful purpose.

The remaining rats turned tail, swam to the shore and emerged dripping. As they neared the light, their comrades greeted them with shrill cries, with what sounded like a derisive note predominating. They answered angrily and mingled with their fellows. From the several tussles that broke out, they resented being ridiculed for their failure to capture the ship.

But all this did nothing to get us out of our jail. The small ship could not approach, but steamed around the light at a safe distance, and the tower must have seemed fantastic, some weird, many-mouthed beast hurling defiance at them.

Finally, seeing the rats running in and out of the tower through the door and the windows, those on the ship decided that we had perished and were about to leave when Itchoua, regaining his senses, thought of using the light as a signal. He lit it and, using a plank placed and withdrawn before the beam to form the dots and dashes, quickly sent out our story to those on the vessel.

Our reply came quickly. When they understood our position, how we could not get rid of the rats, Le Gleo's mind going fast, Itchoua and myself covered with bites; cornered in the lantern-room without food or water, they had a signal-man send us their reply.

His arms swinging like those of a windmill, he quickly spelled out:

"Don't give up, hang on a little longer! We'll get you out of this!"

Then she turned and steamed at top speed for the coast, leaving us little reassured.

She was back at noon, accompanied by the supply ship, two small coast guard boats, and the fire boat—a small squadron. At twelve-thirty the battle was on.

After a short reconnaissance, the fire boat picked her way slowly through the reefs until she was close to us, then turned her powerful jet of water on the rats. The heavy stream tore the rats from their places, hurled them screaming into the water where the sharks gulped them down. But for every ten that were dislodged, seven swam ashore, and the stream could do nothing to the rats within the tower. Furthermore, some of them, instead of returning to the rocks, boarded the fire boat and the men were forced to battle them hand to hand. They were true rats of Holland, fearing no man, fighting for the right to live!

Nightfall came, and it was as if nothing had been done, the rats were still in possession. One of the patrol boats stayed by the island, the rest of the flotilla departed for the coast. We had to spend another night in our prison. Le Gleo was sitting on the floor, babbling about skeletons and as I turned to Itchoua, he fell unconscious from his wounds. I was in no better shape and could feel my blood flaming with fever.

Somehow the night dragged by, and the next afternoon I saw a tug, accompanied by the fire boat, come from the mainland with a huge barge in tow. Through my glasses, I saw that the barge was filled with meat.

Risking the treacherous reefs, the tug dragged the barge as close to the island as possible. To the last rat, our besiegers deserted the rock, swam out and boarded the barge reeking with the scent of freshly cut meat. The tug dragged the barge about a mile from shore, where the fire boat drenched the barge with gasoline. A well placed incendiary shell from the patrol boat set her on fire.

The barge was covered with flames immediately and the rats took to the water in swarms, but the patrol boat bombarded them with shrapnel from a safe distance, and the sharks finished off the survivors.

A whaleboat from the patrol boat took us off the island and left three men to replace us. By nightfall we were in the hospital in Cayenne. What became of my friends?

Well, Le Gleo's mind had cracked and he was raving mad. They sent him back to France and locked him up in an asylum, the poor devil; Itchoua died within a week; a rat's bite is dangerous in that hot, humid climate, and infection sets in rapidly.

As for me—when they fumigated the light and repaired the damage done by the rats, I resumed my service there. Why not? No reason why such an incident should keep me from finishing out my service there, is there?

Besides—I told you I liked the place—to be truthful, I've never had a post as pleasant as that one, and when my time came to leave it forever, I tell you that I almost wept as Three Skeleton Key disappeared below the horizon.

Shipwreck of the Whaleship Essex

BY OWEN CHASE

I f you've ever been inclined to think that the images of the great white whale Moby-Dick taking out the whaleship *Pequod* with a slam-dunk move seemed a bit far-fetched, you might owe Mister Herman Melville an apology. As subsequent history has revealed, it seems old Herm got the original germ of the idea for his great novel from real life—a Nantucket whaleship named *Essex* that got the deep six in an attack by a sperm whale in the Pacific. Twenty men survived the sinking of the *Essex* by taking to three open lifeboats, but only eight of these shipwreck survivors lived to tell the story of what happened during the sea journey. For three months and three thousand miles the whaling men suffered the worst ordeals of hunger and thirst imaginable in their epic journey for survival. One of the boats was lost at sea, and eventually the other two became separated. Before they reached the haven of rescue, the survivors resorted to cannibalism to sustain life.

Owen Chase was the first mate of the *Essex* and was one of the eight survivors. Twenty years after his narrative of the ordeal was originally published, Herman Melville borrowed a copy from Chase's son and read it while at sea on a whaling vessel in the South Pacific. "The reading of the wondrous story upon the landless sea and very close to the very latitude of the shipwreck had a surprising effect on me," Melville later wrote. He actually started writing *Moby-Dick* eight years after reading Chase's book.

This excerpt of the Owen Chase narrative is from the edition published by The Lyons Press in 1999, with an introduction by Tim Cahill. Two separate sections are excerpted. The first describes the actual attack of the whale, and the crew taking to the boats on November 20, 1820. As the second part of the excerpt begins, the whalers are struggling to stay alive on Henderson Island deep in the South Pacific, far west of Easter Island and actually not too far from Pitcairn Island, famous as the last stop of the H.M.S. *Bounty.* When the men arrived on the island on December 20, they thought their prayers had been answered, but subsequent exploration has shown that the place is virtually barren of food and water. Thoughts of resuming their dreadful ocean voyage are rampart.

★   ★   ★   ★   ★

I have not been able to recur to the scenes which are now to become the subject of description, although a considerable time has elapsed, without feeling a mingled emotion of horror and astonishment at the almost incredible destiny that has preserved me and my surviving companions from a terrible death. Frequently, in my reflections on the subject, even after this lapse of time, I find myself shedding tears of gratitude for our deliverance, and blessing God, by whose divine aid and protection we were conducted through a series of unparalleled suffering and distress, and restored to the bosoms of our families and friends. There is no knowing what a stretch of pain and misery the human mind is capable of contemplating, when it is wrought upon by the anxieties of preservation; nor what pangs and weaknesses the body is able to endure, until they are visited upon it; and when at last deliverance comes, when the dream of hope is realized, unspeakable gratitude takes possession of the soul, and tears of joy choke the utterance. We require to be taught in the school of some signal suffering, privation, and despair, the great lessons of constant dependence upon an almighty forbearance and mercy. In the midst of the wide ocean, at night, when the sight of the heavens was shut out, and the dark tempest came upon us, then it was that we felt ourselves ready to exclaim, "Heaven have mercy upon us, for nought but that can save us now." But I proceed to the recital.—On the 20th of November (cruising in latitude 0°40′S., longitude 119° 0′W.), a shoal of whales was discovered off the lee-bow. The weather at this time was extremely fine and clear, and it was about 8 o'clock in the morning that the man at the mast-head gave the usual cry of, "There she blows." The ship was immediately put away, and we ran down in the direction for them. When we had got within half a mile of the place where they were observed, all our boats were lowered down, manned, and we started in pursuit of them. The ship, in the meantime, was brought to the wind, and the main-top-sail hove aback, to wait for us. I had the harpoon in the second boat; the captain preceded me in the first. When I arrived at the spot where we calculated they were, nothing was at first to be seen. We lay on our oars in anxious expectation of discovering them come up somewhere near us. Presently one rose, and spouted a short distance ahead of my boat; I made all speed towards it, came up with, and struck it; feeling the harpoon in him, he threw himself, in agony, over

towards the boat (which at that time was up alongside of him), and, giving a severe blow with his tail, struck the boat near the edge of the water, amidships,
and stove a hole in her. I immediately took up the boat hatchet, and cut the
line, to disengage the boat from the whale, which by this time was running off
with great velocity. I succeeded in getting clear of him, with the loss of the
harpoon and line; and finding the water to pour fast in the boat, I hastily
stuffed three or four of our jackets in the hole, ordered one man to keep constantly bailing, and the rest to pull immediately for the ship; we succeeded in
keeping the boat free, and shortly gained the ship. The captain and the second
mate, in the other two boats, kept up the pursuit, and soon struck another
whale. They being at this time a considerable distance to leeward, I went forward, braced around the mainyard, and put the ship off in a direction for them;
the boat which had been stove was immediately hoisted in, and after examining the hole, I found that I could, by nailing a piece of canvas over it, get her
ready to join in a fresh pursuit, sooner than by lowering down the other remaining boat which belonged to the ship. I accordingly turned her over upon
the quarter, and was in the act of nailing on the canvas, when I observed a very
large spermaceti whale, as well as I could judge about eighty-five feet in
length; he broke water about twenty rods off our weather-bow, and was lying
quietly, with his head in a direction for the ship. He spouted two or three
times, and then disappeared. In less than two or three seconds he came up
again, about the length of the ship off, and made directly for us, at the rate of
about three knots. The ship was then going with about the same velocity. His
appearance and attitude gave us at first no alarm; but while I stood watching
his movements, and observing him but a ship's length off, coming down for us
with great celerity, I involuntarily ordered the boy at the helm to put it hard
up; intending to sheer off and avoid him. The words were scarcely out of my
mouth, before he came down upon us with full speed, and struck the ship with
his head, just forward of the fore-chains*; he gave us such an appalling and
tremendous jar, as nearly threw us all on our faces. The ship brought up as suddenly and violently as if she had struck a rock, and trembled for a few seconds
like a leaf. We looked at each other with perfect amazement, deprived almost
of the power of speech. Many minutes elapsed before we were able to realize
the dreadful accident; during which time he passed under the ship, grazing her
keel as he went along, came up alongside of her to leeward, and lay on the top
of the water (apparently stunned with the violence of the blow) for the space
of a minute; he then suddenly started off, in a direction to leeward. After a few

---

*Between the platform where the foremast shrouds were secured and the bow of the ship.

moments reflection, and recovering, in some measure, from the sudden consternation that had seized us, I of course concluded that he had stove a hole in the ship, and that it would be necessary to set the pumps going. Accordingly they were rigged, but had not been in operation more than one minute before I perceived the head of the ship to be gradually settling down in the water; I then ordered the signal to be set for the other boats, which, scarcely had I despatched, before I again discovered the whale, apparently in convulsions, on the top of the water, about one hundred rods to leeward. He was enveloped in the foam of the sea, that his continual and violent thrashing about in the water had created around him, and I could distinctly see him smite his jaws together, as if distracted with rage and fury. He remained a short time in this situation, and then started off with great velocity, across the bows of the ship, to windward. By this time the ship had settled down a considerable distance in the water, and I gave her up for lost. I, however, ordered the pumps to be kept constantly going, and endeavoured to collect my thoughts for the occasion. I turned to the boats, two of which we then had with the ship, with an intention of clearing them away, and getting all things ready to embark in them, if there should be no other resource left; and while my attention was thus engaged for a moment, I was aroused with the cry of a man at the hatchway, "Here he is—he is making for us again." I turned around, and saw him about one hundred rods directly ahead of us, coming down apparently with twice his ordinary speed, and to me at that moment, it appeared with tenfold fury and vengeance in his aspect. The surf flew in all directions about him, and his course towards us was marked by a white foam of a rod in width, which he made with the continual violent thrashing of his tail; his head was about half out of water, and in that way he came upon, and again struck the ship. I was in hopes when I descried him making for us, that by a dexterous movement of putting the ship away immediately, I should be able to cross the line of his approach, before he could get up to us, and thus avoid what I knew, if he should strike us again, would prove our inevitable destruction. I bawled out to the helmsman, "Hard up!" but she had not fallen off more than a point, before we took the second shock. I should judge the speed of the ship to have been at this time about three knots, and that of the whale about six. He struck her to windward, directly under the cathead,* and completely stove in her bows. He passed under the ship again, went off to leeward, and we saw no more of him. Our situation at this juncture can be more readily imagined than described. The shock to our feelings was such, as I am sure none can have an adequate conception of that

---

*A projecting timber near the bow, to which the anchor is hoisted.

were not there: the misfortune befell us at a moment when we least dreamt of any accident; and from the pleasing anticipations we had formed, of realizing the certain profits of our labour, we were dejected by a sudden, most mysterious, and overwhelming calamity. Not a moment, however, was to be lost in endeavouring to provide for the extremity to which it was now certain we were reduced. We were more than a thousand miles from the nearest land, and with nothing but a light open boat, as the resource of safety for myself and companions. I ordered the men to cease pumping, and every one to provide for himself; seizing a hatchet at the same time, I cut away the lashings of the spare boat, which lay bottom up across two spars directly over the quarter deck, and cried out to those near me to take her as she came down. They did so accordingly, and bore her on their shoulders as far as the waist of the ship. The steward had in the meantime gone down into the cabin twice, and saved two quadrants, two practical navigators,* and the captain's trunk and mine; all which were hastily thrown into the boat, as she lay on the deck, with the two compasses which I snatched from the binnacle.† He attempted to descend again; but the water by this time had rushed in, and he returned without being able to effect his purpose. By the time we had got the boat to the waist, the ship had filled with water, and was going down on her beam-ends: we shoved our boat as quickly as possible from the plank-shear* into the water, all hands jumping in her at the same time, and launched off clear of the ship. We were scarcely two boat lengths distant from her, when she fell over to windward, and settled down in the water.

Amazement and despair now wholly took possession of us. We contemplated the frightful situation the ship lay in, and thought with horror upon the sudden and dreadful calamity that had overtaken us. We looked upon each other, as if to gather some consolatory sensation from an interchange of sentiments, but every countenance was marked with the paleness of despair. Not a word was spoken for several minutes by any of us; all appeared to be bound in a spell of stupid consternation; and from the time we were first attacked by the whale, to the period of the fall of the ship, and of our leaving her in the boat, more than ten minutes could not certainly have elapsed! God only knows in what way, or by what means, we were enabled to accomplish in that short time what we did; the cutting away and transporting the boat from where she was

---

*Probably Nathaniel Bowditch's *New American Practical Navigator;* the fourth edition was issued in 1817.
†A non-magnetic stand for the compass.
*A timber around a vessel's hull at deck line.

deposited would of itself, in ordinary circumstances, have consumed as much time as that, if the whole ship's crew had been employed in it. My companions had not saved a single article but what they had on their backs; but to me it was a source of infinite satisfaction, if any such could be gathered from the horrors of our gloomy situation, that we had been fortunate enough to have preserved our compasses, navigators, and quadrants. After the first shock of my feelings was over, I enthusiastically contemplated them as the probable instruments of our salvation; without them all would have been dark and hopeless. Gracious God! what a picture of distress and suffering now presented itself to my imagination. The crew of the ship were saved, consisting of twenty human souls. All that remained to conduct these twenty beings through the stormy terrors of the ocean, perhaps many thousand miles, were three open light boats. The prospect of obtaining any provisions or water from the ship, to subsist upon during the time, was at least now doubtful. How many long and watchful nights, thought I, are to be passed? How many tedious days of partial starvation are to be endured, before the least relief or mitigation of our sufferings can be reasonably anticipated. We lay at this time in our boat, about two ship lengths off from the wreck, in perfect silence, calmly contemplating her situation, and absorbed in our own melancholy reflections, when the other boats were discovered rowing up to us. They had but shortly before discovered that some accident had befallen us, but of the nature of which they were entirely ignorant. The sudden and mysterious disappearance of the ship was first discovered by the boat-steerer in the captain's boat, and with a horror-struck countenance and voice, he suddenly exclaimed, "Oh, my God! where is the ship?" Their operations upon this were instantly suspended, and a general cry of horror and despair burst from the lips of every man, as their looks were directed for her, in vain, over every part of the ocean. They immediately made all haste towards us. The captain's boat was the first that reached us. He stopped about a boat's length off, but had no power to utter a single syllable: he was so completely overpowered with the spectacle before him that he sat down in his boat, pale and speechless. I could scarcely recognise his countenance, he appeared to be so much altered, awed, and overcome with the oppression of his feelings, and the dreadful reality that lay before him. He was in a short time however enabled to address the inquiry to me, "My God, Mr. Chase, what is the matter?" I answered, "We have been stove by a whale." I then briefly told him the story. After a few moment's reflection he observed that we must cut away her masts, and endeavour to get something out of her to eat. Our thoughts were now all accordingly bent on endeavours to save from the wreck whatever we might possibly want, and for this purpose we rowed up and got on to her. Search was

made for every means of gaining access to her hold; and for this purpose the
lanyards were cut loose, and with our hatchets we commenced to cut away the
masts, that she might right up again, and enable us to scuttle her decks. In
doing which we were occupied about three quarters of an hour, owing to our
having no axes, nor indeed any other instruments, but the small hatchets be-
longing to the boats. After her masts were gone she came up about two-thirds
of the way upon an even keel. While we were employed about the masts the
captain took his quadrant, shoved off from the ship, and got an observation. We
found ourselves in latitude 0° 40′S., longitude 119° W. We now commenced to
cut a hole through the planks, directly above two large casks of bread, which
most fortunately were between decks, in the waist of the ship, and which being
in the upper side, when she upset, we had strong hopes was not wet. It turned
out according to our wishes, and from these casks we obtained six hundred
pounds of hard bread. Other parts of the deck were then scuttled, and we got
without difficulty as much fresh water as we dared to take in the boats, so that
each was supplied with about sixty-five gallons; we got also from one of the
lockers a musket, a small canister of powder, a couple of files, two rasps, about
two pounds of boat nails, and a few turtles. In the afternoon the wind came on
to blow a strong breeze; and having obtained every thing that occurred to us
could then be got out, we began to make arrangements for our safety during
the night. A boat's line was made fast to the ship, and to the other end of it one
of the boats was moored, at about fifty fathoms to leeward; another boat was
then attached to the first one, about eight fathoms astern; and the third boat,
the like distance astern of her. Night came on just as we had finished our operations; and such a night as it was to us! so full of feverish and distracting inqui-
etude, that we were deprived entirely of rest. The wreck was constantly before
my eyes. I could not, by any effort, chase away the horrors of the preceding day
from my mind: they haunted me the live-long night. My companions—some
of them were like sick women; they had no idea of the extent of their deplorable situation. One or two slept unconcernedly, while others wasted the
night in unavailing murmurs. I now had full leisure to examine, with some degree of coolness, the dreadful circumstances of our disaster. The scenes of yesterday passed in such quick succession in my mind that it was not until after
many hours of severe reflection that I was able to discard the idea of the cata-
strophe as a dream. Alas! it was one from which there was no awaking; it was
too certainly true, that but yesterday we had existed as it were, and in one short
moment had been cut off from all the hopes and prospects of the living! I have
no language to paint out the horrors of our situation. To shed tears was indeed
altogether unavailing, and withal unmanly; yet I was not able to deny myself
the relief they served to afford me. After several hours of idle sorrow and repin-

ing I began to reflect upon the accident, and endeavoured to realize by what unaccountable destiny or design (which I could not at first determine) this sudden and most deadly attack had been made upon us: by an animal, too, never before suspected of premeditated violence, and proverbial for its insensibility and inoffensiveness. Every fact seemed to warrant me in concluding that it was anything but chance which directed his operations; he made two several attacks upon the ship, at a short interval between them, both of which, according to their direction, were calculated to do us the most injury, by being made ahead, and thereby combining the speed of the two objects for the shock; to effect which, the exact manoeuvres which he made were necessary. His aspect was most horrible, and such as indicated resentment and fury. He came directly from the shoal which we had just before entered, and in which we had struck three of his companions, as if fired with revenge for their sufferings. But to this it may be observed, that the mode of fighting which they always adopt is either with repeated strokes of their tails, or snapping of their jaws together; and that a case, precisely similar to this one, has never been heard of amongst the oldest and most experienced whalers. To this I would answer, that the structure and strength of the whale's head is admirably designed for this mode of attack; the most prominent part of which is almost as hard and as tough as iron; indeed, I can compare it to nothing else but the inside of a horse's hoof, upon which a lance or harpoon would not make the slightest impression. The eyes and ears are removed nearly one-third the length of the whole fish, from the front part of the head, and are not in the least degree endangered in this mode of attack. At all events, the whole circumstances taken together, all happening before my own eyes, and producing, at the time, impressions in my mind of decided, calculating mischief on the part of the whale (many of which impressions I cannot now recall) induce me to be satisfied that I am correct in my opinion. It is certainly, in all its bearings, a hitherto unheard of circumstance, and constitutes, perhaps, the most extraordinary one in the annals of the fishery.

★   ★   ★   ★   ★

Editor's Note: As this section begins, the survivors of the *Essex's* sinking are on Henderson Island, where they landed on Dec. 20, 1820. At this point in the narrative, it is obvious to them that the landfall they thought would be their salvation for food and water is not unlike a desert wasteland. They realize they will have to sail on . . . and keep hoping.

★   ★   ★   ★   ★

December 23rd. At 11 o'clock A.M., we again visited our spring: the tide had fallen to about a foot below it, and we were able to procure, before it rose again, about twenty gallons of water. It was at first a little brackish, but soon became fresh, from the constant supply from the rock and the departure of the sea. Our observations this morning tended to give us every confidence in its quantity and quality, and we, therefore, rested perfectly easy in our minds on the subject, and commenced to make further discoveries about the island. Each man sought for his own daily living, on whatsoever the mountains, the shore, or the sea, could furnish him with; and every day, during our stay there, the whole time was employed in roving about for food. We found, however, on the twenty-fourth, that we had picked up, on the island, every thing that could be got at, in the way of sustenance; and, much to our surprise, some of the men came in at night and complained of not having gotten sufficient during the day to satisfy the cravings of their stomachs. Every accessible part of the mountain, contiguous to us, or within the reach of our weak enterprise, was already ransacked, for birds' eggs and grass, and was rifled of all that they contained: so that we began to entertain serious apprehensions that we should not be able to live long here; at any rate, with the view of being prepared, as well as possible, should necessity at any time oblige us to quit it, we commenced, on the twenty-fourth, to repair our boats, and continued to work upon them all that and the succeeding day. We were enabled to do this, with much facility, by drawing them up and turning them over on the beach, working by spells of two or three hours at a time, and then leaving off to seek for food. We procured our water daily, when the tide would leave the shore: but on the evening of the twenty-fifth, found that a fruitless search for nourishment had not repaid us for the labors of a whole day. There was no one thing on the island upon which we could in the least degree rely, except the peppergrass, and of that the supply was precarious, and not much relished without some other food. Our situation here, therefore, now became worse than it would have been in our boats on the ocean; because, in the latter case, we should be still making some progress towards the land, while our provisions lasted, and the chance of falling in with some vessel be considerably increased. It was certain that we ought not to remain here unless upon the strongest assurances in our own minds, of sufficient sustenance, and that, too, in regular supplies, that might be depended upon. After much conversation amongst us on this subject, and again examining our navigators, it was finally concluded to set sail for Easter Island, which we found to be E.S.E. from us in latitude 27° 9'S., longitude 109° 35'W. All we knew of this island was that it existed as laid down in the books; but of its extent, productions, or inhabitants, if any, we were entirely ignorant; at any rate, it was nearer by eight hundred and fifty miles to the coast, and could not be worse in its productions than the one we were about leaving.

The twenty-sixth of December was wholly employed in preparations for our departure; our boats were hauled down to the vicinity of the spring, and our casks, and everything else that would contain it, filled with water.

There had been considerable talk between three of our companions about their remaining on this island, and taking their chance both for a living, and an escape from it; and as the time drew near at which we were to leave, they made up their minds to stay behind. The rest of us could make no objection to their plan, as it lessened the load of our boats, allowed us their share of the provisions, and the probability of their being able to sustain themselves on the island was much stronger than that of our reaching the mainland. Should we, however, ever arrive safely, it would become our duty, and we so assured them, to give information of their situation, and make every effort to procure their removal from thence; which we accordingly afterwards did.

Their names were William Wright of Barnstable, Massachusetts, Thomas Chapple of Plymouth, England, and Seth Weeks of the former place. They had begun, before we came away, to construct a sort of habitation, composed of the branches of trees, and we left with them every little article that could be spared from the boats. It was their intention to build a considerable dwelling, that would protect them from the rains, as soon as time and materials could be provided. The captain wrote letters, to be left on the island, giving information of the fate of the ship, and that of our own; and stating that we had set out to reach Easter Island, with further particulars, intended to give notice (should our fellow sufferers die there, and the place be ever visited by any vessel) of our misfortunes. These letters were put in a tin case, enclosed in a small wooden box, and nailed to a tree, on the west side of the island, near our landing place. We had observed, some days previously, the name of a ship, *The Elizabeth,* cut out in the bark of this tree, which rendered it indubitable that one of that name had once touched here. There was, however, no date to it, or anything else, by which any further particulars could be made out.

December 27th. I went, before we set sail this morning, and procured for each boat a flat stone, and two armfuls of wood, with which to make a fire in our boats, should it become afterwards necessary in the further prosecution of our voyage; as we calculated we might catch a fish, or a bird, and in that case be provided with the means of cooking it; otherwise, from the intense heat of the weather, we knew they could not be preserved from spoiling. At ten o'clock A.M., the tide having risen far enough to allow our boats to float over the rocks, we made all sail, and steered around the island, for the purpose of making a little further observation, which would not detain us any time, and might be productive of some unexpected good fortune. Before we started we missed our three companions, and found they had not come down, either to assist us to get off, nor to take any kind of leave of us. I walked up the beach towards their rude dwelling, and informed them that we were then about to set sail, and should probably never see them more. They seemed to be very much affected, and one of them shed tears. They wished us to write to their relations, should Providence safely direct us again to our homes, and said but little else. They had every confidence in being able to procure a subsistence there as long as they remained: and, finding them ill at heart about taking any leave of us, I hastily bid them "good-bye," hoped they would do well, and came away. They followed me with their eyes until I was out of sight, and I never saw more of them.

On the N.W. side of the island we perceived a fine white beach, on which we imagined we might land, and in a short time ascertain if any further useful discoveries could be effected, or any addition made to our stock of provisions; and having set ashore five or six of the men for this purpose, the rest of us shoved off the boats and commenced fishing. We saw a number of sharks, but all efforts to take them proved ineffectual; and we got but a few small fish, about the size of a mackerel, which we divided amongst us. In this business we were occupied for the remainder of the day, until six o'clock in the afternoon, when the men, having returned to the shore from their search in the mountains, brought a few birds, and we again set sail and steered directly for Easter Island. During that night, after we had got quite clear of the land, we had a fine strong breeze from the N.W.; we kept our fires going, and cooked our fish and birds, and felt our situation as comfortable as could be expected. We continued on our course, consuming our provisions and water as sparingly as possible, without any material incident, until the thirtieth, when the wind hauled out E.S.E. directly ahead, and so continued until the thirty-first, when it again came to the northward, and we resumed our course.

On the third of January we experienced heavy squalls from the W.S.W. accompanied with dreadful thunder and lightning, that threw a gloomy and cheerless aspect over the ocean, and incited a recurrence of some of those heavy and desponding moments that we had before experienced. We commenced from Ducie's Island to keep a regular reckoning, by which, on the fourth of January, we found we had got to the southward of Easter Island, and the wind prevailing E.N.E. we should not be able to get on to the eastward, so as to reach it. Our birds and fish were all now consumed, and we had begun again upon our short allowance of bread. It was necessary, in this state of things, to change our determination of going to Easter Island, and shape our course in some other direction, where the wind would allow of our going. We had but little hesitation in concluding, therefore, to steer for the island of Juan Fernandez, which lay about E.S.E. from us, distant two thousand five hundred miles. We bent our course accordingly towards it, having for the two succeeding days very light winds, and suffering excessively from the intense heat of the sun. The seventh brought us a change of wind to the northward, and at twelve o'clock we found ourselves in latitude 30° 18′S., longitude 117° 29′W. We continued to make what progress we could to the eastward.

January 10th. Matthew P. Joy, the second mate, had suffered from debility, and the privations we had experienced, much beyond any of the rest of us, and was on the eighth removed to the captain's boat, under the impression that he would be more comfortable there, and more attention and pains be bestowed in nursing and endeavouring to comfort him. This day being calm, he manifested a desire to be taken back again; but at 4 o'clock in the afternoon, after having been, according to his wishes, placed in his own boat, he died very suddenly after his removal. On the eleventh, at six o'clock in the morning, we sewed him up in his clothes, tied a large stone to his feet, and, having brought all the boats to, consigned him in a solemn manner to the ocean. This man did not die of absolute starvation, although his end was no doubt very much hastened by his sufferings. He had a weak and sickly constitution, and complained of being unwell the whole voyage. It was an incident, however, which threw a gloom over our feelings for many days. In consequence of his death, one man from the captain's boat was placed in that from which he died, to supply his place, and we stood away again on our course.

On the 12th of January we had the wind from the N.W. which commenced in the morning, and came on to blow before night a perfect gale. We were obliged to take in all sail and run before the wind. Flashes of lightning were quick and vivid, and the rain came down in cataracts. As, however, the gale blew us fairly on our course, and our speed being great during the day, we derived, I may say, even pleasure from the uncomfortableness and fury of the storm. We were apprehensive that in the darkness of this night we should be separated, and made arrangements, each boat to keep an E.S.E. course all night. About eleven o'clock my boat being ahead a short distance of the others, I turned my head back, as I was in the habit of doing every minute, and neither of the others were to be seen. It was blowing and raining at this time as if the heavens were separating, and I knew not hardly at the moment what to do. I hove my boat to the wind, and lay drifting about an hour, expecting every moment they would come up with me, but not seeing anything of them, I put away again, and stood on the course agreed upon, with strong hopes that daylight would enable me to discover them again. When the morning dawned, in vain did we look over every part of the ocean for our companions; they were gone! and we saw no more of them afterwards. It was folly to repine at the circumstance; it could neither be remedied, nor could sorrow secure their return; but it was impossible to prevent ourselves feeling all the poignancy and bitterness that characterizes the separation of men who have long suffered in each other's company, and whose interests and feelings fate had so closely linked together. By our observation, we separated in latitude 32° 16′S., longitude 112° 20′W. For many days after this accident, our progress was attended with dull and melancholy reflections. We had lost the cheering of each other's faces, that which strange as it is, we so much required in both our mental and bodily distresses. The 14th January proved another very squally and rainy day. We had now been nineteen days from the island, and had only made a distance of about 900 miles: necessity began to whisper us, that still further reduction of our allowance must take place, or we must abandon altogether the hopes of reaching the land, and rely wholly on the chance of being taken up by a vessel. But how to reduce the daily quantity of food, with any regard to life itself, was a question of the utmost consequence. Upon our first leaving the wreck, the demands of the stomach had been circumscribed to the smallest possible compass; and subsequently before reaching the island, a diminution had taken place of nearly one-half; and it was now, from a reasonable calculation, become necessary even to curtail that at least one-half; which must, in a short time, reduce us to mere skeletons again. We had a full allowance of water, but it only served to contribute to our debility; our bodies deriving but the scanty support which an ounce and a half of bread for each man afforded. It required a great effort to bring matters to this dreadful alternative, either to feed our bodies and our hopes a little longer, or in the agonies of hunger to seize upon and devour our provisions, and coolly await the approach of death.

We were as yet, just able to move about in our boats, and slowly perform the necessary labors appertaining to her; but we were fast wasting away with the relaxing effects of the water, and we daily almost perished under the torrid rays of a meridian sun; to escape which, we would lie down in the bottom of the boat, cover ourselves over with the sails, and abandon her to the mercy of the waves. Upon attempting to rise again, the blood would rush into the head, and an intoxicating blindness come over us, almost to occasion our suddenly falling down again. A slight interest was still kept up in our minds by the distant hopes of yet meeting with the other boats, but it was never realized. An accident occurred at night, which gave me a great cause of uneasiness, and led me to an unpleasant rumination upon the probable consequences of a repetition of it. I had laid down in the boat without taking the usual precaution of securing the lid of the provision chest, as I was accustomed to do, when one of the white men awoke me, and informed me that one of the blacks had taken some bread from it. I felt at the moment the highest indignation and resentment at such conduct in any of our crew and immediately took my pistol in my hand, and charged him if he had taken any, to give it up without the least hesitation, or I should instantly shoot him!—He became at once very much alarmed, and trembling, confessed the fact, pleading the hard necessity that urged him to it: he appeared to be very penitent for his crime, and earneastly swore that he would never be guilty of it again. I could not find it in my soul to extend towards him the least severity on this account, however much, according to the strict imposition which we felt upon ourselves, it might demand it. This was the first infraction; and the security of our lives, our hopes of redemption from our sufferings, loudly called for a prompt and signal punishment; but every humane feeling of nature plead in his behalf, and he was permitted to escape, with the solemn injunction that a repetition of the same offence would cost him his life.

I had almost determined upon this occurrence to divide our provisions, and give to each man his share of the whole stock; and should have done so in the height of my resentment had it not been for the reflection that some might, by imprudence, be tempted to go beyond the daily allowance, or consume it all at once, and bring on a premature weakness or starvation: this would of course disable them for the duties of the boat, and reduce our chances of safety and deliverance.

On the 15th of January, at night, a very large shark was observed swimming about us in a most ravenous manner, making attempts every now and then upon different parts of the boat, as if he would devour the very wood with hunger; he came several times and snapped at the steering oar, and even the stern-post. We tried in vain to stab him with a lance, but we were so weak as not to be able to make any impression upon his hard skin; he was so much larger than an ordinary one, and manifested such a fearless malignity, as to make us afraid of him; and our utmost efforts, which were at first directed to kill him for prey, became in the end self-defense. Baffled however in all his hungry attempts upon us, he shortly made off.

On the 16th of January, we were surrounded with porpoises in great numbers, that followed us nearly an hour, and which also defied all manoeuvres to catch them. The 17th and 18th proved to be calm; and the distresses of a cheerless prospect and a burning hot sun were again visited upon our devoted heads.

We began to think that Divine Providence had abandoned us at last; and it was but an unavailing effort to endeavour to prolong a now tedious existence. Horrible were the feelings that took possession of us!—The contemplation of a death of agony and torment, refined by the most dreadful and distressing reflections, absolutely prostrated both body and soul. There was not a hope now remaining to us but that which was derived from a sense of the mercies of our Creator. The night of the 18th was a despairing era in our sufferings; our minds were wrought up to the highest pitch of dread and apprehension for our fate, and all in them was dark, gloomy, and confused. About 8 o'clock, the terrible noise of whale spouts near us sounded in our ears: we could distinctly hear the furious thrashing of their tails in the water, and our weak minds pictured out their appalling and hideous aspects. One of my companions, the black man, took an immediate fright, and solicited me to take out the oars, and endeavour to get away from them. I consented to his using any means for that purpose; but alas! it was wholly out of our power to raise a single arm in our own defense. Two or three of the whales came down near us, and went swiftly off across our stern, blowing and spouting at a terrible rate; they, however, after an hour or two disappeared, and we saw no more of them. The next day, the 19th of January, we had extremely boisterous weather, with rain, heavy thunder and lightning, which reduced us again to the necessity of taking in all sail and lying to. The wind blew from every point of the compass within the twenty-four hours, and at last towards the next morning settled at E.N.E. a strong breeze.

January 20th. The black man, Richard Peterson, manifested today symptoms of a speedy dissolution; he had been lying between the seats in the boat, utterly dispirited and broken down, without being able to do the least duty, or hardly to place his hand to his head for the last three days, and had this morning made up his mind to die rather than endure further misery: he refused his allowance; said he was sensible of his approaching end, and was perfectly ready to die: in a few minutes he became speechless, the breath appeared to be leaving his body without producing the least pain, and at four o'clock he was gone. I had two days previously conversations with him on the subject of religion on which he reasoned very sensibly, and with much composure; and begged me to let his wife know his fate, if ever I reached home in safety. The next morning we committed him to the sea, in latitude 35° 07′ S., longitude 105° 46′ W. The wind prevailed to the eastward until the 24th of January, when it again fell calm. We were now in a most wretched and sinking state of debility, hardly able to crawl around the boat, and possessing but strength enough to convey our scanty morsel to our mouths. When I perceived this morning that it was calm, my fortitude almost forsook me. I thought to suffer another scorching day, like the last we had experienced, would close before night the scene of our miseries; and I felt many a despairing moment that day, that had well nigh proved fatal. It required an effort to look calmly forward, and contemplate what was yet in store for us, beyond what I felt I was capable of making; and what is was that buoyed me above all the terrors which surrounded us, God alone knows. Our ounce and a half of bread, which was to serve us all day, was in some cases greedily devoured, as if life was to continue but another moment; and at other times, it was hoarded up and eaten crumb by crumb, at regular intervals during the day, as if it was to last us for ever. To add to our calamities, biles* began to break out upon us, and our imaginations shortly became as diseased as our bodies. I laid down at night to catch a few moments of oblivious sleep, and immediately my starving fancy was at work. I dreamt of being placed near a splendid and rich repast, where there was every thing that the most dainty appetite could desire; and of contemplating the moment in which we were to commence to eat with enraptured feelings of delight; and just as I was about to partake of it, I suddenly awoke to the cold realities of my miserable situation. Nothing could have oppressed me so much. It set such a longing frenzy for victuals in my mind, that I felt as if I could have wished the dream to continue for ever, that I never might have awoke from it. I cast a sort of vacant stare about the boat, until my eyes rested upon a bit of tough cowhide, which was fastened to one of the oars; I eagerly seized and commenced to chew it, but there was no substance in it, and it only severed to fatigue my weak jaws, and add to my bodily pains. My fellow sufferers murmured very much the whole time, and continued to press me continually with questions upon the probability of our reaching land again. I kept constantly rallying my spirits to enable me to afford them comfort. I encouraged them to bear up against all evils, and if we must perish, to die in our own cause, and not weakly distrust the providence of the Almighty by giving ourselves up to despair. I reasoned with them, and told them that we would not die sooner by keeping up our hopes; that the dreadful sacrifices and privations we endured were to preserve us from death, and were not to be put in competition with the price which we set upon our lives, and their value to our families: it was, besides, unmanly to repine at what neither admitted of alleviation nor cure; and withal, that it was our solemn duty to recognise in our calamities an overruling divinity, by whose mercy we might be suddenly snatched from peril, and to rely upon him alone, "Who tempers the wind to the shorn lamb."

---

*Boils

The three following days, the 25th, 26th, and 27th, were not distinguished by any particular circumstances. The wind still prevailed to the eastward, and by its obduracy, almost tore the very hopes of our hearts away: it was impossible to silence the rebellious repinings of our nature, at witnessing such a succession of hard fortune against us. It was our cruel lot not to have had one bright anticipation realized—not one wish of our thirsting souls gratified. We had, at the end of these three days, been urged to the southward as far as latitude 36° into a chilly region, where rains and squalls prevailed; and we now calculated to tack and stand back to the northward: after much labor, we got our boat about; and so great was the fatigue attending this small exertion of our bodies, that we all gave up for a moment and abandoned her to her own course.—Not one of us had now strength sufficient to steer, or indeed to make one single effort towards getting the sails properly trimmed, to enable us to make any headway. After an hour or two of relaxation, during which the horrors of our situation came upon us with a despairing force and effect, we made a sudden effort and got our sails into such a disposition as that the boat would steer herself; and we then threw ourselves down, awaiting the issue of time to bring us relief, or to take us from the scene of our troubles. We could now do nothing more; strength and spirits were totally gone; and what indeed could have been the narrow hopes, that in our situation, then bound us to life?

January 28th. Our spirits this morning were hardly sufficient to allow of our enjoying a change of the wind, which took place to the westward.—It had nearly become indifferent to us from what quarter it blew: nothing but the slight chance of meeting a vessel remained to us now: it was this narrow comfort alone that prevented me from lying down at once to die. But fourteen days stinted allowance of provisions remained, and it was absolutely necessary to increase the quantity to enable us to live five days longer: we therefore partook of it, as pinching necessity demanded, and gave ourselves wholly up to the guidance and disposal of our Creator.

The 29th and 30th of January, the wind continued west, and we made considerable progress until the 31st, when it again came ahead, and prostrated all our hopes. On the 1st of February, it changed again to the westward, and on the 2nd and 3rd blew to the eastward; and we had it light and variable until the 8th of February. Our sufferings were now drawing to a close; a terrible death appeared shortly to await us; hunger became violent and outrageous, and we prepared for a speedy release from our troubles; our speech and reason were both considerably impaired, and we were reduced to be at this time certainly the most helpless and wretched of the whole human race. Isaac Cole, one of our crew, had the day before this, in a fit of despair, thrown himself down in the boat, and was determined there calmly to wait for death. It was obvious that he had no chance; all was dark he said in his mind, not a single ray of hope was left for him to dwell upon; and it was folly and madness to be struggling against what appeared so palpably to be our fixed and settled destiny. I remonstrated with him as effectually as the weakness both of my body and understanding would allow of; and what I said appeared for a moment to have a considerable effect: he made a powerful and sudden effort, half rose up, crawled forward and hoisted the jib, and firmly and loudly cried that he would not give up; that he would live as long as the rest of us—but alas! this effort was but the hectic fever of the moment, and he shortly again relapsed into a state of melancholy and despair. This day his reason was attacked, and he became about 9 o'clock in the morning a most miserable spectacle of madness: he spoke incoherently about everything, calling loudly for a napkin and water, and then, lying stupidly and senselessly down in the boat again, would close his hollow eyes, as if in death. About 10 o'clock, we suddenly perceived that he became speechless; we got him as well as we were able upon a board, placed on one of the seats of the boat, and covering him up with some old clothes, left him to his fate. He lay in the greatest pain and apparent misery, groaning piteously until four o'clock, when he died, in the most horrid and frightful convulsions I ever witnessed. We kept his corpse all night, and in the morning my two companions began as a course to make preparations to dispose of it in the sea; when after reflecting on the subject all night, I addressed them on the painful subject of keeping the body for food!! Our provisions could not possibly last us beyond three days, within which time, it was not in any degree probable that we should find relief from our present sufferings, and that hunger would at last drive us to the necessity of casting lots. It was without any objection agreed to, and we set to work as fast as we were able to prepare it so as to prevent its spoiling. We separated his limbs from his body, and cut all the flesh from the bones; after which, we opened the body, took out the heart, and then closed it again—sewed it up as decently as we could, and committed it to the sea. We now first commenced to satisfy the immediate cravings of nature from the heart, which we eagerly devoured, and then ate sparingly of a few pieces of the flesh; after which we hung up the remainder, cut in thin strips about the boat, to dry in the sun: we made a fire and roasted some of it, to serve us during the next day. In this manner did we dispose of our fellow sufferer; the painful recollection of which brings to mind at this moment, some of the most disagreeable and revolting ideas that it is capable of conceiving. We knew not then to whose lot it would fall next, either to die or be shot, and eaten like the poor wretch we had just dispatched. Humanity must shudder at the dreadful recital. I have no language to paint the anguish of our souls in this dreadful dilemma. The next morning, the 10th of February, we found that the flesh had become tainted, and had turned of a greenish color upon which we concluded to make a fire and cook it at once, to prevent its becoming so putrid as not to be eaten at all: we accordingly did so, and by that means preserved it for six or seven days longer; our bread during the time remained untouched; as that would not be liable to spoil, we placed it carefully aside for the last moments of our trial. About three o'clock this afternoon a strong breeze set in from the N.W. and we made very good progress, considering that we were compelled to steer the boat by management of the sails alone: this wind continued until the thirteenth, when it changed again ahead. We contrived to keep soul and body together by sparingly partaking of our flesh, cut up in small pieces and eaten with salt water. By the fourteenth, our bodies became so far recruited, as to enable us to make a few attempts at guiding our boat again with the oar; by each taking his turn, we managed to effect it, and to make a tolerable good course. On the fifteenth, our flesh was all consumed, and we were driven to the last morsel of bread, consisting of two cakes; our limbs had for the last two days swelled very much, and now began to pain us most excessively. We were still, as near as we could judge, three hundred miles from the land, and but three days of our allowance on hand. The hope of a continuation of the wind, which came out at west this morning, was the only comfort and solace that remained to us: so strong had our desires at last reached in this respect, that a high fever had set in, in our veins, and a longing that nothing but its continuation could satisfy. Matters were now with us at their height; all hope was cast upon the breeze; and we tremblingly and fearfully awaited its progress, and the dreadful development of our destiny. On the sixteenth, at night, full of the horrible reflections of our situation, and panting with weakness, I laid down to sleep, almost indifferent whether I should ever see the light again. I had not lain long, before I dreamt I saw a ship at some distance off from us, and strained every nerve to get to her, but could not. I awoke almost overpowered with the frenzy I had caught in my slumbers, and stung with the cruelties of a diseased and disappointed imagination. On the seventeenth, in the afternoon, a heavy cloud appeared to be settling down in an E. by N. direction from us, which in my view, indicated the vicinity of some land, which I took for the island of Mas Afuera. I concluded it could be no other; and immediately upon this reflection, the life blood began to flow again briskly in my veins. I told my companions that I was well convinced it was land, and if so, in all probability we should reach it before two days more. My words appeared to comfort them much; and by repeated assurances of the fafourable appearance of things, their spirits acquired even a degree of elasticity that was truly astonishing. The dark features of our distress began now to diminish a little, and the countenance, even amid the gloomy bodings of our hard lot, to assume a much fresher hue. We directed our course for the cloud, and our progress that night was extremely good. The next morning, before daylight, Thomas Nicholson, a boy about seventeen years of age, one of my two companions who had thus far survived with me, after having bailed the boat, laid down, drew a piece of canvas over him, and cried out that he then wished to die immediately. I sw that he had given up, and I attempted to speak a few words of comfort and encouragement to him, and endeavoured to persuade him that it was a great weakness and even wickedness to abandon a reliance upon the Almighty, while the least hope, and a breath of life remained; but he felt unwilling to listen to any of the consolatory suggestions which I made to him; and, notwithstanding the extreme probability which I stated there was of our gaining the land before the end of two days more, he insisted upon lying down and giving himself up to despair. A fixed look of settled and forsaken despondency came over his face: he lay for some time silent, sullen, and sorrowful—and I felt at once satisfied that the coldness of death was fast gathering upon him: there was a sudden and unaccountable earnestness in his manner that alarmed me, and made me fear that I myself might unexpectedly be overtaken by a like weakness, or dizziness of nature, that would bereave me at once of both reason and life; but Providence willed it otherwise.

At about seven o'clock this morning, while I was lying asleep, my companion who was steering, suddenly and loudly called out *"There's a Sail!"* I know not what was the first movement I made upon hearing such an unexpected cry: the earliest of my recollections are that immediately I stood up, gazing in a state of abstraction and ecstasy upon the blessed vision of a vessel about seven miles off from us; she was standing in the same direction with us, and the only sensation I felt at the moment was, that of a violent and unaccountable impulse to fly directly towards her. I do not believe it is possible to form a just conception of the pure, strong feelings, and the unmingled emotions of joy and gratitude, that took possession of my mind on this occasion: the boy, too, took a sudden and animated start from his despondency, and stood up to witness the probable instrument of his salvation. Our only fear was now that she would not discover us, or that we might not be able to intercept her course: we, however, put our boat immediately, as well as we were able, in a direction to cut her off; and found, to our great joy, that we sailed faster than she did. Upon observing us, she shortened sail, and allowed us to come up to her. The captain hailed us, and asked who we were. I told him we were from a wreck, and he cried out immediately for us to come alongside the ship. I made an effort to assist myself along to the side, for the purpose of getting up, but strength failed me altogether, and I found it impossible to move a step further without help. We must have formed at that moment, in the eyes of the captain and his crew, a most deplorable and affecting picture of suffering and misery. Our cadaverous countenances, sunken eyes, and bones just starting through the skin, with the ragged remnants of clothes stuck about our sun burnt bodies, must have produced an appearance to him affecting and revolting in the highest degree. The sailors commenced to remove us from our boat, and we were taken to the cabin, and comfortably provided for in every respect. In a few minutes we were permitted to taste of a little thin food, made from tapioca, and in a few days, with prudent management, we were considerably recruited. This vessel proved to be the brig *Indian,* Captain William Crozier, of London; to whom we are indebted for every polite, friendly, and attentive disposition towards us, that can possibly characterize a man of humanity and feeling. We were taken up in latitude 33° 45′S., longitude 81° 03′W. At twelve o'clock this day we saw the island of Mas Afuera, and on the 25th of February, we arrived at Valparaiso in utter distress and poverty. Our wants were promptly relieved there.

The Most Dangerous Game

BY RICHARD CONNELL

Wilderness survival in the face of hunger, thirst, extreme weather, dangerous wildlife, and disease would seem to be quite a challenge for any human being. Toss in one additional element, however, and the dramatic stew really begins to boil.

What if, let's say, you are facing all of the above-mentioned calamities and you suddenly find yourself in the clutches of a lunatic—I mean a certifiable whacko!?

That's exactly the concoction served up in Richard Connell's rousing short story, "The Most Dangerous Game," which has knocked around with lasting vigor in various anthologies since it first appeared in 1924. This little gem of a tale has been filmed three times: first in 1932 with Joel McCrea; then in 1946 as *A Game of Death*; and again in 1956 under the title *"Run for the Sun"* with Richard Widmark.

★   ★   ★   ★   ★

"Off there to the right—somewhere—is a large island," said Whitney. "It's rather a mystery—"

"What island is it?" Rainsford asked.

"The old charts call it 'Ship-Trap Island,'" Whitney replied. "A suggestive name, isn't it? Sailors have a curious dread of the place. I don't know why some superstition—"

"Can't see it," remarked Rainsford, trying to peer through the dank tropical night that was palpable as it pressed its thick, warm blackness in upon the yacht.

"You've good eyes," said Whitney, with a laugh, "and I've seen you pick off a moose moving in the brown fall bush at four hundred yards, but even you can't see four miles or so through a moonless Caribbean night."

"Not four yards," admitted Rainsford. "Ugh! It's like moist black velvet."

"It will be light enough where we're going," promised Whitney. "We should make it in a few days. I hope the jaguar guns have come. We'll have good hunting up the Amazon. Great sport, hunting."

"The best sport in the world," agreed Rainsford.

"For the hunter," amended Whitney. "Not for the jaguar."

"Don't talk rot, Whitney," said Rainsford. "You're a big-game hunter, not a philosopher. Who cares how a jaguar feels?"

"Perhaps the jaguar does," observed Whitney.

"Bah! They've no understanding."

"Even so, I rather think they understand one thing—fear. The fear of pain and the fear of death."

"Nonsense," laughed Rainsford. "This hot weather is making you soft, Whitney. Be a realist. The world is made up of two classes—the hunters and the hunted. Luckily, you and I are hunters. Do you think we've passed that island yet?"

"I can't tell in the dark. I hope so."

"Why?" asked Rainsford.

"The place has a reputation—a bad one."

"Cannibals?" suggested Rainsford.

"Hardly. Even cannibals wouldn't live in such a God-forsaken place. But it's got into sailor lore, somehow. Didn't you notice that the crew's nerves seemed a bit jumpy today?"

"They were a bit strange, now you mention it. Even Captain Nielson—"

"Yes, even that tough-minded old Swede, who'd go to the devil himself and ask him for a light. Those fishy blue eyes held a look I never saw there before. All I could get out of him was: 'This place has an evil name among seafaring men, sir.' Then he said to me, very gravely: 'Don't you feel anything?'—as if the air about us was actually poisonous. Now you mustn't laugh when I tell you this—I did feel something like a sudden chill.

"There was no breeze. The sea was as flat as a plateglass window. We were drawing near the island then. What I felt was a—a mental chill; a sort of sudden dread."

"Pure imagination," said Rainsford. "One superstitious sailor can taint the whole ship's company with his fear."

"Maybe. But sometimes I think sailors have an extra sense that tells them when they are in danger. Sometimes I think evil is a tangible thing—

with wave lengths, just as sound and light have. An evil place can, so to speak, broadcast vibrations of evil. Anyhow, I'm glad we're getting out of the zone. Well, I think I'll turn in now, Rainsford."

"I'm not sleepy," said Rainsford. "I'm going to smoke another pipe up on the afterdeck."

"Good night, then, Rainsford. See you at breakfast."

"Good night, Whitney."

There was no sound in the night as Rainsford sat there but the muffled throb of the engine that drove the yacht swiftly through the darkness, and the swish and ripple of the wash of the propeller.

Rainsford, reclining in a steamer chair, indolently puffed on his favorite briar. The sensuous drowsiness of the night was on him. "It's so dark," he thought, "that I could sleep without closing my eyes; the night would be my eyelids—"

An abrupt sound startled him. Off to the right he heard it, and his ears, expert in such matters, could not be mistaken. Again he heard the sound, and again. Somewhere, off in the blackness, someone had fired a gun three times.

Rainsford sprang up and moved quickly to the rail, mystified. He strained his eyes in the direction from which the reports had come, but it was like trying to see through a blanket. He leaped upon the rail and balanced himself there, to get greater elevation; his pipe, striking a rope, was knocked from his mouth. He lunged for it; a short, hoarse cry came from his lips as he realized he had reached too far and had lost his balance. The cry was pinched off short as the blood-warm waters of the Caribbean Sea closed over his head.

He struggled up to the surface and tried to cry out, but the wash from the speeding yacht slapped him in the face and the salt water in his open mouth made him gag and strangle. Desperately he struck out with strong strokes after the receding lights of the yacht, but he stopped before he had swum fifty feet. A certain cool-headedness had come to him; it was not the first time he had been in a tight place. There was a chance that his cries could be heard by someone aboard the yacht, but that chance was slender, and grew more slender as the yacht raced on. He wrestled himself out of his clothes, and shouted with all his power. The lights of the yacht became faint and ever-vanishing fireflies; then they were blotted out entirely by the night.

Rainsford remembered the shots. They had come from the right, and doggedly he swam in that direction, swimming with slow, deliberate strokes, conserving his strength. For a seemingly endless time he fought the sea. He began to count his strokes; he could do possibly a hundred more and then—

Rainsford heard a sound. It came out of the darkness, a high, screaming sound, the sound of an animal in an extremity of anguish and terror.

He did not recognize the animal that made the sound—he did not try to; with fresh vitality he swam toward the sound. He heard it again; then it was cut short by another noise, crisp, staccato.

"Pistol shot," muttered Rainsford, swimming on.

Ten minutes of determined effort brought another sound to his ears—the most welcome he had ever heard—the muttering and growling of the sea breaking on a rocky shore. He was almost on the rocks before he saw them; on a night less calm he would have been shattered against them. With his remaining strength he dragged himself from the swirling waters. Jagged crags appeared to jut into the opaqueness; he forced himself upward, hand over hand. Gasping, his hands raw, he reached a flat place at the top. Dense jungle came down to the very edge of the cliffs. What perils that tangle of trees and underbrush might hold for him did not concern Rainsford just then. All he knew was that he was safe from his enemy, the sea, and that utter weariness was on him. He flung himself down at the jungle edge and tumbled headlong into the deepest sleep of his life.

When he opened his eyes he knew from the position of the sun that it was late in the afternoon. Sleep had given him new vigor; a sharp hunger was picking at him. He looked about him, almost cheerfully.

"Where there are pistol shots, there are men. Where there are men, there is food," he thought. But what kind of men, he wondered, in so forbidding a place? An unbroken front of snarled and jagged jungle fringed the shore.

He saw no sign of a trail through the closely knit web of weeds and trees; it was easier to go along the shore, and Rainsford floundered along by the water. Not far from where he had landed, he stopped.

Some wounded thing, by the evidence a large animal, had thrashed about in the underbrush; the jungle weeds were crushed down and the moss was lacerated; one patch of weeds was stained crimson. A small, glittering object not far away caught Rainsford's eye and he picked it up. It was an empty cartridge.

"A twenty-two," he remarked. "That's odd. It must have been a fairly large animal too. The hunter had his nerve with him to tackle it with such a light gun. It's clear that the brute put up a good fight. I suppose the first three shots I heard were when the hunter flushed his quarry and wounded it. The last shot was when he trailed it here and finished it."

He examined the ground closely and found what he had hoped to find—the print of hunting boots. They pointed along the cliff in the direction he had been going. Eagerly he hurried along, now slipping on a rotten log or a loose stone, but making headway. Night was beginning to settle down on the island.

Bleak darkness was blacking out the sea and jungle when Rainsford sighted the lights. He came upon them as he turned a crook in the coast line, and his first thought was that he had come upon a village, for there were many lights. But as he forged along he saw to his great astonishment that all the lights were in one enormous building—a lofty structure with pointed towers plunging upward into the gloom. His eyes made out the shadowy outlines of a palatial château; it was set on a high bluff, and on three sides of it cliffs dived down to where the sea licked greedy lips in the shadows.

"Mirage," thought Rainsford. But it was no mirage, he found, when he opened the tall spiked iron gate. The steps were real enough; the massive door with a leering gargoyle for a knocker was real enough; yet about it all hung an air of unreality.

He lifted the knocker, and it creaked up stiffly, as if it had never before been used. He let it fall, and it startled him with its booming loudness. He thought he heard steps within; the door remained closed. Again Rainsford lifted the heavy knocker, and let it fall. The door opened then, opened as suddenly as if it were on a spring, and Rainsford stood blinking in the river of glaring gold light that poured out. The first thing his eyes discerned was the largest man he had ever seen—a gigantic creature, solidly made and black-bearded to the waist. In his hand the man held a long-barreled revolver, and he was pointing it straight at Rainsford's heart.

Out of the snarl of beard two small eyes regarded Rainsford.

"Don't be alarmed," said Rainsford, with a smile which he hoped was disarming. "I'm no robber. I fell off a yacht. My name is Sanger Rainsford of New York City."

The menacing look in the eyes did not change. The revolver pointed as rigidly as if the giant were a statue. He gave no sign that he understood Rainsford's words, or that he had even heard them. He was dressed in uniform, a black uniform trimmed with gray astrakhan.

"I'm Sanger Rainsford of New York," Rainsford began again. "I fell off a yacht. I am hungry."

The man's only answer was to raise with his thumb the hammer of his revolver. Then Rainsford saw the man's free hand go to his forehead in a military salute, and he saw him click his heels together and stand at attention. Another man was coming down the broad marble steps, an erect, slender man in evening clothes. He advanced and held out his hand.

In a cultivated voice marked by a slight accent that gave it added precision and deliberateness, he said: "It is a very great pleasure and honor to welcome Mr. Sanger Rainsford, the celebrated hunter, to my home." Automatically Rainsford shook the man's hand.

"I've read your book about hunting snow leopards in Tibet, you see," explained the man. "I am General Zaroff."

Rainsford's first impression was that the man was singularly handsome; his second was that there was an original, almost bizarre quality about the general's face. He was a tall man, past middle age, for his hair was a vivid white; but his thick eyebrows and pointed military mustache were as black as the night from which Rainsford had come. His eyes, too, were black and very bright. He had high cheekbones, a sharp-cut nose, a spare, dark face, the face of a man used to giving orders, the face of an aristocrat. Turning to the giant in uniform, the general made a sign. The giant put away his pistol, saluted, withdrew.

"Ivan is an incredibly strong fellow," remarked the general, "but he has the misfortune to be deaf and dumb. A simple fellow, but, I'm afraid, like all his race, a bit of a savage."

"Is he Russian?"

"He is a Cossack," said the general, and his smile showed red lips and pointed teeth. "So am I.

"Come," he said, "we shouldn't be chatting here. We can talk later. Now you want clothes, food, rest. You shall have them. This is a most restful spot."

Ivan had re-appeared, and the general spoke to him with lips that moved but gave forth no sound.

"Follow Ivan, if you please, Mr. Rainsford," said the general. "I was about to have my dinner when you came. I'll wait for you. You'll find that my clothes will fit you, I think."

It was to a huge, beam-ceilinged room with a canopied bed big enough for six men that Rainsford followed the silent giant. Ivan laid out an evening suit, and Rainsford, as he put it on, noticed that it came from a London tailor who ordinarily cut and sewed for none below the rank of a duke.

The dining room to which Ivan conducted him was in many ways remarkable. There was a medieval magnificence about it; it suggested a baronial hall of feudal times with its oaken panels, its high ceiling, its vast refectory table where two score men could sit down to eat. About the hall were the mounted heads of many animals—lions, tigers, elephants, moose, bears; larger or more perfect specimens Rainsford had never seen before. At the great table the general was sitting, alone.

"You'll have a cocktail, Mr. Rainsford," he suggested. The cocktail was surpassingly good; and, Rainsford noted, the table appointments were of the finest—the linen, the crystal, the silver, the china.

They were eating *borsch,* the rich, red soup with whipped cream so dear to Russian palates. Half apologetically General Zaroff said: "We try to preserve the amenities of civilization here. Please forgive any lapses. We are well off the beaten track, you know. Do you think the champagne has suffered from its long ocean trip?"

"Not in the least," declared Rainsford. He was finding the general a most thoughtful and affable host, a true cosmopolite. But there was one trait of the general's that made Rainsford uncomfortable. Whenever he looked up he found the general studying him, appraising him narrowly.

"Perhaps," said General Zaroff, "you were surprised that I recognized your name. You see, I read all books on hunting published in English, French, and Russian. I have but one passion in my life, Mr. Rainsford, and it is the hunt."

"You have some wonderful heads here," said Rainsford as he ate a particularly well-cooked filet mignon. "That Cape buffalo is the largest I ever saw."

"Oh, that fellow. Yes, he was a monster."

"Did he charge you?"

"Hurled me against a tree," said the general. "Fractured my skull. But I got the brute."

"I've always thought," said Rainsford, "that the Cape buffalo is the most dangerous of all big game."

For a moment the general did not reply; he was smiling his curious red-lipped smile. Then he said slowly: "No. You are wrong, sir. The Cape buffalo is not the most dangerous big game." He sipped his wine. "Here in my preserve on this island," he said in the same slow tone, "I hunt more dangerous game."

Rainsford expressed his surprise. "Is there big game on this island?"

The general nodded. "The biggest."

"Really?"

"Oh, it isn't here naturally, of course. I have to stock the island."

"What have you imported, General?" Rainsford asked. "Tigers?"

The general smiled. "No," he said. "Hunting tigers ceased to interest me some years ago. I exhausted their possibilities, you see. No thrill left in tigers, no real danger. I live for danger, Mr. Rainsford."

The general took from his pocket a gold cigarette case and offered his guest a long black cigarette with a silver tip; it was perfumed and gave off a smell like incense.

"We will have some capital hunting, you and I," said the general. "I shall be most glad to have your society."

"But what game—" began Rainsford.

"I'll tell you," said the general. "You will be amused, I know. I think I may say, in all modesty, that I have done a rare thing. I have invented a new sensation. May I pour you another glass of port, Mr. Rainsford?"

"Thank you, General."

The general filled both glasses, and said: "God makes some men poets. Some He makes kings, some beggars. Me He made a hunter. My hand was made for the trigger, my father said. He was a very rich man with a quarter of a million acres in the Crimea, and he was an ardent sportsman. When I was only five years old he gave me a little gun, specially made in Moscow for me, to shoot sparrows with. When I shot some of his prize turkeys with it, he did not punish me; he complimented me on my marksmanship. I killed my first bear in the Caucasus when I was ten. My whole life had been one prolonged hunt. I went into the army—it was expected of noblemen's sons—and for a time commanded a division of Cossack cavalry, but my real interest was always the hunt. I have hunted every kind of game in every land. It would be impossible for me to tell you how many animals I have killed."

The general puffed at his cigarette.

"After the debacle in Russia I left the country, for it was imprudent for an officer of the Czar to stay there. Many noble Russians lost everything. I, luckily, had invested heavily in American securities, so I shall never have to open a tearoom in Monte Carlo or drive a taxi in Paris. Naturally, I continued to hunt—grizzlies in your Rockies, crocodiles in the Ganges, rhinoceroses in East Africa. It was in Africa that the Cape buffalo hit me and laid me up for six months. As soon as I recovered, I started for the Amazon to hunt jaguars, for I had heard they were unusually cunning. They weren't." The Cossack sighed. "They were no match at all for a hunter with his wits about him, and a high-powered rifle. I was bitterly disappointed. I was lying in my tent with a splitting headache one night when a terrible thought rushed into my mind. Hunting was beginning to bore me! And hunting, remember, had been my life. I have heard that in America businessmen often go to pieces when they give up the business that has been their life."

"Yes, that's so," said Rainsford.

The general smiled. "I had no wish to go to pieces," he said. "I must do something. Now, mine is an analytical mind, Mr. Rainsford. Doubtless that is why I enjoy the problems of the chase."

"No doubt, General Zaroff."

"So," continued the general, "I asked myself why the hunt no longer fascinated me. You are much younger than I am, Mr. Rainsford, and have not hunted as much, but you perhaps can guess the answer."

"What was it?"

"Simply this: hunting had ceased to be what you call a 'sporting proposition.' It had become too easy. I always got my quarry. Always. There is no greater bore than perfection."

The general lit a fresh cigarette.

"No animal had a chance with me any more. That is no boast; it is a mathematical certainty. The animal had nothing but his legs and his instinct. Instinct is no match for reason. When I thought of this, it was a tragic moment for me, I can tell you."

Rainsford leaned across the table, absorbed in what his host was saying.

"It came to me as an inspiration what I must do," the general said.

"And that was?"

The general smiled the quiet smile of one who has faced an obstacle and surmounted it with success. "I had to invent a new animal to hunt," he said.

"A new animal? You're joking."

"Not at all," said the general. "I never joke about hunting. I needed a new animal. I found one. So I bought this island, built this house, and here I do my hunting. The island is perfect for my purposes—there are jungles with a maze of trails in them, hills, swamps—"

"But the animal, General Zaroff?"

"Oh," said the general, "it supplies me with the most exciting hunting in the world. No other hunting compares with it for an instant. Every day I hunt, and I never grow bored now, for I have a quarry with which I can match my wits."

Rainsford's bewilderment showed in his face.

"I wanted the ideal animal to hunt," explained the general. "So I said: 'What are the attributes of an ideal quarry?' And the answer was, of course: 'It must have courage, cunning, and, above all, it must be able to reason.' "

"But no animal can reason," objected Rainsford.

"My dear fellow," said the general, "there is one that can."

"But you can't mean—" gasped Rainsford.

"And why not?"

"I can't believe you are serious, General Zaroff. This is a grisly joke."

"Why should I not be serious? I am speaking of hunting."

"Hunting? Good God, General Zaroff, what you speak of is murder."

The general laughed with entire good nature. He regarded Rainsford quizzically. "I refuse to believe that so modern and civilized a young man as you harbors romantic ideas about the value of human life. Surely your experiences in the war—"

"Did not make me condone cold-blooded murder," finished Rainsford stiffly.

Laughter shook the general. "How extraordinarily droll you are!" he said. "One does not expect nowadays to find a young man of the educated class, even in America, with such a naïve and, if I may say so, mid-Victorian point of view. It's like finding a snuffbox in a limousine. Ah, well, doubtless you had Puritan ancestors. So many Americans appear to have had. I'll wager you'll forget your notions when you go hunting with me. You've a genuine new thrill in store for you, Mr. Rainsford."

"Thank you, I'm a hunter, not a murderer."

"Dear me," said the general, quite unruffled, "again that unpleasant word. But I think I can show you that your scruples are quite unfounded."

"Yes?"

"Life is for the strong, to be lived by the strong, and, if needs be, taken by the strong. The weak of the world were put here to give the strong pleasure. I am strong. Why should I not use my gift? If I wish to hunt, why should I not? I hunt the scum of the earth—sailors from tramp ships—lascars, blacks, Chinese, whites, mongrels—a thoroughbred horse or hound is worth more than a score of them."

"But they are men," said Rainsford hotly.

"Precisely," said the general. "That is why I use them. It gives me pleasure. They can reason, after a fashion. So they are dangerous."

"But where do you get them?"

The general's left eyelid fluttered down in a wink. "This island is called Ship Trap," he answered. "Sometimes an angry god of the high seas sends them to me. Sometimes, when Providence is not so kind, I help Providence a bit. Come to the window with me."

Rainsford went to the window and looked out toward the sea.

"Watch! Out there!" exclaimed the general, pointing into the night. Rainsford's eyes saw only blackness, and then, as the general pressed a button, far out to sea Rainsford saw the flash of lights.

The general chuckled. "They indicate a channel," he said, "where there's none: giant rocks with razor edges crouch like a sea monster with wide-open jaws. They can crush a ship as easily as I crush this nut." He dropped a walnut on the hardwood floor and brought his heel grinding down on it. "Oh, yes," he said, casually, as if in answer to a question, "I have electricity. We try to be civilized here."

"Civilized? And you shoot down men?"

A trace of anger was in the general's black eyes, but it was there for but a second, and he said, in his most pleasant manner: "Dear me, what a righteous young man you are! I assure you I do not do the thing you suggest. That would be barbarous. I treat these visitors with every consideration. They get plenty of good food and exercise. They get into splendid physical condition. You shall see for yourself tomorrow."

"What do you mean?"

"We'll visit my training school," smiled the general. "It's in the cellar. I have about a dozen pupils down there now. They're from the Spanish bark, 'San Lucar,' that had the bad luck to go on the rocks out there. A very inferior lot, I regret to say. Poor specimens and more accustomed to the deck than to the jungle."

He raised his hand, and Ivan, who served as waiter, brought thick Turkish coffee. Rainsford, with an effort, held his tongue in check.

"It's a game, you see," pursued the general blandly. "I suggest to one of them that we go hunting. I give him a supply of food and an excellent hunting knife. I give him three hours' start. I am to follow, armed only with a pistol of the smallest caliber and range. If my quarry eludes me for three whole days, he wins the game. If I find him," the general smiled, "he loses."

"Suppose he refuses to be hunted?"

"Oh," said the general, "I give him his option, of course. He need not play that game if he doesn't wish to. It he does not wish to hunt I turn him over to Ivan. Ivan once had the honor of serving as official knouter to the Great White Czar, and he has his own ideas of sport. Invariably, Mr. Rainsford, invariably they choose the hunt."

"And if they win?"

The smile on the general's face widened. "To date I have not lost," he said.

Then he added, hastily: "I don't wish you to think me a braggart, Mr. Rainsford. Many of them afford only the most elementary sort of problem. Occasionally I strike a tartar. One almost did win. I eventually had to use the dogs."

"The dogs?"

"This way, please. I'll show you."

The general steered Rainsford to a window. The lights from the window sent a flickering illumination that made grotesque patterns on the courtyard below, and Rainsford could see moving about there a dozen or so huge black shapes; as they turned toward him, their eyes glittered greenly.

"A rather good lot, I think," observed the general. "They are let out at seven every night. If anyone should try to get into my house—or out of it—something extremely regrettable would occur to him." He hummed a snatch of song from the *Folies Bergère*.

"And now," said the general, "I want to show you my new collection of heads. Will you come with me to the library?"

"I hope," said Rainsford, "that you will excuse me tonight, General Zaroff. I'm really not feeling at all well."

"Ah, indeed?" the general inquired solicitously. "Well, I suppose that's only natural, after your long swim. You need a good, restful night's sleep. To-morrow you'll feel like a new man, I'll wager. Then we'll hunt, eh? I've one rather promising prospect—"

Rainsford was hurrying from the room.

"Sorry you can't go with me tonight," called the general. "I expect rather fair sport—a big, strong black. He looks resourceful—well, good night, Mr. Rainsford; I hope you have a good night's rest."

The bed was good, and the pajamas of the softest silk, and he was tired in every fiber of his being, but nevertheless Rainsford could not quiet his brain with the opiate of sleep. He lay, eyes wide open. Once he thought he heard stealthy steps in the corridor outside his room. He sought to throw open the door; it would not open. He went to the window and looked out. His room was high up in one of the towers. The lights of the château were out now, and it was dark and silent; but there was a fragment of sallow moon, and by its wan light he could see, dimly, the courtyard; there, weaving in and out in the pattern of shadow, were black, noiseless forms; the hounds heard him at the window and looked up, expectantly, with their green eyes. Rainsford went back to the bed and lay down. By many methods he tried to put himself to sleep. He had achieved a doze when, just as morning began to come, he heard, far off in the jungle, the faint report of a pistol.

General Zaroff did not appear until luncheon. He was dressed faultlessly in the tweeds of a country squire. He was solicitous about the state of Rainsford's health.

"As for me," sighed the general, "I do not feel so well. I am worried, Mr. Rainsford. Last night I detected traces of my old complaint."

To Rainsford's questioning glance the general said: "Ennui. Boredom."

Then, taking a second helping of Crêpes Suzette, the general explained: "The hunting was not good last night. The fellow lost his head. He made a straight trail that offered no problems at all. That's the trouble with these sailors; they have dull brains to begin with, and they do not know how to get about in the woods. They do excessively stupid and obvious things. It's most annoying. Will you have another glass of Chablis, Mr. Rainsford?"

"General," said Rainsford firmly, "I wish to leave this island at once."

The general raised his thickets of eyebrows; he seemed hurt. "But, my dear fellow," the general protested, "you've only just come. You've had no hunting—"

"I wish to go today," said Rainsford. He saw the dead black eyes of the general on him, studying him. General Zaroff's face suddenly brightened.

He filled Rainsford's glass with venerable Chablis from a dusty bottle. "Tonight," said the general, "we will hunt—you and I."

Rainsford shook his head. "No, General," he said. "I will not hunt."

The general shrugged his shoulders and nibbled delicately at a hot-house grape. "As you wish, my friend," he said. "The choice rests entirely with you. But may I not venture to suggest that you will find my idea of sport more diverting than Ivan's?"

He nodded toward the corner where the giant stood, scowling, his thick arms crossed on his hogshead of chest.

"You don't mean—" cried Rainsford.

"My dear fellow," said the general, "have I not told you I always mean what I say about hunting? This is really an inspiration. I drink to a foeman worthy of my steel—at last."

The general raised his glass, but Rainsford sat staring at him.

"You'll find this game worth playing," the general said enthusiastically. "Your brain against mine. Your woodcraft against mine. Your strength and stamina against mine. Outdoor chess. And the stake is not without value, eh?"

"And if I win—" began Rainsford huskily.

"I'll cheerfully admit myself defeated if I do not find you by midnight of the third day," said General Zaroff. "My sloop will place you on the mainland near a town."

The general read what Rainsford was thinking.

"Oh, you can trust me," said the Cossack. "I will give you my word as a gentleman and a sportsman. Of course you, in turn, must agree to say nothing of your visit here."

"I'll agree to nothing of the kind," said Rainsford.

"Oh," said the general, "in that case— But why discuss that now? Three days hence we can discuss it over a bottle of Veuve Cliquot, unless—"

The general sipped his wine.

Then a businesslike air animated him. "Ivan," he said to Rainsford, "will supply you with hunting clothes, food, a knife. I suggest you wear moccasins; they leave a poorer trail. I should suggest too that you avoid the big swamp in the southeast corner of the island. We call it Death Swamp. There's quicksand there. One foolish fellow tried it. The deplorable part of it was that Lazarus followed him. You can imagine my feelings, Mr. Rainsford. I loved Lazarus; he was the finest hound in my pack. Well, I must beg you to excuse me now. I always take a siesta after lunch. You'll hardly have time for a nap, I fear. You'll want to start, no doubt. I shall not follow till dusk. Hunting at night is so much more exciting than by day, don't you think? Au revoir, Mr. Rainsford, au revoir."

General Zaroff, with a deep, courtly bow, strolled from the room.

From another door came Ivan. Under one arm he carried khaki hunting clothes, a haversack of food, a leather sheath containing a long-bladed hunting knife; his right hand rested on a cocked revolver thrust in the crimson sash around his waist. . . .

Rainsford had fought his way through the bush for two hours. "I must keep my nerve. I must keep my nerve," he said through his tight teeth.

He had not been entirely clear-headed when the château gates snapped shut behind him. His whole idea at first was to put distance between himself and General Zaroff, and, to this end, he had plunged along, spurred on by the sharp rowels of something very like panic. Now he had got a grip on himself, had stopped, and was taking stock of himself and the situation.

He saw that straight flight was futile; inevitably it would bring him face to face with the sea. He was in a picture with the frame of water, and his operations, clearly, must take place within that frame.

"I'll give him a trail to follow," muttered Rainsford, and struck off from the rude path he had been following into the trackless wilderness. He executed a series of intricate loops; he doubled on his trail again and again, recalling all the lore of the fox hunt, and all the dodges of the fox. Night found him leg-weary, with hands and face lashed by the branches, on a thickly wooded ridge. He knew it would be insane to blunder on through the dark, even if he had the strength. His need for rest was imperative and he thought: "I have played the fox, now I must be the cat of the fable." A big tree with a thick trunk and outspread branches was near by, and taking care to leave not the slightest mark, he climbed up into the crotch and, stretching out on one of the broad limbs, after a fashion, rested. Rest brought him new confidence and almost a feeling of security. Even so zealous a hunter as General Zaroff could not trace him there, he told himself; only the devil himself could follow that complicated trail through the jungle after dark. But perhaps the general was a devil—

An apprehensive night crawled slowly by like a wounded snake, and sleep did not visit Rainsford, although the silence of a dead world was on the jungle. Toward morning when a dingy gray was varnishing the sky, the cry of some startled bird focused Rainsford's attention in that direction. Something was coming through the bush, coming slowly, carefully, coming by the same winding way Rainsford had come. He flattened himself down on the limb, and through a screen of leaves almost as thick as tapestry, he watched. The thing that was approaching was a man.

It was General Zaroff. He made his way along with his eyes fixed in utmost concentration on the ground before him. He paused almost beneath the tree, dropped to his knees, and studied the ground before him. Rainsford's impulse was to hurl himself down like a panther, but he saw that the general's right hand held something small and metallic—an automatic pistol.

The hunter shook his head several times as if he were puzzled. Then he straightened up and took from his case one of his black cigarettes; its pungent incense-like smoke floated up to Rainsford's nostrils.

Rainsford held his breath. The general's eyes had left the ground and were traveling inch by inch up the tree. Rainsford froze there, every muscle tensed for a spring. But the sharp eyes of the hunter stopped before they reached the limb where Rainsford lay; a smile spread over his brown face. Very deliberately he blew a smoke ring into the air; then he turned his back on the tree and walked carelessly away, back along the trail he had come. The swish of the underbrush against his hunting boots grew fainter and fainter.

The pent-up air burst hotly from Rainsford's lungs. His first thought made him feel sick and numb. The general could follow a trail through the woods at night; he could follow an extremely difficult trail; he must have uncanny powers; only by the merest chance had the Cossack failed to see his quarry.

Rainsford's second thought was even more terrible. It sent a shudder of cold horror through his whole being. Why had the general smiled? Why had he turned back?

Rainsford did not want to believe what his reason told him was true, but the truth was as evident as the sun that had by now pushed through the morning mists. The general was playing with him. The general was saving him for another day's sport! The Cossack was the cat; he was the mouse. Then it was that Rainsford knew the full meaning of terror.

"I will not lose my nerve. I will not."

He slid down from the tree, and struck off again into the woods. His face was set and he forced the machinery of his mind to function. Three hundred yards from his hiding place he stopped where a huge dead tree leaned precariously on a smaller living one. Throwing off his sack of food, Rainsford took his knife from its sheath and began to work with all his energy.

The job was finished at last, and he threw himself down behind a fallen log a hundred feet away. He did not have to wait long. The cat was coming again to play with the mouse.

Following the trail with the sureness of a bloodhound came General Zaroff. Nothing escaped those searching black eyes, no crushed blade of grass, no bent twig, no mark, no matter how faint, in the moss. So intent was the Cossack on his stalking that he was upon the thing Rainsford had made before he saw it. His foot touched the protruding bough that was the trigger. Even as he touched it, the general sensed his danger and leaped back with the agility of an ape. But he was not quite quick enough; the dead tree, delicately adjusted to rest on the cut living one, crashed down and struck the general a glancing blow on the shoulder as it fell; but for his alertness, he must have been smashed beneath it. He staggered, but he did not fall; nor did he drop his revolver. He stood there rubbing his injured shoulder, and Rainsford, with fear again gripping his heart, heard the general's mocking laugh ring through the jungle.

"Rainsford," called the general, "if you are within sound of my voice, as I suppose you are, let me congratulate you. Not many men know how to make a Malay mancatcher. Luckily, for me, I too have hunted in Malacca. You are proving interesting, Mr. Rainsford. I am going now to have my wound dressed; it's only a slight one. But I shall be back. I shall be back."

When the general, nursing his bruised shoulder, had gone, Rainsford took up his flight again. It was flight now, a desperate, hopeless flight, that carried him on for some hours. Dusk came, then darkness, and still he pressed on. The ground grew softer under his moccasins; the vegetation grew ranker, denser; insects bit him savagely. Then, as he stepped forward his foot sank into the ooze. He tried to wrench it back, but the muck sucked viciously at his foot as if it were a giant leech. With a violent effort, he tore his foot loose. He knew where he was now. Death Swamp and its quicksand.

His hands were tight closed as if his nerve were something tangible that someone in the darkness was trying to tear from his grip. The softness of the earth had given him an idea. He stepped back from the quicksand a dozen feet or so and, like some huge prehistoric beaver, he began to dig.

Rainsford had dug himself in in France when a second's delay meant death. That had been a placid pastime compared to his digging now. The pit grew deeper; when it was above his shoulders, he climbed out and from some hard saplings cut stakes and sharpened them to a fine point. These stakes he planted in the bottom of the pit with the points sticking up. With flying fingers he wove a rough carpet of weeds and branches and with it covered the mouth of the pit. Then, wet with sweat and aching with tiredness, he crouched behind the stump of a lightning-charred tree.

He knew his pursuer was coming; he heard the padding sound of feet on the soft earth, and the night breeze brought him the perfume of the general's cigarette. It seemed to Rainsford that the general was coming with unusual swiftness; he was not feeling his way along, foot by foot. Rainsford, crouching there, could not see the general, nor could he see the pit. He lived a year in a minute. Then he felt an impulse to cry aloud with joy, for he heard the sharp crackle of the breaking branches as the cover of the pit gave way; he heard the sharp scream of pain as the pointed stakes found their mark. He leaped up from his place of concealment. Then he cowered back. Three feet from the pit a man was standing, with an electric torch in his hand.

"You've done well, Rainsford," the voice of the general called. "Your Burmese tiger pit has claimed one of my best dogs. Again you score, I think, Mr. Rainsford, I'll see what you can do against my whole pack. I'm going home for a rest now. Thank you for a most amusing evening."

At daybreak Rainsford, lying near the swamp, was awakened by a sound that made him know that he had new things to learn about fear. It was a distant sound, faint and wavering, but he knew it. It was the baying of a pack of hounds.

Rainsford knew he could do one of two things. He could stay where he was and wait. That was suicide. He could flee. That was postponing the inevitable. For a moment he stood there, thinking. An idea that held a wild chance came to him, and tightening his belt, he headed away from the swamp. The baying of the hounds grew nearer, then still nearer, nearer, ever nearer. On a ridge, Rainsford climbed a tree. Down a watercourse, not a quarter of a mile away, he could see the bush moving. Straining his eyes, he saw the lean figure of General Zaroff; just ahead of him Rainsford made out another figure whose wide shoulders surged through the jungle weeds; it was the giant Ivan, and he seemed pulled forward by some unseen force; Rainsford knew that Ivan must be holding the pack in leash.

They would be on him any minute now. His mind worked frantically. He thought of a native trick he had learned in Uganda. He slid down the tree. He caught hold of a springy young sapling and to it he fastened his hunting knife, with the blade pointing down the trail; with a bit of wild grapevine he tied back the sapling. Then he ran for his life. The hounds raised their voices as they hit the fresh scent. Rainsford knew now how an animal at bay feels.

He had to stop to get his breath. The baying of the hounds stopped abruptly, and Rainsford's heart stopped too. They must have reached the knife.

He shinned excitedly up a tree and looked back. His pursuers had stopped. But the hope that was in Rainsford's brain when he climbed died, for he saw in the shallow valley that General Zaroff was still on his feet. But Ivan was not. The knife, driven by the recoil of the springing tree, had not wholly failed.

Rainsford had hardly tumbled to the ground when the pack resumed the chase.

"Nerve, nerve, nerve!" he panted, as he dashed along. A blue gap showed between the trees dead ahead. Ever nearer drew the hounds. Rainsford forced himself on toward that gap. He reached it. It was the shore of the sea. Across a cove he could see the gloomy gray stone of the château. Twenty feet below him the sea rumbled and hissed. Rainsford hesitated. He heard the hounds. Then he leaped far out into the sea. . . .

When the general and his pack reached the place by the sea, the Cossack, stopped. For some minutes he stood regarding the blue-green expanse of water. He shrugged his shoulders. Then he sat down, took a drink of brandy from a silver flask, lit a perfumed cigarette, and hummed a bit from *Madame Butterfly.*

General Zaroff had an exceedingly good dinner in his great paneled dining hall that evening. With it he had a bottle of Pol Roger and a half bottle of Chambertin. Two slight annoyances kept him from perfect enjoyment. One was the thought that it would be difficult to replace Ivan; the other was that his quarry had escaped him; of course, the American hadn't played the game—so thought the general as he tasted his after-dinner liqueur. In his library he read, to soothe himself, from the works of Marcus Aurelius. At ten we went up to his bedroom. He was deliciously tired, he said to himself, as he locked himself in. There was a little moonlight, so, before turning on his light, he went to the window and looked down at the courtyard. To the great hounds he called: "Better luck another time!" Then he switched on the light.

"Rainsford!" screamed the general. "How in God's name did you get here?"

"Swam," said Rainsford. "I found it quicker than walking through the jungle."

The general sucked in his breath and smiled. "I congratulate you," he said. "You have won the game."

Rainsford did not smile. "I am still a beast at bay," he said, in a low voice. "Get ready, General Zaroff."

The general made one of his deepest bows. "I see," he said. "Splendid! One of us is to furnish a repast for the hounds. The other will sleep in this very excellent bed. On guard, Rainsford!" . . .

He had never slept in a better bed, Rainsford decided.

"Rikki-Tikki-Tavi"

BY RUDYARD KIPLING

O ne of the greatest storytellers of all time . . . a classic confrontation of two of nature's most interesting creatures . . . a tale to survive the ages.

★   ★   ★   ★   ★

At the hole where he went in
Red-Eye called to Wrinkle-Skin
Hear what little Red-Eye saith: —
'Nag, come up and dance with death!'
Eye to eye and head to head
　(*Keep the measure, Nag*).
This shall end when one is dead
　(*At thy pleasure, Nag*).
Turn for turn and twist for twist
　(*Run and hide thee, Nag*).
Hah! The hooded Death has missed!
　(*Woe betide thee, Nag!*)

This is the story of the great war that Rikki-tikki-tavi fought single-handed, through the bath-rooms of the big bungalow in Segowlee cantonment. Darzee, the tailor-bird, helped him, and Chuchundra, the musk-rat, who never comes out into the middle of the floor, but always creeps round by the wall, gave him advice; but Rikki-tikki-tavi did the real fighting.

He was a mongoose, rather like a little cat in his fur and his tail, but quite like a weasel in his head and his habits. His eyes and the end of his restless nose were pink; he could scratch himself anywhere he pleased with any leg, front or back, that he chose to use; he could fluff up his tail till it looked like a bottle-brush, and his war-cry as he scuttled through the long grass was: *Rikk-tikk-tikki-tikki-tikki-tchk!*

One day, a high summer flood washed him out of the burrow where he lived with his father and mother, and carried him, kicking and clucking, down a roadside ditch. He found a little wisp of grass floating there, and clung to it till he lost his senses. When he revived, he was lying in the hot sun on the middle of a garden path, very draggled indeed, and a small boy was saying: "Here's a dead mongoose. Let's have a funeral."

"No," said his mother; "let's take him in and dry him. Perhaps he isn't really dead."

They took him into the house, and a big man picked him up between his finger and thumb and said he was not dead but half choked; so they wrapped him in cotton-wool, and warmed him over a little fire, and he opened his eyes and sneezed.

"Now," said the big man (he was an Englishman who had just moved into the bungalow); "don't frighten him, and we'll see what he'll do."

It is the hardest thing in the world to frighten a mongoose, because he is eaten up from nose to tail with curiosity. The motto of all the mongoose family is, "Run and find out"; and Rikki-tikki was a true mongoose. He looked at the cotton-wool, decided that it was not good to eat, ran all round the table, sat up and put his fur in order, scratched himself, and jumped on the small boy's shoulder.

"Don't be frightened, Teddy," said his father. "That's his way of making friends."

"Ouch! He's tickling under my chin," said Teddy.

Rikki-tikki looked down between the boy's collar and neck, snuffed at his ear, and climbed down to the floor, where he sat rubbing his nose.

"Good gracious" said Teddy's mother, "and that's a wild creature! I suppose he's so tame because we've been kind to him."

"All mongooses are like that," said her husband. "If Teddy doesn't pick him up by the tail, or try to put him in a cage, he'll run in and out of the house all day long. Let's give him something to eat."

They gave him a little piece of raw meat. Rikki-tikki liked it immensely, and when it was finished he went out into the veranda and sat in the sunshine and fluffed up his fur to make it dry to the roots. Then he felt better.

"There are more things to find out about in this house," he said to himself, "than all my family could find out in all their lives. I shall certainly stay and find out."

He spent all that day roaming over the house. He nearly drowned himself in the bath-tubs; put his nose into the ink on a writing-table, and burnt it on the end of the big man's cigar, for he climbed up in the big man's lap to see how writing was done. At nightfall he ran into Teddy's nursery to watch how kerosene lamps were lighted, and when Teddy went to bed Rikki-tikki climbed up too; but he was a restless companion, because he had to get up and attend to every noise all through the night, and find out what made it. Teddy's mother and father came in, the last thing, to look at their boy, and Rikki-tikki was awake on the pillow. "I don't like that," said Teddy's mother; "he may bite the child." "He'll do no such thing" said the father. "Teddy's safer with that little beast than if he had a bloodhound to watch him. If a snake came into the nursery now—"

But Teddy's mother wouldn't think of anything so awful.

Early in the morning Rikki-tikki came to early breakfast in the veranda riding on Teddy's shoulder, and they gave him banana and some boiled egg; and he sat on all their laps one after the other, because very well-brought-up mongoose always hopes to be a house-mongoose some day and have rooms to run about in; and Rikki-tikki's mother (she used to live in the General's house at Segowlee) had carefully told Rikki what to do if ever he came across white men.

Then Rikki-tikki went out into the garden to see what was to be seen. It was a large garden, only half cultivated, with bushes, as big as summer-houses, of Marshal Niel roses; lime and orange trees, clumps of bamboos, and thickets of high grass. Rikki-tikki licked his lips. "This is a splendid hunting-ground," he said, and his tail grew bottle-brushy at the thought of it, and he scuttled up and down the garden, snuffing here and there till he heard very sorrowful voices in a thorn-bush. It was Darzee, the tailor-bird, and his wife. They had made a beautiful nest by pulling two big leaves together and stitching them up the edges with fibres, and had filled the hollow with cotton and downy fluff. The nest swayed to and fro, as they sat on the rim and cried.

"What is the matter?" asked Rikki-tikki.

"We are very miserable," said Darzee. "One of our babies fell out of the nest yesterday and Nag ate him."

"H'm!" said Rikki-tikki, "that is very sad—but I am a stranger here. Who is Nag?"

Darzee and his wife only cowered down in the nest without answering, for from the thick grass at the foot of the bush there came a low hiss—a horrid cold sound that made Rikki-tikki jump back two clear feet. Then inch by inch out of the grass rose up the head and spread hood of Nag, the big black cobra, and he was five feet long from tongue to tail. When he had lifted one-third of himself clear of the ground, he stayed balancing to and fro exactly as a dandelion-tuft balances in the wind, and he looked at Rikki-tikki with the wicked snake's eyes that never change their expression, whatever the snake may be thinking of.

"Who is Nag," said he. "*I* am Nag. The great God Brahm put his mark upon all our people, when the first cobra spread his hood to keep the sun off Brahm as he slept. Look, and be afraid!"

He spread out his hood more than ever, and Rikki-tikki saw the spectacle-mark on the back of it that looks exactly like the eye part of a hook-and-eye fastening. He was afraid for the minute; but it is impossible for a mongoose to stay frightened for any length of time, and though Rikki-tikki had never met a live cobra before, his mother had fed him on dead ones, and he knew that all a grown mongoose's business in life was to fight and eat snakes. Nag knew that too and, at the bottom of his cold heart, he was afraid.

"Well," said Rikki-tikki, and his tail began to fluff up again, "marks or no marks, do you think it is right for you to eat fledglings out of a nest?"

Nag was thinking to himself, and watching the least little movement in the grass behind Rikki-tikki. He knew that mongooses in the garden meant death sooner or later for him and his family; but he wanted to get Rikki-tikki off his guard. So he dropped his head a little, and put it on one side.

"Let us talk," he said. "You eat eggs. Why should not I eat birds?"

"Behind you! Look behind you!" sang Darzee.

Rikki-tikki knew better than to waste time in staring. He jumped up in the air as high as he could go, and just under him whizzed by the head of Nagaina, Nag's wicked wife. She had crept up behind him as he was talking, to make an end of him; and he heard her savage hiss as the stroke missed. He came down almost across her back, and if he had been an old mongoose he would have known that then was the time to break her back with one bite; but he was afraid of the terrible lashing return-stroke of the cobra. He bit, indeed, but did not bite long enough, and he jumped clear of the whisking tail, leaving Nagaina torn and angry.

"Wicked, wicked Darzee!" said Nag, lashing up as high as he could reach toward the nest in the thorn-bush; but Darzee had built it out of reach of snakes, and it only swayed to and fro.

Rikki-tikki felt his eyes growing red and hot (when a mongoose's eyes grow red, he is angry), and he sat back on his tail and hind legs like a little kangaroo, and looked all round him, and chattered with rage. But Nag and Nagaina had disappeared into the grass. When a snake misses its stroke, it never says anything or gives any sign of what it means to do next. Rikki-tikki did not care to follow them, for he did not feel sure that he could manage two snakes at once. So he trotted off to the gravel path near the house, and sat down to think. It was a serious matter for him. If you read the old books of natural history, you will find they say that when the mongoose fights the snake and happens to get bitten, he runs off and eats some herb that cures him. That is not true. The victory is only a matter of quickness of eye and quickness of foot,— snake's blow against the mongoose's jump,—and as no eye can follow the motion of a snake's head when it strikes, this makes things much more wonderful than any magic herb. Rikki-tikki knew he was a young mongoose, and it made him all the more pleased to think that he had managed to escape a blow from behind. It gave him confidence in himself, and when Teddy came running down the path, Rikki-tikki was ready to be petted. But just as Teddy was stooping, something wriggled a little in the dust, and a tiny voice said: 'Be careful. I am Death?' It was Karait, the dusty brown snakeling that lies for choice on the dusty earth; and his bite is as dangerous as the cobra's. But he is so small that nobody thinks of him, and so he does the more harm to people.

Rikki-tikki's eyes grew red again, and he danced up to Karait with the peculiar rocking, swaying motion that he had inherited from his family. It looks very funny, but it is so perfectly balanced a gait that you can fly off from it at any angle you please; and in dealing with snakes this is an advantage. If Rikki-tikki had only known, he was doing a much more dangerous thing than fighting Nag, for Karait is so small, and can turn so quickly, that unless Rikki bit him close to the back of the head, he would get the return-stroke in his eye or his lip. But Rikki did not know: his eyes were all red, and he rocked back and forth, looking for a good place to hold. Karait struck out, Rikki jumped sideways and tried to run in, but the wicked little dusty gray head lashed within a fraction of his shoulder, and he had to jump over the body, and the head followed his heels close.

Teddy shouted to the house: "Oh, look here! Our mongoose is killing a snake"; and Rikki-tikki heard a scream from Teddy's mother. His father ran out with a stick, but by the time he came up, Karait had lunged out once too far, and Rikki-tikki had sprung, jumped on the snake's back, dropped his head far between his fore-legs, bitten as high up the back as he could get hold, and rolled away. That bite paralysed Karait, and Rikki-tikki was just going to eat him up from the tail, after the custom of his family at dinner, when he remembered that a full meal makes a slow mongoose, and if he wanted all his strength and quickness ready, he must keep himself thin. He went away for a dust-bath under the castor-oil bushes, while Teddy's father beat the dead

Karait. "What is the use of that?" thought Rikki-tikki; "I have settled it all"; and then Teddy's mother picked him up from the dust and hugged him, crying that he had saved Teddy from death, and Teddy's father said that he was a providence, and Teddy looked on with big scared eyes. Rikki-tikki was rather amused at all the fuss, which, of course, he did not understand. Teddy's mother might just as well have petted Teddy for playing in the dust. Rikki was thoroughly enjoying himself.

That night at dinner, walking to and fro among the wine-glasses on the table, he might have stuffed himself three times over with nice things; but he remembered Nag and Nagaina, and though it was very pleasant to be patted and petted by Teddy's mother, and to sit on Teddy's shoulder, his eyes would get red from time to time, and he would go off into his long war-cry of "*Rikk-tikk-tikki-tikki-tchk!*"

Teddy carried him off to bed, and insisted on Rikki-tikki's sleeping under his chin. Rikki-tikki was too well bred to bite or scratch, but as soon as Teddy was asleep he went off for his nightly walk round the house, and in the dark he ran up against Chuchundra, the musk-rat, creeping round by the wall. Chuchundra is a broken-hearted little beast. He whimpers and cheeps all night, trying to make up his mind to run into the middle of the room; but he never gets there.

"Don't kill me," said Chuchundra, almost weeping. "Rikki-tikki, don't kill me!"

"Do you think a snake-killer kills musk-rats?" said Rikki-tikki scornfully.

"Those who kill snakes get killed by snakes," said Chuchundra, more sorrowfully than ever. "And how am I to be sure that Nag won't mistake me for you some dark night?"

"There's not the least danger," said Rikki-tikki; "but Nag is in the garden, and I know you don't go there."

"My cousin Chua, the rat, told me—" said Chuchundra, and then he stopped.

"Told you what?"

"H'sh! Nag is everywhere, Rikki-tikki. You should have talked to Chua in the garden."

"I didn't—so you must tell me. Quick, Chuchundra, or I'll bite you!"

Chuchundra sat down and cried till the tears rolled off his whiskers. "I am a very poor man," he sobbed. "I never had spirit enough to run out into the middle of the room. H'sh! I mustn't tell you anything. Can't you *hear*, Rikki-tikki?"

Rikki-tikki listened. The house was as still as still, but he thought he could just catch the faintest *scratch-scratch* in the world,—a noise as faint as that of a wasp walking on a window-pane,—the dry scratch of a snake's scales on brickwork.

"That's Nag or Nagaina," he said to himself; "and he is crawling into the bath-room sluice. You're right, Chuchundra; I should have talked to Chua."

He stole off to Teddy's bath-room, but there was nothing there, and then to Teddy's mother's bath-room. At the bottom of the smooth plaster wall there was a brick pulled out to make a sluice for the bath-water, and as Rikki-tikki stole in by the masonry curb where the bath is put, he heard Nag and Nagaina whispering together outside in the moonlight.

"When the house is emptied of people," said Nagaina to her husband, "*he* will have to go away, and then the garden will be our own again. Go in quietly, and remember that the big man who killed Karait is the first one to bite. Then come out and tell me, and we will hunt for Rikki-tikki together."

"But are you sure that there is anything to be gained by killing the people?" said Nag.

"Everything. When there were no people in the bungalow, did we have any mongoose in the garden? So long as the bungalow is empty, we are king and queen of the garden; and remember that as soon as our eggs in the melon-bed hatch (as they may to-morrow), our children will need room and quiet."

"I had not thought of that," said Nag. "I will go, but there is no need that we should hunt for Rikki-tikki afterward. I will kill the big man and his wife, and the child if I can, and come away quietly. Then the bungalow will be empty, and Rikki-tikki will go."

Rikki-tikki tingled all over with rage and hatred at this, and then Nag's head came through the sluice, and his five feet of cold body followed it. Angry as he was, Rikki-tikki was very frightened as he saw the size of the big cobra. Nag coiled himself up, raised his head, and looked into the bath-room in the dark, and Rikki could see his eyes glitter.

"Now, if I kill him here, Nagaina will know; and if I fight him on the open floor, the odds are in his favour. What am I to do?" said Rikki-tikki-tavi.

Nag waved to and fro, and then Rikki-tikki heard him drinking from the biggest water-jar that was used to fill the bath. "That is good," said the snake. "Now, when Karait was killed, the big man had a stick. He may have that stick still, but when he comes in to bathe in the morning he will not have a stick. I shall wait here till he comes. Nagaina—do you hear me?—I shall wait here in the cool till daytime."

There was no answer from outside, so Rikki-tikki knew Nagaina had gone away. Nag coiled himself down, coil by coil, round the bulge at the bottom of the water-jar, and Rikki-tikki stayed still as death. After an hour he began to move, muscle by muscle, towards the jar. Nag was asleep, and Rikki-tikki looked at his big back, wondering which would be the best place for a good hold. "If I don't break his back at the first jump," said Rikki, "he can still fight; and if he fights—O Rikki!" He looked at the thickness of the neck below the hood, but that was too much for him; and a bite near the tail would only make Nag savage.

"It must be the head," he said at last; "the head above the hood; and, when I am once there, I must not let go."

Then he jumped. The head was lying a little clear of the water-jar, under the curve of it; and, as his teeth met, Rikki braced his back against the bulge of the red earthenware to hold down the head. This gave him just one second's purchase, and he made the most of it. Then he was battered to and fro as a rat is shaken by a dog—to and fro on the floor, up and down, and round in great circles, but his eyes were red and he held on as the body cartwhipped over the floor, upsetting the tin dipper and the soap-dish and the flesh-brush, and banged against the tin side of the bath. As he held he closed his jaws tighter and tighter, for he made sure he would be banged to death, and, for the honour of his family, he preferred to be found with his teeth locked. He was dizzy, aching, and felt shaken to pieces when something went off like a thunderclap just behind him; a hot wind knocked him senseless and red fire singed his fur. The big man had been wakened by the noise, and had fired both barrels of a shot-gun into Nag just behind the hood.

Rikki-tikki held on with his eyes shut, for now he was quite sure he was dead; but the head did not move, and the big man picked him up and said: "It's the mongoose again, Alice; the little chap has saved *our* lives now." Then Teddy's mother came in with a very white face, and saw what was left of Nag, and Rikki-tikki dragged himself to Teddy's bedroom and spent half the rest of the night shaking himself tenderly to find out whether he really was broken into forty pieces, as he fancied.

When morning came he was very stiff, but well pleased with his doings. "Now I have Nagaina to settle with, and she will be worse than five Nags, and there's no knowing when the eggs she spoke of will hatch. Goodness! I must go and see Darzee," he said.

Without waiting for breakfast, Rikki-tikki ran to the thorn-bush where Darzee was singing a song of triumph at the top of his voice. The news of Nag's death was all over the garden, for the sweeper had thrown the body on the rubbish-heap.

"Oh, you stupid tuft of feathers!" said Rikki-tikki angrily. "Is this the time to sing?"

"Nag is dead—is dead—is dead!" sang Darzee. "The valiant Rikki-tikki caught him by the head and held fast. The big man brought the bang-stick, and Nag fell in two pieces! He will never eat my babies again."

"All that's true enough; but where's Nagaina?" said Rikki-tikki, looking carefully round him.

"Nagaina came to the bath-room sluice and called for Nag," Darzee went on; "and Nag came out on the end of a stick—the sweeper picked him up on the end of a stick and threw him upon the rubbish-heap. Let us sing about the great, the red-eyed Rikki-tikki!" and Darzee filled his throat and sang.

"If I could get up to your nest, I'd roll your babies out!" said Rikki-tikki. "You don't know when to do the right thing at the right time. You're safe enough in your nest there, but it's war for me down here. Stop singing a minute, Darzee."

"For the great, beautiful Rikki-tikki's sake I will stop," said Darzee. "What is it, O Killer of the terrible Nag?"

"Where is Nagaina, for the third time?"

"On the rubbish-heap by the stables, mourning for Nag. Great is Rikki-tikki with the white teeth."

"Bother my white teeth! Have you ever heard where she keeps her eggs?"

"In the melon-bed, on the end nearest the wall, where the sun strikes nearly all day. She hid them there weeks ago."

"And you never thought it worth while to tell me? The end nearest the wall, you said?"

"Rikki-tikki, you are not going to eat her eggs?"

"Not eat exactly; no. Darzee, if you have a grain of sense you will fly off to the stables and pretend that your wing is broken, and let Nagaina chase you away to this bush? I must get to the melon-bed, and if I went there now she'd see me."

Darzee was a feather-brained little fellow who could never hold more than one idea at a time in his head; and just because he knew that Nagaina's children were born in eggs like his own, he didn't think at first that it was fair to kill them. But his wife was a sensible bird, and she knew that cobra's eggs meant young cobras later on; so she flew off from the nest, and left Darzee to keep the babies warm, and continue his song about the death of Nag. Darzee was very like a man in some ways.

She fluttered in front of Nagaina by the rubbish-heap, and cried out, "Oh, my wing is broken! The boy in the house threw a stone at me and broke it." Then she fluttered more desperately than ever.

Nagaina lifted up her head and hissed, "You warned Rikki-tikki when I would have killed him. Indeed and truly, you've chosen a bad place to be lame in." And she moved toward Darzee's wife, slipping along over the dust.

"The boy broke it with a stone!" shrieked Darzee's wife.

"Well! It may be some consolation to you when you're dead to know that I shall settle accounts with the boy. My husband lies on the rubbish-heap this morning, but before night the boy in the house will lie very still. What is the use of running away? I am sure to catch you. Little fool, look at me!"

Darzee's wife knew better than to do *that,* for a bird who looks at a snake's eyes gets so frightened that she cannot move. Darzee's wife fluttered on, piping sorrowfully, and never leaving the ground, and Nagaina quickened her pace.

Rikki-tikki heard them going up the path from the stables, and he raced for the end of the melon-patch near the wall. There, in the warm litter above the melons, very cunningly hidden, he found twenty-five eggs, about the size of a bantam's eggs, but with whitish skins instead of shells.

"I was not a day too soon," he said; for he could see the baby cobras curled up inside the skin, and he knew that the minute they were hatched they could each kill a man or a mongoose. He bit off the tops of the eggs as fast as he could, taking care to crush the young cobras, and turned over the litter from time to time to see whether he had missed any. At last there were only three eggs left, and Rikki-tikki began to chuckle to himself, when he heard Darzee's wife screaming:

"Rikki-tikki, I led Nagaina toward the house, and she has gone into the veranda, and—oh, come quickly—she means killing!"

Rikki-tikki smashed two eggs, and tumbled backward down the melon-bed with the third egg in his mouth, and scuttled to the veranda as hard as he could put foot to the ground. Teddy and his mother and father were there at early breakfast; but Rikki-tikki saw that they were not eating anything. They sat stone-still, and their faces were white. Nagaina was coiled up on the matting by Teddy's chair, within easy striking distance of Teddy's bare leg, and she was swaying to and fro, singing a song of triumph.

"Son of the big man that killed Nag," she hissed, "stay still. I am not ready yet. Wait a little. Keep very still, all you three! If you move I strike, and if you do not move I strike. Oh, foolish people, who killed my Nag!"

Teddy's eyes were fixed on his father, and all his father could do was to whisper, "Sit still, Teddy. You mustn't move. Teddy, keep still."

Then Rikki-tikki came up and cried: "Turn round, Nagaina; turn and fight!"

"All in good time," said she, without moving her eyes. "I will settle my account with *you* presently. Look at your friends, Rikki-tikki. They are still and white. They are afraid. They dare not move, and if you come a step nearer I strike."

Look at your eggs," said Rikki-tikki, "in the melon-bed near the wall. Go and look, Nagaina!"

The big snake turned half round, and saw the egg on the veranda. "Ah-h! Give it to me," she said.

Rikki-tikki put his paws one on each side of the egg, and his eyes were blood-red. "What price for a snake's egg? For a young cobra? For a young king-cobra? For the last—the very last of the brood? The ants are eating all the others down by the melon-bed."

Nagaina spun clear round, forgetting everything for the sake of the one egg; and Rikki-tikki saw Teddy's father shoot out a big hand, catch Teddy by the shoulder, and drag him across the little table with the tea-cups, safe and out of reach of Nagaina.

"Tricked! Tricked! Tricked! *Rikk-tck-tck!*" chuckled Rikki-tikki. "The boy is safe, and it was I—I—I—that caught Nag by the hood last night in the bath-room." Then he began to jump up and down, all four feet together, his head close to the floor. "He threw me to and fro, but he could not shake me off. He was dead before the big man blew him in two. I did it! *Rikki-tikki-tck-tck!* Come then, Nagaina. Come and fight with me. You shall not be a widow long."

Nagaina saw that she had lost her chance of killing Teddy, and the egg lay between Rikki-tikki's paws. "Give me the egg, Rikki-tikki. Give me the last of my eggs, and I will go away and never come back," she said, lowering her hood.

"Yes, you will go away, and you will never come back; for you will go to the rubbish-heap with Nag. Fight, widow! The big man has gone for his gun! Fight!"

Rikki-tikki was bounding all round Nagaina, keeping just out of reach of her stroke, his little eyes like hot coals. Nagaina gathered herself together, and flung out at him. Rikki-tikki jumped up and backwards. Again and again and again she struck, and each time her head came with a whack on the matting of the veranda and she gathered herself together like a watch-spring. Then Rikki-tikki danced in a circle to get behind her, and Nagaina spun round to keep her head to his head, so that the rustle of her tail on the matting sounded like dry leaves blown along by the wind.

He had forgotten the egg. It still lay on the veranda, and Nagaina came nearer and nearer to it, till at last, while Rikki-tikki was drawing breath, she caught it in her mouth, turned to the veranda steps, and flew like an arrow down the path, with Rikki-tikki behind her. When the cobra runs for her life, she goes like a whip-lash flicked across a horse's neck. Rikki-tikki knew that he must catch her, or all the trouble would begin again. She headed straight for the long grass by the thorn-bush, and as he was running Rikki-tikki heard Darzee still singing his foolish little song of triumph. But Darzee's wife was wiser. She flew off her nest as Nagaina came along, and flapped her wings about Nagaina's head. If Darzee had helped they might have turned her; but Nagaina only lowered her hood and went on. Still, the instant's delay brought Rikki-tikki up to her, and as she plunged into the rat-hole where she and Nag used to live, his little white teeth were clenched on her tail, and he went down with her—and very few mongooses, however wise and old they may be, care to follow a cobra into its hole. It was dark in the hole; and Rikki-tikki never knew when it might open out and give Nagaina room to turn and strike at him. He held on savagely, and stuck out his feet to act as brakes on the dark slope of the hot, moist earth. Then the grass by the mouth of the hole stopped waving, and Darzee said: "It is all over with Rikki-tikki! We must sing his death-song. Valiant Rikki-tikki is dead! For Nagaina will surely kill him underground."

So he sang a very mournful song that he made up on the spur of the minute, and just as he got to the most touching part the grass quivered again, and Rikki-tikki, covered with dirt, dragged himself out of the hole leg by leg, licking his whiskers. Darzee stopped with a little shout. Rikki-tikki shook some of the dust out of his fur and sneezed. "It is all over," he said. "The widow will never come out again." And the red ants that live between the grass stems heard him, and began to troop down one after another to see if he had spoken the truth.

Rikki-tikki curled himself up in the grass and slept where he was—slept and slept till it was late in the afternoon, for he had done a hard day's work.

"Now," he said, when he awoke, "I will go back to the house. Tell the Coppersmith, Darzee, and he will tell the garden that Nagaina is dead."

The Coppersmith is a bird who makes a noise exactly like the beating of a little hammer on a copper pot; and the reason he is always making it is because he is the town-crier to every Indian garden, and tells all the news to everybody who cares to listen. As Rikki-tikki went up the path, he heard his "attention" notes like a tiny dinner-gong; and then the steady *"Ding-dong-tock! Nag is dead—dong! Nagaina is dead! Ding-dong-tock!"* That set all the birds in the garden singing, and the frogs croaking; for Nag and Nagaina used to eat frogs as well as little birds.

When Rikki got to the house, Teddy and Teddy's mother (she looked very white still, for she had been fainting) and Teddy's father came out and almost cried over him; and that night he ate all that was given him till he could eat no more, and went to bed on Teddy's shoulder, where Teddy mother saw him when she came to look late at night.

"He saved our lives and Teddy's life," she said to her husband. "Just think, he saved all our lives."

Rikki-tikki woke up with a jump, for the mongooses are light sleepers.

"Oh, it's you," said he. "What are you bothering for? All the cobras are dead; and if they weren't, I'm here."

Rikki-tikki had a right to be proud of himself; but he did not grow too proud, and he kept that garden as a mongoose should keep it, with tooth and jump and spring and bite, till never a cobra dared show its head inside the walls.

Darzee's Chaunt
(Sung in Honour of Rikki-Tikki-Tavi)

Singer and tailor am I—
    Doubled the joys that I know—
Proud of my lilt to the sky,
    Proud of the house that I sew.
Over and under, so weave I my music—so weave I the house that I sew.
Sing to your fledglings again,
    Mother, O lift up your head!
Evil that plagued us is slain,
    Death in the garden lies dead.
Terror that hid in the roses is impotent—flung on the dunghill and dead!
Who has delivered us, who?
    Tell me his nest and his name.
Rikki, the valiant, the true,

Tikki, with eyeballs of flame—
Rikki-tikki-tikki, the ivory-fanged, the hunter with eyeballs of flame!
Give him the Thanks of the Birds,
      Bowing with tail-feathers spread,
Praise him with nightingale words—
      Nay, I will praise him instead.
Hear! I will sing you the praise of the bottle-tailed Rikki with eyeballs of red!
(Here Rikki-tikki interrupted, so the rest of the song is lost.)

A First-Rate Tragedy

Robert Falcon Scott and the Race to the South Pole

BY DIANA PRESTON

The expedition started as a race to the South Pole. Then it became a race for life itself. Robert Falcon Scott lost both.

The 1911 expedition of the great British explorer and adventurer has captured the imagination and interest of historians, writers and the public since Scott's and his companions' bodies were discovered in a frozen tent on November 17, 1912, by a rescue team trekking across Antarctica's Great Ice Barrier. Scott and his team had departed the McMurdo Sound area along the Ross Ice Shelf on November 1, 1911, bound for the South Pole, 800 miles away, on a route that would take the party past the furthermost southern point every reached, the spot where Shackleton had turned back just 97 miles from the Pole in the expedition of 1907–09. [Shackleton was to further add to his legends of courage on his research expedition of 1914–16. See our excerpt from his book, *South.*] At the same time Scott was making his bid to be first at the South Pole, the Norwegian explorer Roald Amundsen had launched his own attempt, leaving from the Bay of Wales area. The time was chosen by both parties to coincide with the advent of high summer, when the attempt could be made in daylight as opposed to the continual darkness that falls over the land there in mid-winter. [Remember that in the Southern Hemisphere the seasons are reversed.] But even in summer, the Antarctic is a dreadful place, with winds and temperatures that test the utmost skills and equipment for survival.

Scott had made a shorter Antarctica journey in 1902–03 and was thought to be a strong leader. As a British hero, his name today is synonymous with courage and persistence, but questions abound over many of his key decisions during the journey. Diana Preston's book is arguably the best ever written, a superb and unforgettable reading experience.

This excerpt puts you with Scott during the critical days of his team's journey. For the final push to the Pole, the team has been narrowed down to Scott and four companions, on skis, man-hauling sledges of supplies. The support members of the expedition have turned back to the McMurdo base, leaving caches, "depots," of supplies along the route Scott is to follow on his return journey.

Thanks to the diaries that survived Scott and his companions, and the talents of Diana Preston, you're about to relive one of the greatest survival adventure sagas of all time.

★   ★   ★   ★   ★

The going was becoming increasingly difficult with heavy surfaces, sandy snow and falling crystals. For men already exhausted by manhauling up the Beardmore it was a struggle. There was great satisfaction when on 6 January they passed the site of Shackleton's most southerly camp, but Scott was becoming preoccupied with the difficult terrain: "The vicissitudes of this work are bewildering," he wrote in anguish. They were among sastrugi, "a sea of fish-hook waves," some of them barbed with sharp crystals. This made skiing near-impossible and Scott decided to abandon the skis. However, after marching for a mile the sastrugi disappeared and they returned to fetch their skis, wasting precious time and energy. A rueful Scott concluded that: "I must stick to the ski after this," but his indecision was a symptom of the growing strain he was under. On the same day Wilson was recording the increasingly grim conditions: "We get our hairy faces and mouths dreadfully iced up on the march and often one's hands get very cold indeed holding ski sticks. Evans who cut his knuckle some days ago at the last depot . . . has a lot of pus in it tonight."

The next day a blizzard struck. Scott consoled himself that the rest would be good for Evans's hand and used the enforced break to write a tribute to his companions. His diary turns to eulogy about his sledging comrades:

It is quite impossible to speak too highly of my companions. Each fulfils his office to the party; Wilson, first as doctor, ever on the lookout to alleviate the small pains and troubles incidental to the work; now as cook, quick, careful and dexterous, ever thinking of some fresh expedient to help the camp life; tough as steel on the traces, never wavering from start to finish. Evans, a giant worker with a really remarkable headpiece. It is only now I realise how much has been due to him . . . Little Bowers remains a marvel — he is thoroughly enjoying himself. I leave all the provision arrangement in his hands . . . but not one single mistake has been made. In addition to the stores, he keeps the most thorough and conscientious meterological record, and to this he now adds the duty of observer and photographer . . . Oates had his invaluable period with the ponies; now he is a foot slogger and goes hard the whole time, does his share of camp work, and stands the hardship as well as any of us. I would not like to be without him either. So our five people are perhaps as happily selected as it is possible to imagine.

This Platonic view of an expedition as a mini society where everyone has their particular specialism is shared by more modern explorers. Sit Ranulph Fiennes wrote in his account of his Pole to Pole Transgiobe Expedition that: "much of our strength, despite our lack of experience, lay in our collective ability."

The blizzard lifted and on 9 January Scott was able to note in his diary a triumphant "record"—they had passed Shackleton's farthest south and were truly in terra incognita. However, the party was becoming increasingly weary. The Polar plateau was covered with sandy snow which clogged the runners of the sledge. Relatively warm and sunny conditions made the going worse. His diary shows that Scott now realized that the journey was going to be "a stiff pull *both ways* apparently." On 11 January Scott was writing: "Another hard grind in the afternoon and five miles added. About 74 miles from the Pole—can we keep this up for seven days? It takes it out of us like anything. None of us ever had such hard work before." He was using words like "fearful" and "agonising." The heavy pulling across a monotonous terrain was soul-destroying. "With the surface as it is, one gets horribly sick of the monotony and can easily imagine oneself getting played out . . . It is an effort to keep up the double figures, but if we can do so for another four marches we ought to get through. It is going to be a close thing," wrote a sombre Scott.

They were feeling the cold: "At camping to-night everyone was chilled and we guessed a cold snap, but to our surprise the actual temperature was higher than last night, when we could dawdle in the sun. It is most unaccountable why we should suddenly feel the cold in this manner; partly the exhaustion of the march, but partly some damp quality in the air, I think." From now on the cold becomes a recurring theme—the effect of the climate was aggravated by lack of food. Scott noticed that Oates, in particular, was feeling the chill and the fatigue more than the others. But in spite of these warning signs Scott was buoyed up as they neared the Pole, intent on his goal. On Monday 15 January he wrote like an excited schoolboy: "It is wonderful to think that two long marches would land us at the Pole. We left our depot to-day with nine days" provisions, so that it ought to be a certain thing now, and the only appalling possibility the sight of the Norwegian flag forestalling ours."

Of course, that is exactly what happened. Scott's diary entry for the next day tells how the "appalling possibility" had become reality:

The worst has happened, or nearly the worst. We marched well in the morning . . . and we started off in high spirits in the afternoon, feeling that to-morrow would see us at our destination. About the second hour of the march Bowers's sharp eyes detected what he thought was a cairn; he was uneasy about it, but argued that it must be a sastrugus. Half an hour later he detected a black speck ahead . . . We marched on, found that it was a black flag tied to a sledge bearer; near by the remains of a camp; sledge tracks and ski tracks going and coming and the clear trace of dogs' paws—many dogs. This told us the whole story. The Norwegians have forestalled us and are first at the Pole. It is a terrible disappointment, and I am very sorry for my loyal companions.

Curiously enough on 15 December while out sledging Gran had dreamt accurately that his fellow Norwegian had reached the Pole that day. His companions pooh-poohed it but he insisted on noting it down in Griffith Taylor's copy of Browning. Taylor later ascribed it to extraordinary coincidence rather than the supernatural, as Gran believed, but was clearly struck by the strangeness of it.

The psychological impact of the discovery was tremendous. The shock made it difficult to sleep that night. Scott lay in his sleeping-bag contemplating the weary journey back, all hope gone. His thoughts must have turned to Kathleen, then visiting relations in Berlin and attending lectures given by Nansen. This is the occasion on which Roland Huntford alleges they had an affair. Kathleen certainly enjoyed the company and admiration of this virile explorer who perhaps reminded her of her husband. She may even have been strongly attracted to him. However, she was both too honourable and too sensible to embark on what she must have recognized could become a lasting and destructive liaison. She made no secret of their meeting, writing to Scott in a letter which he would never read: "He really is an adorable person and I will tell you all the lovely times we had together when you get back. He thinks you are marvellous . . ."

The next day, Wednesday 17 January, they at last reached the Pole but, as Scott wrote bitterly, in very different circumstances to those which they had imagined. To make matters worse there was a chill wind blowing and the air seemed curiously damp, penetrating into their bones. Oates, Evans and Bowers all had frostbitten noses and cheeks and Evans's hands were hurting him. They took some sightings but there is nothing but despair in Scott's diary culminating in his anguished cry: "Great God! this is an awful place and terrible enough for us to have laboured to it without the reward of priority." This says it all—the back-breaking struggle, the terrible deprivation, the worry and anxiety had all been for nothing. Whatever Scott may have said and thought earlier he now knew how badly he had wanted to win. "Now for the run home and a desperate struggle. I wonder if we can do it," are his heroic comments in the edited version of his diary which was later published. What he actually wrote at the Pole was: "a desperate struggle to get the news through first." Even if he was not the first at the Pole he still hoped to give the Central News Agency the scoop they expected.

The classic reaction to extreme disappointment or failure, according to psychiatrists, is to try to rationalize the situation. Scott's determination to salvage something is in interesting contrast to his colleagues'. He did not have Wilson's quiet faith that everything turned out as God meant it to. Wilson's own diary is phlegmatic: "He [Amundsen] has beaten us in so far as he made a race of it. We have done what we came for all the same and as our programme was made out." Bowers's letter to his mother was positively chirpy—

Well, here I really am and very glad to be here too. It is a bleak spot—what a place to strive so hard to reach . . . It is sad that we have been forestalled by the Norwegians, but I am glad that we have done it by good British manhaulage. That is the traditional British sledging method and this is the greatest journey done by man . . .

There is a strong hint that their approach based on "honest sweat" was more honourable than Amundsen's. Evans's response is not recorded but it must have been a deep disappointment to him. Victory at the Pole would have set him and his family up for life. Oates's reaction was one of detachment. He mentally shrugged his shoulders: "I must say that that man must have had his head screwed on right. The gear they left was in excellent order and they seem to have had a comfortable trip with their dog teams very different from our wretched man-hauling."

However, despite appearances, the Norwegians had been exhausted too, finding the altitude a struggle. Altitude sickness comes on at lower altitudes near the Pole. On 11 December just four days from the Pole Amundsen had written that: "We'll get our breath back, if only we win." He too realized the psychological boost of winning.

On 18 January, as Scott and his men continued to take observations around the Pole, they came across Amundsen's tent at his most southerly camp. It was a neat compact affair supported by a single bamboo pole. Inside was a letter to King Haakon of Norway and a note from Amundsen asking Scott to make sure it was delivered. Amundsen was covering himself in case some accident overtook him on the way back to Framheim, though on that very day he was within one week of regaining the Bay of Whales. To Scott and his men it must have seemed the ultimate humiliation. Scott pocketed the letter and left a note to say he had visited the tent. The rest of this final day at the Pole was spent in sketching, photography and erecting a small cairn from which to fly "our poor slighted Union Jack." Scott and his men then photographed themselves in front of it; Birdie Bowers used a string to activate the shutter. They are the saddest pictures of the whole expedition and not only because one knows they were doomed—the weariness and sense of futility leap out. Their faces are drawn and weather-beaten and there is no joy in them. Oates looks tired and in pain, leaning heavily on his shorter left leg.

They carried the flag a short distance northwards, fixed it to a stick then helped themselves to some of the surplus equipment left behind by Amundsen— Bowers took a pair of reindeer mitts to replace his lost dogskin ones. Amundsen had considered leaving them a spare can of fuel but had concluded that Scott's party would be so well-provisioned there was little point. Yet, as events were about to prove, this would have been the greatest service he could have rendered his defeated rivals who now prepared for the homeward trek.

So that was that—a banal and humiliating end to an epic journey. Their ambitions had been thwarted and there was only the consolation prize. "Well," Scott wrote, "we have turned our back now on the goal of our ambition and must face our 800 miles of solid dragging—and good-bye to most of the day-dreams!"

Retracing their steps, Scott's weary party trekked past the "ominous black flag" which just three days earlier had blasted their hopes. They took the flagstaff to help make a sail, hoping to use the wind to speed them on their way. It was made of hickory, gave Wilson splinters and was soon discarded. At first they made reasonable progress, picking up their old track, but showers of fine crystals tendered the surface heavy as sand and they were all feeling the cold more than on the outward journey. Scott reflected that: "the return journey is going to be dreadfully tiring and monotonous." Over the next few days his diary is dominated by such gloomy descriptions as "terrible bad," "really awful," "terribly weary." This is in marked contrast to Amundsen's jaunty account of the Norwegians' departure from the Pole: "The going was splendid and all were in good spirits . . ."

Scott's men were not in good spirits. Even Bowers, "an undefeated little sportsman" to the last and engagingly optimistic, was finding the long marches tiring with his short legs and was yearning for his "dear old ski". Oates was clearly suffering from cold and fatigue. However, Scott was determined to keep up a good marching pace to give them the chance to be back in time to catch the ship. He did not yet seriously consider the possibility that they might not return at all. In fact the returning *Terra Nova* was spotted by Tryggve Gran on 20 January, just three days after their departure from the Pole, trying to nose her way in through the pack ice.

They made dogged progress. Bowers recorded how they watched anxiously for the chain of cairns they had built on their outward odyssey: "We are absolutely dependent upon our depots to get off the plateau alive, and so welcome the lonely little cairns gladly." They used the wind when they could. On 23 January Bowers was cheerfully recording that: "Filling the sail we sped along merrily doing 8¼ miles before lunch. In the afternoon it was even stronger and I had to go back on the sledge and act as guide and brakeman. We had to lower the sail a bit, but even then she ran like a bird." However, on the same day they were depressed by Wilson's discovery that Edgar Evans's nose was badly frostbitten—"white and hard," according to Scott. On the *Discovery* expedition Scott had noticed that Evans's nose had always been "the first thing to indicate stress of frost-biting weather," but Evans was no longer joking about his "old blossom" as he had once called his nose. They made camp and cooked up a good hot hoosh, but Scott was worried about his comrade. For the first time, perhaps, he realized that the man he believed to be a Goliath and the strongest of them all had suffered the most from the long haul to the Pole.

Evans was the heaviest and should, in theory, have had larger rations than the others. As Cherry-Garrard observed, larger machines need more fuel to drive them. Dr Michael Stroud, who manhauled to the Pole himself in the Polar summer of 1992–93, calculated that Evans would have lost more weight than anyone else, perhaps over fifteen kilos, by the time he reached the Pole, equivalent to about one-fifth of his body-weight. As he was "in hard condition", the loss would have been mainly to his muscles with consequent effects on his pulling power. A concerned Scott noted that he seemed very run down, with badly blistered fingers and frostbites. He also noticed something more disturbing—Evans seemed "very much annoyed with himself." The usually ebullient and self-reliant Welshman was losing confidence. Unused to physical weakness and afraid of letting his companions down he was becoming depressed and withdrawn. This hesitant, fretful Evans was a far cry from the man who had tumbled down a crevasse with Scott on the *Discovery* expedition and made calm conversation as he dangled over a chilly abyss.

Scott made an anxious survey of the rest of the team. He concluded that he himself, Wilson and Bowers were as fit as possible under the circumstances, though Wilson was suffering the torments of snow-blindness as a result of trying to sketch and was using cocaine ointment as a painkiller. By 24 January Scott was referring to Wilson and Bowers as "my standby," adding: "I don't like the easy way in which Oates and Evans get frostbitten." In fact, one of Oates's big toes had turned black and he was secretly worrying whether it would hinder him from marching. Scott was also increasingly concerned about the blizzards and gales they were encountering: "Is the weather breaking up? If so, God help us, with the tremendous summit journey and scant food." Their late start for the Pole, the result of the decision to use ponies, had inevitably left them on the plateau late in the season and vulnerable to the falling temperatures. The thin air of the plateau did not help. Amundsen's men, better fed and less stressed, had found the conditions difficult enough. Amundsen described how: "The asthmatic condition in which we found ourselves during our six week's stay on the plateau was anything but pleasant." For Scott and his exhausted team it was very debilitating. It would not have comforted Scott to know that on 26 January his rival reached Framheim after a journey that had taken only ninety-nine days and with men and dogs in rude good health. Amundsen and his companions crept into the hut at Framheim at four in the morning and took delight in waking the sleeping inmates with a casual request for coffee.

They marched on—Oates with his bad foot, Evans with badly frostbitten nose and fingers, Wilson with his snow-blindness and all of them increasingly hungry. Lack of vitamins and malnutrition were affecting their mental as well as their physical well-being. Scott was observing how thin everyone looked, particularly Evans. The conversation turned more and more to food—Bowers had begun fantasizing about making a pig of himself at journey's end, but with some seven hundred miles to go he knew such dreams were premature. His more immediate problem was that "I am in tribulation as regards meals now as we have run out of salt one of my favourite commodities."

30 January was a bad day. Wilson strained a tendon in his leg, Oates had revealed that his big toe was turning blue-black while Evans was beginning to lose his fingernails. Scott observed that: "his hands are really bad, and to my surprise he shows signs of losing heart over it." Poor Evans's transformation had continued and he had become a different person, taciturn, introverted, concentrating on keeping going. There were none of his colourful anecdotes or wild curses about the seven blind witches of Egypt to cheer his compan-

ions. Ironically, it was on that very day that a triumphant Amundsen set sail on the *Fram* to take his momentous news to the outside world.

Wilson's leg began to recover, much to Scott's relief. As he noted: "it is trying to have an injured limb in the party." However, Evans continued to decline—"Evans's fingers now very bad, two nails coming off, blisters burst." Yet this was the time when Evans most needed strength and endurance. They were approaching the crazy terrain of crevasses and icefalls heralding the gateway to the Beardmore Glacier. As they attempted to negotiate their way down a steep and slippery slope Scott lost his footing and landed on the point of his shoulder. That meant that there were now "three out of five injured," as Scott ruefully recorded. Interestingly he did not consider Oates to be one of the sick, but the reality was that only Bowers was in reasonable shape, cheered no doubt by the retrieval of his skis on 31 January. Oates had also found the pipe he had dropped on the outward journey which must have comforted him. The party struggled on but had difficulty in picking up their track, adding to their anxiety. Bowers ceased to keep a diary around this time, making his final entry on "Feb 3rd (I suppose)." On 4 February Evans and Scott both fell into a crevasse and had to be hauled out. Scott now wrote: "the party is not improving in condition, especially Evans, who is becoming rather dull and incapable." Also at this time Wilson observed that Oates's other toes were blackening and that his "nose and cheeks are dead yellow."

In this ominous situation Scott relied increasingly on Bowers, who seemed immune from the mishaps: "Bowers is splendid, full of energy and bustle all the time." Scott needed Bowers's resilience to buoy his own flagging spiritis as they looked for their way down the glacier. Their situation was becoming critical. The next days saw them weaving through a perilous maze of crevasses as they tried to find their way to the Upper Glacier Depot and the badly-needed supplies of food stored there. The depot would also point the way down the Beardmore and it was important they descended quickly. Evans was in a very bad way: "Evans is the chief anxiety now; his cuts and wounds suppurate, his nose looks very bad, and altogether he shows considerable signs of being played out." Scott clung to the hope that his condition might improve as they descended the glacier and the temperature rose.

However, the next day there was momentary panic with the discovery that a whole day's biscuit ration was missing. Bowers, who prided himself on his efficiency in looking after their stores, was shaken. However, by early evening they at last reached the Upper Glacier Depot. Their plateau ordeal was over and they could re-provision. They reflected that they had taken twenty-seven days to reach the Pole from this point and twenty-one days to return. Scott wrote: "we have come through our 7 weeks' ice camp journey and most of us are fit, but I think another week might have had a very bad effect on P.O. Evans, who is going steadily downhill."

It seems strange to read in Scott's diary that the party spent a large part of the next day "geologizing." They veered off towards Mount Darwin and Bowers was sent ahead on skis to collect specimens. The task would normally have fallen to Wilson but he was still suffering from his strained tendon. Later on they steered for the moraine under Mount Buckley which Scott found so interesting he decided to make camp there. Scott described a pleasant few hours of pottering: "We found ourselves under perpendicular cliffs of Beacon sandstone, weathering rapidly and carrying veritable coal seams. From the last Wilson, with his sharp eyes, has picked several plant impressions of thick stems, showing cellular structure. In one place we saw the cast of small waves on the sand. To-night Bill has got a specimen of limestone with archeo-cyathus . . . Altogether we have had a most interesting afternoon . . ." Wilson even managed to do some pencil sketches of Mount Buckley.

No doubt the break from manhauling and the relief of being in a sheltered spot out of the harsh summit winds had their effect on hungry and weary men. More important to their morale, however, was the fact that they were doing what they had come for—scientific research. They could regain some pride after the ignominy of their arrival at the Pole, reminding themselves of the differences between their carefully planned programme of scientific work and Amundsen's opportunistic Viking raid. Indeed, on his return journey Amundsen made a conscious decision not to let anything deflect him from making a dash straight back to Framheim, not even the prospect of discovering some new geographical features. Whether Scott's geologizing was a magnificent example of dedication or a foolish diversion depends on your point of view. It added some thirty-five pounds to a sledge already piled with five kitbags, a cooker, an instrument box, biscuit boxes, a paraffin tank and a tent. On the other hand these rocks were to prove for the first time that Antarctica had once been covered in vegetation and had formed part of a great semi-tropical southern continent—the so-called "Gondwanaland"—once believed to be only a myth. As scientists of the British Antarctic Survey have acknowledged:

The plant fossils collected . . . from the Beardmore Glacier and found with their bodies, were of particular significance. Although the expedition failed to reach the Pole first, its scientific achievements were more than sufficient to justify it. Amundsen won the race but his efforts provided virtually nothing in terms of scientific information.

They geologized again the next day during their march, enjoying the milder temperatures now they had left the dreadful Polar plateau. Scott sounds more relaxed and confident: "It is remarkable to be able to stand outside the tent and sun oneself. Our food satisfies now, but we must march to keep in the full ration, and we want rest, yet we shall pull through all right, D.V. We are by no means worn out." There are no references here to the state of Evans or of Oates, suggesting that they too were benefiting from the change in conditions. Alternatively, Scott may have been trying to convince himself that everything would indeed turn out alright. We can never know.

However, on 11 February everything went wrong again. The surface was wretched and their journey rapidly became a nightmare as they became lost in a maze of pressure ridges. It was the worst day of their whole trip and stemmed from a fatal decision to steer to the east in the hope that this would lead them out of the pressure ridges. However, after hours of hauling they seemed to be trapped in a mass of crevasses. twisting this way and that, they at last glimpsed a smoother slope, but it lay far away across a surface riven by deep chasms. At about 10 p.m., after twelve hours of appalling grind, they were back on the right track. However, they had made little progress towards their next depot and food was beginning to run out. They reduced their rations, squeezing an extra meal out of pemmican only meant for three meals and halving their meagre lunch ration.

The next day they again became disorientated, plunging into a labyrinth of crevasses and fissures and wandering about "absolutely lost for hours and hours," as Wilson recorded. There was clearly debate if not argument about what to do. Scott described how: "Divided councils caused our course to be erratic," and they were forced to make camp in "the worst place of all". Oates recorded that: "We are in rather a nasty hole tonight." They were grimly aware that they now had only one meal left. The wording in Scott's diary is tense. He speaks of endurance, of how the group must and will get through and how they can cope with less food.

The next morning brought thick snow cloaking everything around them. The only option was to remain in their sleeping-bags, hungry and anxious. However, they were able to get under way by mid-morning and after struggling through a chaotic expanse of broken ice hit an old moraine track. It was easier to make progress on this smoother surface. Evans, confused by a shadow on the ice, shouted out, believing they had reached the next depot, but not long after Wilson spotted the depot flag. Scott was not exaggerating when he wrote that it was "an immense relief." They now had a further three and a half days' food. Wilson even geologized for an hour or two as they tramped on. They were also relived to learn from messages left for them that the two supporting parties had passed through safely, though Teddy Evans "seems to have got mixed up with pressures like ourselves." In fact at that very moment Teddy Evans was not safe. He had collapsed from scurvy with some hundred miles to go and that day was still on the Barrier.

Scott brooded over the unnerving experiences of the last days: "In future food must be worked so that we do not run so short if the weather fails us. We musn't get into a hole like this again." Recent events had made him feel very insecure and it was being brought home to him that he had cut things too finely. He was revising the opinion he had expressed earlier in the year that: "... it must be sound policy to keep the men of a sledge party keyed up to a high pitch of well-fed physical condition as long as they have animals to drag their loads. The time for short rations ... comes when the men are dependent on their own traction efforts." He also had time to assess the condition of his companions. Bowers and Wilson were suffering badly from snow-blindness. However, the news of Evans was much worse. This once hearty and vigorous giant had "no power to assist with camping work" but Scott does not explain why. Perhaps his wounded and frostbitten hands were preventing him, or perhaps it was a further manifestation of the slowness which Scott noted after Evans fell down the crevasse.

They set off again the next day, carrying their new provisions, but only covered six and a half miles. Scott knew a crisis was coming:

There is no getting away from the fact that we are not going strong. Probably none of us: Wilson's leg still troubles him and he doesn't like to trust himself on ski; but the worst case is Evans who is giving us serious anxiety. This morning he suddenly disclosed a huge blister on his foot. It delayed us on the march ... Sometimes I fear he is going from bad to worse, but I trust he will pick up again when we come to steady work on ski like this afternoon. He is hungry and so is Wilson.

Hunger had also affected the returning Norwegians, but as Amundsen wrote: "Fortunately we were so well supplied that when this sensation of hunger came over us, we could increase our daily rations."

There are hints that their morale was breaking down. All of them must have been reaching the end of their tether, while Scott was becoming frustrated and disappointed with their progress. The goal of reaching the *Terra Nova* in time was slipping away—she was due to sail northwards around the end of February. "We are inclined to get slack and slow," he complained, "... I have talked of the matter tonight and hope for improvement." They were now some thirty miles from the Lower Glacier Depot with nearly three days' food in hand, but on 15 February Scott was again noting that provisions were running low. In desperation he had reduced both their rations and their rest time so they could reach the depot before the rations ran out. Perhaps, as they hauled their heavy sledge, his thoughts turned to home and Kathleen as a source of strength and comfort. In fact, on 15 February, she was lunching with the Prime Minister, Asquith, no doubt in the hope of charming some funds out of him.

The next day heralded tragedy. Scott's diary for 16 February records: "A rather trying position. Evans has nearly broken down in brain, we think. He is absolutely changed from his normal self-reliant self. This morning and this afternoon he stopped the march on some trivial excuse." If this sounds unsympathetic it must be remembered that Scott was under great mental and physical strain. He probably also felt responsible for the poor state of his comrade, and hence guilty. Oates's verdict sounds equally callous: "It is an extraordinary thing about Evans, he has lost his guts and behaves like an old woman or worse," and yet Oates was the most popular officer among the men of the lower deck. Wilson's verdict was that: "Evans's collapse has much to do with the fact that he has never been sick in his life and is now helpless with his hands frost-bitten."

The next day they pressed on, hoping to make the depot, but it was "anxious work with the sick man." The crisis was about to break and it was, in Scott's words, "a very terrible day." Evans had slept well and prepared for the march, gamely declaring, as he always did, that he was fit and well. He took his place in the traces but within half an hour had to drop out because his ski shoes had loosened. The others plodded on with the groaning sledge over a thick treacly surface. Evans slowly caught them up again and once more took his place. However, after half an hour he again dropped out and asked Bowers to lend him some string. Scott told Evans to catch up when he could and the seaman apparently answered him cheerfully.

Again the others continued to haul, anxious to reach the depot, and sweating heavily. At lunchtime they sat and waited, expecting the lonely shambling figure of Evans to come into view. When he failed to appear they went to look for him and caught sight of him still some way behind. It was obvious something was wrong. Scott was the first to reach Evans and was shocked at his appearance: "he was on his knees with clothing disarranged, hands uncovered and frostbitten, and a wild look in his eyes." Asked what had happened he replied that he did not know but thought that he must have fainted. He could no longer walk and was showing signs of complete collapse. Oates remained with him while the others hurried to fetch the sledge. By the time they managed to get him into the tent he was comatose and died quietly that night without regaining consciousness. He had been out from Cape Evans for three and a half months and had marched over twelve hundred miles. In his final letter to his wife he had written: "I am always thinking of you on this great ice platform ten thousand feet above the sea level."

His shocked companions debated the cause of his death. They concluded that he had begun to weaken before reaching the Pole and that his downward spiral had been hastened by the discovery of his frostbitten fingers, his falls on the glacier and his loss of confidence. Wilson believed he must have injured his brain during a fall. Whatever the cause of their companion's death it was a chilling moment for the four survivors, emphasizing their own vulnerability, with so many miles still to go. Yet at the same time it was the solution to a horrible dilemma. As Scott commented: "It is a terrible thing to lose a companion in this way, but calm reflection shows that there could not have been a better ending to the terrible anxieties of the past week . . . what a desperate pass we were in with a sick man on our hands at such a distance from home."

Later on, when Scott knew that he himself was probably going to die, he wrote that Evans's death had spared them a terrible decision since "the safety of the remainder seemed to demand his abandonment." He also noted gratefully that Evans had died a natural death—meaning he had not had to resort to suicide, or even that his comrades had not been required to give him a merciful release with the opium they carried. They would never have left him while he lived, yet it would have been impossible to pull him on the sledge. As it was, both Scott and Wilson could record their pride that their record "was clear."

Scott and his companions kept vigil for two hours after Edgar Evans died—the first victim of a journey that would prove too far for them all. What they did with his body is not recorded.

The next day, as the surviving quartet marched grimly on their way, Kathleen wrote in her diary: "I was very taken up with you all evening. I wonder if anything special is happening to you. Something odd happened to the clocks between 9 and 10 p.m." She felt uncharacteristically depressed and had to shake off a sense of foreboding. There is a story that around this time Peter asked to be lifted down from his rocking-horse and ran to the door holding out his hands and calling: "Hello Daddy," but Kathleen did not believe in the supernatural. She was, however, brooding over Scott's perennial bad luck and told Sir Compton Mackenzie, who was sitting for her at the time, that she feared it would prevent him from reaching the Pole.

After snatching five hours sleep at the Lower Glacier Depot Scott and his three companions reached Shambles Camp, the desolate spot where the last of the ponies had been slaughtered, but a "fine supper" of pony meat revived them a little. As Scott wrote: "New life seems to come with greater food almost immediately." They could take comfort that the plateau and the treacherous glacier lay behind them, but they now faced a slog of nearly four hundred miles across the Barrier where the only certainty would be the mind-numbing monotony of a featureless landscape. They prepared as best they could, swapping their sledge for a new one which had been left at the depot and loading it with pony meat. However, they soon discovered that the surface was coated with soft slushy snow. Scott described it miserably "like pulling over desert sand, not the least glide in the world." He knew they must maintain a reasonable momentum to reach the depots containing the vital supplies, strung out across the Barrier, before their food and fuel ran out. There are echoes here of Shackleton's return from his great southern journey when he wrote the morbid line: "Our food lies ahead, and death stalks us from behind."

Scott pinned his hopes on a change in the weather. A brisk southerly wind would enable them to hoist their sail and be blown across the ice. Even a moderate blizzard would have helped by sweeping away the loose ice crystals which clogged the sledge. Yet no kindly wind came to their aid. As he hauled, Scott pondered whether the absence of the tragic fifth man was a help or a hindrance. He concluded that: "The absence of poor Evans is a help to the commissariat, but if he had been here in a fit state we might have got along faster." On 20 February they staggered into Desolation Camp where the blizzard had imprisoned them for a disastrous four days on their outward journey. They searched hopefully for more pony meat but found none.

Scott was lost in gloom. Trudging on, the only "rays of comfort" were finding the tracks and cairns of the outward journey. This was not easy and they sometimes found themselves veering off course. Scott was on tenterhooks, straining for the sight of each new cairn, anxiously assessing the surface of the Barrier and wondering what the weather held in store. On 24 February Scott set down the challenge: "It is a race between the season and hard conditions and our fitness and good food." He might have added that it was also a race to cover the distance before their fuel ran out. That very day while collecting supplies from the Southern Barrier Depot they had found a worrying shortage of oil. The fuel allowance had been carefully calculated—two one-gallon tins had been left at each depot for the returning parties. However, the oil had been exposed to extremes of heat and cold. In particular, the tins were often left in an accessible place on tope of the cairns and in the sun's warmth the oil vaporized and escaped through the stoppers. The problem was exacerbated by the fact that the leather washers around the stoppers were prone to perish in the cold, and that the tins had been disturbed by being opened by the other returning parties. Scott noted that they would have to be *"very* saving", and from now on his diaries are peppered with worried references to the fuel situation and the need to cover greater distances. Scott's anxiety expressed itself in various ways. The next day he nagged Bowers about his ability to pull the sledge while on skis, writing that he "hasn't quite the trick and is a little hurt at my criticisms, but I never doubted his heart."

As the month drew to a close the temperature dropped steadily. By 27 February Scott was describing it as "desperately cold" and he knew their position was critical. Everything now depended on reaching each depot in time. He made endless calculations—how many days would it take to reach the next depot? How many days' supply of food and fuel was left? Apart from everything else, the Barrier itself depressed him—there was nothing to see, no warmth, no comfort on this great shelf of ice. "There is no doubt the middle of the Barrier is a pretty awful locality," he wrote, in the knowledge that there were nearly three hundred miles to go. Wilson's diary ceased from this time. Living up to his ideal of being "entirely careless of your own soul or body in looking after the welfare of others" left him neither time nor energy to write. Oates had abandoned his diary on 24 February, the day the poor meat-loving "Soldier" had dug up Christopher's head only to find that it had gone rotten. From now on Scott became the only one to record the unfolding tragedy day by day.

On 1 March they reached the Middle Barrier Depot to discover a trio of misfortunes. Firstly, there was a further serious shortage of oil—there was barely enough to carry them on to the next depot over sixty miles away. Secondly, Oates, no longer able to conceal the appalling state of his feet, disclosed his frostbitten gangrenous toes on which the bitter temperatures on the Barrier had taken their toll. Thirdly, that night the temperature fell to below −40°F. Leaving them so chilled that it took an hour and a half to struggle into their footgear the next morning. Scott was not mincing his words when he wrote: "We are in a *very* queer street."

Indeed, from now on Scott's account descends into thinly veiled despair as they battled along, barely managing a mile an hour, although he acknowledged the bravery of his companions: "Amongst ourselves we are unendingly cheerful, but what each man feels in his heart I can only guess. Pulling on foot gear in the morning is getting slower and slower, therefore every day more dangerous." Scott derived his strength and comfort from Wilson and Bowers, knowing he would not be able to cope if they "weren't so determinedly cheerful over things." He was painfully aware of Oates's condition, knowing that a colder snap would spell disaster for "Soldier." On 5 March he was writing: "Our fuel dreadfully low and the poor Soldier nearly done. It is pathetic enough because we can do nothing for him . . ." None of them had expected such dreadfully low temperatures on the Barrier and the one suffering most, after Oates, was Wilson: "mainly, I fear, from his self-sacrificing devotion in doctoring Oates's feet."

By 6 March poor Oates could no longer pull. He never complained and, indeed, was growing daily ever more silent. There seems little doubt that he knew what lay ahead and was coming to terms with the fact that he would never again see Gestingthorpe, nor ride to hounds nor see his mother. He knew he was now a drag on the others. So did Scott, writing: "If we were all fit I should have hopes of getting through, but the poor Soldier has become a terrible hindrance, though he does his utmost and suffers much . . ." The obvious solution stared Oates in the face. He must have remembered his discussions with Ponting at Cape Evans when he had asserted that suicide was the only honourable course for a sledger who was imperilling his companions.

The days that followed were harrowing—three men struggling to pull what had become an impossible load, the fourth wondering how much longer he should continue to be a burden. On 7 March Scott wrote that "the Soldier's" crisis was near but implying that it was fast approaching for them all. He himself was determined to keep going: "I should like to keep the track to the end," he wrote defiantly. Much would depend on what they found at the next depot. Had the dogs been out there with fresh supplies? Would there be enough fuel? Arriving at the depot at Mount Hooper on 9 March they found everything in short supply and only "cold comfort"—"the dogs which would have been our salvation have evidently failed," Scott recorded grimly. The dogs had actually been awaiting the Polar party at One Ton Depot since 3 March, but a week later, after depoting some supplies, their drivers Cherry-Garrard and Dimitri had turned northwards again.

Meanwhile, in early March London was a-buzz with rumours that Scott had been first to the Pole. Kathleen, however, confided in her diary: "I was certain there was something wrong." On 7 March, with Amundsen's arrival in Tasmania, came proof positive that the Norwegian had in fact been the victor. The reaction in Britain was predictably muted and praise of Amundsen was tempered by the suggestion that he had not really played the game. *The Times* declared that his sudden decision to go south rather than north and the secrecy which surrounded it "were felt to be not quite in accordance with the spirit of fair and open competition which had hitherto marked Antarctic exploration." Kathleen reacted with characteristic dignity and generosity to the

Norwegian's triumph, but wrote: "I worked badly and my head rocked. I'm not going to recount what I have been feeling." Perhaps her little son was trying to cheer her up when he said: "Amundsen and Daddy both got to the Pole. Daddy has stopped working now."

Out on the Barrier Oates's crisis was approaching. On 10 March he "asked Wilson if he had a chance this morning, and of course Bill had to say he didn't know. In point of fact he has none," Scott wrote: "Apart from him, if he went under now, I doubt whether we could get through." The next day Scott wrote:

Titus Oates is very near the end, one feels. What we or he will do, God only knows. We discussed the matter after breakfast; he is a brave fine fellow and understands the situation, but he practically asked for advice. Nothing could be said but to urge him to march as long as he could. One satisfactory result to the discussion; I practically ordered Wilson to hand over the means of ending our troubles to us . . . We have 30 opium tabloids apiece and he is left with a tube of morphine. So far the tragical side of our story.

What bleak thoughts were now playing across their minds? They would have agreed with Cherry-Garrard that: "Practically any man who undertakes big polar journeys must face the possibility of having to commit suicide to save his companions . . ." On the winter journey even the indomitable Bowers had "had a scheme of doing himself in with a pickaxe if necessity arose, though how he could have accomplished it I don't know: or, as he said, there might be a crevasse and at any rate there was the medical case." However, Scott had not abandoned hope and was still making frantic calculations. They had seven days' food left and were about fifty-five miles from One Ton Camp. Averaging about six miles a day, the limit of their endurance, they would be just thirteen miles short of the depot when their food ran out. Could they get through?

On 12 March they managed a further few miles at terrible cost. "The surface remains awful, the cold intense, and our physical condition running down. God help us!" They awoke the next day to a strong northerly wind and a temperature of −37°F which they simply could not face. They stayed in camp till afternoon, when they managed just over five miles. The next day brought even lower temperatures of −43°F at midday. Wilson was so horribly cold he could not even take off his skis for some time and: "poor Oates got it again in the foot." Scott wrote: "It must be near the end, but a pretty merciful end." Under the pressure of "tragedy all along the line" Scott was now beginning to lose track of dates and, instead of writing his diary at lunchtime and again at night, was simply making notes at midday. That he kept writing at all is remarkable.

On 16 or 17 March Oates decided he could go on no longer and asked to be left in his sleeping-bag. Wilson had been reading Tennyson's "In Memoriam" earlier on the journey. It contained lines which could have been written for the broken cavalry officer: "This year I slept and woke with pain, I almost wished no more to wake." His comrades persuaded him to continue and he hobbled gamely on but at night his condition was so bad it was clear he could go no farther. Scott recorded his end:

Should this be found I want these facts recorded. Oates's last thoughts were of his Mother, but immediately before he took pride in thinking that his regiment would be pleased with the bold way in which he met his death. We can testify to his bravery. He has borne intense suffering for weeks without complaint . . . He did not—would not—give up hope to the very end. He was a brave soul. This was the end. He slept through the night before last hoping not to wake; but he woke in the morning—yesterday. It was blowing a blizzard. He said, "I am just going outside and may be some time." He went out into the blizzard and we have not seen him since . . . We knew that poor Oates was walking to his death, but though we tried to dissuade him, we knew it was the act of a brave man and an English gentleman. We all hope to meet the end with a similar spirit, and assuredly the end is not far.

The seventeenth of March was Oates's birthday. He was thirty-two.

The forlorn trio marched onward. They had jettisoned their theodolite, Oates's sleeping-bag and a camera, but were still dragging their geological specimens "at Wilson's special request." Scott's feet had become badly frostbitten and Bowers was now the fittest. Both he and Wilson continued to talk of winning through but, Scott wondered, could they really believe it? They were all suffering frostbitten feet and Scott's right foot was so bad that amputation was the least he could fear. However, this seemed increasingly academic—he had begun to write his farewell letters.

By 19 March they were only eleven miles from One Ton Depot but the next day a severe blizzard descended. It was decided that Wilson and Bowers would try to battle through to the depot to fetch fuel but Wilson's letter to Oriana suggests it was a forlorn hope: "Birdie and I are going to try and reach the Depot 11 miles north of us and return to this tent where Captain Scott is lying with a frozen foot . . . I shall simply fall and go to sleep in the snow . . . Don't be unhappy—all is for the best." Bowers's last letter to his mother is in similar vein: "God alone knows what will be the outcome of the 22 miles march we have to make but my trust is still in Him and in the abounding Grace of my Lord . . . There will be no shame however and you will know that I have struggled to the end . . . you will know that for me the end was peaceful as it is only sleep in the cold." It was his firm belief that "nothing that happens to our bodies really matters." A sad little postscript added: "My gear that is not on the ship is at Mrs. Hatfield's Marine Hotel, Sumner, New Zealand."

However, malign fate again took a hand. The blizzard was too thick for any such attempt and their plan changed. They decided they would all march for the depot when the blizzard lifted and die in their tracks if necessary. However, even this was denied them. The blizzard continued to blow and their lives ebbed away with it. Perhaps, as he lay there, Scott reflected on the ill luck during the depot journey and his sensitivity to the ponies' suffering which had resulted in One Ton Depot being laid thirty miles further north than he had originally intended. Perhaps he still hoped against hope to hear the yapping of dog teams loping through the snowstorm to their rescue. Yet in his heart he must have known it was the end. He completed his letters. In his message to Oriana Wilson he paid tribute to Bill and also revealed his sense of guilt: "I should like you to know how splendid he was at the end—everlastingly cheerful and ready to sacrifice himself for others, never a word of blame to me for leading him into this mess . . ." To Bowers's mother he wrote of her son's "dauntless spirit" and that "he has remained cheerful, hopeful, and indomitable to the end . . ." He asked Barrie to help his own wife and child but also appealed for others: ". . . Wilson leaves a widow, and Edgar Evans also a widow in humble circumstances. Do what you can to get their claims recognized." He also wrote to a number of those involved with the expedition, including the treasurer Sir Edgar Speyer and his agent Joseph Kinsey. His "Message to the Public" justified the decisions he had taken, aware that in death, as in life, there would be those to criticize him. He did not write directly to Markham, telling Kathleen: "I haven't time to write to Sir Clements, tell him I thought much of him, and never regretted his putting me in command of the *Discovery*."

Of course, Scott's deepest thoughts and feelings were reserved for his "dear, dear" mother and for Kathleen. As he confessed to Hannah Scott: "For myself I am not unhappy, but for Kathleen, you and the rest of the family hy heart is very sore." In a letter addressed "To my Widow," he wrote: "What lots and lots I could tell you of this journey. How much better has it been than lounging in too great comfort at home. What tales you would have for the boy. But what a price to pay." Inspired perhaps by the faith of his two companions he urged Kathleen to try and make their son believe in a God because: "it is comforting . . ." He also told her to guard their son against indolence. In his dying hours perhaps he though back to his own boyhood, to the little daydreamer they had called "Old Mooney" and to the hardship caused by his father's fecklessness. He urged Kathleen to "make the boy interested in natural history" and encouraged her to remarry: "When the right man comes to help you in life you ought to be your happy self again—I wasn't a very good husband but I hope I shall be a good memory." In fact, as he lay dying Kathleen was giving a party in London, hoping hourly for news of him. Her brother Rosslyn was there and saw the strain she was under, but he also noted that: "A new beam of courage has grown into her face."

On 29 March, believed to be the day of his death although this is by no means certain, Scott made one last entry in his diary, recounting the bitter frustration of their final days as each morning they had prepared to march for "our depot *11 miles* away" only to find that "outside the door of the tent it remains a scene of whirling drift." He was now looking death in the eye: "I do not think we can hope for any better things now. We shall stick it out to the end, but we are getting weaker, of course, and the end cannot be far. It seems a pity, but I do not think I can write more. R. Scott." The diary ends with a raggedly written appeal: "For God's sake look after our people." This has a bitter pathos. Ever since early adulthood Scott had carried the burden of responsibility for others, with all the concomitant feelings of guilt and inadequacy. Now he was leaving mother, wife and child alone as well as the loved ones of those who had followed him unquestioningly to the Pole.

As they lay frozen and starving in their small tent out on the Barrier, Scott, Wilson and Bowers must have wondered whether the outside world would even learn their fate—their tent was neatly pitched along the line of cairns between the depots but would soon be shrouded by drifting snow. In fact it would be eight months before their bodies would be discovered and their stricken comrades would find their letters and diaries and read Scott's spirited "Message to the Public": "Had we lived, I should have had a tale to tell of the hardihood, endurance and courage of my companions which would have stirred the heart of every Englishman. These rough notes and our dead bodies must tell the tale . . ."

Meanwhile at McMurdo Sound the other members of the expedition watched and waited. The first supporting party, consisting of Atkinson, Cherry-Garrard, Wright and Keohane, reached Hut Point safely on 26 January though a ravenous Atkinson had so gorged himself on supplies at One Ton Depot that he was not at all well during the final leg of the journey. The first clue that all might not be well with the Polar party came about three weeks later. At 3:30 a.m. on 19 February the dogs began barking and an exhausted Crean staggered into Hut Point. He had walked thirty miles across crevassed ice to bring news that Teddy Evans was lying dangerously ill with scurvy near Corner Camp with Lashly to nurse him. It was pure chance that Atkinson and

Dimitri happened to be there with the dog teams. Aghast at the news they hastily prepared to go to Evans's aid but a thick blizzard descended within half an hour of Crean's arrival and delayed their departure. In the afternoon they made a dash over the ice and Dimitri spotted the black cloth Lashly had fixed to the sledge to attract attention.

Evans, Lashly and Crean were, of course, the men of the last supporting party. They had bidden farewell to Scott and the Polar team on 4 January, less than one hundred and fifty miles from the Pole, and had faced a return journey of nearly seven hundred miles. Like Scott, they had had an appalling time navigating down the Beardmore Glacier which shook even the phlegmatic Lashly:

We have today experienced what none of us ever wants to be our lot again. I cannot describe the maze we got into and the hairbreadth escapes we have had to pass through today . . . The more we tried to get clear the worse the pressure got; at times it seemed almost impossible for us to get along, and when we had got over the places it was more than we could face to try and retreat.

He wrote of fathomless pits and deep crevasses "where it was possible to drop the biggest ship afloat in and lose her." Teddy Evans removed his goggles to help find the way and suffered agonies of snow-blindness which left him unable to pull. He could only walk helplessly beside the sledge, hoping a poultice of used tea-leaves would bring some relief. The strain took its toll. Evans felt despondent and guilty at having led his men into such a mess. He later wrote of his feelings at seeing silhouetted against the sun "two tiny disconsolate figures, one sitting, one standing . . ." patiently waiting for him to find a way out of the maze.

On 22 January they escaped the toils of the glacier but on this very day Evans began to display symptoms of scurvy, complaining of a stiffness behind the knees. Lashly guessed at once what it was: "Tonight I watched his gums, and I am convinced he is on the point of something anyhow . . . It seems we are in for more trouble now, but let's hope for the best." However, the best did not happen. As the month drew on Evans began to suffer bowel problems. On 29 January Lashly was writing: "His legs are getting worse and we are quite certain he is suffering from scurvy, at least he is turning black and blue and several other colours as well." By early February Evans was in great pain. He had to be strapped on his skis, unable to lift his legs. By the middle of the month he was passing blood and increasingly helpless. As well as his physical weakening he later admitted to some mental anguish: "The disappointment of not being included in the Polar party had not helped me much." Though he hid it from the men, his morale had suffered in much the same way as the Polar party's had done on finding that Amundsen had beaten them. Bowers had written on 1 January: "Teddy was fearfully upset at not going to the Pole—he had set his heart on it so . . . I am sure it was for his wife's sake he wanted to go."

Evans fainted on the march: "Crean and Lashly picked me up, and Crean thought I was dead. His hot tears fell on my face, and as I came to I gave a weak kind of laugh." Their progress was becoming worryingly slow in the low temperatures and Lashly and Crean decided the only solution was to carry Evans on the sledge. They jettisoned everything but the essentials and laid him carefully on it. He asked them to leave him behind but as Lashly wrote: "this we could not think of." By now Lashly was suffering from a frostbitten foot and Evans suggested he place it on his stomach to warm it up. Lashly reluctantly agreed and it worked. He paid tribute to their mutual care for each other in his diary: ". . . I think we could go to any length of trouble to assist one another." He did not know of Evans's later wry comment that: "there is something objectionable about a man's frostbitten clammy foot thrust against one's belly in the middle of the Great Ice Barrier with the thermometer at fifty below." They pressed on, sometimes using a sail to help them along, Evans grinding his teeth with the pain. They were hoping to un into dog teams on their way out to meet the Polar party. On 17 February they thought they spotted a tent in the deceptive light of the Barrier but it turned out to be only a piece of biscuit box. Marching on, they reached one of the abandoned motor sledges which lifted their spirits and they made camp. However, the next morning it was clear that Evans was dying. Crean was almost in tears. They made the wise decision that he should strike out alone to fetch help. He set out with just a little chocolate and a few biscuits, a staunch figure struggling alone and on foot because the skis had been among the equipment jettisoned.

Evans's account of their wait shows what Scott and his companions must have gone through in their last days: "The end had nearly come, and I was past caring; we had no food, except a few paraffin saturated biscuits, and Lashly in his weakened state without food could never have marched in. He took it very quietly—a noble, steel true man . . ." However, on 20 February they heard a sound which made their hearts leap. Lashly described the wonderful moment: "Hark! from us both. Yes, it is the dogs near. Relief at last." One of the dogs rushed into the tent and slobbered over the prostrate Evans: "Perhaps to hide my feelings I kissed his old hairy, Siberian face with the kiss that was meant for Lashly. We were both dreadfully affected at our rescue."

In fact, the delight which greeted the rescue of the last supporting party, coupled with their news that on parting from Scott he had been marching strongly for the Pole, obscured the significance of what had happened to Teddy Evans. Tryggve Gran, however, hit the nail on the head:

My conversation with Evans had not lasted long, but from what I heard . . . the prospects of our five-man polar party were not so bright as most of the members of the expedition imagined. Evans's frightful return journey was a pointer to what Scott and his men would be bound to undergo. There was also another matter which caused me anxiety. Since the Beardmore Glacier's suitability for dogs had been established, I took it for granted that Amundsen had reached the Pole before Scott. The consequence would probably be a fall in morale for our polar party. Of course I kept these dark broodings to myself for . . . my pessimism could only cause damage.

It was some time before the rest of the party at Cape Evans began to worry seriously about Scott. The main preoccupation was what to do about sending dog teams to meet the Polar party. The various messages sent back by Scott had caused some confusion. There had been plans for Meares and his dog teams to take extra rations for the returning parties and dog biscuit out to One Ton Depot provided they returned from the Polar trip in the first half of December. However, they did not return to Cape Evans in time. As a result, some of the extra rations but no dog biscuit were manhauled to One Ton Depot by Day, Nelson, Clissold and Hooper. It was not until 13 February that the dog teams set out again, under Atkinson since Meares was returning on the *Terra Nova*. Their mission was to run further supplies south to One Ton Depot for the returning party. The fateful encounter with Crean at Hut Point meant that Atkinson was now required to nurse Teddy Evans.

Cherry-Garrard took his place, arriving with Dimitri at One Ton Depot on 3 March. He wondered whether he would find Scott already there. Of course, he was not. He was still over one hundred miles away with poor Oates fast approaching his end. Faced with a lack of dog food and heavy winds Cherry-Garrard decided the best course was to wait at the depot. If he headed south there was every chance he might miss Scott. It never crossed his mind that the Polar party would be running out of food and fuel—as far as he knew adequate provisions had been left at the depots. Also, Atkinson had stressed that the Polar party was not dependent on the dogs to get them home and had reminded him of Scott's orders that under no circumstances were the dogs to be risked. The only way Cherry-Garrard could take the dogs south was to kill them for dog food as he went. He therefore waited six days until, on 10 March, dwindling supplies and the fact that Dimitri was suffering from the cold, forced him to turn his face northwards again. As he later learned, Scott was just sixty miles away. It was a decision for which he would never forgive himself.

Scott had been expected back at any time from early March, and by the end of the month at the latest. The men at Cape Evans waited for a signal from Hut Point to say that they were in. The telephone cable had been washed out to sea so they had agreed that rockets would be fired. However, as the month drew on there was an ominous silence from Hut Point, while the storms and blizzards which raged around Cape Evans boded ill for anyone out on the Barrier. As Gran wrote: "It can't be easy to travel on the Barrier in such God-forsaken weather." Sometimes the dogs would "sing," something they often did when a party was approaching. The men in the hut would rush outside only to find that there was nothing. The position became more critical with every day that passed: "Atkinson and I look at one another, and he looks, and I feel, quite haggard with anxiety. He says he does not think they have scurvy," wrote Cherry-Garrard. Atkinson and Keohane made a sortie out on to the Barrier but could find no trace of any living thing and dared not venture much beyond Corner Camp. Their return to Cape Evans with Dimitri sparked false hopes. As Gran described: ". . . I heard someone shout, 'The polar party's coming.' I rushed into the hut to the gramophone to get out the national anthem to greet Scott. I stood and waited long, but no one came. I went out again, and there stood three men, bearded, and coated with ice, dirty as sweeps." A mournful Cherry-Garrard confided to his diary in early April: "We have got to face it now. The Pole Party will not in all probability ever get back. And there is no more that we can do."

Atkinson had taken command as the only naval officer left. Teddy Evans had returned on the *Terra Nova,* while Campbell and his men were marooned in an igloo at Evans Coves, along the coast from Cape Adare where they had landed after finding Amundsen ensconced at the Bay of Whales. Atkinson now led an abortive attempt to get through to Campbell. However, on 24 April the sun disappeared and with it any realistic hope of rescuing anybody. The members of the expedition tried to keep busy and not fall prey to morbid thoughts. However, it must have been eerie faced with the empty bunks of their companions. There was no Scott sitting at his lino-covered table calculating sledging rations with the eager little Birdie, no wise Uncle Bill to look up from his sketching and dispense some kind word, no Oates to tease the scientists and indulge in horseplay and no Edgar Evans to roar his way around the mess-deck. The men with the most striking personalities, as Ponting had remarked, were gone forever.

The dilemma facing Atkinson was whether to devote his resources to rescuing Campbell or to try and discover what fate had overtaken Scott once the sledging season came round again. He had put the question to Cherry-Garrard at the beginning of the winter and his reply had been to go for Campbell: ". . . just then it seemed to me unthinkable that we should leave live men to search for those who were dead." However, the *Terra Nova* might have managed to pick up Campbell and his men on her voyage north. Alternatively, if Campbell had not been rescued but had survived the winter, the *Terra Nova* should be able to reach him on her way back to Cape Evans, although a land party might reach them earlier.

Scott and his companions had undoubtedly perished. The general view was that they had fallen down a crevasse, probably in the hellish labyrinth of the Beardmore, though Lashly and Crean believed they had contracted scurvy. However, dead or alive, there was surely a duty to try to discover what had happened. As Cherry-Garrard observed: "The first object of the expedition had been the Pole. If some record was not found, their success or failure would for ever remain uncertain." Even if the chance of finding the bodies was remote Scott had been meticulous about leaving notes at the depots. On Midwinter Day Atkinson gathered the whole party round the table and put the arguments. The decision was unanimous. When the weather permitted they would go south and seek the fate of the Polar party. It was a decision that would be vindicated. Campbell and his party returned safely under their own steam in mid November.

And so it was that towards the end of October the search-party set out. On 12 November, eleven miles south of One Ton Depot, they made their grim discovery. Wright saw what he thought was a cairn with something black by its side to his right and veered off towards it. "It is the tent," he said quietly to the others who had hurried in his wake. Someone brushed off an overhanging pile of snow to reveal the green flap of the ventilator. Atkinson crawled in, taking Lashly with him because he was the oldest member of the party and the last to have seen Scott and the Polar party. When he came out Lashly did not say a word but tears were rolling from his eyes.

Cherry-Garrard described what they had found:

Bowers and Wilson were sleeping in their bags. Scott had thrown back the flaps of his bag at the end. His left hand stretched over Wilson, his life-long friend. Beneath the head of his bag, beneath the bag and the floor-cloth, was the green wallet in which he carried his diary. The brown books of diary were inside: and on the floor-cloth were some letters.

Scott lay between his two companions whose appearance was serene, as if they had died very quietly. Bowers was lying flat, his arms crossed, Wilson was half-reclining, his head and upper body against the tent pole, and "traces of a sweet smile" on his lips. Scott, with arm outflung looked as if he had "fought hard at the moment of death." Their skin was yellow and glassy and scarred by frostbite. By Scott's side was a lamp made from a tin where he had burned the remnants of the methylated spirit as he wrote. Some tobacco and a bag of tea lay by his head. The tent itself was well-pitched and shipshape. No snow had penetrated the inner lining and all their equipment was neatly stowed—pannikins, spare clothing, chronometers, finnesko, socks and a flag as well as more letters, and, movingly, the "chatty little notes" the supporting parties had left for Scott as they returned to Cape Evans. There were also detailed records. Despite all the obstacles and hardships a meteorological log had been kept until some two weeks before their death.

Scott had left instructions on the cover of his diary that the finder was to read it and then bring it home. Atkinson read enough to discover what had happened to the Polar party. He then gathered his comrades around him and read Scott's "Message to the Public" and the account of Oates's death which Scott had expressly asked to be made known.

It seemed sacrilege to move the bodies. The months during which they had lain beneath their canopy of snow had made them as one with the white and hostile world on which they had trespassed. Instead, the bamboos of the tent were removed and the tent itself collapsed over them. The men then built a cairn on which they placed a cross made by Lashly from Gran's skis, and Atkinson read the lesson from the Burial Service from Corinthians, and other prayers for the dead. Cherry-Garrard was deeply affected and left a description of Arthurian grandeur:

I do not know how long we were there, but when all was finished, and the chapter of Corinthians had been read, it was midnight . . . The sun was dipping low above the Pole, the Barrier was almost in shadow. And the sky was blazing . . . sheets and sheets of iridescent clouds. The cairn and Cross stood dark against a glory of burnished gold.

Atkinson wrote his own tribute: "There alone in their greatness they will lie without change or bodily decay, with the most fitting tomb in the world above them."

After a miserable and eerie night, an abortive attempt was made to locate Oates's body. However, only his sleeping-bag was found with the great slit down its front which he had made so that he could keep his frostbitten feet frozen while he slept and spare himself the agony of them thawing. The party erected a cairn to him at the point where he had walked out to meet his death, and left a note recording how this "very gallant gentleman" had sacrificed himself for his comrades. The search-party then retraced its steps, minds still be-numbed with the horror of their discovery and the knowledge that the party had died just eleven miles from One Ton Depot. Gran wore Scott's skis so that they completed the journey. The note they left at the cairn gave the cause of death as "inclement weather and lack of fuel," but there was more to it than that.

Two Mountain Men

BY GEORGE LAYCOCK

Published by The Lyons Press in 1966, George Laycock's *The Mountain Men,* with illustrations by Tom Beecham, is one of the best books you can get your hands on if you want to read vivid portraits of life as it was lived boldly by the early fur trappers in the Rockies. Here is life as it was experienced in the open by a restless, freedom-loving breed of men who took on everything the wilderness and the hostile Indians of that day could throw at them. Preceded only by Lewis and Clark, surviving on fish and game and their skills, these men saw an American wilderness virgin and unspoiled, vast and challenging. Their stories, all of them, make amazing reading.

Two of my personal favorites are presented here. In the first, you will learn why the Yellowstone Region was sometimes called "Colter's Hell." In the second, the epic journey of Huge Glass will bring you a new meaning of the word tough.

★　　★　　★　　★　　★

For Love of the Wild Places

Through the soft days of early October, the easterner moved swiftly along the woodland trails, always headed west, up and over the mountains. His trip turned out to be an adventure as wild as any North American outdoorsman has ever known.

The mountainsides around him and the forest giants forming their canopy over his trail were splashed with fiery autumn colors. He must have watched the gray squirrels gathering nuts for the winter, the wild turkeys walking in the forest, the deer and the black bear hurrying out of sight. But he was in a hurry too. Word was out that Captain Meriwether Lewis was signing on hunters and boatmen for a grand journey into the distant Rocky Mountains, to places new to the white man.

The traveler's immediate destination was Limestone, Kentucky, a settlement on the south bank of the Ohio River, fifty miles or so upstream from Cincinnati. The little riverside village was already famous as a landing for flatboats and keelboats bringing people down the Ohio to the western frontier.

In Limestone, which we now call Maysville, the woodsman soon spotted a keelboat tied to the bank. He introduced himself to the captain and outlined his qualifications. He had been a hunter, trapper, and horseman since he was a boy on the farm in Virginia. Captain Lewis sized him up. The applicant stood five feet ten inches tall, looked strong, and seemed to be quiet and reserved but quick-witted and decisive in his manner. The captain noticed that this stranger was not the loudmouthed braggart often found along the rivers. He was instead somewhat inclined to weigh his words. When the keelboat eased into the current to head on down the Ohio toward Louisville, a new member was aboard. Captain Lewis had signed on John Colter, and apparently neither of them ever regretted the decision.

The deeper Lewis and Clark traveled into the wilderness with their little band of explorers, the more they came to rely on the skills of Private John Colter. They frequently relieved him of his other duties and sent him with Drouillard to roam the countryside on foot or horseback and supply the company with meat. Colter was a specialist in traveling alone in the wilderness, sometimes for days or weeks at a time, always finding his way back.

As Lewis and Clark were returning to St. Louis near the end of their two-year-long journey, Colter seemed in no rush to return to civilization. The Lewis and Clark party was within six weeks of reaching St. Louis when it tied up beside a little two-man camp on the banks of the Missouri.

The two strangers explained that they had come into the mountains from their homes in Illinois in 1804, to trap beaver. They found beaver aplenty in the mountains, but Indians had robbed them so often that they had little to show for the time and work. They still nurtured their dreams of growing rich trapping furs in the western mountains.

Colter was especially interested when the two trappers, Forrest Hancock and Joe Dixon, said they were headed back toward the wilderness, up the Yellowstone River, where the beaver lived. Furthermore, they needed a partner who knew the Yellowstone country. There was then probably no white person anywhere who knew it better than John Colter did.

Colter took the idea to Captain Lewis and Captain Clark. Would they perhaps discharge him here on the Missouri instead of back in St. Louis? Lewis and Clark considered the long months of faithful service Colter had rendered. Why not? They took the matter up with the rest of their crew. They would release Colter, providing no others in the party would make similar requests before reaching St. Louis. The chances are good that no other man in the group gave serious thought anyhow to turning back into the mountains with St. Louis so close at hand.

The Lewis and Clark party moved off downstream and was soon out of sight. The three trappers, Hancock, Dixon, and Colter, turned upstream toward the distant peaks and ridges. They spent that winter of 1806–1807 in the upper Yellowstone where, it is believed, they built a shelter and waited out the worst of the weather.

None of these three pioneering mountain men was strong on writing. Little can be known for sure of what they saw. But their association was not especially profitable and did not last long. By the following spring, Colter had carved himself a dugout canoe from a cottonwood log and was soon headed downstream alone, once more St. Louis bound.

By this time, however, Manuel Lisa, the crusty fur trader who guided the fortunes of his Missouri Fur Company, was moving toward the Rocky Mountains in pursuit of beaver plews. In due time Lisa's party had wrestled his keelboats up the Missouri River as far as the mouth of the Platte, and were tied up there when John Colter's little canoe slid into view around the bend.

Colter, the mountain man, once more turned his back on St. Louis and headed for the mountains, this time working for Manuel Lisa.

Lisa moved his party up the Missouri as far as the Yellowstone, then turned up that tributary and followed it to where the Bighorn River fed into it sixty miles or so downstream from where Billings, Montana, stands today. Here Lisa's men began felling timbers and constructing an unimpressive shelter that became the first fur trading post in the upper Missouri country. It was probably close to where Colter, Dixon, and Hancock had wintered the year before.

Although Lisa intended to send his own trappers out on the beaver waters, he also expected to barter for furs with the Indians of surrounding tribes. He had, with Colter's guidance, selected a good location. People of the Crow nation wintered in this region, and so did large numbers of wild game animals that would provide food for the trappers.

But unless someone went out among the Indians to spread the word about Lisa's arrival, and his new commercial enterprise, there would be few furs. This may have been the hazardous assignment Lisa had in mind for Colter from the first. Nowhere could he have found a better qualified person.

Colter said he would travel alone. He liked being alone in the mountains, depending on his own survival skills, making his own decisions, going where he pleased. He would seek out the Indians in their wintering camps, and he would spread the word—there was now a trading post at the mouth of the Bighorn. He put together the essentials—powder, lead, flint and steel, sharpening stone, jerky, some lightweight trade goods, a blanket or robe, in a pack weighing thirty pounds—picked up his rifle, and set out on a five-hundred-mile winter hike through the mountain stronghold of the Crows.

About where Cody, Wyoming, stands today he came upon an Indian village of perhaps a thousand people. They talked with the lightly equipped trapper and allowed him to go on. This camp was on the Shoshone River, which was then called the "Stinking Water." It was near here that Colter witnessed springs bubbling from the ground and filling the air with their sulfurous odor. When he later described the scene to his fellow trappers, they laughed and slapped their buckskin leggins, declaring, "That's some, that is! This child's heard it all now. Old Colter's found his hell, sure enough 'er I wouldn't say so." In due time, the springs of Colter's Hell subsided.

Colter crossed the mountains over Shoshone Pass and down into the Wind River Range, then turned northwest toward Yellowstone. Among the mysteries surrounding Colter's life are the details of the route he followed on the remainder of this journey. But there is agreement that he crossed the area that later became Yellowstone National Park. He skirted Yellowstone Lake. Then traveling north, he went down the Yellowstone River and finally turned east again to cross the mountains and come down into the headwaters of Clark's Fork of the Yellowstone. He was now making his way back toward Cody.

There are no records telling us how long Colter needed for this winter hike of more than five hundred miles. He may not have considered the time important and surely did not anticipate that researchers would one day scour old records, hoping to uncover bits and pieces of information revealing the details of his life and travels. To the mountain man, his trip on foot, while living off the land, was a job, and he did it.

Spring was probably at hand by the time Colter returned to Lisa's fort. But soon, he was sent off again on another journey as ambassador to the Indians. He was going about his business visiting with the Crows, when the Crows' traditional enemies, the Blackfeet, attacked. An attack by the Blackfeet was always a serious matter. On that spring day in 1808, Colter had little choice: he joined his hosts in their efforts to repel the Blackfeet.

Some historians believe that the Blackfeet held a grudge from that moment on against not only Colter but all white men. At any rate, this marked the beginning for John Colter of a series of almost unbelievable close encounters.

Coming from Joe Meek, Jim Beckwourth, or some other trapper famed for his storytelling skills, the account of Colter's amazing escape might have been questioned. But the quiet Colter was known for his honesty. He later told the story to Thomas James, and James wrote it down. He also vouched for Colter. "His veracity was never questioned among us," wrote James, "and his character was that of a true American back woodsman . . . of the Daniel Boone stamp. Nature had formed him, like Boone, for hardy endurance of fatigue, privations, and perils. He had gone with a companion named Potts to the Jefferson river which is the most western of the three forks, and runs near the base of the mountains."

Colter and Potts, each in his own canoe, were working their way slowly upstream, running their beaver sets, and Colter was edgy because they were deep into Blackfoot territory. He had good reason for his uneasiness. Suddenly several hundred Indians materialized on the east shore of the river and there was little hope that the white trappers could escape.

When the chiefs ordered the trappers to come ashore, Colter obeyed, figuring that he would thereby add, at least briefly, to his life span. Killing him where he sat in his canoe would be easy enough for this many warriors. He no sooner touched shore than the squaws began ripping the clothes off his body and soon he stood before the yelling warlike Indians, stripped of all clothing and weapons.

The chiefs again demanded that Colter tell Potts to come on in. Colter relayed the message. He also advised Potts to do as he was told. Potts said something akin to, "Wagh. Them red devils will kill this child, sure enough, same's they're fixin' to do you and from here I can leastways take one of 'em with me." With this, one of the Indians put a ball in Pott's shoulder.

Potts did what he said he would do; he recovered enough to lift his gun and kill the Indian who shot him. In the next minute Potts was, in Colter's words, "made a riddle of."

The screaming Indians now dragged Potts's body from the river while others turned their fury on Colter. He fully expected to black out, permanently, from the quick blow of one of the tomahawks being lifted against him, but the chiefs managed to push back the young warriors. Meanwhile, some of the Indians were hacking off chunks of Potts. One of the squaws walked up close to Colter and threw Potts's penis and testicles in his face. They continued pelting him with various bloody parts of his partner's body, using for the purpose, as Tom James wrote, "the entrails, heart, lungs, etc."

Then came a squabble about what to do with their white captive. Colter figured maybe Potts had taken the best way out after all. But his wits were still with him, and given the slightest opportunity, he was keyed up for escape.

One of the chiefs walked up to Colter. Was he a good runner? Not very, Colter lied. The satisfied chief, surrounded by powerful young men eager to prove how fast they could run, gave Colter his instructions. He led the naked trapper out behind the main group of warriors onto the open plain, and told Colter to start running.

Colter noticed, in a glance, that the warriors were stripping themselves of all clothing and extra weight and now he fully understood the odds against him. He dashed off across the flatlands toward the river six miles away.

Perhaps no runner ever had greater motivation than John Colter did in that hour. Ignoring the thorns of the prickly pear cactus through which is bare feet raced, Colter, toughened by his years in the mountains, ran at his fastest speed. Glancing over his shoulder, he saw the band of runners racing along silently, each intent on being first to come within spear-throwing range of the white man.

Colter got his second wind. He did not slow his pace. Blood began flowing from his nose. It spattered against his sweating chest, dropping onto his bare legs. He raced on beneath the brilliant sun, oblivious to everything but maintaining his grueling pace.

One by one, the exhausted Indians fell far behind. One of them, however, was an exceptionally strong runner and Colter knew that the warrior was closing the distance between them.

When it became obvious that he could not outrun the Indian, Colter took a bold chance. He jerked to a halt, and wheeled to meet the Indian, calling to him to stop and talk the matter over. The Indian kept coming and, as he drew near, he raised his spear over his head and lunged at the trapper. Colter side-stepped, grabbed the spear, and put enough pressure on it to throw the off-balance Indian to the ground. The tumbling Indian was no sooner rolling on the ground than Colter ran him through with the spear point, pinning him to mother earth.

He grabbed the Indian's blanket and, once more, began running. He was now well ahead of the nearest warrior. At last he came to the river and, for the first time, began to think that he might have a good chance of escaping. He swam to the end of a small island where he dove under a pile of tangled driftwood that had washed up against the land.

Within minutes, dozens of Indians were running up and down the riverbank. They probed each hiding place with their spears, and searched around the roots of the cottonwoods. They even swam out to search the island. They climbed onto the pile of logs beneath which Colter clung in the darkness with his head barely above water. He waited for them to drive their spears through the brush pile, or set it afire.

The search continued throughout much of the day. Darkness settled over the river. At last the Indians withdrew, and Colter slipped from beneath his shelter and swam the river. Instead of crossing the mountain pass, which was the easiest way out of the valley, but probably guarded by the frustrated Indians, he climbed the nearly vertical slope to the distant ridge. For the next eleven days he stopped only to sleep or to gather the roots and plants that sustained him. When he reached Lisa's Fort, the other trappers scarcely recognized him.

Colter told the story of his escape in detail to Tom James and others on a later trip as they traveled through the area where he had made his unforgettable run for freedom. He pointed out the mountain he had scaled. As Colter quietly related the details of that day, his companions grew silent. One of the trappers listening to the story, fully aware that they were in hostile country said, "I never felt fear before, but now I feel it." His fear should have been a warning. A few days later this trapper was caught by the Blackfeet and killed.

Those traps Colter had quietly dropped overboard when the large band of Blackfeet discovered him and Potts were very much on his mind. Traps were hard to come by in the mountains and there was no substitute for them if a man was to take plews. The possibility of recovering the traps lured Colter back to the scene. He had stopped to cook supper and rest, and as he settled down he heard the sound of rustling leaves in the darkness.

The mountain man, like the hunted animal, lived with all senses alert. Every sign was weighed for what it might mean in terms of survival. Now, he heard a noise the meaning of which was known to him instantly; beyond his campfire guns were being cocked.

He leaped over the fire and raced off through the brush as shots rattled around him. Once more he scaled the mountain to avoid the pass, and once more John Colter escaped. But he was beginning to get the message. He came back to the fort this time saying that he had made a promise to his Maker; providing he could survive, he would leave the country.

He still had one test ahead of him. He was finally on his way downriver with a companion headed for the distant sights and sounds of St. Louis when the Blackfeet attacked. This time Colter and his companion hid in the bushes, and the Indians, who had high respect for the trappers' rifles, did not come after them.

John Colter never counted coup. He was no braggart and no bully. Perhaps in all his years in the mountains he killed only one Indian, and that time to save his own life. For all this, he had little to show. He came down from the mountains without much more than memories. He moved to a farm near where Dundee, Missouri, is today. He married, and all we know of his wife is that he called her Sally.

Colter, the pioneering trapper and explorer, who specialized in traveling alone, had spent six years in the mountains. He had played his role in the historic adventures of Lewis and Clark, traveled where no white man had gone before, discovered on his own the wonders of Yellowstone, and set an example for hundreds of fur trappers who would soon follow him to the mountains. John Colter, the soft-spoken mountain man, became a legend in his own day. He died in bed in November 1813, of jaundice.

A Grizzly Problem

The first white man the wilderness grizzly bear saw was simply another animal, and the grizzly had never met the animal it feared. Even when the great bears learned that these newcomers could hurt them, they still attacked any man who surprised them or pushed them too far.

The mountain men, meanwhile, saw in the grizzlies an ultimate challenge to their skills and bravery—the highest test of manhood—so they sought the grizzly out in his native haunts and carried the challenge to him. Consequently, stories of the early trappers are laced with accounts of unforgettable conflicts between man and bear. Few, if any, of these encounters could match the legendary struggle that began one September day, in 1823, in what is now the northwestern corner of South Dakota.

Major Andrew Henry was leading a party of thirteen men in an overland shortcut away from the Missouri to go almost straight west up the valley of the Grand River toward the Yellowstone country. He always tried to keep his little band of trappers in the best position to avoid nasty surprises by Indians. There was security to be gained by staying within sound of your fellow trappers. But in Henry's party was Hugh Glass, an independent spirit who had a habit of straying away from the group whenever he chose. Trapper Jim Clyman was aware of this when he wrote in his journal for September 1823, that ". . . a Mr. Hugh Glass . . . who could not be restrained . . . went off the line of march one afternoon and met with a large grizzly bear which he shot and wounded."

Parts of the legend of Hugh Glass, born of that impulsive shot from a muzzleloader, remain fuzzy to this day. Some have speculated that the whole tale of his unfortunate encounter was the product of frontier imaginations. There is, however, widespread belief that the legend of Hugh Glass is true. It is admittedly the kind of bear story that could grow from campfire to campfire, and in the final analysis, one is free to make his own decisions on what he believes of this unforgettable frontier adventure. John Myers concludes his book *The Saga of Hugh Glass, Pirate, Pawnee, and Mountain Man* by finding the incredible story "thoroughly true."

The background of Hugh Glass, before his beaver-trapping years, is filled with questions. Glass may once have found temporary employment as a pirate. It is said that he sailed on a ship that was overwhelmed by the infamous privateer Jean Lafitte, who specialized in preying on Spanish ships in the Gulf of Mexico. Although Glass rarely spoke of those times, it seems probable that, in preference to execution at the hands of Lafitte, he chose to serve his apprenticeship as a pirate, biding his time, and reasoning that as long as he was alive and kept his wits, there was hope.

Glass's career as a pirate terminated one dark night off the coast of Texas when he and a buddy slipped over the side and swam for shore. On land, the big problem was staying alive in a world dominated by hostile Indians. The two men, slipping along northwestward, as swiftly as they could, while watching for signs of natives, made it all the way to Kansas before their luck ran out. There they had the misfortune to be discovered by a band of Pawnees, who were bad news anytime.

The Pawnees lived in lodges made of earth, and around their dwellings planted corn and squash to supplement the food taken by their hunters. They were proud and powerful warriors noted for their nasty tempers. They fought all the neighboring tribes at every opportunity and were recognized experts in creating unusual ways to torture their captives.

The jubilant Indians hustled their two white captives back to their village in high anticipation of the festive occasion ahead. The ceremony was soon in progress. The Indians chose Glass's companion for their first sacrifice. Instead of simply building a fire and putting him on it, they pushed numerous slivers of dry resinous pine into sensitive parts of this body and Glass was forced to watch his companion burn slowly. By intermission time, when this first act ended, Glass had a vivid picture of what lay ahead for him.

Instead of cringing and pleading, Glass forced himself to remain calm and appear unconcerned. This made a deep impression on the Pawnees, who considered bravery the greatest of virtues. Glass even offered the chief a gift. In the few trade items he had carried along was a small waterproof pack of vermilion, which was always considered of extreme value among the Indians.

The chief was impressed; he decided that this brave and generous white man would make an outstanding Pawnee, so he brought Glass into the tribe by the simple process of adopting him as his son. Once more, Glass the survivor was willing to make the most of this development and for the next could of years lived as a Pawnee. He sharpened his survival skills. He learned the Indian techniques of living off the land.

His opportunity to desert the tribe came unexpectedly. When his "father," the chief, set out for St. Louis to confer with the Indian agent, Glass was taken along. When the rest of his tribe set off for home, Glass stayed behind.

He was still in St. Louis when Ashley and Henry began organizing their second historic trip into the mountains for beaver in 1823.

By this time, Glass was older than most of the mountain men, perhaps forty, but by any measure he was tough, resolute, and a most capable outdoorsman. He was also said to be something of a loner and independent by nature, but still a dependable partner in times of trouble. Here was the kind of man Ashley and Henry needed if they were to succeed in their new enterprise and deliver substantial payloads of furs back to St. Louis. Soon the party, including Hugh Glass, was deep into hostile country.

In autumn, the bears feed constantly, adding fat ahead of the coming winter. They eat all manner of foods, both plant and animal. One of their favorites is ripe fruit; they were especially fond of the wild plums growing in thickets along the streams. On this day, an old female grizzly and her husky cubs were busy gathering fruit in the heart of the thicket toward which Glass was headed.

He came upon the bear suddenly, or more accurately, she came upon him. She smelled him or heard him, or both, and his presence in her territory was an invasion of her space. She reacted in the only way she knew as she crashed through the brush toward the trapper. Glass waited as long as he dared, then gave her one in the heart.

The single shot lacked power to do the job and the grizzly came on without breaking stride. There was no time for reloading. The furious grizzly was on Glass almost immediately, her teeth chomping and claws raking whatever they could reach, while Glass made futile slashes at her with his butcher knife.

She was still at her job when the first of Glass's companions, responding to his loud calls for help, arrived on the scene out of breath. They shot the bear until she dropped and lay still beside the man she had mauled. One glance was all the trappers needed. Anyone could see that Old Glass was going under. He was torn apart and bleeding from numerous wounds and there was precious little anybody was going to be able to do about it.

They tried to make him comfortable in what they believed were his final moments. Then, after standing around quietly for a while waiting for him to die, it began to dawn on them that the tough old Hugh Glass was a long way from becoming wolf meat. He lived on through that night; then, according to George C. Yount, a mountain man who talked with Glass about the event, his companions moved on, carrying their silent and helpless companion on a litter. To this day people living in the wilderness far from help are drawn close together in case of emergency. They depend on each other. Yount spoke of this quality in the mountain men. "Among those rude & rough trappers of the wilderness, fellow feeling and devotion to each others wants is a remarkable & universal feature or characteristics."

For several days the trappers carried the litter. But Henry knew that the burden was eating into his crew's fall trapping time and that their slow progress increased the threat of Indian attack. He reasoned that he had little choice—he must leave Hugh Glass behind. But one does not abandon a helpless companion to die in the wilderness. Henry asked for volunteers who would stay with Glass until he died, see to it that he got a decent burial, then catch up with the main party.

This was not a detail for which anyone would volunteer lightly. Henry offered extra pay to any two men who would stay. Most accounts tell us that one who stepped forward was Jim Bridger, although events that followed seem out of character. The other was named Fitzgerald. They watched solemnly as the rest of their party struck camp, loaded their equipment, and disappeared in the distance.

They waited for Glass to grow weaker and die, but he lived on, day after day. Fitzgerald and Bridger grew restless. Perhaps Fitzgerald argued that Glass couldn't last much longer anyhow and that they should move out and save themselves. And perhaps the younger Bridger finally went along. Nobody will ever know the details of this conversation, but in the end the two trappers loaded up and departed. Glass, watching them make ready, was unable to speak to them because of injuries in his throat. He may have been conscious and awake when they took his equipment, including his rifle. Once Glass died, he would have no further need for the rifle and someone was certain to ask about it.

The two had not reckoned with the rawhide toughness of this man they abandoned. Here perhaps the most incredible story in the colorful history of the American West began. Glass had water within reach, and he may have managed to pick a few berries. He rested and regained some of his strength.

At first, he was so weak that he could not rise to his feet, so he began to crawl. Yard by yard, he worked his way back down the valley of the Grand

River toward the Missouri. How far can a half-starved man, broken and bleeding, crawl in a day over rocky cactus-studded country? At first, Glass was marking his progress in yards.

Hunger plagued him. At one point, he killed a fat rattlesnake with a rock and dined on its flesh. There were sometimes berries to pick. His biggest break came the day a pack of wolves brought down a buffalo calf near him. The salivating Glass considered ways to take the treasure away from the wolves. Perhaps he hid in the bushes and waited until the wolves were sluggish on fresh meat, then chased them off with rocks. The meat strengthened him and he stayed beside it, resting and eating, as long as he could. Using his razor, he could have cut strips of it to dry in the sun and carried the jerky off in the pockets of his tattered clothes.

Eventually Glass was able to rise to his feet and walk. As his strength grew, his progress improved. He would probably find the culprits at Fort Kiowa where Henry's partner Ashley was headed, so he started back downstream planning to turn up the Missouri when he came to that river again. Eventually, a band of Sioux Indians befriended him and helped him reach Fort Kiowa.

He soon learned that the two who had abandoned him were no longer there, so he set off again following his party up the Missouri. One story says that he hitched a ride on a supply boat. The Arikaras were still attacking river travelers whenever they had the opportunity, and Indians scouts soon spotted the boat on which Glass traveled. In the attack that followed, the Indians killed everyone on board. Typically, Glass escaped; he was on shore at the time. Once more he was traveling alone.

When he finally reached Fort Henry, where the Bighorn River empties into the Yellowstone, the mountains were in winter's grip. Here he encountered Jim Bridger, the first of the two men he wanted.

Bridger might already have heard rumors that Glass lived. Or perhaps the old trapper, his frayed buckskins flecked with fresh snow and a satanic look on his scowling face, pushed open the heavy door and walked in out of the winter night like a ghost, to stand before the unbelieving trappers. Bridger was young and apparently Glass was more intent on finding the older man— Fitzgerald. It was sometimes written that Glass shamed the young Bridger and delivered an unforgettable tongue lashing. Nobody will ever know. But Glass was not done traveling yet.

Eventually, he tracked Fitzgerald to Council Bluffs, only to learn that he had joined the army. After tracking his former companion for hundreds of miles he took his satisfaction in confronting Fitzgerald with a shame that could not be lived down. Glass resisted the temptation to kill a United States soldier. But the trip may have been worth it to Glass.

To fur trappers, Glass had proved himself to be an iron man and his story, true or not, was repeated in trading posts and around campfires as long as beaver trappers worked the mountains. He began wearing his hair long to cover some of the scars the grizzly gave him. Other than that, he displayed little outward evidence of the attack, or his astounding campaign to survive. On a winter day, after Glass returned to trapping, he was surprised again by Indians. They caught up with him as he worked along the Yellowstone River. This time his luck ran out. The trapper who had survived Jean Lafitte, the Pawnees, a grizzly attack, and an incredible journey, died that day fighting his old enemies, the Arikara.

Three Days

Because I love the outdoors so much, I have this rather active fantasy life in which I sometimes imagine myself as a self-sufficient wilderness dweller—hunting, fishing, gardening. And trapping. Could I hack it out there? Would my meager skills be sufficient? Or do I know just enough to likely get myself killed?

Fortunately for my wife, children, and various employers, I will never have to answer that question, and one of the reasons why is that I've settled for reading about these experiences rather than trying to live them.

One man who *has* lived them, even in the so-called "modern" age, is John Haines, a poet and writer of extraordinary talent. Haines' memoir of life as a trapper in the Alaska wilderness from the late 1940s through the 1960s is called *The Stars, the Snow, the Fire*. Published by Graywolf Press of Saint Paul, Minnesota, in 1989, the book is one of the most superbly written accounts of life in the outdoors I have ever read. Haines is the author of other books and volumes of poetry, but *The Stars, the Snow, the Fire* is my personal favorite. In this piece from that work, you'll go with John Haines as he runs his trapline.

★   ★   ★   ★   ★

I

Six o'clock on a January morning. I wake, look into the darkness overhead, and then to the half-lighted windows. I listen. No sound comes to me from the world outside. The wind is quiet.

I get out of bed, pulling the stiffness from my body. Jo is still sleeping under the big down robe, turned toward the wall. I go to the window with a flashlight and look out at the thermometer. It is minus thirty-one, clear, and no moon. It will not be light for another three hours.

I put on a jacket and pair of slippers, and go outside. The door creaks on its frosty hinges, the latch is cold to my hand. One of our dogs emerges from his house in the yard and shakes himself, rattling his chain.

The stars are bright, Orion gone down the west. The Dipper has turned, Arcturus above the hill. The sky and the snow give plenty of light, and I can easily see the outlines of the river channel below the house, and the dark crests of the hills around me. The air is sharp and clean, it will be a good day.

I gather up a few sticks of wood from the porch and go back indoors. Laying the wood on the floor beside the stove, I go to a table by the south window, find a match, and light the lamp. I turn the wick up slowly, letting the chimney warm.

Light gathers in the room, reflecting from the window glass and the white enamel of a washpan. I open the stove door and the damper in the pipe. With a long poker I reach into the big firebox and rake some of the hot coals forward. I lay kindling on them, dry slivers of spruce, and two or three dry sticks on top of these. I close the door and open the draft. Air sucks through the draft holes, and in no time the fire is burning, the wood crackling. I fill the big kettle with water from a bucket near at hand, and set it on the back of the stove. It will soon be singing.

By now Jo is awake and beginning to function. I sit on the edge of the bed, putting thoughts together. The lamp makes shadows in the small room; heat is beginning to flow from the stove.

Today I am going back to our cabin below Banner Dome, to look at my traps. I have not been out for over a week, and must surely have caught something by now. While Jo makes breakfast, I begin to dress. We talk a little; the mornings here are quiet, the days also.

I put on heavy wool trousers over my underwear, and two wool shirts. Over the wool trousers I sometimes wear another light cotton pair to break the wind or to keep off the snow. I put on socks—three pair of wool, and the felt oversock; two pair of insoles, and last the moosehide moccasins. I tie them at the top; they are a loose fit, soft and light on my feet. I made them six years ago from the hide of a big moose, and though worn by now, they are still the best I have.

I go out to the storehouse, find my big basket, and begin to pack. I will need my small axe, a few traps, and perhaps a few snares. That piece of dried moose paunch I have been saving—it is strong-smelling and will make good bait. What else? Something needed for the cabin—a candle, some kerosene in a bottle. I put it all together in the basket.

We eat our breakfast slowly, there is no hurry. Half-frozen blueberries with milk, oatmeal, bread, and plenty of coffee. We listen to the stove, to the kettle buzzing. How many winters have gone by like this? Each morning that begins in the same quiet way—the darkness, the fire, the lamp, the stirring within. We talk a little, what she will do when I am gone. Food will have to be cooked for the dogs, there is plenty of wood. I am not sure when I will return; in three days, maybe.

By seven-thirty I am ready. I get my stuff together—into the basket now goes a light lunch, some bread for the cabin. I put on my old green army parka with its alpaca lining buttoned into it. It is heavily patched, and by now almost a homemade thing, the hood sewn large and trimmed with fur to shield my face from the wind. I take two wool caps, one for my head, and another in the basket in case I should need it. My big mittens also go into the pack; to start with, I will need only a pair of canvas gloves.

I say goodbye at the door, and walk up the hill. The dogs think that they may be going too, and the four of them begin to bark, waiting for the harness and tugging at their chains. But today I am going on foot; I want to take my time, to look around and set new traps. My dogs are too much in a hurry.

I begin the long climb through the birchwoods to the ridge. The trail goes steeply the first few hundred yards, but it soon takes an easier grade, turning north and away from the river. The woods are still dark, but there is light in the snow, and perhaps a brightening in the sky above the trees. Morning and evening come on slowly this time of year, a gradual twilight. I carry a light walking stick made of birch in one hand as I go along. It comes in handy, to knock snow off the brush, to test the ice when I cross a creek, or to kill an animal with when I find one alive in a trap.

It is a winter of light snowfall, with barely ten inches on the ground, and I do not need my snowshoes. The trail is packed hard underfoot, and is easy walking, but away in the woods the snow is still loose and powdery under a thin crust; in the dim light I see that it is littered with dry, curled leaves and small, winged seeds from the alders and birches.

The air is sharp on my face, and it pinches my nose, but I soon begin to feel warm from climbing. I open my parka and push the cap back on my head; I take off my gloves and put them into one of my pockets. It won't do to get overheated.

Behind me now I hear an occasional mournful howl from one of our dogs, sunken and distant in the timber. Otherwise, there is not a sound in the woods this morning, and no air moving in the trees; but now and then the quiet snap of something contracting or expanding in the frost. At other times I have walked this trail in deep snow and bright moonlight, when the birch shadows made another transparent forest on the snow. There were shadows within the shadows, and now and then something would seem to move there—rabbit or lynx, or only a shape in my mind.

Partway up the hill I come to a marten set. Earlier in the season I caught a marten here, close to home, but there is nothing in the trap this morning. In the grey light I see that nothing has come to it, and all the tracks in the snow around it are old.

Frost bristles on the trap, a dense white fur over the jaws, the pan and the trigger. I put my gloves back on, spring the trap and bang it a couple of times against the pole to knock the frost from it.

I have two ways of setting traps for marten—one on the snow, and the other on a pole above the snow. This is a pole set. To make it, I have cut down a young birch four feet above the snow, and drawn the trunk of the tree forward a couple of feet to rest in the vee of the stump. I split the end of it to take a piece of bait, and the trap is set back a short space on top of the pole and held in place with a piece of light wire or string. It is a good way in heavy snow; once caught, the marten will always be found hanging from the pole.

Satisfied that the trap is working properly, I reset it, tying the wire loosely in place again. I go on, walking at a steady pace as the trail levels and climbs, winding among the birches.

Within half an hour I come out of the trees and into the open on the long, cleared ridge that rises behind the homestead. Light is stronger here, and I can see the cold, blue height of Banner Dome to the north beyond a range of hills. I have a long ways to go.

I begin to cool off now that I am on top, so I wear my gloves and button the front of my parka. As I stride along in the lightly drifted snow, I savor once more the cold stillness of this winter morning—my breath blown in a long plume before me, and no sound but the soft crunch of my moccasins, and the grating of my stick in the snow.

This ridge like a true watershed divides what I like to think of as my country; for in a way I own it, having come by it honestly, and nearly its oldest resident now. To the south of me, all the way down to the river, it is mostly dry hillside with birch and aspen. To the north, falling way into Redmond and Banner creeks, it is spruce country, mossy and wet. Years ago, when I first lived here, this ridge was heavily wooded; the trail wound through the timber, companionable and familiar, with small clearings and berry patches. Then, eight years ago, came a pipeline crew clearing the ridges and hillsides into Fairbanks. And later they built a powerline to run beside it, from Fairbanks to Delta. The cleared way is overgrown with grass, with alders and raspberries, and the pipe is buried in the ground; but the ridge is windy now, and the trail drifts badly in heavy snow. Because of this, few fur animals come here, and I have no traps on this ridge.

I see some much-trampled snow at the edge of the timber, and turn aside to look. Moose have been feeding here at night, and the tops of many of the smaller trees are pulled down, broken and bitten. I find a couple of hard-packed beds in the snow, and piles of black, frozen droppings. The moose must be close by, but they are out of sight, bedded down in the timber. I stand very still and listen, but hear nothing.

I cover a good mile of steady walking as the light grows and the snow brightens; the trail visible now some distance ahead of me where it follows the open ridge, paced by the power poles, dipping and curving with the slope of the hills. And then near the top of the last rise of hill the trail swings sharply north, and I go down into the woods again. The country changes swiftly, becomes dense and shaggy, the scrubby black spruce dominant, with alder and a few scattered birches. The trail is narrow, rutted and uneven to walk. There is more snow here on a north slope, and I soon see marten sign, their characteristic tracks crossing my trail at intervals.

I have gone only a short distance when I find a marten dead in a trap. It is frozen, hanging head down at the end of the trap chain—a female, small, and with dull orange splashes over its neck and shoulders, a grizzled mask on its frost-pinched face. I release it from the trap and put the hard, stiff body in my pack. I cut a fresh piece of bait and reset the trap—where one marten has been caught, the chances are good for another.

Encouraged by my luck and in good spirits, I go on, following the trail through the woods, turning and climbing, past windfalls and old, rotted firestumps under the snow. A small covey of spruce hens startles me, flying up from the snow into the trees with a sudden flurry of wings. I hear an alarmed clucking, and see one of the big black and grey birds perched on a spruce bough, sitting very still but watching me with one bright eye.

On a point of hill where a stand of birches form an open grove, I stop for a short time to rest and reset a trap. The sun is up now, just clearing the hills to the south. There is light in the trees, a gold light laid on the blue and white of the snow, and luminous shadows. Frost-crystals glitter in the still air wherever a shaft of sunlight pierces the forest.

This hill is open to the north, and I can see, closer now, the rounded summit of Banner Dome, rose and gold in the low sunlight. The Salchaket hills rising beyond it stand out clearly in the late morning sunlight. I can just see part of the shoulder of hill that rises above the cabin I am going to, six miles yet by this trail. The valleys of Redmond and Glacier creeks lie below me, still in a deep, cold shadow. The sun will not reach there for another month.

I keep a cache on this hill, a fifty-gallon oil drum with a tight lid bolted to it. I brought it here on the sled a couple of years ago, on the last snow of the season. It stands upright between two birches, with its rusty grey paint a little out of place here in the woods, but to me familiar. Inside it I keep a few traps, a spare axe, and some cans of emergency rations in case I should need them. Whatever I leave there stays dry and is safe from bears.

I stand with my pack off for a moment, leaning on my stick. A little wind from somewhere stirs in the birches overhead. I have sometimes thought of building a small camp here, a shelter under these trees. There are places we are attracted to more than others, though I do not always know why. Here, it is the few strong birches, the airy openness of the woods, the view, and the blueberry shrubs under the trees where in good years we have come to pick them. If I were to begin again in some more distant part of the country, to build a home, this is one place I would consider. Perhaps because I know it so well, it is already part of what I think of as home.

I take up my pack and stick, ready to go on. I have put on my mittens, finally; my gloves have gotten damp and become icy and stiff on my hands. From here the trail descends the long north slope into Redmond, a wandering, downhill track through stubby open spruce and over much boggy ground, the longest hill I have to walk. As soon as I start down I am out of the sunlight and into shadow again. It feels at once colder, with a chill blue light in the snowy hummocks.

It is six years now since I cut this part of the trail, and it is worn deep in the moss from our summer walking. So little snow this winter, it makes hard foot and sled travel over the humps and holes. So I walk, going from one side of the trail to the other, springing from hummock to hummock, and balancing myself with my stick. I go at a good pace, anxious to cover the remaining ground before the day is over.

I am halfway down the hill when I find another marten in a trap set on the snow under a spruce. The marten is still alive, tugging at the end of the trap chain, angry and snarling. For a moment I stand and look at the animal. No larger than a house cat, but supple and snaky in body, it lunges at me as if it would bite me.

I take off my pack and approach the marten with my stick. I hit it a sharp blow across its nose, and it falls twitching in the snow. I quickly turn it on its back, lay my stick across its throat and hold it there with one foot, while

I place my other foot on its narrow chest. I can feel the small heart beating through the sole of my moccasin.

As I stand bending over it, the marten partly revives and attempts to free itself, kicking and squirming. But in a short time its heart stops and the slim body relaxes. I remove my foot and the stick, open the trap jaws, and lay the marten out in the snow. It is a large, dark male with thick fur.

It is better to find them dead and frozen, I do not like to kill them this way. Mostly they do not live long when caught in a trap in cold weather; another few hours, and this one too would have frozen.

I reset the trap at the bottom of the tree, placing it on two small dry sticks. I arrange the toggle stick so that the marten will have to step over it and into the trap. I cut a fresh piece of moose gut, and with my axehead I nail it to the tree a foot above the trap. To shield the bait from birds, I break off large twigs of spruce and stand them in the snow around the trap, but leave a small opening for the marten. Finally, I gather some fresh dry snow in the palm of my mitten and sprinkle it around the trap. Thinking that it will do, I put the dead marten into my basket, and go on my way, walking downhill into the cold bottom of Redmond.

The day passes, another hour, another mile. I walk, watching the snow, reading what is written there, the history of the tribes of mice and voles, of grouse and weasel, of redpoll and chickadee, hunter and prey. A scurry here, a trail ended there—something I do not understand, and stop to ponder. I find a trap sprung and nothing in it. I catch another marten, another male, so dark it is almost black. I am in luck today.

Already sunlight is fading from the hilltops. I look at my watch—it is past one, and I still have a good three miles to go. The air feels much colder here in this boggy creek bottom. I do not have a thermometer, but I judge it to be at least in the mid-thirties. There is some ice-fog in this valley, a thin haze in the air above the creek, and that is always a sign of cold and stagnant air.

The trail is slick in places where spring water has seeped up through the snow and frozen into a pale yellow ice. We call it "overflow" or "glaciering," and it is common here in winter. I watch carefully while crossing; the ice is firm, but where ice and snow meet, a little water sometimes steams in the cold air. I feel with my stick as I go, suspecting more water under the snow.

At times while traveling like this, absent in mind or misjudging the snow, I have broken through thin ice and plunged halfway to my knees in slushy water. I have always climbed out quickly, and with so many socks on my feet I have never been wet to my skin. All the same, there is some danger in it, and I do not want to walk the rest of a day with frozen socks and trousers and icy moccasins. Today I am careful, and only once, while crossing a short stretch of overflow, do I look behind me and see water seeping into my tracks from the thin snow.

Twilight comes on slowly across the hills and through the forest; there are no more shadows. I stop again in a stand of spruce above the crossing on Glacier Creek. I have been feeling hungry for some time, so I nibble a frozen cookie from my pack. I have no water to drink, but I remove one of my mittens, and with the warm, bare hand ball up some snow until it is ice, and suck it:

Five years ago we camped here in a tent while hunting moose. That was before we built the cabin, and before I had cut a trail across the creek. The four dogs were with us, tied here among the trees. It was late in the fall, and below zero much of the time, but the tent with its big canvas fly and sheet-iron stove was warm enough. The tent poles still stand here, ready for use, and our cache is still here, a rough platform built into the trees eight feet above me.

I put the three marten I have caught in a sack, tie it, and hang it from a spike high in the cache. I will pick them up on my way home.

I take my pack and go off downhill to the creek—there is no water on the ice, and I am across safely and dry. Then on through the woods and through the swamp, across a low saddle between two hills, tired now, and glad to be getting to the end of it. Fresh marten sign in the snow, and one more marten caught.

I am within half a mile of the cabin, when I find a lynx alive in a marten trap. It has not been caught long, the toes of one big forefoot barely held in the small steel jaws. The animal backs away from me, crouched and growling, its big tawny eyes fastened upon me, and its tufted ears laid back.

I take off my pack, approach carefully, and when I am close enough I hit the lynx hard on its head with my stick. Stunned, the animal sags in the snow. I turn the stick and hit it again with the heavier end, and strike it again, until the lynx sprawls and relaxes, and I am sure that it is dead. For so large an animal, they are easy to kill, but I wait to be certain—I do not want it coming alive in my hands.

Sure that it is dead, I release it from the trap. It is a big male, pale, and a choice fur. I hang the trap in a tree and shoulder my pack. Pleased with this unexpected catch, I drag the big lynx by one hind foot the rest of the way to the cabin, leaving a thread of blood behind me in the snow.

II

The cabin is hidden in a dense stand of spruce on a bench overlooking a small, brushy creek. The creek has no name on the maps, but I have called it Cabin

Creek for the sake of this camp. The ground is perhaps 1700 feet in elevation, and from the cabin I can look up and see the clear slope of Banner Dome another thousand feet above.

With its shed roof sloping north, the cabin sits low and compact in the snow, a pair of moose antlers nailed above a window in the high south wall. There are four dog houses to the rear of it, each of them roofed with a pile of snow-covered hay. A meat rack stands to one side, built high between two stout spruces, and a ladder made of dry poles leans against a tree next to it. A hindquarter of moose hangs from the rack; it is frozen rock hard and well wrapped with canvas to keep it from birds. Just the same, I see that camp-robbers have pecked at it and torn a hole in the canvas. Nothing else can reach it there, seven feet above the ground.

Nothing has changed since I was last here, and there has been no new snow. Squirrel and marten tracks are all around the cabin, and some of them look fresh; I must set a trap somewhere in the yard.

I leave the dead lynx in the snow beside the cabin; I will skin it later. I lean my walking stick by the door and ease the pack from my shoulders—I am a little stiff from the long walk, and it feels good to straighten my back. A thermometer beside the door reads thirty below.

I open the door, go inside, and set my pack down by the bunk. The cabin is cold, as cold as the outdoors, but there is birch bark and kindling by the stove, and I soon have a fire going. The small sheet-iron stove gets hot in a hurry; I watch the pipe to see that it does not burn.

As the cabin warms up I take off my parka, shake the frost from it, and hang it from a hook near the ceiling. The last time I was here I left a pot of moose stew on the floor beside the stove. Now I lift the pot and set it on the edge of the stove to thaw.

I will need water. Much of the time here I scoop up buckets of clean snow to melt on the stove. There is not much water in a bucketful of dry snow, even when the snow is packed firm, and many buckets are needed to make a gallon or two of water. But this year the snow is shallow, and it is dirty from the wind, with dust and twigs and cones from the trees around the cabin.

And so while the light stays I take a bucket and an ice-chisel, and go down to a small pond below the cabin. Under the snow the ice is clear, and in a short time I chop enough of it to fill the bucket. There is water under the ice, but I know from past use of it that the ice itself is cleaner and has a fresher taste.

Before going back up to the cabin I stand for a moment and take in the cold landscape around me. The sun has long gone, light on the hills is deepening, the gold and rose gone to a deeper blue. The cold, still forest, the slim, black spruce, the willows and few gnarled birches are slowly absorbed in the darkness. I stand here in complete silence and solitude, as alone on the ice of this small pond as I would be on the icecap of Greenland. Only far above in the blue depth of the night I hear a little wind on the dome.

I stir myself and begin walking back up the hill to the cabin with my bucket of ice. Before it is dark completely I will want to get in more wood. There are still a few dry, standing poles on the slope behind the cabin, and they are easy to cut. There will be time for that.

Past three o'clock, and it is dark once more. I am done with my chores. Inside the cabin I light a kerosene lamp by the window, and hang my cap and mittens to dry above the stove. The ice has half-melted in the bucket, and the stew is hot and steaming. I have eaten little this day, and I am hungry. I put on the kettle for tea, set out a plate, and cut some bread. The stew is thick and rich; I eat it with the bread and cold, sweetened cranberries from a jar beneath the table.

Fed and feeling at ease, I sit here by the window, drinking tea, relaxing in the warmth of the cabin. The one lamp sends a soft glow over the yellow, peeled logs. When we built this cabin I set the windows low in the walls so that we could look out easily while sitting. That is the way of most old cabins in the woods, where windows must be small and we often sit for hours in the winter, watching the snow. Now I look out the double panes of glass; there is nothing to see out there but the warm light from the window falling to the snow. Beyond that light there is darkness.

I get up from my chair, to put another stick of wood in the stove and more water in the kettle. I am tired from the long walk, and sleepy with the warmth and food. I take off my moccasins and lie down on the bunk with a book, one of a half dozen I keep here. It is Virgil's *Aeneid,* in English. I open the book to the beginning of the poem and read the first few lines. Almost immediately I fall asleep. When I wake up, it is nearly six o'clock; the fire has burned down and the cabin is chilly.

I feel lazy and contented here with nothing urgent to do, but I get up anyway and feed more wood to the stove. On my feet again, moving around, I find that I am still hungry—all day out in the cold, one uses a lot of fuel. So I heat up what remains of the stew and finish it off. Tomorrow I will cut more meat from the quarter hanging outside, and make another pot. What I do not eat, I will leave here to freeze for another day.

Having eaten and rested, I feel a surge of energy. I go outside to bring in the lynx, intending to skin it; I don't want to carry that heavy carcass home. The lynx is already stiff, beginning to freeze. I carry it in and lay it on the floor near the stove to thaw, while I make myself another cup of tea. When I can move its legs easily, I pull one of the big hind feet into my lap and begin to cut with my pocket knife below the heel where the foot-pad begins. The skin is stiff and cold under thick fur as it comes slowly free from the sinew.

But soon in the warmth of the room I begin to see fleas, red fleas, crawling out of the fur. One of them, suddenly strong, jumps onto me, and then to the bunk. That is enough. I put down my knife and take the lynx back outdoors. I will leave it here to freeze, and when I come again the fleas will be dead. I am in no hurry about it, and I do not want fleas in my clothing and in my bunk. Already I begin to itch.

Outside, I leave the lynx in the snow once more, and for a brief time I stand in front of the cabin, to watch and listen. The cold air feels good on my bare skin. The stars are brilliant—Polaris and the Dipper overhead. Through a space in the trees to the south I can see part of the familiar winter figure of Orion, his belt and sword; in the north I see a single bright star I think is Vega. I hear an occasional wind-sigh from the dome, and now and then moving air pulls at the spruces around me.

What does a person do in a place like this, so far away and alone? For one thing, he watches the weather—the stars, the snow and the fire. These are the books he reads most of all. And everything that he does, from bringing in firewood and buckets of snow, to carrying the waste water back outdoors, re-quires that he stand in the open, away from his walls, out of his man-written books and his dreaming head for a while. As I stand here, refreshed by the still-ness and closeness of the night, I think it is a good way to live.

But now the snow is cold through my stocking feet, and I go back in-doors. I wash the dishes and clean the small table, putting things away for the night. I hang up my trousers and wool shirts, and hang my socks on a line near the ceiling. There is still some hot water in the kettle; I pour it into a basin, cool it with a cup of cold water from the bucket, and wash my face and hands. Having dried myself and brushed my teeth, I am ready for bed.

Lying on the bunk once more, with the lamp by my left shoulder, I pick up my book and try to read again. A page, and then another. My mind fills with images: a fire in the night, Aeneas, and the flight from Troy. I drowse, then wake again. I remember Fred Campbell lying on his cot in the Lake cabin that good fall many years ago, the Bible held overhead in his hand as he tried to read. And soon he was sleeping, the book fallen to his chest. The same page night after night. I was amused at him then, but older now I see the same thing happens to me. It is the plain life, the air, the cold, the hard work; and having eaten, the body rests and the mind turns to sleep.

I wake once more and put away my book. I get up from the bunk and bank the fire, laying some half-green sticks of birch on the coals, and close down the draft. Ice has melted in the bucket, there is plenty of water for the morning.

I blow out the lamp and settle down in the sleeping bag, pulling it around my shoulders. I look into the dark cabin, and to the starlight on the snow outside. At any time here, away from the river and the sound of traffic on the road, I may hear other sounds—a moose in the creek bottom, breaking brush, a coyote on a ridge a mile away, or an owl in the spruce branches above the cabin. Often it is the wind I hear, a whispering, rushy sound in the boughs. Only sometimes when the wind blows strongly from the south I hear a diesel on the road toward Fairbanks, changing gears in the canyon. And once, far away on a warm south wind, the sound of dogs barking at Richardson.

I spend another day at the cabin, taking my time. I loaf and read, cut more wood and chop some ice. I thaw and skin the one marten, and roll the fur in a sack to take with me; it will mean a pound or two less to carry, and more room in the basket. With the ladder and a block and tackle, I take down the moose quarter, unwrap it, and saw a piece of meat from the round. It was killed late, and is not fat meat, but having hung frozen for so long it is tender enough. The outside of the meat is darkened and dried and will need to be trimmed. I put the piece I have cut on a board near the stove to thaw.

In the afternoon I go up the creek to look at some snares I have set there. I find that nothing has come but one lynx, and he pushed a snare aside. It may have been the one I caught.

From the creek I climb a couple of miles up the ridge toward the dome. It is easy walking in the light snow, and here on higher ground there is bright sunlight and the air seems to be warmer. There is plenty of marten sign in the open spruce mixed with aspen, and I set two traps.

I mark the days on a calendar, drawing a circle around the dates. The calendar shows a ship, full-rigged in the old romantic style of the sea, hard-driven from Cape Horn, or following the trades homeward. This calendar comes from Canada, and bears the trade name of *John Leckie & Company, Ltd., Edmonton, Alberta. Marine Supplies and Hardware.* Three years ago I bought a whitefish net from them by mail, and now each year they send me a calendar. Since we have others at home, I bring them here. They look fine against the log walls, and brighten their place by the window.

I remember how we built this cabin, the many hours here, the long walks in the rain that turned into snow. I had the big wall tent pitched in the woods, near where the cabin is now, a cot to sleep on, and the small iron stove with its pipe stuck through a piece of sheet metal in the tent roof. I would come here from home in the afternoons, packing some food, lumber and tools. I worked on the cabin until dark, and slept overnight in the tent. Again the next morning, from the first light, I worked hard, trimming and fitting the logs, then walked home in the afternoon over the wet hills.

I worked from early August until mid–October, a few hours or a day at a time. Fall came early that year, and toward the end of it I was scraping frozen bark from the roof poles, determined to make a clean job of it. There was no dry sod for the roof, so we went to the creek to cut big batts of half-frozen moss and carry them up the hill one at a time. And finally we had a roof on the cabin, the door hung and windows fitted, and a fire in the stove.

That fall I shot a moose from the front of the cabin just at dusk. It was a long shot down into the flat below the hill, the moose only a dark shape in the frozen grass. Then came the work that evening and part of the next day, cutting the meat into quarters and dragging them up the hill to the camp. We hung the meat high on the rack I built that morning behind the cabin. We had a long walk home that afternoon in wet snow, carrying with us a chunk of the ribs, the tongue, the heart, the kidneys and liver. It was a hard fall, in many ways the hardest and poorest year I have spent in the north.

But the time and work was worth it, for here is the cabin now, snug and warm. No matter how long it stands here, it will always seem like a new thing, strange to come upon far in these hills at the end of a long hike, and to know we have built it.

I look around me, at the floor, at the walls, at the ceiling, the logs and poles. When the cabin was first built we had only hay for a floor, a deep bed of it spread on the moss. There was nothing to sweep or to clean, and each fall I brought in a few armloads of new hay to freshen the floor. But as cheery and rustic as it was, there were things about that hay floor I never liked. Frost was deep in the ground beneath the hay, and because the cabin went unoccupied for many weeks in winter, it was cold and damp to live in until the fire had thawed it. Mice and squirrels tunneled through the moss and into the cabin, and made a mess in the bedding. And so one spring before the trail went soft, I brought sledloads of lumber here. In August of that year I came and worked three days, putting in a proper floor. Now it is dry and warm, and the mice stay out. I sweep it now and then.

There is only the one room, eight feet by twelve feet, but it is large enough for a camp in the woods. The door opens west, and the two windows face north and south. Overhead I have cut a round hole in one wall for a vent, and fitted it with a metal lid. The peeled poles of the ceiling are still clean and bright yellow; smoke has not darkened them and the roof has never leaked.

Here at the back of the room I have built two bunks, one above the other, with a small ladder at one end to reach the upper. The table I eat from and the work table across the room are both fashioned from two-inch wooden pegs driven into auger holes in the logs. Boards are laid across the pegs and nailed in place. The few shelves are made in the same way. It is a simple means of making the essential furniture, and there are no table legs to get in the way underfoot.

Here and there I have driven nails and spikes into the walls; some odds and ends of clothing hung there, a few traps, a piece of rope. A .22 rifle is propped on a couple of spikes at the foot of the lower bunk. Behind the stove hang pots and washpans, and into one log by the door I have driven a twelve-inch spike from which I hang the dog harness to dry.

There have been other winters here, not easy ones. I have come after a heavy snowfall, with the dogs dead-tired and me walking behind or in front of the sled, breaking trail. We were five or six hours getting here, the traps buried, something caught but hard to find in the snow. And then would come the journey home the next day over a soft, half-broken trail with a load of meat and three dogs; me again walking behind, steering, holding the snubline while the dogs pulled ahead.

Fifty years ago in the twilight of the goldrush, wagon roads and freight trails were still in use here. Though they are badly overgrown now and deeply rutted, I can still walk parts of them for a short distance; they go up the creek, across the divide and down Shamrock, to the Salcha River and Birch Lake, many miles from here. It is strange to think of it then, the country still busy with people coming and going, the dogs and horses, freight and men.

No one comes here now but Jo and myself, the dogs and us, the moose and the marten. Only once, three years ago, two men came from Banner Creek with a Cat to prospect on Glacier Creek, two miles over the hill. They cleared a small piece of ground on the beach above the creek, but they found nothing there and did not come back. I am glad of that, I like having this country to myself.

I am living out a dream in these woods. Old dreams of the Far North, old stories read and absorbed: of snow and dogs, of moose and lynx, and of all that is still native to these unpeople places. Nothing I have yet done in life pleases me as much as this. And yet it seems only half-deliberate, as if I had followed a scent on the wind and found myself in this place. Having come, I will have to stay, there's no way back.

The hunting and fishing, the wild fruit, the trapping, the wood that we burn and the food that we eat—it is all given to us by the country. The fur of this marten is lovely when held in the light, shaken so that the hair stands from the pelt. And meat of the moose is good to have; it keeps us fed and warm inside, and I pay no butcher for it. Yet I cannot trap and kill without thought or emotion, and it may be that the killing wounds me also in some small but deadly way. Life is here equally in sunlight and frost, in the thriving blood and sap of things, in their decay and sudden death.

It can be hard and cruel sometimes, as we are prepared to see it clearly. I put the beats to death for my own purposes, as the lynx kills the rabbit, the marten the squirrel, and the weasel the mouse. Life is filled with contradictions—confused and doubting in the heart of a man, or it is straight as an arrow and full of purpose.

I look at my hands and flex my fingers. They have handled much, done things I hardly dreamed of doing when I was younger. I have woven my nets with them and made my snares. I have pulled the trigger of my rifle many times and watched a bird fall or a moose crumple to the ground. And with these hands I have gone deep into the hot body of the animal, and torn from it the still-quivering tissue of lungs, heart, liver and guts. There is blood under the nails, dirt and grease in the cracks of the finger joints.

I have learned to do these things, and do them well, as if I'd come into something for which I had a native gift. And a troubling thought will return sometimes: having done so much, would I kill a man? I do not know. I might if I had to, in anger, perhaps, passion of defense or revenge. But not, I think, in the cold, judging light of the law. I have seen a war, a dead man floating in the sea off a Pacific island, and I was there. By my presence alone, I took part in many deaths. I cannot pretend that I am free and guiltless. Justice evades us; the forest with all its ancient scarcity and peril is still within us, and it may be that we will never know a world not haunted in some way by a return to that night of the spirit where the hangman adjusts his noose and the executioner hones his axe to perfection.

I put these thoughts away, and look out the window to the sunlit snow on the hillside across the creek. In this wilderness life I have found a way to touch the world once more. One way. To live the life that is here to be lived, as nearly as I can without that other—clock hands, hours and wages. I relive each day the ancient expectation of the hunt—the setting out, and the trail at dawn. What will we find today?

I leave some of my mankindness behind me for a while and become part tree, a creature of the snow. It is a long way back, and mostly in shadow. I see a little there, not much, but what I see will never be destroyed.

I may not always be here in these woods. The trails I have made will last a long time; this cabin will stand twenty years at least before it falls. I can imagine a greater silence, a deeper shadow where I am standing, but what I have loved will always be here.

Night, and the day passes. Evening, another pot of stew—rice and chunks of meat, dried vegetables, onions, a little fat, and spice for flavor. The weather holding steady, still twenty-nine below. I continue to hear some wind on the dome.

I rise early on the morning of the third day, make my breakfast by lamplight. Oats and bread, some meat in the frypan. Might as well feed up, it will be another long day. I take my time this morning, dressing slowly, putting things away. I bring in more wood and stack it by the stove. Outside in the clear frost I hang the frozen lynx high on the rack; nothing will bother it there. Dawn comes slowly over the hills, lighting the snowy dome.

I pack my gear—the small axe again, a few traps. One marten skin to carry, three marten to pick up on the way. My pack will be as heavy as before.

The fire slowly dies and the cabin grows cool again. I fill a shallow pan with the remaining water and place it on the stove. It will freeze, and I will have water quickly the next time here. I put away my saw and the big axe; there is bark and kindling at hand when I come again. I close the door and latch it. I look around with care, at the cabin and the yard—everything is in place. I will be back in a week or ten days.

It is minus twenty-four degrees this morning; some thin clouds are forming, it may snow by evening. I take my pack and, stick in hand, set off up the trail toward Glacier Creek.

III

It is evening again, and I have come home by the river from Banner Creek. I came by another trail today, over the long divide between Redmond and Banner, another part of the country. It was hard walking in places; much of it is steep sidehill scraped and gouged by a Cat trail made many years ago, with several small springs and water under the snow.

I met with some wind on a high and open ridge where I could look east into the rose-grey morning sunlight. I felt too warm from climbing, and stopped to take the lining out of my parka. The wind came only now and then, not cold, a little loose snow blowing across the open trail.

Few traps and no marten there, but plenty of moose sign in the willows going down into Banner. One big red fox caught somehow in a trap set
for marten, caught by the toes only, and not for long. He watched me as I came
near, stretched out on the short chain, his eyes enormous with alertness and
fear. I thought of trying to knock him out with a blow from my stick, so that I
could free him from the trap and let him go. But I finally killed him, breaking
his neck as I have learned to do. I put him into my pack with the others, tying
him down, and took the trap with me.

I was close to Banner Creek, walking slowly on a straight and open
stretch of the trail, when I came upon a set of wolf tracks. They were soon
joined by others, and I saw that two, possibly three wolves had come out of the
dense, sloping spruce wood to the north, and finding my foot trail, had turned
to follow it.

Thinking they might return in a few days, I set two heavy snares in
that open place, a few yards apart from each other. I propped the nooses over
my trail, supporting them with some brush cut from the woods close by and
stuck down in the scant snow. I tried to make the sets appear as natural as I
could, and looking at them afterwards from a distance, it seemed to me that
they might work. Yet somehow I do not expect much from them; the wind
may blow them down, or the wolves go around them.

I went on down Banner Creek, walking the old road between the
spruce and the birch, the snow so light this winter it hardly fills the frozen ruts.
A side path turning off into the woods brought me into a brushy flat where I
keep an ancient and tilting cabin. I stopped there to build a fire in the stove and
make some tea. My feet were sore from walking that hard trail in soft moccasins, and it felt good to take off the pack and rest for a while. The cabin is old
and damp and does not heat well, but it is better than no camp at all.

Afterwards I searched the brushed-in trails near the cabin where I
have set snares for lynx. But I have caught nothing there this winter. Today
one snare was missing; something had made off with it—what? The snow told
me nothing.

In late afternoon I walked the last mile home along the Tanana,
through the woods on the steep hillside between the river and the highway.
The sun was gone, and light on the river, on the ice, a steely grey. Clouds were
building a heavy darkness in the west. Sounds came to me along the river:
water running somewhere out on the ice, a dog barking at Richardson. A car
went by on the road, going to Fairbanks, going to Delta. People.

I sit here now, the long day over and the pack gone from my shoulders
at last. My heavy clothing removed, moccasins hung up to dry, gloves and mit-

tens drying on the rack above the stove. Half-sleepy, warmed by the fire, while Jo makes supper, and we talk. What happened while I was gone? Yesterday, today, the day before. A moose on the hill, water and wood, and no one came. The world is still the same, it will be the same tomorrow.

I am happy deep inside. Not the mind-tiredness of too much thought, of thoughts that pursue each other endlessly in that forest of nerves, anxiety and fear. But a stretching kind of tiredness, the ease and satisfaction of the time well spent, and of the deep self renewed.

Tomorrow, marten to skin and meat to cut. What else? It is two degrees below zero this evening. The wind is blowing.

The Open Boat

S tephen Crane (1871–1900) burst upon the literary scene of his day
with a firecracker of a novel, *The Red Badge of Courage,* published in
1895. Although he had never seen war, Crane's evocative tale of the
Civil War was an immediate triumph and remains an American classic
to this day.

Ambrose Bierce, one of the most popular writers of that era, said of
Crane, "This young man has the power to feel. He knows nothing of war, yet
he is drenched in blood. Most beginners who deal with this subject spatter
themselves with ink."

Crane's success with *The Red Badge of Courage* led to his later career as
a war correspondent. A shipwreck off Cuba inspired this autobiographical
story. The experiences that enabled Crane to write "The Open Boat" resulted
in health problems which contributed to Crane's early demise from consump-
tion in 1900.

Among the many striking qualities of this story, the first paragraph
strikes me as one of the best short story openings ever written.

★　★　★　★　★

None of them knew the color of the sky. Their eyes glanced level, and were
fastened upon the waves that swept toward them. These waves were of the hue
of slate, save for the tops, which were of foaming white, and all of the men
knew the colors of the sea. The horizon narrowed and widened, and dipped
and rose, and at all times its edge was jagged with waves that seemed thrust up
in points like rocks. Many a man ought to have a bath-tub larger than the boat
which here rode upon the sea. These waves were most wrongfully and bar-

barously abrupt and tall, and each froth top was a problem in small boat navigation.

The cook squatted in the bottom and looked with both eyes at the six inches of gunwale which separated him from the ocean. His sleeves were rolled over his fat forearms, and two flaps of his unbuttoned vest dangled as he bent to bail out the boat. Often he said: "Gawd! That was a narrow clip." As he remarked it he invariably gazed eastward over the broken sea.

The oiler, steering with one of the two oars in the boat, sometimes raised himself suddenly to keep clear of water that swirled in over the stern. It was a thin little oar and it seemed often ready to snap.

The correspondent, pulling at the other oar, watched the waves and wondered why he was there.

The injured captain, lying in the bow, was at this time buried in that profound dejection and indifference which comes, temporarily at least, to even the bravest and most enduring when, willy-nilly, the firm fails, the army loses, the ship goes down. The mind of the master of a vessel is rooted deep in the timbers of her, though he commanded for a day or a decade, and this captain had on him the stern impression of a scene in the grays of dawn of seven turned faces, and later a stump of a top mast with a white ball on it that slashed to and fro at the waves, went low and lower, and down. Thereafter there was something strange in his voice. Although steady, it was deep with mourning, and of a quality beyond oration or tears.

"Keep 'er a little more south, Billie," said he.

" 'A little more south,' sir," said the oiler in the stern.

A seat in this boat was not unlike a seat upon a bucking broncho, and by the same token, a broncho is not much smaller. The craft pranced and reared, and plunged like an animal. As each wave came, and she rose for it, she seemed like a horse making at a fence outrageously high. The manner of her scramble over these walls of water is a mystic thing, and, moreover, at the top of them were ordinarily these problems in white water, the foam racing down from the summit of each wave, requiring a new leap, and a leap from the air. Then, after scornfully bumping a crest, she would slide, and race, and splash down a long incline, and arrive bobbing and nodding in front of the next menace.

A singular disadvantage of the sea lies in the fact that after successfully surmounting one wave you discover that there is another behind it just as important and just as nervously anxious to do something effective in the way of swamping boats. In a ten-foot dingey one can get an idea of the resources of the sea in the line of waves that is not probable to the average experience which is never at sea in a dingey. As each slatey wall of water approached, it shut all else from the view of the men in the boat, and it was not difficult to imagine that this particular wave was the final outburst of the ocean, the last effort of the grim water. There was a terrible grace in the move of the waves, and they came in silence, save for the snarling of the crests.

In the wan light, the faces of the men must have been gray. Their eyes must have glinted in strange ways as they gazed steadily astern. Viewed from a balcony, the whole thing would doubtless have been weirdly picturesque. But the men in the boat had no time to see it, and if they had had leisure there were other things to occupy their minds. The sun swung steadily up the sky, and they knew it was broad day because the color of the sea changed from slate to emerald green, streaked with amber lights, and the foam was like tumbling snow. The process of the breaking day was unknown to them. They were aware only of this effect upon the color of the waves that rolled toward them.

In disjointed sentences the cook and the correspondent argued as to the difference between a life-saving station and a house of refuge. The cook had said: "There's a house of refuge just north of the Mosquito Inlet Light, and as soon as they see us, they'll come off in their boat and pick us up."

"As soon as who see us?" said the correspondent.

"The crew," said the cook.

"Houses of refuge don't have crews," said the correspondent. "As I understand them, they are only places where clothes and grub are stored for the benefit of shipwrecked people. They don't carry crews."

"Oh, yes, they do," said the cook.

"No, they don't," said the correspondent.

"Well, we're not there yet, anyhow," said the oiler, in the stern.

"Well," said the cook, "perhaps it's not a house of refuge that I'm thinking of as being near Mosquito Inlet Light. Perhaps it's a life-saving station."

"We're not there yet," said the oiler, in the stern.

II

As the boat bounced from the top of each wave, the wind tore through the hair of the hatless men, and as the craft plopped her stern down again the spray splashed past them. The crest of each of these waves was a hill, from the top of which the men surveyed, for a moment, a broad tumultuous expanse, shining and wind-driven. It was probably splendid. It was probably glorious, this play of the free sea, wild with lights of emerald and white and amber.

"Bully good thing it's an on-shore wind," said the cook. "If not, where would we be? Wouldn't have a show."

"That's right," said the correspondent.

The busy oiler nodded his assent.

Then the captain, in the bow, chuckled in a way that expressed humor, contempt, tragedy, all in one. "Do you think we've got much of a show now, boys?" said he.

Whereupon the three were silent, save for a trifle of hemming and hawing. To express any particular optimism at this time they felt to be childish and stupid, but they all doubtless possessed this sense of the situation in their mind. A young man thinks doggedly at such times. On the other hand, the ethics of their condition was decidedly against any open suggestion of hopelessness. So they were silent.

"Oh, well," said the captain, soothing his children, "We'll get ashore all right."

But there was that in his tone which made them think, so the oiler quoth: "Yes! If this wind holds!"

The cook was bailing: "Yes! If we don't catch hell in the surf."

Canton flannel gulls flew near and far. Sometimes they sat down on the sea, near patches of brown seaweed that rolled on the waves with a movement like carpets on a line in a gale. The birds sat comfortably in groups, and they were envied by some in the dingey, for the wrath of the sea was no more to them than it was to a covey of prairie chickens a thousand miles inland. Often they came very close and stared at the men with black bead-like eyes. At these times they were uncanny and sinister in their unblinking scrutiny, and the men hooted angrily at them, telling them to be gone. One came, and evidently decided to alight on the top of the captain's head. The bird flew parallel to the boat and did not circle, but made short sidelong jumps in the air in chicken fashion. His black eyes were wistfully fixed upon the captain's head. "Ugly brute," said the oiler to the bird. "You look as if you were made with a jack-knife." The cook and the correspondent swore darkly at the creature. The captain naturally wished to knock it away with the end of the heavy painter; but he did not dare do it, because anything resembling an emphatic gesture would have capsized this freighted boat, and so with his open hand, the captain gently and carefully waved the gull away. After it had been discouraged from the pursuit the captain breathed easier on account of his hair, and others breathed easier because the bird struck their minds at this time as being somehow gruesome and ominous.

In the meantime the oiler and the correspondent rowed. And also they rowed.

They sat together in the same seat, and each rowed an oar. Then the oiler took both oars; then the correspondent took both oars; then the oiler; then the correspondent. They rowed and they rowed. The very ticklish part of the business was when the time came for the reclining one in the stern to take his turn at the oars. By the very last star of truth, it is easier to steal eggs from under a hen than it was to change seats in the dingey. First the man in the stern slid his hand along the thwart and moved with care, as if he were of Sèvres. Then the man in the rowing seat slid his hand along the other thwart. It was all done with the most extraordinary care. As the two sidled past each other, the whole party kept watchful eyes on the coming wave, and the captain cried: "Look out now! Steady there!"

The brown mats of seaweed that appeared from time to time were like islands, bits of earth. They were traveling, apparently, neither one way nor the other. They were, to all intents, stationary. They informed the men in the boat that it was making progress slowly toward the land.

The captain, rearing cautiously in the bow, after the dingey soared on a great swell, said that he had seen the lighthouse at Mosquito Inlet. Presently the cook remarked that he had seen it. The correspondent was at the oars then, and for some reason he too wished to look at the lighthouse, but his back was toward the far shore and the waves were important, and for some time he could not seize an opportunity to turn his head. But at last there came a wave more gentle than the others, and when at the crest of it he swiftly scoured the western horizon.

"See it?" said the captain.

"No," said the correspondent slowly, "I didn't see anything."

"Look again," said the captain. He pointed. "It's exactly in that direction."

At the top of another wave, the correspondent did as he was bid, and this time his eyes chanced on a small still thing on the edge of the swaying horizon. It was precisely like the point of a pin. It took an anxious eye to find a lighthouse so tiny.

"Think we'll make it, captain?"

"If this wind holds and the boat don't swamp, we can't do much else," said the captain.

The little boat, lifted by each towering sea, and splashed viciously by the crests, made progress that in the absence of seaweed was not apparent to those in her. She seemed just a wee thing wallowing, miraculously top up, at the mercy of five oceans. Occasionally, a great spread of water, like white flames, swarmed into her.

"Bail her, cook," said the captain serenely.

"All right, captain," said the cheerful cook.

III

It would be difficult to describe the subtle brotherhood of men that was here established on the seas. No one said that it was so. No one mentioned it. But it dwelt in the boat, and each man felt it warm him. They were a captain, an oiler, a cook and a correspondent, and they were friends, friends in a more curiously iron-bound degree than may be common. The hurt captain, lying against the water jar in the bow, spoke always in a low voice and calmly, but he could never command a more ready and swiftly obedient crew than the motley three of the dingey. It was more than a mere recognition of what was best for the common safety. There was surely in it a quality that was personal and heartfelt. And after this devotion to the commander of the boat there was this comradeship that the correspondent, for instance, who had been taught to be cynical of men, knew even at the time was the best experience of his life. But no one said that it was so. No one mentioned it.

"I wish we had a sail," remarked the captain. "We might try my overcoat on the end of an oar and give you two boys a chance to rest." So the cook and the correspondent held the mast and spread wide the overcoat. The oiler steered, and the little boat made good way with her new rig. Sometimes the oiler had to scull sharply to keep a sea from breaking into the boat, but otherwise sailing was a success.

Meanwhile the lighthouse had been growing slowly larger. It had now almost assumed color, and appeared like a little gray shadow on the sky. The man at the oars could not be prevented from turning his head rather often to try for a glimpse of this little gray shadow.

At last, from the top of each wave the men in the tossing boat could see land. Even as the lighthouse was an upright shadow on the sky, this land seemed but a long black shadow on the sea. It certainly was thinner than paper. "We must be about opposite New Smyrna," said the cook, who had coasted this shore often in schooners. "Captain, by the way, I believe they abandoned that life-saving station there about a year ago."

"Did they?" said the captain.

The wind slowly died away. The cook and the correspondent were not now obliged to slave in order to hold high the oar. But the waves continued their old impetuous swooping at the dingey, and the little craft, no longer under way, struggled woundily over them. The oiler or the correspondent took the oars again.

Shipwrecks are *àpropos* of nothing. If men could only train for them and have them occur when the men had reached pink condition, there would be less drowning at sea. Of the four in the dingey none had slept any time worth mentioning for two days and two nights previous to embarking in the dingey, and in the excitement of clambering about the deck of a foundering ship they had also forgotten to eat heartily.

For these reasons, and for others, neither the oiler nor the correspondent was fond of rowing at this time. The correspondent wondered ingenuously how in the name of all that was sane could there be people who thought it amusing to row a boat. It was not an amusement; it was a diabolical punishment, and even a genius of mental aberrations could never conclude that it was anything but a horror to the muscles and a crime against the back. He mentioned to the boat in general how the amusement of rowing struck him, and the weary-faced oiler smiled in full sympathy. Previously to the foundering, by the way, the oiler had worked double-watch in the engine-room of the ship.

"Take her easy, now, boys," said the captain. "Don't spend yourselves. If we have to run a surf you'll need all your strength, because we'll sure have to swim for it. Take your time."

Slowly the land arose from the sea. From a black line it became a line of black and a line of white, trees and sand. Finally, the captain said that he could make out a house on the shore. "That's the house of refuge, sure," said the cook. "They'll see us before long, and come out after us."

The distant lighthouse reared high. "The keeper ought to be able to make us out now, if he's looking through a glass," said the captain. "He'll notify the life-saving people."

"None of those other boats could have got ashore to give word of the wreck," said the oiler, in a low voice. "Else the lifeboat would be out hunting us."

Slowly and beautifully the land loomed out of the sea. The wind came again. It had veered from the northeast to the southeast. Finally, a new sound struck the ears of the men in the boat. It was the low thunder of the surf on the shore. "We'll never be able to make the lighthouse now," said the captain. "Swing her head a little more north, Billie," said he.

" 'A little more north,' sir," said the oiler.

Whereupon the little boat turned her nose once more down the wind, and all but the oarsman watched the shore grow. Under the influence of this expansion doubt and direful apprehension was leaving the minds of the men. The management of the boat was still most absorbing, but it could not prevent a quiet cheerfulness. In an hour, perhaps, they would be ashore.

Their backbones had become thoroughly used to balancing in the boat, and they now rode this wild colt of a dingey like circus men. The correspondent thought that he had been drenched to the skin, but happening to feel in the top pocket of his coat, he found therein eight cigars. Four of them were soaked with sea water; four were perfectly scatheless. After a search, somebody produced three dry matches, and thereupon the four waifs rode impudently in their little boat, and with an assurance of an impending rescue shining in their eyes, puffed at the big cigars and judged well and ill of all men. Everybody took a drink of water.

IV

"Cook," remarked the captain, "there don't seem to be any signs of life about your house of refuge."

"No," replied the cook. "Funny they don't see us!"

A broad stretch of lowly coast lay before the eyes of the men. It was of dunes topped with dark vegetation. The roar of the surf was plain, and sometimes they could see the white lip of a wave as it spun up the beach. A tiny house was blocked out black upon the sky. Southward, the slim lighthouse lifted its little gray length.

Tide, wind, and waves were swinging the dingey northward. "Funny they don't see us," said the men.

The surf's roar was here dulled, but its tone was, nevertheless, thunderous and mighty. As the boat swam over the great rollers, the men sat listening to this roar. "We'll swamp sure," said everybody.

It is fair to say here that there was not a life-saving station within twenty miles in either direction, but the men did not know this fact, and in consequence they made dark and opprobrious remarks concerning the eyesight of the nation's life-savers. Four scowling men sat in the dingey and surpassed records in the invention of epithets.

"Funny they don't see us."

The lightheartedness of a former time had completely faded. To their sharpened minds it was easy to conjure pictures of all kinds of incompetency and blindness and, indeed, cowardice. There was the shore of the populous land, and it was bitter and bitter to them that from it came no sign.

"Well," said the captain, ultimately, "I suppose we'll have to make a try for ourselves. If we stay out here too long, we'll none of us have strength left to swim after the boat swamps."

And so the oiler, who was at the oars, turned the boat straight for the shore. There was a sudden tightening of muscle. There was some thinking.

"If we don't all get ashore—" said the captain. "If we don't all get ashore, I suppose you fellows know where to send news of my finish?"

They then briefly exchanged some addresses and admonitions. As for the reflections of the men, there was a great deal of rage in them. Perchance they might be formulated thus: "If I am going to be drowned—if I am going to be drowned—if I am going to be drowned, why, in the name of the seven mad gods who rule the sea, was I allowed to come thus far and contemplate sand and trees? Was I brought here merely to have my nose dragged away as I was about to nibble the sacred cheese of life? It is preposterous. If this old ninny woman, Fate, cannot do better than this, she should be deprived of the management of men's fortunes. She is an old hen who knows not her intention. If she has decided to drown me, why did she not do it in the beginning and save me all this trouble? The whole affair is absurd. . . . But no, she cannot mean to drown me. She dare not drown me. She cannot drown me. Not after all this work." Afterward the man might have had an impulse to shake his fist at the clouds: "Just you drown me, now, and then hear what I call you!"

The billows that came at this time were more formidable. They seemed always just about to break and roll over the little boat in a turmoil of foam. There was a preparatory and long growl in the speech of them. No mind unused to the sea would have concluded that the dingey could ascend these sheer heights in time. The shore was still afar. The oiler was a wily surfman. "Boys," he said swiftly, "she won't live three minutes more, and we're too far out to swim. Shall I take her to sea again, captain?"

"Yes! Go ahead!" said the captain.

This oiler, by a series of quick miracles, and fast and steady oarsmanship, turned the boat in the middle of the surf and took her safety to sea again.

There was a considerable silence as the boat bumped over the furrowed sea to deeper water. Then somebody in gloom spoke. "Well, anyhow, they must have seen us from the shore by now."

The gulls went in slanting flight up the wind toward the gray desolate east. A squall, marked by dingy clouds, and clouds brick red, like smoke from a burning building, appeared from the southeast.

"What do you think of those life-saving people? Ain't they peaches?"

"Funny they haven't seen us."

"Maybe they think we're out here for sport! Maybe they think we're fishin'. Maybe they think we're damned fools."

It was a long afternoon. A changed tide tried to force them southward, but the wind and wave said northward. Far ahead, where coastline, sea, and sky formed their mighty angle, there were little dots which seemed to indicate a city on the shore.

"St. Augustine?"

The captain shook his head. "Too near Mosquito Inlet."

And the oiler rowed, and then the correspondent rowed. Then the oiler rowed. It was a weary business. The human back can become the seat of more aches and pains than are registered in books for the composite anatomy of a regiment. It is a limited area, but it can become the theater of innumerable muscular conflicts, tangles, wrenches, knots, and other comforts.

"Did you ever like to row, Billie?" asked the correspondent.

"No," said the oiler. "Hang it!"

When one exchanged the rowing seat for a place in the bottom of the boat, he suffered a bodily depression that caused him to be careless of everything save an obligation to wiggle one finger. There was cold sea water swashing to and fro in the boat, and he lay in it. His head, pillowed on a thwart, was within an inch of the swirl of a wave crest, and sometimes a particularly obstreperous sea came in-board and drenched him once more. But these matters did not annoy him. It is almost certain that if the boat had capsized he would have tumbled comfortably out upon the ocean as if he felt sure that it was a great soft mattress.

"Look! There's a man on the shore!"

"Where?"

"There! See 'im? See 'im?"

"Yes, sure! He's walking along."

"Now he's stopped. Look! He's facing us!"

"He's waving at us!"

"So he is! By thunder!"

"Ah, now we're all right! Now we're all right! There'll be a boat out here for us in half an hour."

"He's going on. He's running. He's going up to that house there."

The remote beach seemed lower than the sea, and it required a searching glance to discern the little black figure. The captain saw a floating stick and they rowed to it. A bath towel was by some weird chance in the boat, and, tying this on the stick, the captain waved it. The oarsman did not dare turn his head, so he was obliged to ask questions.

"What's he doing now?"

"He's standing still again. He's looking, I think. . . . There he goes again. Toward the house. . . . Now he's stopped again."

"Is he waving at us?"

"No, not now! he was, though."

"Look! There comes another man!"

"He's running."

"Look at him go, would you."

"Why, he's on a bicycle. Now he's met the other man. They're both waving at us. Look!"

"There comes something up the beach."

"What the devil is that thing?"

"Why it looks like a boat."

"Why, certainly it's a boat."

"No, it's on wheels."

"Yes, so it is. Well, that must be the life-boat. They drag them along shore on a wagon."

"That's the life-boat, sure."

"No, by—, it's—it's an omnibus."

"I tell you it's a life-boat."

"It is not! It's an omnibus. I can see it plain. See? One of these big hotel omnibuses."

"By thunder, you're right. It's an omnibus, sure as fate. What do you suppose they are doing with an omnibus? Maybe they are going around collecting the life-crew, hey?"

"That's it, likely. Look! There's a fellow waving a little black flag. He's standing on the steps of the omnibus. There come those other two fellows. Now they're all talking together. Look at the fellow with the flag. Maybe he ain't waving it."

"That ain't a flag, is it? That's his coat. Why, certainly, that's his coat."

"So it is. It's his coat. He's taken it off and is waving it around his head. But would you look at him swing it."

"Oh, say, there isn't any life-saving station there. That's just a winter resort hotel omnibus that has brought over some of the boarders to see us drown."

"What's that idiot with the coat mean? What's he signaling, anyhow?"

"It looks as if he were trying to tell us to go north. There must be a life-saving station up there."

"No! He thinks we're fishing. Just giving us a merry hand. See? Ah, there, Willie!"

"Well, I wish I could make something out of those signals. What do you suppose he means?"

"He don't mean anything. He's just playing."

"Well, if he'd just signal us to try the surf again, or to go to sea and wait, or go north, or go south, or go to hell—there would be some reason in it. But look at him. He just stands there and keeps his coat revolving like a wheel. The ass!"

"There come more people."

"Now there's quite a mob. Look! Isn't that a boat?"

"Where? Oh, I see where you mean. No, that's no boat."

"That fellow is still waving his coat."

"He must think we like to see him do that. Why don't he quit it? It don't mean anything."

"I don't know. I think he is trying to make us go north. It must be that there's a life-saving station there somewhere."

"Say, he ain't tired yet. Look at 'im wave."

"Wonder how long he can keep that up. He's been revolving his coat ever since he caught sight of us. He's an idiot. Why aren't they getting men to bring a boat out? A fishing boat—one of those big yawls—could come out here all right. Why don't he do something?"

"Oh, it's all right, now."

"They'll have a boat out here for us in less than no time, now that they've seen us."

A faint yellow tone came into the sky over the low land. The shadows on the sea slowly deepened. The wind bore coldness with it, and the men began to shiver.

"Holy smoke!" said one, allowing his voice to express his impious mood, "if we keep on monkeying out here! If we've got to flounder out here all night!"

"Oh, we'll never have to stay here all night! Don't you worry. They've seen us now, and it won't be long before they'll come chasing out after us."

The shore grew dusky. The man waving a coat blended gradually into this gloom, and it swallowed in the same manner the omnibus and the group of people. The spray, when it dashed uproariously over the side, made the voyagers shrink and swear like men who were being branded.

"I'd like to catch the chump who waved the coat. I feel like soaking him one, just for luck."

"Why? What did he do?"

"Oh, nothing, but then he seemed so damned cheerful."

In the meantime the oiler rowed, and then the correspondent rowed, and then the oiler rowed. Gray-faced and bowed forward, they mechanically, turn by turn, plied the leaden oars. The form of the lighthouse had vanished from the southern horizon, but finally a pale star appeared, just lifting from the sea. The streaked saffron in the west passed before the all-merging darkness, and the sea to the east was black. The land had vanished, and was expressed only by the low and drear thunder of the surf.

"If I am going to be drowned—if I am going to be drowned—if I am going to be drowned, why, in the name of the seven mad gods who rule the sea, was I allowed to come thus far and contemplate sand and trees? Was I brought here merely to have my nose dragged away as I was about to nibble the sacred cheese of life?"

The patient captain, drooped over the water jar, was sometimes obliged to speak to the oarsman.

"Keep her head up! Keep her head up!"

" 'Keep her head up,' sir." The voices were weary and low.

This was surely a quiet evening. All save the oarsman lay heavily and listlessly in the boat's bottom. As for him, his eyes were just capable of noting the tall black waves that swept forward in a most sinister silence, save for an occasional subdued growl of a crest.

The cook's head was on a thwart, and he looked without interest at the water under his nose. He was deep in other scenes. Finally he spoke. "Billie," he murmured, dreamily, "what kind of pie do you like best?"

V

"Pie," said the oiler and the correspondent, agitatedly. "Don't talk about those things, blast you!"

"Well," said the cook. "I was just thinking about ham sandwiches, and—"

A night on the sea in an open boat is a long night. As darkness settled finally, the shine of the light, lifting from the sea in the south, changed to full gold. On the northern horizon a new light appeared, a small bluish gleam on the edge of the waters. These two lights were the furniture of the world. Otherwise there was nothing but waves.

Two men huddled in the stern, and distances were so magnificent in the dingey that the rower was enabled to keep his feet partly warmed by thrusting them under his companions. Their legs indeed extended far under the rowing seat until they touched the feet of the captain forward. Sometimes, despite the efforts of the tired oarsman, a wave came piling into the boat, an icy wave of the night, and the chilling water soaked them anew. They would twist their bodies for a moment and groan, and sleep the dead sleep once more, while the water in the boat gurgled about them as the craft rocked.

The plan of the oiler and the correspondent was for one to row until he lost the ability, and then arouse the other from his sea water couch in the bottom of the boat.

The oiler plied the oars until his head drooped forward, and the overpowering sleep blinded him. And he rowed yet afterward. Then he touched a man in the bottom of the boat and called his name. "Will you spell me for a little while?" he said meekly.

"Sure, Billie," said the correspondent, awakening and dragging himself to a sitting position. They exchanged places carefully, and the oiler, cuddling down in the sea water at the cook's side, seemed to go to sleep instantly.

The particular violence of the sea had ceased. The waves came without snarling. The obligation of the man at the oars was to keep the boat headed so that the tilt of the rollers would not capsize her, and to preserve her from filling when the crests rushed past. The black waves were silent and hard to be seen in the darkness. Often one was almost upon the boat before the oarsman was aware.

In a low voice the correspondent addressed the captain. He was not sure that the captain was awake, although this iron man seemed to be always awake. "Captain, shall I keep her making for that light north, sir?"

The same steady voice answered him. "Yes. Keep it about two points off the port bow."

The cook had tied a life belt around himself in order to get even the warmth which this clumsy cork contrivance could donate, and he seemed almost stove-like when a rower, whose teeth invariably chattered wildly as soon as he ceased his labor, dropped down to sleep.

The correspondent, as he rowed, looked down at the two men sleeping under foot. The cook's arm was around the oiler's shoulders, and, with their fragmentary clothing and haggard faces, they were the babes of the sea, a grotesque rendering of the old babes in the wood.

Later he must have grown stupid at his work, for suddenly there was a growling of water, and a crest came with a roar and a swash into the boat, and it was a wonder that it did not set the cook afloat in his life belt. The cook continued to sleep, but the oiler sat up, blinking his eyes and shaking with the new cold.

"Oh, I'm awful sorry, Billie," said the correspondent contritely.

"That's all right, old boy," said the oiler, and lay down again and was asleep.

Presently it seemed that even the captain dozed, and the correspondent thought that he was the one man afloat on all the oceans. The wind had a voice as it came over the waves, and it was sadder than the end.

There was a long, loud swishing astern of the boat, and a gleaming trail of phosphorescence, like blue flame, was furrowed on the black waters. It might have been made by a monstrous knife.

Then there came a stillness, while the correspondent breathed with the open mouth and looked at the sea.

Suddenly there was another swish and another long flash of bluish light, and this time it was alongside the boat, and might almost have been reached with an oar. The correspondent saw an enormous fin speed like a shadow through the water, hurling the crystalline spray and leaving the long glowing trail.

The correspondent looked over his shoulder at the captain. His face was hidden, and he seemed to be asleep. He looked at the babes of the sea. They certainly were asleep. So, being bereft of sympathy, he leaned a little way to one side and swore softly into the sea.

But the thing did not then leave the vicinity of the boat. Ahead or astern, on one side or the other, at intervals long or short, fled the long sparkling streak, and there was to be heard the whirroo of the dark fin. The speed and power of the thing was greatly to be admired. It cut the water like a gigantic and keen projectile.

The presence of this biding thing did not affect the man with the same horror that it would if he had been a picnicker. He simply looked at the sea dully and swore in an undertone.

Nevertheless, it is true that he did not wish to be alone. He wished one of his companions to awaken by chance and keep him company with it. But the captain hung motionless over the water jar, and the oiler and the cook in the bottom of the boat were plunged in slumber.

VI

"If I am going to be drowned—if I am going to be drowned—if I am going to be drowned, why, in the name of the seven mad gods who rule the sea, was I allowed to come thus far and contemplate sand and trees?"

During this dismal night, it may be remarked that a man would conclude that it was really the intention of the seven mad gods to drown him, despite the abominable injustice of it. For it was certainly an abominable injustice to drown a man who had worked so hard, so hard. The man felt it would be a crime most unnatural. Other people had drowned at sea since galleys swarmed with painted sails, but still—

When it occurs to a man that nature does not regard him as important, and that she feels she would not maim the universe by disposing of him, he at first wishes to throw bricks at the temple, and he hates deeply the fact that there are no bricks and no temples. Any visible expression of nature would surely be pelleted with his jeers.

Then, if there be no tangible thing to hoot he feels, perhaps, the desire to confront a personification and indulge in pleas, bowed to one knee, and with hands supplicant, saying: "Yes, but I love myself."

A high cold star on a winter's night is the word he feels that she says to him. Thereafter he knows the pathos of his situation.

The men in the dingey had not discussed these matters, but each had, no doubt, reflected upon them in silence and according to his mind. There was seldom any expression upon their faces save the general one of complete weariness. Speech was devoted to the business of the boat.

To chime the notes of his emotion, a verse mysteriously entered the correspondent's head. He had even forgotten that he had forgotten this verse, but it suddenly was in his mind.

"A soldier of the Legion lay dying in Algiers,
　　There was a lack of woman's nursing, there was dearth of woman's
　　　　tears;
　　But a comrade stood beside him, and he took that comrade's hand,
　　And he said: 'I shall never see my own, my native land.' "

In his childhood, the correspondent had been made acquainted with the fact that a soldier of the Legion lay dying in Algiers, but he had never regarded the fact as important. Myriads of his school fellows had informed him of the soldier's plight, but the dinning had naturally ended by making him perfectly indifferent. He had never considered it his affair that a soldier of the Legion lay dying in Algiers, nor had it appeared to him as a matter for sorrow. It was less to him than the breaking of a pencil's point.

Now, however, it quaintly came to him as a human, living thing. It was no longer merely a picture of a few throes in the breast of a poet, meanwhile drinking tea and warming his feet at the grate; it was an actuality—stern, mournful, and fine.

The correspondent plainly saw the soldier. He lay on the sand with his feet out straight and still. While his pale left hand was upon his chest in an attempt to thwart the going of his life, the blood came between his fingers. In the far Algerian distance, a city of low square forms was set against a sky that was faint with the last sunset hues. The correspondent, plying the oars and dreaming of the slow and slower movements of the lips of the soldier, was moved by a profound and perfectly impersonal comprehension. He was sorry for the soldier of the Legion who lay dying in Algiers.

The thing which had followed the boat and waited, had evidently grown bored at the delay. There was no longer to be heard the slash of the cut water, and there was no longer the flame of the long trail. The light in the north still glimmered, but it was apparently no nearer to the boat. Sometimes the boom of the surf rang in the correspondent's ears, and he turned the craft seaward then and rowed harder. Southward, someone had evidently built a watch fire on the beach. It was too low and too far to be seen, but it made a shimmering, roseate reflection upon the bluff back of it, and this could be discerned from the boat. The wind came stronger, and sometimes a wave suddenly raged out like a mountain cat, and there was to be seen the sheen and sparkle of a broken crest.

The captain, in the bow, moved on his water jar and sat erect. "Pretty long night," he observed to the correspondent. He looked at the shore. "Those life-saving people take their time."

"Did you see that shark playing around?"

"Yes, I saw him. He was a big fellow, all right."

"Wish I had known you were awake."

Later the correspondent spoke into the bottom of the boat.

"Billie!" There was a slow and gradual disentanglement. "Billie, will you spell me?"

"Sure" said the oiler.

As soon as the correspondent touched the cold comfortable sea water in the bottom of the boat, and had huddled close to the cook's life belt he was deep in sleep, despite the fact that his teeth played all the popular airs. This sleep was so good to him that it was but a moment before he heard a voice call his name in a tone that demonstrated the last stages of exhaustion. "Will you spell me?"

"Sure, Billie."

The light in the north had mysteriously vanished, but the correspondent took his course from the wide-awake captain.

Later in the night they took the boat farther out to sea, and the captain directed the cook to take one oar at the stern and keep the boat facing the seas.

He was to call out if he should hear the thunder of the surf. This plan enabled the oiler and the correspondent to get respite together. "We'll give those boys a chance to get into shape again," said the captain. They curled down and, after a few preliminary chatterings and trembles, slept once more the dead sleep. Neither knew they had bequeathed to the cook the company of another shark, or perhaps the same shark.

As the boat caroused on the waves, spray occasionally bumped over the side and gave them a fresh soaking, but this had no power to break their repose. The ominous slash of the wind and the water affected them as it would have affected mummies.

"Boys," said the cook, with the notes of every reluctance in his voice, "she's drifted in pretty close. I guess one of you had better take her to sea again." The correspondent, aroused, heard the crash of the toppled crests.

As he was rowing, the captain gave him some whisky and water, and this steadied the chills out of him. "If I ever get ashore and anybody shows me even a photograph of an oar—"

At last there was a short conversation.

"Billie. . . . Billie, will you spell me?"

"Sure," said the oiler.

VII

When the correspondent again opened his eyes, the sea and the sky were each of the gray hue of the dawning. Later, carmine and gold was painted upon the waters. The morning appeared finally, in its splendor, with a sky of pure blue, and the sunlight flamed on the tips of the waves.

On the distant dunes were set many little black cottages, and a tall white windmill reared above them. No man, nor dog, nor bicycle appeared on the beach. The cottages might have formed a deserted village.

The voyagers scanned the shore. A conference was held in the boat. "Well," said the captain, "if no help is coming we might better try a run through the surf right away. If we stay out here much longer we will be too weak to do anything for ourselves at all." The others silently acquiesced in this reasoning. The boat was headed for the beach. The correspondent wondered if none ever ascended the tall wind tower, and if then they never looked seaward. This tower was a giant, standing with its back to the plight of the ants. It represented in a degree, to the correspondent, the serenity of nature amid the struggles of the individual—nature in the wind, and nature in the vision of men. She did not seem cruel to him then, nor beneficent, nor treacherous, nor wise. But she was indifferent, flatly indifferent. It is, perhaps, plausible that a man in this situation, impressed with the unconcern of the universe, should see the innumerable flaws of his life, and have them taste wickedly in his mind and wish for another chance. A distinction between right and wrong seems absurdly clear to him, then, in this new ignorance of the grave edge, and he understands that if he were given another opportunity he would mend his conduct and his words, and be better and brighter during an introduction or at a tea.

"Now, boys," said the captain, "she is going to swamp, sure. All we can do is to work her in as far as possible, and then when she swamps, pile out and scramble for the beach. Keep cool now, and don't jump until she swamps sure."

The oiler took the oars. Over his shoulders he scanned the surf. "Captain," he said, "I think I'd better bring her about, and keep her head-on to the seas and back her in."

"All right, Billie," said the captain. "Back her in." The oiler swung the boat then and, seated in the stern, the cook and the correspondent were obliged to look over their shoulders to contemplate the lonely and indifferent shore.

The monstrous in-shore rollers heaved the boat high until the men were again enabled to see the white sheets of water scudding up the slanted beach. "We won't get in very close," said the captain. Each time a man could wrest his attention from the rollers, he turned his glance toward the shore, and in the expression of the eyes during this contemplation there was a singular quality. The correspondent, observing the others, knew that they were not afraid, but the full meaning of their glances was shrouded.

As for himself, he was too tired to grapple fundamentally with the fact. He tried to coerce his mind into thinking of it, but the mind was dominated at this time by the muscles, and the muscles said they did not care. It merely occurred to him that if he should drown it would be a shame.

There were no hurried words, no pallor, no plain agitation. The men simply looked at the shore. "Now, remember to get well clear of the boat when you jump," said the captain.

Seaward the crest of a roller suddenly fell with a thunderous crash, and the long white comber came roaring down upon the boat.

"Steady now," said the captain. The men were silent. They turned their eyes from the shore to the comber and waited. The boat slid up the incline, leaped at the furious top, bounced over it, and swung down the long back of the wave. Some water had been shipped and the cook bailed it out.

But the next crashed also. The tumbling, boiling flood of white water caught the boat and whirled it almost perpendicular. Water swarmed in from all sides. The correspondent had his hands on the gunwale at this time, and when the water entered at that place he swiftly withdrew his fingers, as if he objected to wetting them.

The little boat, drunken with this weight of water, reeled and snuggled deeper into the sea.

"Bail her out, cook! Bail her out," said the captain.

"All right, captain," said the cook.

"Now, boys, the next one will do for us, sure," said the oiler. "Mind to jump clear of the boat."

The third wave moved forward, huge, furious, implacable. It fairly swallowed the dingey, and almost simultaneously the men tumbled into the sea. A piece of life belt had lain in the bottom of the boat, and as the correspondent went overboard he held this to his chest with his left hand.

The January water was icy, and he reflected immediately that it was colder than he had expected to find it on the coast of Florida. This appeared to his dazed mind as a fact important enough to be noted at the time. The coldness of the water was sad; it was tragic. This fact was somehow so mixed and confused with his opinion of his own situation that it seemed almost a proper reason for tears. The water was cold.

When he came to the surface he was conscious of little but the noisy water. Afterward he saw his companions in the sea. The oiler was ahead in the race. He was swimming strongly and rapidly. Off to the correspondent's left, the cook's great white and corked back bulged out of the water, and in the rear the captain was hanging with his one good hand to the keel of the overturned dingey.

There is a certain immovable quality to a shore, and the correspondent wondered at it amid the confusion of the sea.

It seemed also very attractive, but the correspondent knew that it was a long journey, and he paddled leisurely. The piece of life preserver lay under him, and sometimes he whirled down the incline of a wave as if he were on a hand-sled.

But finally he arrived at a place in the sea where travel was beset with difficulty. He did not pause swimming to inquire what manner of current had caught him, but there his progress ceased. The shore was set before him like a bit of scenery on a stage, and he looked at it and understood with his eyes each detail of it.

As the cook passed, much farther to the left, the captain was calling to him, "Turn over on your back, cook! Turn over on your back and use the oar."

"All right, sir." The cook turned on his back, and, paddling with an oar, went ahead as if he were a canoe.

Presently the boat also passed to the left of the correspondent with the captain clinging with one hand to the keel. He would have appeared like a man raising himself to look over a board fence, if it were not for the extraordinary gymnastics of the boat. The correspondent marveled that the captain could still hold to it.

They passed on, nearer to shore—the oiler, the cook, the captain—and following them went the water jar, bounding gayly over the seas.

The correspondent remained in the grip of this strange new enemy—a current. The shore, with its white slope of sand and its green bluff, topped with little silent cottages, was spread like a picture before him. It was very near to him then, but he was impressed as one who in a gallery looks at a scene from Brittany or Holland.

He thought: "I am going to drown? Can it be possible? Can it be possible? Can it be possible?" Perhaps an individual must consider his own death to be the final phenomenon of nature.

But later a wave perhaps whirled him out of this small, deadly current, for he found suddenly that he could again make progress toward the shore. Later still, he was aware that the captain, clinging with one hand to the keel of the dingey, had his face turned away from the shore and toward him, and was calling his name. "Come to the boat! Come to the boat!"

In his struggle to reach the captain and the boat, he reflected that when one gets properly wearied, drowning must really be a comfortable arrangement, a cessation of hostilities accompanied by a large degree of relief, and he was glad of it, for the main thing in his mind for some months had been horror of the temporary agony. He did not wish to be hurt.

Presently he saw a man running along the shore. He was undressing with most remarkable speed. Coat, trousers, shirt, everything flew magically off him.

"Come to the boat," called the captain.

"All right, captain." As the correspondent paddled, he saw the captain let himself down to bottom and leave the boat. Then the correspondent performed his one little marvel of the voyage. A large wave caught him and flung him with ease and supreme speed completely over the boat and far beyond it. It struck him even then as an event in gymnastics, and a true miracle of the sea. An overturned boat in the surf is not a plaything to a swimming man.

The correspondent arrived in water that reached only to his waist, but his condition did not enable him to stand for more than a moment. Each wave knocked him into a heap, and the undertow pulled at him.

Then he saw the man who had been running and undressing, and undressing and running, come bounding into the water. He dragged the ashore cook, and then waded towards the captain, but the captain waved him away, and sent him to the correspondent. He was naked, naked as a tree in winter, but a halo was about his head, and he shone like a saint. He gave a strong pull, and a long drag, and a bully heave at the correspondent's hand. The correspondent, schooled in the minor formulae, said: "Thanks, old man." But suddenly the man cried: "What's that?" He pointed a swift finger. The correspondent said: "Go."

In the shallows, face downward, lay the oiler. His forehead touched sand that was periodically, between each wave, clear of the sea.

The correspondent did not know all that transpired afterward. When he achieved safe ground he fell, striking the sand with each particular part of his body. It was as if he had dropped from a roof, but the thud was grateful to him.

It seems that instantly the beach was populated with men with blankets, clothes, and flasks, and women with coffee pots and all the remedies sacred to their minds. The welcome of the land to the men from the sea was warm and generous, but a still and dripping shape was carried slowly up the beach, and the land's welcome for it could only be the different and sinister hospitality of the grave.

When it came night, the white waves paced to and fro in the moonlight, and the wind brought the sound of the sea's great voice to the men on shore, and they felt that they could then be interpreters.

The Long Walk

BY SLAVOMIR RAWICZ

P ublished in America by The Lyons Press in 1997, *The Long Walk* brought to new generations of readers one of the most remarkable statements ever made about man's desire to be free.

In 1941, Slavomir Rawicz and a small group of fellow prisoners escaped a Soviet labor camp. Their march out of Siberia, through China, the Gobi Desert, Tibet, and over the Himalayas to British India was a journey "positively Homeric," as Cyril Connoly described it in *The London Times*.

Of Polish descent, Rawicz today lives in England and receives a constant stream of letters from readers of various editions of his book eager to salute his courage and thank him for sharing his amazing story.

No single excerpt can do this great book justice, but I find this particular section particularly vivid. At this point in the trek, the group's survivors have entered Mongolia and are making their way into the one of the most formidable obstacles they must cross: the Gobi Desert.

★　★　★　★　★

Two days without water in the hillocky, sand-covered, August furnace of the Gobi and I felt the first flutterings of fear. The early rays of the sun rising over the rim of the world dispersed the sharp chill of the desert night. The light hit the tops of the billowing dunes and threw sharp shadows across the deep-sanded floors of the intervening little valleys. Fear came with small fast-beating wings and was suppressed as we sucked pebbles and dragged our feet on to make maximum distance before the blinding heat of noon. From time to time one or other of us would climb one of the endless knolls and look south to see the same deadly landscape stretching to the horizon. Towards midday we stuck our long clubs in the sand and draped our jackets over them to make a shelter.

Alarm about our position must have been general but no one voiced it. My own feeling was that we must not frighten the girl and I am sure the others kept silent for the same reason.

The heat enveloped us, sucking the moisture from our bodies, putting ankle-irons of lethargy about our legs. Each one of us walked with his and her own thoughts and none spoke, dully concentrating on placing one foot ahead of the other interminably. Most often I led the way, Kolemenos and the girl nearest to me and the others bunched together a few yards behind. I was driving them now, making them get to their feet in the mornings, forcing them to cut short the noon rest. As we still walked in the rays of the setting sun the fear hit me again. It was, of course, the fundamental, most oppressive fear of all—that we should die here in the burning wilderness. I struggled against a panicky impulse to urge a return the way we had come, back to water and green things and life. I fought it down.

We flopped out against a tall dune and the cold stars came out to look at us. Our bone-weariness should have ensured the sleep of exhaustion but, tortured with thirst, one after another twisted restlessly, rose, wandered around and came back. Some time after midnight I suggested we start off again to take advantage of the cool conditions. Everybody seemed to be awake. We hauled ourselves upright and began again the trudge south. It was much easier going. We rested a couple of hours after dawn—and still the southerly prospect remained unaltered.

After this one trial there were no more night marches. Makowski stopped it.

"Can you plot your course by the stars?" he asked me. The others turned haggard faces towards me.

I paused before answering. "Not with complete certainty," I confessed.

"Can any of us?" he persisted. No one spoke.

"Then we could have been walking in circles all through the night," he said heavily.

I sensed the awful dismay his words had caused. I protested that I was sure we had not veered off course, that the rising sun had proved us still to be facing south. But in my own mind, even as I argued, I had to admit the possibility that Makowski was right. In any case, the seed of doubt had been sown and we just could not afford to add anything to the already heavy burden of apprehension.

So we went on through the shimmering stillness. Not even a faint zephyr of air came up to disperse the fine dust hanging almost unseen above the desert, the dust that coated our faces and beards, entered into our cracked lips and reddened the rims of eyes already sore tried by the stark brightness of the sun.

The severely-rationed dried fish gave out on about the fifth day and still we faced a lifeless horizon. In all this arid world only eight struggling human specks and an occasional snake were alive. We could have ceased to move quite easily and lain there and died. The temptation to extend the noon-day halt, to go on dozing through the hot afternoon until the sun dropped out of sight, invited our dry, aching bodies. Our feet were in a pitiable state as the burning sand struck through the thin soles of our worn moccasins. I found myself croaking at the others to get up and keep going. There is nothing here, I would say. There is nothing for days behind us. Ahead there must be something. There must be *something*. Kristina would stand up and join me, and Kolemenos. Then the others in a bunch. Like automatons we would be under way again, heads bent down, silent, thinking God knows what, but moving one foot ahead of the other hour after desperate hour.

On the sixth day the girl stumbled and, on her knees, looked up at me. "That was foolish of me, Slav. I tripped myself up." She did not wait for my assistance. She rose slowly from the sand and stepped out beside me. That afternoon I found to my faint surprise and irritation I was on my knees. I had not been conscious of the act of falling. One moment I was walking, the next I had stopped. On my knees, I thought . . . like a man at prayer. I got up. No one had slackened pace for me. They probably hardly noticed my stumble. It seemed to take me a very long time to regain my position at the head again. Others were falling, too, I noticed from time to time. The knees gave and they knelt there a few unbelieving seconds until realisation came that they had ceased to be mobile. They came on again. There was no dropping out. These were the signs of growing, strength-sapping weakness, but it would have been fatal to have acknowledged them for what they were. They were the probing fingers of death and we were not ready to die yet.

The sun rose on the seventh day in a symphony of suffused pinks and gold. Already we had been plodding forward for an hour in the pale light of the false dawn and dully I looked at Kristina and the other shambling figures behind me and was struck with the unconquerable spirit of them all. Progress now was a shuffle; the effort to pick up the feet was beyond our strength.

Without much hope we watched Kolemenos climb laboriously to the top of a high mound. One or other of us did this every morning as soon as the light was sufficient to give clear visibility southwards to the horizon. He stood there for quite a minute with his hand over his eyes, and we kept walking, expecting the usual hopeless shrug of the shoulders. But Kolemenos made no move to come down, and because he was staring intently in one direction, a few degrees to the east of our course, I dragged to a stop. I felt Kristina's hand lightly on my arm. She, too, was gazing up at Kolemenos. Everybody halted. We saw him rub his eyes, shake his head slowly and resume his intent peering in the same direction, eyes screwed up. I wanted to shout to him but stayed quiet. Instead I started to climb up to him. Zaro and the girl came with me. Behind came the American and Marchinkovas. The two Poles, Paluchowicz and Makowski, leaned on their clubs and watched us go.

As I reached Kolemenos I was telling myself, "It will be nothing. I must not get excited. It surely can't be anything." My heart was pounding with the exertion of the slight climb.

Kolemenos made no sound. He flung out his right arm and pointed. My sight blurred over. For some seconds I could not focus. I did what I had seen Kolemenos do. I rubbed my eyes and looked again. There was *something,* a dark patch against the light sand. It might have been five miles distant from us. Through the dancing early morning haze it was shapeless and defied recognition. Excitement grew as we looked. We began to talk, to speculate. Panting and blowing, the two Poles came up to us. They, too, located the thing.

"Could it be an animal?" asked the Sergeant.

"Whatever it is, it is not sand," Mister Smith replied. "Let's go and investigate."

It took us a good two hours to make the intervening distance. Many times we lost sight of the thing we sought as we plunged along in the sandy depressions. We climbed more often than we would otherwise have done because we could not bear the idea that somehow the smudge on the landscape might disappear while we were cut off from view of it. It began to take shape and definition and hope began to well up in us. And hope became certainty. There were *trees*—real, live, growing, healthy trees, in a clump, outlined against the sand like a blob of ink on a fresh-laundered tablecloth.

"Where there are trees there is water," said the American.

"An oasis," somebody shouted, and the word fluttered from mouth to mouth.

Kristina whispered, "It is a miracle. God has saved us."

If we could have run we would have done so. We toiled that last half-mile as fast as we could flog our legs along. I went sprawling a few times. My tongue was dry and swollen in my mouth. The trees loomed larger and I saw they were palms. In their shade was a sunken hollow, roughly oval-shaped, and I knew this must be water. A few hundred yards from the oasis we crossed an east-west caravan track. On the fringe of the trees we passed an incongruous pile of what looked like rusting biscuit tins like some fantastic mid-desert junk yard. In the last twenty yards we quickened our pace and I think we managed a lope that was very near a run.

The trees, a dozen or more of them, were arranged in a crescent on the south side of the pool, and threw their shadow over it for most part of the day. The wonderful cool water lay still and inviting in an elliptical depression hemmed round with big, rough-worked stones. At this time, probably the hottest season, the limits of the water had receded inwards from the stone ring, and we had to climb over to reach it. The whole, green, life-giving spot could have been contained inside half-an-acre.

Zaro had the mug but we could not wait for him to fill it and hand it round. We lay over the water lapping at it and sucking it in like animals. We allowed it to caress our fevered faces. We dabbed it around our necks. We drank until someone uttered the warning about filling our empty bellies with too much liquid. Then we soaked our food sacks and, sitting on the big stones, gently laved our cracked and lacerated feet. For blissful minutes we sat with the wet sacking draped about our feet. With a mugful of water at a time we rinsed from our heads and upper bodies some of the accumulated sand and dust of the six-and-a-half days of travail. The very feel and presence of water was an ecstasy. Our spirits zoomed. We had walked out of an abyss of fear into life and new hope. We chatted and laughed as though the liquid we had drunk was heady champagne. We wondered what hands had brought these stones and planted these palms to make of this miraculous pool a sign that could be seen from afar by thirst-tortured men.

The full extent of our good fortune was yet to be discovered. Some twenty yards east of the pool, on the opposite side from which we had approached, there were the remains of a still-warm fire and the fresh tracks of camels and many hoof-marks, telling of the recent halt of a big caravan. It had probably departed at sunrise. These men, whoever they were, had cooked and eaten meat, and the bones, as yet quite fresh and untainted, were scattered around the wood ashes. They were the bones of one large and one small animal and the meat had been sliced from them with knives, leaving small, succulent pieces still adhering. We shared out the bones and tore at them with our teeth, lauding our luck. Poor toothless Paluchowicz borrowed the knife from me and did as well as anybody. When there was no more meat we cracked each bone with the axe and sucked out the marrow.

For two or three hours during the heat of the afternoon we lay stretched out near the water under the blessed shade of the palms. Kolemenos, who had that rare gift of complete relaxation in any situation, snored with his arms behind his head and his cap pulled down over one eye. The sun's rays began to slant and I came out of a sleep haunted by blazing light and never-ending desert. I picked up the mug, climbed over the stones, scooped up water and drank again. The American stood up, stretched and joined me. Soon we were all up and about.

Zaro moved away. "I'm going to have a look at that pile of tins," he called back. "Maybe we'll find one we can carry water in."

The puzzle of that dump of civilised junk in the heart of the South Gobi must remain unsolved. There were about a hundred of the box-like metal containers and they had been there so long that, even in the dry air of that place, they had rusted beyond use. We turned them over one by one but could find nothing to indicate what they had contained or from where they had come. As we examined them we stacked them on one side. Beneath the pile, half-buried in the sand, Zaro pulled out a complete coil of rust-covered quarter-inch wire held together by circlets of thinner wire which broke away at a touch. I held a handful of sand in a fold of my sack and rubbed away at the heavy wire until I cleared the rust. The coating was thin; the wire was strong and sound.

That night we made a low-walled shelter from the tins, searched around for small pieces of wood and lit a fire. I lay awake for a long time trying to decide how long we should remain in this place, but the answer would not come. Sleep when it did come was dreamless and complete. I opened my eyes, according to the habit of the desert, about an hour before dawn, and Zaro was already pottering around, tugging tentatively at the free end of the coil of wire.

A conference of suggestion and counter-suggestion developed about that length of wire. We lugged it over to the pool and began pulling it out and rubbing it down with sand. No one had any clear notion what to do with it but there was unanimity on its probable usefulness to us some time in the future. Any metal object was precious. We just could not bring ourselves to leave treasure behind. Since we had to take it with us, the discussion finally boiled down to shaping it into an easily-portable form. That was how we came to spend hours of that day cutting off about four-feet lengths, turning the ends into hooks and making loops which could be slung around the neck. The metal was tough and bending it caused hard work with the back of the axe-head while the wire ends were jammed and firmly held in interstices between the close-set stones. When each of us had been supplied with a loop, Zaro and a couple of others made a few metal spikes about two feet long, one end beaten out to a point and the other looped to hang on the belt. Plenty of wire still remained when we had finished, but we thought we had all we could conveniently carry. The operation gave us a sense of achievement. To use our hands and our skill again was stimulating, and there was, too, the prisoner's fierce pride of possession, be the object only a loop of discarded wire.

Inevitably came the question of when to depart. Two of our problems were insoluble. The oasis had water but no food. We had nothing in which to carry water, except our metal mug. Makowski argued that if we waited here a few days we stood a chance of meeting a caravan and securing ourselves a stock of food for the next stage. But I wanted to go. I said that, as we had just missed one caravan, there might not be another for weeks. We would wait on for days until we were too weak from lack of food to move at all and the next travellers might find us dead from starvation. In the light of what was to come, I hope I may be forgiven for my insistence. Yet I think I may have been right. But there is no way of judging the issue now, nor was there then. There was no acrimony about the debate. We were in desperate straits and we had to decide immediately one way or the other. The thing was decided late that evening. We would set out before dawn.

We were on our way when the sun came up and for half a day we could look back and see the trees of the oasis. I was glad when I could no longer see their shape against the skyline. For hours Zaro carried the mug, one hand underneath, the other over the top. He had filled it with water after we had all taken our final drinks and as he walked it slopped warm against his palm and little trickles escaped down the sides. When we halted at midday he had lost nearly half the quantity through spillage and evaporation and was complaining about the cramping of his arms in holding so tightly to the can. So, very carefully, sitting up under the small shade of our jackets slung over our clubs, we handed the water round and disposed of it a sip at a time.

This was the pre-oasis journey all over again, but this time we were deprived of even the scant sustenance of a few dried fish. For the first three days I thought we moved surprisingly well. On the fourth day the inescapable, strength-draining heat began quite suddenly to take its toll. Stumbles and falls became increasingly frequent, the pace slowed, speech dried up into short grunted phrases. I remember Makowski saying, "Hell can't be hotter than this bloody desert."

On the fifth day Kristina went to her knees. I turned slowly round to look at her, expecting her to get to her feet as she had done before. She remained kneeling, her fair head bowed down on her chest. She was very still. I moved towards her and Kolemenos stepped back at the same time. Before we could reach her she swayed from the hips and slumped forward, her face in the sand. We reached her at the same time and turned her on her back. She was unconscious. I opened the neck of her dress and started talking to her, gently shaking her, while Mister Smith set to with sticks and *fufaikas* to make shade for her.

She came to quickly. She looked at our anxious ring of faces, sat up, smiled through split lips and said, "I feel better now. I must have fallen over—I don't know how it happened."

"Don't worry," I consoled her. "We'll rest here a while and then you'll be all right again."

She leaned forward and lightly patted the back of my hand. "I won't fall down again."

We sat there a while. Kristina reached down to scratch her ankle and my eyes idly followed the hand. The ankle was swollen so that the skin pressed outward against the narrow-fitting ends of her padded trousers.

"Has anything bitten you, Kristina?"

"No, Slav. Why?"

"Your leg looks swollen."

She pulled up the trouser leg and looked, turning her foot about as she did so. "I hadn't noticed it before," she said.

We struggled on for a couple more hours. She seemed to be refreshed. Then she fell again and this time her knees buckled and her face hit the sand in almost one movement without even the action of putting her arms out to break the fall.

We turned her over again and wiped away the sand which had been forced into her nose and mouth. We put up the shelter. She lay with eyes closed, breathing in harsh gasps through her mouth. I looked at her ankles and they were a pitiful sight. Both were badly discoloured and so swollen that it seemed they would burst the restricting bottoms of the trousers. I took out my knife and slit the cloth upwards. The skin appeared to be distended by water right up to the knees. I touched the swelling and the mark of my fingers remained for some seconds.

Kristina was unconscious for an hour while we tried to stifle our gnawing anxiety with banalities like, "It must be just a touch of sunstroke." I had a feeling like lead in the pit of my stomach. I was frightened.

She was quite cheerful when she came round. "I am becoming a nuisance," she said. "What can be the matter with me?" We fussed around her.

Kristina got to her feet. "Come on. We are wasting time."

I walked alongside her. She stopped suddenly and glanced down at her legs, her attention attracted by the flapping of slit trousers about her legs.

"My legs are getting quite thick, Slav."

"Do they hurt you, Kristina?"

"No, not at all. They must be swelling because I have walked so far."

The time was afternoon on the fifth day. She walked on for hours without more than an occasional small stumble and was still keeping up with Kolemenos and I when the sun had gone and we stopped for the night. Sitting there among us she stole frequent looks at her legs. She said nothing and we affected not to notice.

It was a disturbed night. All except Kolemenos seemed too weary and worried for sleep, Kristina lay still but I sensed she remained awake. I chewed on the pebble in my mouth. My teeth ached, my gums were enlarged and tender. Thoughts of flowing water constantly invaded my mind. I had clear pictures of the sampans I had seen on those northern rivers. I had little fits of shivering that made me stand up and walk around. My head felt constricted. I ached from head to foot.

For the first two hours of the sixth day the air was cool and walking was as pleasant as ever it can be in the desert. But soon the sun began to blaze at us out of a sky empty of clouds.

I took Kristina's elbow. "Can you keep going in this?"

"Yes, I think so."

Five minutes later she had folded up and was out, face down in the sand. Again we ministered to her and waited for her to open her eyes. She appeared to be breathing quite normally, like a tired child.

I stood a few steps away from her and the others came over to me. "She is very swollen," I said. "Do any of you know what that means?" Nobody knew the symptoms. We went back to her and waited. I flapped my cap over her face to make some air.

She smiled at us. "I am being a trouble again." We shook our heads. "I am afraid you had better leave me this time."

We all broke into protest at once. Kolemenos dropped down on his knees beside her. "Don't say that. Don't be a silly little girl. We shall never leave you." She lay there for another half-an-hour and when she tried to force herself up on her elbows she fell back again.

I spoke to Kolemenos. "We must give her a hand." We lifted her to her feet. "I can walk if you stay near me," she said.

Amazingly she walked, Kolemenos and I lightly holding her elbows. After a quarter of a mile we felt her start to fall forward. We steadied her and she went on again. She pulled herself erect and there was not a sound of distress, not a whimper. The next time she slumped forward we could not hold her. She had played herself utterly out and even the gallant will in that frail body could not produce another torturing effort. We were all in a bunch around her as the sun climbed up over our heads. Kolemenos and I each put an arm about her and, half-carrying, half-dragging her, set off again. A mile or so of that and I had no reserve of strength to give her. We stopped and I bent double fighting for breath.

"Stick beside me, Slav," said Kolemenos. "I am going to carry her." And he lifted her into his arms, swayed for a moment as he adjusted himself to the weight, and staggered off. He carried her for fully two hundred yards and I was there to ease her down when he paused for a rest.

"Please leave me, Anastazi," she begged. "You are wasting your strength." He looked at her but could not bring himself to speak.

We made a shelter there and stayed for perhaps three hours through the worst heat of the day. She lay still—I do not think she could move. The ugly swelling was past the knees and heavy with water. Kolemenos was flat on his back, restoring his strength. He knew what he was going to do.

The sun began to decline. Kolemenos bent down and swung her into his arms and trudged off. I stayed with him and the rest were all about us. He covered fully a quarter of a mile before he put her down that first time. He picked her up again and walked, her head pillowed on his great shoulder. I can never in my life see anything so magnificent as the blond-bearded giant Kolemenos carrying Kristina, hour after hour, towards darkness of that awful sixth day. His ordeal lasted some four hours. Then she touched his cheek.

"Put me on the ground, Anastazi. Just lay me down on the ground."

I took her weight from him and together we eased her down. We gathered round her. A wisp of a smile hovered about the corners of her mouth. She looked very steadily at each one of us in turn and I thought she was going to speak. Her eyes were clear and very blue. There was a great tranquility about her. She closed her eyes.

"She must be very tired," said Sergeant Paluchowicz. "The poor, tired little girl."

We stood around for several minutes, dispirited and at a loss to know what to do next. The shoulders of Kolemenos were sagging with exhaustion. We exchanged glances but could think of nothing to say. I looked down at Kristina. I looked at the open neck of her dress, and in a second I was down at her side with my ear over her heart. There was no beat. I did not believe it. I turned my head and applied the other ear. I lifted my head and picked up her thin wrist. There was no pulse. They were all looking at me intently. I dropped her hand and it thumped softly into the sand.

The American spoke, hardly above a whisper. I tried to answer but the words would not come. Instead the tears came, the bitter salt tears. And the sobs were torn from me. In that God-forsaken place seven men cried openly because the thing most precious to us in all the world had been taken from us. Kristina was dead.

I think we were half crazy there beside her body in the desert. We accused ourselves of having brought her here to her death. More personally, Makowski, speaking in Polish, blamed me for having insisted on leaving the shelter of the oasis.

The American intervened, his voice cold and flat. "Gentlemen, it is no use blaming ourselves. I think she was happy with us." The talk ceased. He went on, "Let us now give her a decent burial."

We scraped a hole in the sand at the base of a dune. Little pieces of stone that we sifted from the grains as we dug deeper we laid apart. I slit open a food sack and laid the double end gently under her chin. We lowered the body. On her breast lay her little crucifix. We stood around with our caps in our hands. There was no service, but each man spoke a prayer in his own language. Mister Smith spoke in English, the first time I had heard him use it. I opened out the sacking and lifted it over her face and I could not see for tears. We covered her with sand and we dotted the mound round with the little stones.

And Kolemenos took her tall stick and chopped a piece off it with his axe and bound the one piece to the other with a leather thong to make a cross.

So we said goodbye to her and went our empty way.

The awful thing was that there was so little but the girl to think about. Walking was sheer painful habit—it required no thought to perform. The sun beating down hour after hour would addle my brains and check the orderly sequence of thinking. I found I could imagine she was still there, just behind my shoulders and I could scuff along for miles seeing her. But there always came a time when the idea of her presence was so strong that I must turn my head, and bitter grief would knife at me all over again. I came slowly out of a troubled, thirst-ridden sleep that night and I was sure once more that she remained with us. And each fresh realisation of her death renewed dumb agony.

It took another tragedy to dull the sharp edges of our memory of her. Oddly, too, it relieved some of the load of guilt I felt about her death.

On the eighth day out from the oasis Sigmund Makowski pitched over into the sand. His arms were still at his sides when his face thumped down and he had made no effort to use his stick to prevent the fall. He lay there a minute or two and was barely conscious. We looked down at him and saw the tell-tale sign. Over the top of his moccasins the flesh was soft and puffy. We exchanged glances and said nothing. We turned him round and flapped our sacks in his face and he recovered quickly. He got to his feet, shook his head from side to side, grabbed his stick and plunged off. He keeled over again and again, but he kept going. And all the time the sickening flabby swelling grew upwards and weighed upon his legs.

Makowski lasted longer after the first onset than Kristina had done. On the ninth day he must have slumped down half-a-dozen times in a couple of hours. Then, lying flat and heaving desperately with his arms to get himself to his knees, he called out the name of Kolemenos. Both Kolemenos and I knelt down beside him.

"If you give me a hand to get to my feet, I can keep going."

Kolemenos took one arm, I took the other. We got Makowski upright. Feebly he shook our hands off and stood swaying. I felt myself choking as he staggered off like a drunken man, still going forward, but weaving from side to side, stabbing his stick into the yielding sand as he went. The six of us stood there hopelessly and watched him go.

"Mustn't let him fall again," Kolemenos said to me.

It was not difficult to catch up with him. Kolemenos took his stick from him and we took an arm each. We put his arms about our shoulders and stepped out. He swung his head round to each of us in turn and gave a bit of a smile. He kept his legs moving, but progressively more weakly so that towards the end of the day he was an intolerable, sagging burden about our necks.

That night he seemed to sleep peacefully and in the morning of the tenth day he was not only still alive but appeared to have regained some strength. He set off with the rest of us dragging his feet but unaided. He moved for half-an-hour before his first fall, but thereafter he pitched over repeatedly until Kolemenos and I again went to his rescue. When the time came to make our noonday halt he was draped about our shoulders like a sack and his legs had all but ceased to move. Mister Smith and Paluchowicz eased his weight away from us and gently laid him down on his back. Then we put up the shelter and squatted down around him. He lay quite still and only his eyes seemed to be alive.

After a while he closed his eyes and I had thought he had gone, but he was still breathing quietly. He opened his eyes again. The lids came down and this time he was dead. There was no spasm, no tremor, no outward sign to show that life had departed the body. Like Kristina, he had no words for us at the end.

The dossier for Sigmund Makowski, aged 37, ex-captain of the Polish frontier forces, *Korpus Ochrony Pogranicza,* was closed. Somewhere in Poland he had a wife. I would like her some day to know he was a brave man. We buried him there in the Gobi. The first grave we scratched out was too small and we had to lift out the body and enlarge the hole. We laid his sack, empty of food for so long, that he had carried with him for two thousand or more miles, over his face, and scooped the sand over him. Kolemenos made another small wooden cross, we said our prayers and we left him.

I tried hard to keep count of the days. I tried, too, to remember if I had ever read how long a man can keep alive without food and water. My head ached with the heat. Often the blackest pall of despair settled on me and I felt we were six doomed men toiling inevitably to destruction. With each hopeless dawn the thought recurred: Who will be next? We were six dried-out travesties of men shuffling, shuffling. The sand seemed to get deeper, more and more reluctant to let our ill-used feet go. When a man stumbled he made a show of getting quickly on his legs again. Quite openly now we examined our ankles for the first sign of swelling, for the warning of death.

In the shadow of death we grew closer together than ever before. No man would admit to despair. No man spoke of fear. The only thought spoken out again and again was that there must be water soon. All our hope was in this. Over every arid ridge of hot sand I imagined a tiny stream and after each waterless vista there was always another ridge to keep the hope alive.

Two days after Makowski's death we were reaching the limits of endurance. I think it was about the twelfth day out from the oasis. We walked only for about six hours on that day. We moved along in pairs now. There was no effort to choose partners. The man next to you was your friend and you took each other's arms and held each other up and kept moving. The only life we saw in the desert about us were snakes which lay still, heads showing and the length of their bodies hidden in deep holes in the sand. I wondered how they lived. They showed no fear of us and we had no desire to molest them. Once we did see a rat, but generally the snakes seemed to have the desert to themselves.

At the end of that twelfth day I was arm-in-arm with Zaro. Mister Smith and Paluchowicz were helping each other along and Kolemenos walked with Marchinkovas. In the middle of the night I felt a fever of desire to get moving again. I think I knew that if the miracle did not happen within the next twenty-four hours we could not expect to survive. I stuck it out until a couple of hours before dawn. Marchinkovas, Zaro and the American were awake, so I shook Kolemenos and Paluchowicz. I rasped at them through my dry and aching throat. I stood up. No one argued. As I started away they were with me. Paluchowicz stumbled a little at first because he was still not quite awake and his legs were stiff, but soon we were paired off again and making distance south.

It was easy to imagine in those pre-dawn hours that we were re-covering ground we had trudged over before, but the first light of the rising sun showed we were on course. We tacked from side to side as we walked, two by two, but it seemed to me we had made a remarkable number of tortured miles by the time the heat forced us to stop and rest. It was almost too much trouble to erect our flimsy canopy, but we did it because it was by now one of the habits of survival.

We sweated it out for about three hours in throbbing discomfort, mouths open, gasping in the warm desert air over enlarged, dust-covered tongues. I eased the sticky pebble round my sore gums to create a trickle of saliva so that I could swallow. I was at my lowest ebb, working on the very dregs of stamina and resolution. It was the devil's own job to haul ourselves up-right again. We were all perilously weak and dangerously near death.

All my visions of water had been of exquisite cool ponds and mur-muring streams. The water that saved our lives was an almost dried-out creek, the moisture compounded with the mud at the bottom of a channel not more than a couple of yards wide. We came over the last ridge and failed to see it. We were looking for water and this was no more than a slimy ooze which the killing desert was reluctant to reveal to us. We were almost on it before we saw it. We fell on our faces and sucked at the mud and dabbled our hands in it. For a few minutes we acted like demented men. We chewed mud for the moisture it contained and spat out the gritty residue.

It was the American who got the right idea. He swung his sack off his back and thrust a corner of it down into the mud. He waited some minutes, pulled out the sack and sucked at the damp corner. We followed his example. The amount of water we obtained in this way was infinitesimal compared with our raging, thirteen-day-old thirst, but it was something and it gave us hope. We began to talk again for the first time for days, to exchange suggestions. We decided to walk along the watercourse with the idea that if at this point there was dampness, somewhere there must be real water.

The creek narrowed until it was a mere crack in the ground and here we found water collected in tiny pools in the mud. By pressing down our cupped hands, palms uppermost, we were able to drink, really to drink again, to feel water trickling down our parched throats. We drank it, sand, mud and all, in ecstasy. It was probably as well that we were prevented from gulping it down in large quantities. After each drink there was a waiting period of several minutes before the little hollows filled again with upseeping water. My split, puffed and bleeding lips burned as the water touched them. I held the water in my mouth before swallowing and washed it about my tongue, my tender gums and aching teeth.

For a couple of hours we lay sprawled out exhausted close against the creek. Then we drank some more. Late in the afternoon Zaro pulled off his moccasins and sat with his feet deep in the cool mud. He smiled through his broken lips at the bliss of it and called out to us to join him. We sat round in a rough circle. After those never-ending hot days with blistered and cracked feet being pushed on and on through the burning sand, this was an experience of wonderful relief. After a while I felt the water slowly trickling through into the depressions made by my feet. The balm of it seemed even to ease the aching bones. Now and again I pulled out my feet just for the joy of dropping them back again into the squelching mud.

Sitting there in the only comfort we had known since the far distant oasis, we began to talk, to face up to our still bleak future and to plan. The first fact was that we were starving and near the end of our strength. The second was that, in spite of this God-sent ribbon of moisture, we were still in the desert and the prospect was unchanged for as many miles ahead as we could see. The first decision reached was that we would stay here for a night and a day. This night we would sleep and in the morning we would make an extended exploration along the creek, hoping to find at some point flowing water. Where there was water, we reasoned, there might be life, something we could eat.

Early next morning we piled our *fufaikas* in a mound, split into two trios and set off in opposite directions along the creek. Kolemenos, the American and I in one party walked a mile or more eastward and found nothing. At times the watercourse disappeared entirely, as though it had gone underground. When we found it again it was still only a damp trail. Reluctantly we concluded that if there was flowing water it must be in some spring below ground and inaccessible to us. Two remarkably healthy-looking snakes were the only sign of life we encountered. We turned back and arrived at the meeting point. We had some time to wait for Zaro, Marchinkovas and Paluchowicz, and had begun to entertain some hopes that their delayed return might mean good tidings when we saw them approaching. Zaro stretched out his hands palms downwards to indicate that the investigation had produced nothing.

"No luck," said Marchinkovas as they came up to us.

"We found nothing, either," I told them.

We drank more of the brown, turgid water. We bathed our feet again and watched the sun mounting in the sky.

Kolemenos spoke. "All this bloody desert and only us and a few snakes to enjoy it. They can't eat us and we can't eat them."

"Only half-true, that statement." It was Mister Smith. "It is not unknown for men to eat snakes."

There was an immediate ripple of interest.

Mister Smith stroked his greying beard thoughtfully. "American Indians eat them. I have seen tourists in America tempted into trying them. I never tried to eat snake myself. I suppose it's a natural human revulsion against reptiles."

We sat in silence a while thinking over what he had said.

He broke in on our thoughts. "You know, gentlemen, I think snakes are our only chance. There's hardly anything a starving man can't eat."

The idea fascinated and repelled at the same time. We talked for a while about it but I think we all knew we were going to make the experiment. There was no choice.

"We need a forked stick to catch them," said Marchinkovas, "and we haven't got one."

"No difficulty about that," I told him. "We'll split the bottoms of a couple of our sticks and jam a small pebble into the cleft."

Kolemenos got up off his haunches. "Let's make a start with the sticks straightaway."

We decided to use Zaro's and Paluchowicz's. The splitting was done by Kolemenos with the axe. The wood was bound with thongs above the split and the small stones rammed home. The result was two efficient-looking instruments.

"How shall we know if the snakes are poisonous? Shall we be able to eat the poisonous kind?" This was Paluchowicz, and he was echoing a doubt that existed in most of our minds.

"There is nothing to worry about," said the American. "The poison is contained in a sac at the back of the head. When you cut off the head you will have removed the poison."

Apart from catching our meal, there remained one problem—fuel for a fire to do the cooking. We turned out our bags for the bits of tinder we always carried. Heaped together the pile was bigger than we had expected. From the bottom of his sack Zaro brought out three of four pats of dried animal dung and solemnly placed them on the collection or hoarded fuel. On another occasion we might have laughed, but smiling through split lips was painful.

"I picked it up at the oasis," said Zaro. "I thought it might be needed for fires some time."

I was sorry that we all had not done as Zaro had done back there. This dried animal waste was excellent fuel which burned slowly and produced fair heat. There had been occasions, too, since the oasis when we had come across little heaps of sun-dried debris deposited by the swirling, dancing whirlwinds which we had seen spiralling across the desert. But we had been too intent on our plodding progress to stop and gather these tiny harvests of the wind. From now on the search for tinder was to be a preoccupation ranking almost in importance with the hunt for snakes.

Smith and I got down to the job of preparing a fire while the others went off with the two forked sticks. We scratched down through the powdery top sand to the layer of bigger grains below and through that to the bed of small stones beneath. We were looking for a thin flat stone on which to cook our snake. It was fully an hour before we found one. Among the surrounding dunes we had glimpses of the others creeping quietly around in their quest for some unsuspecting reptile. In the way of things in this life, they spent a couple of hours without seeing a sign of one. When we cared nothing for them we seemed always to be finding them.

The fire was laid. In the blazing sun the flat stone seemed already hot enough for cooking (certainly I think it would have fried an egg easily). Marchinkovas came back to us droop-shouldered. "The snakes must have heard we had changed our minds about them," he said wryly. The three of us sat around the unlighted fire in silence for about another half-an-hour. There came suddenly a great yell from Zaro. We could not see him but we saw Kolemenos and Paluchowicz running in the direction of the sound. We got up and ran, too.

About fifty yards away Zaro had his snake. His stick was firmly about the writhing body a couple of inches behind the head and Zaro was sweating with the exertion of holding it there. We could not judge the size of the creature because all but about six inches of it was hidden in a hole in the sand and the wriggling power of the concealed length was slowly inching the stick back towards the hole. We were tired, weak, slow and clumsy and we ran around and got in one another's way in an effort to help Zaro. Then Paluchowicz jabbed his stick a couple of inches behind Zaro's. I pulled a thong from about my waist, slipped a loop about the snake against the hole and heaved. But there was too much snake inside and too little outside. It was stalemate.

Kolemenos settled the issue. The bright blade of his axe swished down and separated the snake's head from its body. The still wriggling length was hauled into the sunlight. The thing was nearly four feet long. It was as thick as a man's wrist, black above, with a creamy-brown belly lightening to a dull cream-white at the throat.

Zaro struck a pose. "There's your dinner, boys."

The thing still twitched as we carried it back to the fire. We laid it on my sack and, under the direction of the American, I started to skin it. The beginning of the operation was tricky. Smith said the skin could be peeled off entire but I could get no grip at the neck. Eventually I slit the skin a few inches down and with difficulty started to part the snake from its tight sheath. I had never seen an unclothed snake before. The flesh was whitish at first, but in the sun it turned a little darker while we waited for the fire to bring the flat stone to the right heat. We cut the body lengthwise and cleaned it out.

There was still a little reflex of life left as we curled the meat up on the stone over the fire. It sizzled pleasantly. Fat trickled down off the stone and made the fire spit. We streamed sweat as we sat around the fire. We could not take our eyes off the snake. With our sticks we lifted the stone off, turned the meat and put it back for the final stage of grilling. When we thought it was ready to eat we lifted it, stone and all, on to the sand to cool a little.

It lay eventually on my sack a yard or two away from the dying fire. We squatted round it but nobody seemed in a hurry to start carving it up. We looked at one another. Kolemenos spoke. "I am bloody hungry." He reached forward. We all went for it at the same time. Paluchowicz, the man without teeth, stretched his hand out to me for the knife. We ate. It was not long before the snake was reduced to a skeleton. The flesh was close-packed and filling. I had thought the taste might be powerful, even noxious. It was in fact mild, almost tasteless. It had no odour. I was faintly reminded of boiled, unseasoned fish.

"I wish I had thought of snakes earlier," said Mister Smith.

We drank some more of the muddy water. We watched the sun drop from its zenith. We knew that soon we must move again, and we were reluctant to go, to leave this precious ribbon of moisture and launch out again into the unknown, heat-baked country ahead. Sprawled out there, my stomach rumbling as it contended with its barbaric new meal, I longed for a smoke. We still had newspaper but the tobacco had long gone.

No one wanted to bring up the subject of when we should leave, so we talked about other things. For the first time we exchanged ideas freely about Kristina and Makowski. Why should death have overtaken them and left the rest of us still with the strength to carry on? There was no answer to this question, but we mulled it over. We talked of them with sadness and affection. It was, I suppose, an act of remembrance for two absent friends. And it took some of the heavy load of their great loss from us.

I found myself looking at the five of them, taking stock of them, trying to assess our chances. We were all sick men. Kolemenos had his moccasins off and I could see the inflamed raw patches where blisters had formed on punctured blisters, and I knew he was no worse off in this respect than any other of us. All our faces were so disfigured that our nearest relatives would have had difficulty in recognising us. Lips were grotesquely swollen and deeply fissured. Cheeks were sunk in. Brows overhung red-rimmed eyes which seemed to have fallen back in their sockets. We were in an advanced state of scurvy. Only the toothless Paluchowicz escaped the discomfort of teeth rocking loose in sore gums. Already Kolemenos had pulled two aching teeth out between finger and thumb for Marchinkovas and he was to practise his primitive dentistry several times more in the future for others of the party.

Lice, scurvy and the sun had played havoc with our skin. The lice had multiplied with the filthy prolificacy of their kind and swarmed about us. They fed and grew to an obscenely large size. We scratched and scratched at our intolerably irritated bodies until we broke the skin and then our sweat-soaked clothes and untended dirty finger-nails caused the tiny cuts to become septic. This unclean affliction, superficial though it was, was a constant source of depression and misery. I killed the lice when I caught them with savage joy. They were pre-eminently the symbol of our fugitive degradation.

In the end no one took the initiative over our departure. There came a time when Kolemenos and Zaro stood up together. We all rose. We adjusted the wire loops about our necks, picked up our sacks. Into my sack went the flat cooking stone. The American carefully stowed away the little pile of fuel. Grimacing, Kolemenos pulled on his moccasins. We drank a little more water. And in the late afternoon we started off.

Many miles we walked that day, until the light of day faded out and until the stars came out in a purple-black sky. We slept huddled close together and were awake before dawn to start again.

Half-an-hour later Paluchowicz stopped with a groan, clutching his belly, doubled up. In the next hour we were all seized with the most violent, griping pains. All of us were assailed with diarrhoea of an intensity that left us weak and groaning. With the frequent stops we could not have covered more than five miles by late afternoon, when the attacks began to subside.

What had caused it—the snake-meat or the water? We asked one another this question.

Said Mister Smith, "It might well have been the dirty water. But most probably it arises simply from the fact that our empty stomachs are reacting against the sudden load of food and water."

"There's one good way to find out," Kolemenos said. "We'll eat some more snake. I am still hungry."

Marchinkovas shrugged his shoulders. "It will be snakes or nothing."

Paluchowicz gasped with another spasm of stomach ache.

"May God help us," he said, fervently.

Unquestionably the snakes of the Gobi saved us from death. We caught two within minutes of each other the next day. One was like the common European grass snake, the other arrayed in the brilliance of a silver-grey skin marked down the back with a dull red broad stripe flanked closely parallel with two thin lines of the same colour. Profiting by the experience of my difficulty in skinning the first specimen, we clubbed these two to death and held the heads in Zaro's forked stick while I stripped off the skins.

We did not like these two coloured snakes as much as we had the first capture. They were thinner-bodied and we imagined they tasted less pleasantly. I think the colours affected our judgment. The big black was not unlike a conger eel in appearance and in the texture of the flesh. Thereafter we sought specially for this species and counted ourselves lucky when we found one.

The clear fat which oozed out over the heat of the fire we used as a balm for our lips, our sore eyes and our feet and the soothing effect lasted for hours.

Two days after leaving the creek we had visitors. First there wheeled lazily over us half-a-dozen ravens. They stayed with us throughout the morning and then made a leisurely departure as we erected our shelter at midday. We were wondering what had prompted their departure when two great shadows skimmed along the sand. We looked up and saw not twenty feet above a pair of magnificent, long-necked eagles, their plumage looking black against the sun. They passed over us several times and then alighted on the top of a sandy hillock twenty yards away and looked down on us. The spread of wings as they came into land was enormous.

"What do you think *they* want?" someone asked.

The American considered. "It's fairly obvious, I think, that they saw the ravens and came to investigate the prospects of food."

Zaro said, "Well, they're not having *me*."

"Don't worry," I assured him. "They won't attack us."

Zaro stood up and shouted at the great birds. He made motions of throwing. The pair disdained to notice his antics. He scratched away at the sand and produced a couple of pebbles. He aimed carefully and threw. The stone sent up a puff of sand a yard short of them. One held its ground and the other did an ungainly single hop. Zaro hurled the second stone wide of its mark and the two eagles sat unmoved. They took off in their own good time as we dismantled the shelter and followed us for about an hour, high in the sky, before swinging away to the south and disappearing.

"Eagles live in mountains," said the American. "Perhaps we haven't far to go to get out of the desert."

We could see a long way ahead and there were no distant mountains. "They can also fly great distances," I said.

For three or four days we were tormented with stomach pain and its attendant diarrhoea; then, as we began to long for water again, the stomach trouble passed away. As we trudged on there were days when we caught not a glimpse of a snake. Another day and we would pick up a couple basking in the sun in a morning's search. We ate them as soon as we found them. There was a red-letter day when we caught two of the kind we called Big Blacks within half-an-hour. The days dragged by. We were inspected again by both the ravens and the eagles. We were able now to make a fix on a couple of bright stars and sometimes walked long after dark. We began again to dream longing dreams of water.

I lost count of the days again. My fitful sleep was invaded by visions of reptiles so tenacious of life that though I beat at them with my club in a frenzy they still hissed at me and crawled. All my fears came bursting through in dreams. Worst of all was the picture of myself staggering on alone, shouting for the others and knowing that I should never see them again. I would wake shivering in the morning cold and be happily reassured to see Smith, Kolemenos, Zaro, Marchinkovas and Paluchowicz close about me.

Almost imperceptibly the terrain was changing. The yellow sand was deepening in colour, the grains were coarser, the smooth topped dunes taller. The sun still burned its shrivelling way across the blue, unclouded heavens but now there were days when a gentle breeze sighed out from the south and there was a hint of coolness in its caress. The nights were really cold and I had the impression that we were day by day gradually climbing out of the great heat-bowl.

It might have been a week or eight days after leaving the creek that we aoke to discover in a quickening of excitement and hope a new horizon. The day was sharply clear. Far over to the east, perhaps fifty miles away, shrouded in a blue haze like lingering tobacco smoke, a mountain range towered. Directly ahead there were also heights but they were mere foothills compared with the eastward eminences. So uniformed were we of Central Asian geography that we speculated on the possibility that the tall eastern barrier could be the Himalayas, that somehow we had by-passed them to the west, that we might now even be on the threshold of India. We were to learn that the whole considerable north-to-south expanse of Tibet, ruggedly harsh and mountainous, lay between us and the Himalayas.

We plodded on for two more exhausting, heart-breaking days before we reached firm ground, a waste of lightly-sanded rocks. We lay there in the extremity of our weakness and looked back at our tracks through the sand. There were no defined footmarks, only a dragging trail such as skis make in snow. Lifeless and naked the rocky ridge sloped easily into the distance above us. In my mind was the one thought that over the hump there might be water. We rested a couple of hours before we tackled the drag upwards. We took off our moccasins and emptied them of sand. We brushed the fine dust from between our toes. Then we went up and out of the Gobi.

Over the ridge there was more desolation. By nightfall we had dropped down into a stone-strewn valley. We might have struggled on longer but Marchinkovas fell and banged his knee. In the morning he showed us a big bruise and complained of a little stiffness but was able to walk. The pain passed off as he exercised it and he experienced no more trouble from the injury. We climbed again. There was no talking because none of us could spare the breath and movement of the lips was agony. We hauled ourselves along through a faint dawn mist and did not reach this next summit for several hours. From the top there was the view again of the great range to the east, looking even more formidable than at our first sight of it. Ahead there seemed to be an unbroken succession of low ridges corrugating the country as far as we could see. Below us the floor of the valley appeared to be covered with sand and we decided to get down before dark to search for snakes.

It was the merest accident that we did not miss the water on our way down. We had all passed it when Zaro turned round and yelled the one wonderful word. It was no more than a trickle from a crack in a rock but it glinted like silver. It crept down over the curve of a big round boulder and spread thinly over a flat rock below. Kolemenos and I had been picking our way down the slope some twenty yards ahead of Zaro when his shout arrested us. We turned quickly and scrambled back. We found that the source of the little spring was a crack just wide enough to take the fingers of one hand. The water was sparkling, clean and ice-cold. We channeled the tiny stream to a point where we could lead it into our battered and much travelled metal mug and sat down impatiently to watch it fill. The operation took fully ten minutes.

I said to Zaro, "You had passed this point. What made you turn round and find it?"

Zaro spoke quite seriously. "I think I must have smelt it. It was quite a strong impulse that made me turn my head."

The water tinkled musically into the mug until it was brimming. Carefully Zaro lifted it away and I noticed his hand was trembling a little so that some of the water spilled over. He faced Smith and with a bow, and, in imitation of the Mongolian etiquette of serving the senior first, handed him the water. The mug was passed round and each man took a gulp. No nectar of the gods could have tasted so wonderful. Again and again we filled the mug and drank. And then we left it, full and running over, under the life-giving spring so that any of us could drink whenever he felt like it.

The time was around the middle of the day. We agreed readily that we should stay close to the spring for another twenty-four hours, but up here on the hillside nothing lived—and we were very hungry. I volunteered to go down into the sandy valley to search for a snake and Zaro said he would come with me. We took the two forked sticks and set off, turning at intervals to look back and fix the position of the squatting group about the spring.

The descent took us over an hour and the heat shimmered off the sandy, boulder-strewn floor of the valley. Our hopes were immediately raised by seeing a snake about a yard long slither away at our approach and disappear under a rock but we foraged around well into the afternoon after that without seeing another living thing. Then we parted and went opposite ways and I had almost decided it was time to give up the quest when I heard Zaro let out a whoop of triumph. I ran to him and found him pinning down a Big Black which was thrashing about desperately in an effort to break free. I reversed my stick and battered it to death. I put my arm about Zaro's shoulders and congratulated him. He was always our Number One snake-catcher.

Zaro wore his capture like a trophy about his neck as we toiled back up the hillside. We were soaked with sweat and exhausted by the time we reached the spring and Kolemenos took over my usual job of skinning and preparing the snake for the fire. Paluchowicz had laid a fire from our few remaining sticks on which was placed the last piece of camel dung which Zaro had gathered at the oasis. There was not enough heat to cook the meat thoroughly but we were too hungry to be squeamish. We ate and we drank as the sun went down. Only Kolemenos slept well that night; for the rest of us it was too cold for comfort.

The next morning we were on our way again. This time there were no stomach cramps, which led us to believe that we owed at least some of the previous trouble to the muddy creek. We travelled down the long slope, across the hot valley and up the hillside facing us—a total of at least fifteen miles. From the top of the ridge we took fresh bearings. Directly ahead were some formidable heights, so we set our course over easier ground about ten degrees east of the line due south. Towards evening we were heartened by the discovery of the first vegetation we had seen since the oasis. It was a rough, spiky grass clinging hardily to dry rootholds in fissures between the rocks. We pulled up a clump, handed it round and closely examined it like men who had never seen grass before.

The wearing trek went on day after day. Our diet was still confined to an occasional snake—we lived on them altogether for upwards of three weeks from the time of our first sampling back in the desert. The nights set in with a chill which produced a frosty white rime on the stones of the upper hillsides. In vain we looked for signs of animal life, but there were birds: from time to time a pair of hovering hawks, some gossiping magpies and our old acquaintances the ravens. The wiry mountain grass grew more abundant with each passing day and its colour was greener. Then the country presented us with struggling low bushes and lone-growing dwarf trees, ideal fuel for the fires which we now started to light every night. The spectre of thirst receded as we found clear-running rivulets. It was rare now that we had to go waterless for longer than a day.

There came a day when we breasted the top of a long rise and looked unbelievingly down into a wide-spreading valley which showed far below the lush green of grazing grass. Still more exciting, there were, crawling like specks five miles or more distant from and below us, a flock of about a hundred sheep. We made the descent fast, slipping and sliding in our eagerness to get down. As we got nearer we heard the bleating and calling of the sheep. We had about a quarter of a mile to go to reach the flock when we saw the two dogs, long-coated liver-and-white collie types. They came racing round the flock to take up station between us and their charges.

Zaro called out to them, "Don't worry, we won't hurt them. Where's your master?" The dogs eyed him warily.

Kolemenos growled, "I only need to get near enough to a sheep for one swing of my old axe. . . ."

"Don't get impatient, Anastazi," I told him. "It is fairly obvious the shepherd has sent his dogs over here to intercept us. Let us swing away from the flock and see if they will lead us to their master."

We turned pointedly away. The dogs watched us closely for a couple of minutes. Then, apparently satisfied, they had headed us away from the sheep, ran off at great speed together towards the opposite slope of the valley. My eyes followed the line of their run ahead of them and then I shouted and pointed. A mile or more away rose a thin wisp of smoke.

"A fire at midday can only mean cooking," said Marchinkovas hopefully.

The fire was burning in the lee of a rocky outcrop against which had been built a one-man shelter of stones laid one above the other as in an old cairn. Seated there was an old man, his two dogs, tongues lolling, beside him. He spoke to his dogs as we neared him and they got up and raced off back across the valley to the flock. Steaming over the fire was a black iron cauldron.

The American went to the front and approached bowing. The old man rose smiling and returned the bow and then went on to bow to each of us in turn.

He was white-bearded. The high cheek-bones in his broad, square face showed a skin which had been weathered to the colour of old rosewood. He wore a warm goatskin cap with ear-flaps turned up over the crown in the fashion of the Mongols we had met in the north. His felt boots were well made and had stout leather soles. His unfastened three-quarter-length sheepskin coat was held to the body by a woven wool girdle and his trousers were bulkily padded, probably with lamb's-wool. He leaned his weight on a five-feet-tall wooden staff, the lower end of which was iron-spiked and the upper part terminating in a flattened "V" crutch formed by the bifurcation of the original branch. In a leather-bound wooden sheath he carried a bone-handled knife which I later observed was double-edged and of good workmanship. To greet us he got up from a rug of untreated sheepskin. There was no doubt of his friendliness and his pleasure at the arrival of unexpected visitors.

He talked eagerly and it was a minute or two before he realised we did not understand a word. I spoke in Russian and he regarded me blankly. It was a great pity because he must have been looking forward to conversation and the exchange of news. I think he was trying to tell us he had seen us a long way off and had prepared food against our arrival. He motioned us to sit near the fire and resumed the stirring of the pot which our coming had interrupted. I looked into the stone shelter and saw there was just room for one man to sleep. On the floor was a sleeping mat fashioned from bast.

As he wielded his big wooden spoon he made another attempt at conversation. He spoke slowly. It was no use. For a while there was silence. Mister Smith cleared his throat. He gestured with his arm around the group of us. "We," he said slowly in Russian, "go to Lhasa." The shepherd's eyes grew intelligent. "Lhasa, Lhasa," Smith repeated, and pointed south. From inside his jacket the old fellow pulled out a prayer-wheel which looked as if it had been with him for many years. The religious signs were painted on parchment, the edges of which were worn with use. He pointed to the sun and made circles, many of them, with his outstretched arm.

"He is trying to tell us how many days it will take us to reach Lhasa," I said.

"His arm's going round like a windmill," observed Zaro. "It must be a hell of a long way from here."

We bowed our acknowledgment of the information. From his pocket he produced a bag of salt—good quality stuff and almost white—and invited us to look into the cauldron as he sprinkled some in. We crowded round and saw a bubbling, greyish, thick gruel. He stirred again, brought out a spoonful, blew on it, smacked his lips, tasted and finally thrust out his tongue and ran it round his lips. He chuckled at us like a delighted schoolboy and his good humour was so infectious that we found ourselves laughing aloud in real enjoyment for the first time for months.

The next move by the old man had almost a ritualistic air. From his shack he produced an object wrapped in a linen bag. He looked at us, eyes twinkling, and I could not help thinking of a conjuror building up suspense for the trick which was to astound his audience. I think we all looked suitably impressed as he opened the bag and reached into it. Into the sunlight emerged a wooden bowl about five inches in diameter and three inches deep, beautifully turned, shining with care and use, of a rich walnut brown colour. He blew on it, brushed it with his sleeve and handed it round. It was indeed a thing of which a man could be proud, the work of a craftsman. We handed it back with murmurs of appreciation.

Into the bowl he ladled a quantity of gruel and laid it on the skin rug. He disappeared into the shack and came out holding an unglazed earthenware jar, dark-brown and long-necked. It held about a gallon of ewe's milk, a little of which he added to the gruel in the bowl. He made no attempt at working out our seniority but handed the bowl and spoon to Zaro, who was seated nearest to him. Zaro ate a spoonful, smacked his lips and made to pass the bowl around, but the shepherd gently held his arm and indicated he was to finish the portion.

Zaro made short but evidently highly enjoyable work of it. "By God, that tastes wonderful," he exclaimed.

It was my turn next. The main ingredient seemed to be barley, but some kind of fat had been added. The sweet, fresh milk had cooled the mixture down a little and I fairly wolfed it down. I could feel the soothing warmth of it reaching my ill-treated stomach. I belched loudly, smacked my lips and handed back the bowl.

He saw to the needs of each of us in turn before he ate himself. To what was left in the cauldron he added several pints of milk and started stirring again, making enough extra to give us each another bowlful.

He took the cauldron off the fire to cool off, moving it with some difficulty because it had no handle, although I noticed there were the usual two holes in the rim. To our unspeakable joy he then produced tobacco from a skin pouch and handed us each enough for two or three cigarettes. Out came the pieces of hoarded newspaper. We lit up with glowing brands from the fire. We were happy in that moment and brimming over with gratitude towards a supremely generous host. And he, bless him, sat there cross-legged and basked in our smiles.

Away he went after about half-an-hour, refusing offers of help, to wash the cauldron and the precious bowl at a nearby spring. He came back, stoked up the fire and made us tea, Tibetan style, and this time we even faintly approved the taste of the rancid butter floating in globules on the surface.

I felt I wanted to do something for the old man. I said to Kolemenos, "Let's make him a handle for his cauldron out of one of the spare wire loops." Everybody thought it an excellent idea. It took us only about thirty minutes to break off a suitable length, shape it and fasten it. Our host was delighted.

We tried to think of some other service we could render. Someone suggested we forage for wood for the fire. We were away about an hour and came back with a pile of stuff, including a complete small tree which Kolemenos had hacked down with his axe. The shepherd had been waiting for our return. As we came in he was finishing sharpening his knife on a smooth piece of stone. He had his two dogs with him again. He made us sit down and, with his dogs at his heels, strode off.

He returned shortly dragging by the wool between its horns a young ram, the dogs circling him in quiet excitement as he came. In something like five minutes the ram was dead, butchered with practised skill. He wanted no help from us on this job. He skinned and gutted the carcase with a speed which made my own abilities in this direction seem clumsy. The carcase finally was quartered. Salt was rubbed in one fore and one hind quarter, which were hung inside the stone hut. He threw the head and some other oddments to the dogs.

Half the sheep was roasted on wooden spits over the blazing fire that night and we ate again to repletion. We made signs that we would like to stay overnight and he seemed only too willing that we should. The six of us slept warm around the fire, while the shepherd lay the night inside his hut.

From somewhere he produced the next morning a batch of rough barley cakes—three each was our share. There was more tea and, to our astonishment, because we thought the limit of hospitality must already have been reached, the rest of the ram was roasted and shared out, and a little more tobacco distributed.

We left him in the early afternoon, after first restocking his fuel store. We did not know how to thank him for his inestimable kindness. Gently we patted his back and smiled at him. I think we managed to convey to him that he had made half-a-dozen most grateful friends.

At last we stood off a few feet from him and bowed low, keeping our eyes, according to custom, on his face. Gravely he returned the salute. We turned and walked away. When I turned he was sitting with his back to us, his dogs beside him. He did not look round.

Alive

BY PIERS PAUL READ

I t has been called a "classic in the literature of survival," and surely Piers Paul Read's account of the highly publicized Andes plane crash disaster and survival epic of 1972 merits that description. The book, first published in 1974, was a huge bestseller all over the world and was made into a popular film. If you have never read the complete book, I heartily urge you to do so, for this excerpt, while very powerful and moving, cannot possibly capture the entire detailed drama of the full story.

For those who are not already familiar with the story, now almost thirty years old, a bit of scene-setting is in order.

The location is high in the mighty Andes Mountains, separating Chile and Argentina. On October 12, 1972, a Fairchild P-227 (twin-engine turbo-prop commuter-type aircraft) chartered to carry an amateur rugby team, set off from Montevideo in Uruguay for Santiago in Chile. This was early spring in the Southern Hemisphere, and bad, unstable weather caused the plane to be diverted to Mendoza on the Argentinean side of the mountains. The plane remained overnight and set out again the next day but never reached its destination. The crash was devastating. The tail section of the plane broke away, and the main fuselage skidded on the snow down a remote mountain pass. Forty-five passengers, including the crew, were aboard the plane. There were 32 survivors, several seriously injured. The pilots were dead.

Despite frantic and repeated search missions, the plane was never found. The plane crash survivors were forced to endure unending pain and hunger. Slowly, irrevocably, their ranks began to dwindle, as one after the other died of their privations. As the weeks went by, some attempted to leave the site and trek to safety, but they were beaten back by the snows and terrain. Finally, ten weeks after the ordeal began, two of the boys, leaving 14 of their mates behind at the plane, made a heroic trek through the mountains and stumbled upon a Chilean peasant tending his cattle. Soon the world knew the story. That

16 had survived the disaster seemed a miracle. Then the details began to make more news headlines: The survivors had been forced to resort to cannibalism.

The excerpt which follows was chosen because it gives a vivid look at what life was like at the crash site during the ordeal. The action takes place when the plane had been down for about a month, and time for hope and rescue was clearly running out.

★   ★   ★   ★   ★

November 23 was Bobby Francois's twenty-first birthday. He received as a present from his sixteen companions an extra pack of cigarettes. Meanwhile Canessa and Parrado set about the task of removing the radio from the panel of instruments which remained half buried in the pilot's chest.

The earphones and the microphone were connected to a black metal box about the size of a portable typewriter which came out quite easily with the removal of a few screws. They realized, however, that it had no dial and so could only be part of the VHF radio; it also had sixty-seven wires coming out of the back, which they thought must connect it to the missing half. The plane was so full of instruments that it was not easy to decide what might be part of the radio and what might not, but eventually, behind a plastic panel in the wall of the luggage compartment, they found the transmitter. This was much more difficult to get at and separate from all the other instruments—especially as there was no light to work by. Their only tools were a screwdriver, a knife, and a pair of pliers, and with these, after several days of effort, they eventually extracted it.

Their hunch that this was the part which matched the box they had taken from the instrument panel was confirmed by a cable which ran out the back with sixty-seven different wires. The difficulty which faced them was their ignorance of which wire on one piece of equipment matched which wire on the other. With sixty-seven wires on each, there were many million permutations. Then they discovered that the wires had faint markings on them which enabled them to make the correct connections.

Canessa was the most enthusiastic about the radio. He thought it insane for any of them to risk their lives by setting off over the mountains if there was any chance that they could make contact with the outside world. The majority agreed with him, though many were more or less skeptical about the outcome. Pedro Algorta did not think they would ever make it work, but he said nothing which might make the optimists despondent. Roy Harley himself, who was supposed to be their radio expert, was the most doubtful of all.

He knew best the limits of his own expertness upon which they based their hopes—some old afternoons fiddling around with the stereo set of a friend—and insisted repeatedly in a whining voice that this in no way qualified him to dismantle and then reassemble a VHF radio.

The other boys discounted his diffidence as the byproduct of his physical and mental debility. His large face was fixed in a permanent expression of misery and despair, and his body, which had once been solid and strong, had shrunk to the wizened dimensions of an Indian fakir. The expeditionaries and the cousins therefore asked him to train for the journey to the tail by walking around the plane, but he was too weak. (They did not consider it appropriate to increase his ration of flesh.) The more insistent they became, the more Roy resisted the idea. He wept and pleaded and told them over and over again that he knew no more about radios than anyone else. Their authority, however, was difficult to resist, and he was under another kind of pressure from another source. "You must go," his friend Francois said to him, "because the radio may be our only chance. If we have to walk out of here—people like Coche, Moncho, Alvaro, you, and me—we just won't make it."

With enormous reluctance Roy gave in to this argument and agreed to go. Their departure, however, was not imminent because several of them were still struggling with the shark's-fin antenna, riveted on the roof of the plane above the pilots' cabin. They had to remove the rivets with only a screwdriver, and the task was made more difficult by twists in the metal caused by the fall of the plane.

Even when it was removed and lay on the snow beside the different parts of the radio, Canessa spent hour upon hour just staring at it and snapped at anyone who asked him what more there was to do that he was not ready to go. The others became impatient, but they were all wary of Canessa's temper. If he had not been an expeditionary—and the most inventive of the three—they might not have put up with him; as it was, they did not wish to antagonize him. All the same, his procrastination seemed unreasonable, and they began to suspect that he was protracting the experiment with the radio to postpone the moment when he might have to set off in the snow.

At last the three Strauch cousins became exasperated. They told him that he must take the radio and go. Canessa could think of no further excuse for delay, and at eight o'clock the next morning a small column assembled for the descent to the tail. First came Vizintín, loaded as usual like a packhorse; then Harley, with his hands in his pockets, and finally the two figures of Canessa and Parrado, with sticks and knapsacks like two winter sportsmen.

They set off down the mountain, and the thirteen they left behind were delighted to see them go. Not only were they spared the irritable and bullying presence of Canessa and Vizintín but also, with the four absent, they could sleep much more comfortably. Above all they could dream again that rescue was at hand.

They were in no position, however, to sit back and wait for their dreams to come true. For the first time since they had taken their decision to eat the flesh of the dead, they were running short of supplies. The problem was not that sufficient bodies did not exist but that they could not find them; those who had died in the accident and had been left outside the plane were now, as a result of the avalanche, buried deep beneath the snow. One or two still remained of those who had died in the avalanche, but they knew that quite soon they would have to find the earlier victims. It was also a consideration that those who had died in the accident would be fatter and their livers better stocked with the vitamins they all needed to survive.

They therefore set about searching for bodies. Carlitos Páez and Pedro Algorta were in charge of this operation, but all the other boys joined in. Their method was to dig a shaft down into the snow on the spot where they remembered a body had lain, but these holes would often go deep without anything coming to light. On other occasions they would be more successful, but often with frustrating consequences. It was thought, for instance, that a body lay somewhere around the entrance to the plane, and Algorta spent many days methodically digging a hole there, with steps going down into it. It was difficult work because the snow was hard and Pedro, like all the others, had grown increasingly weak, so it was something like finding gold when the piece of aluminum which acted as a shovel uncovered the fabric of what seemed to be a shirt. Pedro dug faster around the legs and feet of the body but suddenly saw, as he uncovered them, that the toenails were painted with red varnish. Instead of a boy's body he had found Liliana Methol, and in deference to Javier's feelings they had agreed not to eat her.

Another method of sinking an exploratory shaft was for all the boys to urinate onto a single spot. It was an effective method, if only they could contain themselves each morning for long enough to reach the appointed place. Alas, many of them awoke with bladders so taut that they were forced to relieve themselves as soon as they left the plane. Algorta often slept with his three pairs of trousers unbuttoned, and even then he sometimes did not make it out of the plane. It was a pity, because it was easier to piss into a hole than to dig one.

Many of the boys felt themselves too weak to do any labor of any kind. Some had learned to live with their uselessness, but other did not admit to themselves that they made no contribution to the welfare of the group. Carlitos once rebuked Sabella for not doing any work, whereupon the enfeebled Moncho fell to digging a hole with such hysterical frenzy that those who watched him feared for his life, but his exertions only led him to collapse with exhaustion. Here indeed was a case where the spirit was willing but the flesh weak. Moncho would have loved to be counted among the heroic cousins and expeditionaries, but his body betrayed him; he had no choice but to be one of the spectators.

At the same time as the boys dug into the snow in search of the buried bodies, the corpses that they had preserved nearer the surface began to suffer from the stronger sun which melted the thin layer of snow which covered them. The thaw had truly set in—the level of the snow had fallen far below the roof of the Fairchild—and the sun in the middle of the day became so hot that any meat left exposed to it would quickly rot. Added, then, to the labors of digging, cutting, and snow melting was that of covering the bodies with snow and then shielding them from the sun with sheets of cardboard and plastic.

As the supplies grew short, an order went out from the cousins that there was to be no more pilfering. This edict was no more effective than most others which seek to upset an established practice. They therefore sought to make what food they had last longer by eating parts of the human body which previously they had left aside. The hands and feet, for example, had flesh beneath the skin which could be scraped off the bone. They tried, too, to eat the tongue off one corpse but could not swallow it, and one of them once ate the testicles.

On the other hand they all took to the marrow. When the last shred of meat had been scraped off a bone it would be cracked open with the ax and the marrow extracted with a piece of wire or a knife and shared. They also ate the blood clots which they found around the hearts of almost all the bodies. Their texture and taste were different from that of the flesh and fat, and by now they were sick to death of this staple diet. It was not just that their senses clamored for different tastes; their bodies too cried out for those minerals of which they had for so long been deprived—above all, for salt. And it was in obedience to these cravings that the less fastidious among the survivors began to eat those parts of the body which had started to rot. This had happened to the entrails of even those bodies which were covered with snow, and there were also the remains of previous carcasses scattered around the plane which were unprotected from the sun. Later everyone did the same.

What they would do was to take the small intestine, squeeze out its contents onto the snow, cut it into small pieces, and eat it. The taste was strong and salty. One of them tried wrapping it around a bone and roasting it in the fire. Rotten flesh, which they tried later, tasted like cheese.

The last discovery in their search for new tastes and new sources of food were the brains of the bodies which they had hitherto discarded. Canessa had told them that, while they might not be of particular nutritional value, they contained glucose which would give them energy; he had been the first to take a head, cut the skin across the forehead, pull back the scalp, and crack open the skull with the ax. The brains were then either divided up and eaten while still frozen or used to make the sauce for a stew; the liver, intestine, muscle, fat, heart, and kidneys, either cooked or uncooked, were cut up into little pieces and mixed with the brains. In this way the food tasted better and was easier to eat. The only difficulty was the shortage of bowls suitable to hold it, for before this the meat had been served on plates, trays, or pieces of aluminum foil. For the stew Inciarte used a shaving bowl, while others used the top halves of skulls. Four bowls made from skulls were used in this way—and some spoons were made from bones.

The brains were inedible when putrid, so all the heads which remained from the corpses they had consumed were gathered together and buried in the snow. The snow was also combed for other parts which had previously been thrown away. Scavenging took on an added value—especially for Algorta, who was the chief scavenger among them. When he was not digging holes or helping the cousins cut up the bodies, his bent figure could be seen hobbling around the plane, poking into the snow with an iron stick. He looked so much like a tramp that Carlitos gave him the nickname of Old Vizcacha★—but his dedication was not without its rewards, because he found many pieces of old fat, some with a thin strip of flesh. These he would place on his part of the roof. If they were waterlogged, they would dry out in the sun, forming a crust which made them more palatable. Or, like the others, he would put them on a piece of metal which caught the sun and in this way warm what he was eating; once, when the sun was exceptionally strong, he actually cooked them.

★. . . a land-louping scapegrace, hung with rags,
That lived like a leech in the fens and quags,
A gully-raking veteran scamp,
Bad-biled as a mangy boar.
—José Hernández,
The Gaucho Martín Fierro, II, xiv, translated by Walter Owen
(Oxford: Basil Blackwell, 1935)

It was a relief to Algorta that the expeditionaries were no longer there to help themselves to what he had so carefully scavenged and prepared. On the other hand, he did share what he had found with Fito. Alongside his bit of the roof there was Fito's and between the two was an area for food which they shared. It was Algorta who kept this common larder stocked with extra food. He had attached himself to Fito in the same way that Zerbino had become, as Inciarte put it, "the German's page boy." It particularly annoyed Inciarte that Zerbino would give cigarettes to Eduardo even when he still had some of his own, but Zerbino remembered the days after the first expedition, when Eduardo had let him sleep with his swollen feet on his shoulders.

As the division between the two groups of workers and work-shy, provident and improvident, grew wider, Coche Inciarte's role became more important. By performance and inclination he was firmly in the camp of the parasites; on the other hand he was an old friend of Fito Strauch and Daniel Fernández. He also had the kind of pure and witty character that it was impossible to dislike. Whether he was coaxing Carlitos to cook on a windy day or shooting a pint of pus out of his dreadfully infected leg, he would always smile himself and make others smile at what he was doing. His condition, like Numa Turcatti's, was increasingly serious because both were reluctant to eat raw meat. Coche even became delirious at times and told the boys in all seriousness that there was a little door in the side of the plane where he slept which led out into a green valley. Yet when he announced one morning, as Rafael Echavarren had done, that he was going to die that day, no one took him seriously. Next day, when he awoke again, they all laughed at him and said, "Well, Coche, what's it like to be dead?"

Cigarettes were, as always, the chief source of tension. Those like the cousins, who had sufficient control of themselves to space their smoking and make their ration last, would find toward the end of the second day that each puff was watched by a dozen pairs of envious eyes. The improvident—and Coche was among the most improvident—would exhaust their own supply the first day and then try and bum cigarettes off those who still had some. Pedro Algorta, who smoked less than the others, would move around with lowered eyes for fear of intercepting one of Coche's importuning glances, yet if he avoided them for long enough, Coche would say to him, "Pedro, when we get back to Montevideo, I'll invite you to eat some *gnocchi* at our uncle's house," at which the hungry Algorta would look up and be caught by the large, pleading, laughing eyes.

Pancho Delgado was also unable to ration himself and would sidle up to Sabella, say, and talk to him about his school days with his brother on the off chance that a cigarette might come out of it. Or he would be sent by Inciarte to persuade Fernández to give them an advance ration. "You see," he would say, "Coche and I are especially nervous people. . . ."

There had been a time when Delgado himself had been in charge of the cigarettes, which was something like putting an alcoholic in charge of a bar. One night the storm outside was so dreadful that snow blew right into the plane. Delgado and Zerbino, who had been sleeping by the door, moved up the cabin to talk and smoke cigarettes with Coche and Carlitos. Most of the boys had stayed awake, smoking and listening to the rumble of avalanches, but in the morning, when they awoke all white from the snow, some doubted that they had smoked quite as many cigarettes as Pancho maintained.

There was another occasion when Fernández and Inciarte quarreled over cigarettes. Fernández, who had charge of one of the three lighters, ignored Coche when he repeatedly asked to use it, because he thought Coche smoked too much. This made Coche furious, and for the rest of that day he refused to speak to Fernández. At night, as usual, they lay next to each other, but every time Fernández's head lolled over onto Coche's shoulder, Coche would shrug it off. Then Fernández said, "Come on, Coche," and Coche gave up his petulant rage. He was too good-natured to sustain it.

Their improvidence with cigarettes reinforced a bond which had already existed between Coche and Pancho. They either bummed alone—Pancho taking some of Numa Turcatti's ration because he felt that smoking was doing him no good, while Coche tried to catch Algorta's eye—or, as we have seen, presented a common front to get an advance from Daniel Fernández. They also talked together about life in Montevideo and weekends in the country with Gaston Costemalle, who had been their mutual friend. Pancho, with his natural eloquence, described the scene of their former happiness so well that Coche would be transported away from the damp, stinking confines of the wrecked plane to the green pastures of his dairy farm. Then, when the story ended, he would suddenly find himself back in the foul reality, which would so depress him that he would sit like a corpse with glazed eyes.

Because of this, the Strauches and Daniel Fernández tried to keep Coche away from Delgado. They felt that these escapist conversations would lower his morale to such an extent that he would lose the will to survive. Also, they were coming increasingly to mistrust Delgado. There was an incident when some of the boys were outside the plane and called to those inside to send someone out to fetch their ration of meat. Pancho appeared and, while taking the pieces of meat, asked Fito if he could take a piece for himself.

"Of course," said Fito.

"The best piece?"

"If you like."

Fito and the others had remained on the roof eating their portions of flesh, and after delivering the rest to the others, Pancho had come out to join them. When Fito had eventually gone in, Daniel Fernández, who had cut the meat Pancho brought into smaller pieces, said to him, "Hey, you didn't give us much to eat."

"I cut twelve pieces," said Fito.

"More like eight. I had to cut them all up again."

Fito shrugged his shoulders and said nothing more, for to have expressed what he suspected would have been against his better judgment. It was essential to the group that there should be no real dissension.

Carlitos, on the other hand, felt less compunction. "I wonder where the ghost is, then," he said, staring at Pancho, "who took the four other pieces?"

"What do you mean?" said Pancho. "What are you suggesting? Don't you trust me?"

They might have said more, but Fito and Daniel Fernández told Carlitos to let the matter go.

While these developments were taking place in the plane, the three expeditionaries and Roy Harley were in the tail. Their journey down had only taken them one and a half hours, and on the way they had found a suitcase which had belonged to Parrado's mother. They found candy inside and two bottles of Coca-Cola.

They spent the rest of that first day at the tail resting and looking through the suitcases which had appeared from under the melting snow since they were last there. Among other things Parrado found a camera loaded with film and his airline bag with the two bottles of rum and liqueur which his mother had bought in Mendoza and asked him to carry for her. Neither was broken, and they opened one of them but saved the other for the expedition they would have to make if they could not get the radio to work.

Canessa and Harley set about that task next morning. It seemed at first that it would not be difficult, because the sockets in the back of the transmitter were marked BAT and ANT to show where the wires to the batteries and antenna should be fixed. Unfortunately there were other wires whose connections were not so clear. Above all they could not make out which wires were positive and which negative, so often when they made a connection sparks flew into their eyes.

Their hopes of success were raised when Vizintín found an instruction manual for the Fairchild lying in the snow beside the tail. They looked at the index for some reference to the radio and discovered that the whole of chapter thirty-four was devoted to "Communications," but when they came to look for this section they discovered that certain pages had been torn out of the book by the wind and it was just these pages which made up the chapter they needed.

They had no choice, therefore, but to return to trial and error. It was a painstaking business, and while the others worked Parrado and Vizintín would rummage around rifling all the baggage for a second time, or light a fire to cook the meat. Though there were only four of them, they were not exempt from the tensions which existed up in the fuselage. It irritated Roy Harley, for example, that Parrado would not give him the same ration as the others. It seemed clear that since he was on an expedition he should eat the same amount as an expeditionary. Parrado, on the other hand, held that Roy was only an auxiliary; if the radio failed he would not have to walk out through the mountains. Therefore he should eat only what was necessary to survive.

Nor would he let Roy smoke cigarettes. His reasoning was that they only had one lighter with them and they would need it for any final expedition; but it was also true that neither Parrado, Canessa, nor Vizintín smoked themselves but all were intolerably irritated by Roy's whimpering and wailing. Thus they told him that he could only smoke when they lit a fire. On one occasion, however, when Roy came to light a cigarette at the fire, Parrado, who was cooking, told him to get out of his way and come back when he had finished. But when Roy came back the fire had gone out. He was so angry that he picked up the lighter which Parrado had left on some cardboard and lit a cigarette. When the three expeditionaries saw what he had done they went for him like a pack of zealous school prefects. They cursed him and might have snatched the cigarette out of his mouth had not Canessa thought better of it and stopped them. "Leave him alone," he said to the other two. "Don't forget that Roy may be the one to save the lives of us all by getting this damned radio to work."

It was clear by the third day that they had not brought enough meat to last them the time it would take to set up the radio. Therefore Parrado and Vizintín set off for the plane again, leaving Harley and Canessa at the tail. The ascent, as before, was a thousand times more difficult than the descent had been. After reaching the top of the hillock which lay just east of the plane, Parrado was assaulted by a momentary but profound despair; instead of the fuselage and its thirteen inhabitants, there was nothing but a huge expanse of snow.

He assumed at once that there must have been another avalanche which had completely covered the plane, but he looked up and saw no signs of a fresh fall of snow on the sides of the mountains above him. He walked on and to his immense relief found the plane on the other side of the next hill.

The boys had not expected them and had no meat prepared. Also, they were all almost too weak to dig for the bodies that would have to be found if the expeditionaries were to restock their larder. Therefore Parrado and Vizintín themselves set about digging. They found a corpse from which the cousins cut meat and stuffed it into rugby socks, and after two nights up in the plane they returned to the tail.

There they found that Harley and Canessa had made all the necessary connections between battery and radio and radio and shark's-fin antenna but still could not pick up any signal on the earphones. They thought that perhaps the antenna was faulty, so they tore out strands of cable from the electrical circuits of the plane and linked them together. One end of this they tied to the tail, the other to a bag filled with stones which they placed on a rock high on the side of the mountain, making an aerial more than sixty feet long. When they connected it to the transistor radio which they had brought with them, they could pick up many radio stations in Chile, Argentina, and Uruguay. When they connected it to the Fairchild's radio, however, nothing came through at all. They therefore reconnected the transistor, found a program which played some cheerful music, and went back to work.

Suddenly there was a shout from Parrado; he had found in one of the suitcases a photograph of a child at a birthday party. It was a little girl, and she was sitting at a table piled with sandwiches, cakes, and crackers. Parrado clutched the photograph and devoured the food with his eyes, but soon the other three, alerted by his cry, came up behind him and joined in the feast. "Just look at that cake," said Canessa, groaning and rubbing his stomach.

"What about the sandwiches?" said Parrado. "I think I'd even rather have the sandwiches."

"The crackers," Vizintín moaned. "Just give me the crackers. . . ."

On the transistor radio that they had attached to their antenna, the four of them heard a news bulletin in which it was announced that the search was to be resumed by a Douglas C-47 of the Uruguayan Air Force. They received the news in different ways. Harley was ecstatic with hope and joy. Canessa too looked relieved. Vizintín showed no particular reaction, while Parrado looked almost disappointed. "Don't get too optimistic," he warned the others. "Just because they're looking again doesn't mean they'll find us."

They decided, all the same, that it would be a good idea to make a large cross in the snow by the tail, and they did so with the suitcases that lay scattered all around. By now they had almost given up hope of the radio, though Canessa still pottered with it and prevaricated about a return to the plane. Parrado and Vizintín, on the other hand, already had their minds on the expedition, for it has been decided up in the plane that if the radio failed the expeditionaries would set off straight up the mountain in obedience to the only thing of which they were sure—that Chile was to the west. Thus Vizintín removed the rest of the material which was wound around the Fairchild's heating system in the dark locker at the base of the tail which had contained the batteries. It was light and yet designed by the most technologically sophisticated industry in the world to contain heat; sewn together into a large sack, it would make an excellent sleeping bag and solve the one outstanding problem which had beset them—how to keep warm at night without the shelter of either tail or plane.

All the time they had been at the tail the snow had been melting around them—all, that is, except the snow immediately beneath the tail, which was shaded from the sun. As a result, the tail had been left as if on a pillar of snow which made it not only more difficult to enter but also perilously unsteady as they moved about inside. On the last night it wobbled so much that Parrado became terrified that it would fall over and shoot down the mountainside. The four lay as still as they could, but there was a wind which made the tail sway and Parrado could not sleep. "Hey," he said at last to the others, "don't you think we'd better sleep outside?"

Vizintín grunted and Canessa said, "Look, Nando. If we're going to die, we're going to die, so let's at least get a good night's sleep."

The tail was in the same place the next morning, but it was clearly no longer safe. It was equally obvious that no more tinkering with the radio would make it work. They therefore made up their minds to return to the plane. Before they left they loaded themselves once again with cigarettes, and Harley—as an expression of all the misery and frustration he had felt in those eight days—kicked to pieces the different components of the radio they had so painstakingly put together.

He was wrong to waste his energy. The 45-degree climb back to the plane was almost a mile. At first it was not so difficult, because the surface of the snow was hard. Later, when it became mushy and they either sank up to their thighs or strapped on the heavy and cumbersome cushions that they used as snowshoes, it needed an almost super-human effort which poor Roy was not in a condition to provide. Though they rested every thirty paces, he soon lagged behind, but Parrado stayed with him—cajoling, cursing, begging him to come on. Roy would try and then fall back into the snow with despair and exhaustion. His voice whined higher than ever before; tears flowed more freely. He begged to be left there to die, but Parrado would not leave him. He swore at him and insulted him to put fire into his blood. He cursed him as he had never cursed anyone before.

The insults were extreme but they worked. They drove Roy on until it came to a point where he no longer responded to either oath or insult. Then Parrado returned to him and spoke quietly, saying, "Listen. It isn't much farther now. Don't you think it's worth making one last little effort for the sake of seeing your mother and father again?"

Then he took his hand and helped Roy to his feet. Once again he staggered up the mountain, resting on Parrado's arm, and when they came to a slope of snow so steep that no effort of will could drive Roy to surmount it, Parrado gripped him with the enormous strength he still seemed to possess and brought him up toward the Fairchild.

They reached the plane between half past six and seven in the evening. There was a cold wind blowing, with a slight flurry of snow. The thirteen had already gone inside, and they gave the expeditionaries a depressed reception.

Canessa, however, was less struck by their unfriendliness than by the desolation of the spectacle they presented. After eight days away he saw with some objectivity just how thin and haggard the bearded faces of his friends had become. He had seen too, with a fresh eye, the horror of the filthy snow strewn with gutted carcasses and split skulls, and he thought to himself that before they were rescued they must do something to tidy it up.

Toward the end of the first week in December, after fifty-six days on the mountain, two condors appeared in the sky and circled above the seventeen survivors. These two enormous birds of prey with bald necks and head, a collar of white down, and a wingspan of nine feet were the first sign of any life but their own that they had seen for eight weeks. The survivors were immediately afraid that they would descend and carry off the carrion. They would have shot at them with the revolver but were afraid that the sudden noise might cause another avalanche.

At times the condors would leave them but then reappear the next morning. They watched the movements of the human beings but never swooped on them, and after some days they disappeared altogether. They were followed, however, by other signs of life. A bee once flew into the fuselage and then out again; later still, one or two flies and finally a butterfly were seen around the plane.

It was now warm during the day; indeed, at midday it was so hot that their skin became burned and their lips were cracked and bleeding. Some of them tried to make a tent to shelter them from the sun with the poles from the hammocks and a bale of cloth that Liliana Methol had bought in Mendoza to make a dress for her daughter. They also thought it would make a useful signal to any plane that flew overhead, for this possibility was uppermost in their minds. When Roy and the expeditionaries had returned from the tail, they had told the thirteen who had stayed in the plane that they had heard on their transistor that the search had been restarted.

The boys were determined that this should not tempt the expeditionaries to abandon the idea of further expedition. They had had no high hopes for the radio and were not thrown into despair when Harley, Canessa, Parrado, and Vizintín returned, but they were impatient that the last three should leave again almost immediately. It soon became evident, however, that while the news of the C-47 in no way affected Parrado's determination to leave, it produced in Canessa a certain reluctance to risk his life on the mountainside. "It would be absurd for us to leave now," he said, "with this specially equipped plane on its way to find us. We should give them at least ten days and then, perhaps, set out. It's crazy to risk our lives if it isn't necessary."

The others were thrown into a fury by this procrastination. They had not pampered Canessa and suffered his intolerable temper for so long only to be told by him that he was not going. Nor were they so optimistic that the C-47 would find them, for they heard on the radio first that it had been forced to land in Buenos Aires, then that it had had to have its engines overhauled in Los Cerrillos. There was also the shortage of food that was upon them, for though they knew that corpses were hidden in the snow beneath them, they either could not find them or only found those they had agreed not to eat.

There was another factor too, which was their sense of pride in what they had already achieved. They had survived now for eight weeks in the most extreme and inhuman conditions. They wanted to prove that they could also escape on their own initiative. They all loved to think of the expression on the face of the first shepherd or farmer they found as he was told that the three expeditionaries were survivors from the Uruguayan Fairchild. All of them practiced in their minds the nonchalant tone they would adopt when telephoning their parents in Montevideo.

Fito's impatience was more practical. "Don't you realize," he said to Canessa, "that they aren't looking for survivors? They're looking for dead bodies. And the special equipment they talk about is photographic equipment. They take aerial photographs and then go back, develop them, study them. . . . It'll take weeks for them to find us, even if they do fly directly overhead."

This argument seemed to convince Canessa. Parrado did not need to be persuaded, and Vizintín always went along with what the other two decided. They therefore set to work to prepare the final expedition. The cousins cut flesh off the bodies not just for their daily needs but to set up a store for the journey. The others were set to sewing the insulating material from the tail into a sleeping bag. It was difficult. They ran out of thread and had to use wire from the electric circuits.

Parrado would have helped them do this, but he was not skilled with his hands. He therefore took photographs with the camera they had found in the tail and collected together the clothes and equipment he would need for the expedition. He filled a knapsack made from a pair of jeans with the plane's compass, his mother's rug, four spare pairs of socks, his passport, four hundred U.S. dollars, a bottle of water, a pocket knife, and a woman's lipstick for his broken lips.

Vizintín put his shaving kit into his knapsack, not so much because he intended to shave before reaching civilization but because it had been a present from his father and he did not want to leave it behind. He also packed the plane's charts, a bottle of rum, a bottle of water, dry socks, and the revolver.

Canessa's rucksack was filled with all the medicines he thought they might conceivably need on their journey—adhesive bandages, a tube of dental floss, aspirin, pills against diarrhea, antiseptic cream, caffeine pills, muscle-warming ointment, and a large pill whose function was not known. He added to this a woman's foundation cream to protect his skin, toothpaste, his documents, including his vaccination certificate, Methol's penknife, a spoon, a piece of paper, a length of wire, and an elephant hair as a good-luck charm.

December 8 was the Feast of the Immaculate Conception. To honor the Virgin, and to persuade her to intercede for the success of their final expedition, the boys in the Fairchild decided to pray the full fifteen mysteries of the rosary. Alas, soon after they had finished five their voices grew thinner and fewer, and one by one they dropped off to sleep. They therefore made up the rest the next evening, the ninth, which was also Parrado's twenty-third birthday. It was a mildly melancholy occasion, for they had so often planned the party they would have in Montevideo. To celebrate here on the mountain, the community gave Parrado one of the Havana cigars that had been found in the tail. Parrado smoked it, but he took more pleasure from the warmth it provided than from the aroma.

On December 10, Canessa still insisted that the expedition was not ready to leave. The sleeping bag was not sewn to his satisfaction, nor had he collected together everything he would need. Yet instead of applying himself to what was still to be done, Canessa lay around "conserving his energy" or insisted on treating the boils that Roy Harley had developed on his legs. He also quarreled with the younger boys. He told Francois that at the tail Vizintín had wiped his backside on Bobby's best Lacoste T-shirt, which put Bobby into an unusual rage. He even quarreled with his great friend and admirer Alvaro Mangino, for that morning, while defecating onto a seat cover in the plane (he had diarrhea from eating putrid flesh), he told Mangino to move his leg. Mangino said that it had been cramped all night and so he would not. Canessa shouted at Mangino. Mangino cursed Canessa. Canessa lost his temper and grabbed Mangino by the hair. He was about to hit him but simply threw Alvaro back against the wall of the plane instead.

"Now you're not my friend any more," Mangino said, sobbing.

"I'm sorry," said Canessa, sitting back, his temper once more under control. "It's just that I'm feeling so ill. . . ."

He was no one's friend that day. The cousins thought he was deliberately procrastinating and were especially angry with him. That night they did not keep his special place as an expeditionary, and he had to sleep by the door. The only one who had any influence on him was Parrado, and his determination was as great as it had ever been. That morning, as they lay in the plane waiting to go out, he suddenly said, "You know, if that plane flies over us, it might not see us. We should make a cross." And without waiting for anyone else to take up his idea, he went out of the plane and surveyed an area of pristine snow where a cross could be best constructed. The other boys followed him, and soon all those who could walk without pain were stamping the ground along preordained lines to make a giant cross in the snow.

In the middle, where the two lines crossed, they put the upturned trash can which Vizintín had brought up on the trial expedition. They also laid out the bright yellow and green jackets of the pilots. Realizing that movement would attract a flier's attention, they drew up a plan whereby they would run in circles as soon as a plane was sighted overhead.

That night Fito Strauch went to Parrado and said that if Canessa would not leave on the expedition then he would.

"No," said Parrado. "Don't worry. I've talked to Muscles. He'll go. He must go. He's much better trained than you are. All we have to do now is finish the sleeping bag."

The next morning the Strauches rose early and set to work on the sleeping bag. They were determined that by that evening there should be no possible excuse for any further delay. But something was to happen that day which would make their threats and admonitions superfluous.

Numa Turcatti had been getting weaker every day. His health, along with that of Roy Harley and Coche Inciarte, caused the greatest concern to the two "doctors," Canessa and Zerbino. Though Numa, who was so pure in spirit, was loved by all on the plane, his closest friend before the accident had been Pancho Delgado, and it was Delgado who took it upon himself to look after him. He brought Numa's ration of food into the plane, made water for him, tried to stop him from smoking cigarettes because Canessa had said they were bad for him, and fed him little smears of toothpaste from a tube which Canessa had brought from the tail.

For all this care Numa continued to decline, and Delgado decided that something further should be done. He made up his mind to get extra food for his patient and, true to his nature, fell upon the method of stealth. He felt, perhaps, that had he asked the cousins outright, they might have refused. There came a day, however, when Canessa had diarrhea and was sitting near where Numa lay inside the plane. Delgado went out to fetch the food and came in with three dishes. Canessa had decided not to eat, because of his diarrhea, but it was a day when they had cooked a stew, and when he saw what Delgado had brought in he asked to taste it. Delgado let him, willingly; Canessa tasted it and then decided that after all he would have his ration.

Canessa went up to Eduardo, who was serving it out, and asked for his ration. Eduardo said, "But I gave your portion to Pancho."

"Well, he never gave it to me."

Eduardo was quick to lose his temper, and he lost it now. He began to vilify Delgado, and as he did so Delgado came out the plane.

"Are you talking about me?"

"I am. Did you think we wouldn't notice how you sneaked an extra ration?"

Delgado blushed and said, "I don't know how you can think such a thing of me."

"Then why didn't you give Muscles his ration?"

"Do you think I kept it for myself?"

"Yes."

"It was for Numa. You may not realize it, but Numa is growing weaker every day. If he doesn't have extra food he will die."

Eduardo was taken aback. "Then why didn't you ask us?"

"I thought you might refuse."

The cousins let it pass, but they remained suspicious of Delgado. They knew, for instance, that on the days when the meat was raw Numa could hardly be persuaded to eat one ration, let alone two. Nor did it escape their notice that those cigarettes Delgado so conscientiously prevented Numa from smoking, he smoked himself.

Even with an extra ration, Numa's condition did not improve. Instead he grew weaker. As he grew weaker, he grew more listless, and as he grew more listless he bothered less about feeding himself, which in its turn made him weaker still. He also developed a bedsore on his coccyx, and it was when he asked Zerbino to come and look at it that Zerbino realized how drastically thin he had become. Until then his face had been covered by a beard and his whole body by clothes. Removing the clothes to examine the sore, Zerbino could see that there was practically no flesh left between the skin and the spine. Numa had become a skeleton, and Zerbino told the others afterward that he only gave him a few more days to live.

Like Inciarte and Sabella, Numa was intermittently delirious, but on the night of December 10 he slept peacefully. In the morning Delgado went out to sit in the sun. He had been told that Numa might die but his mind would not accept it. Later in the morning, however, Canessa came out and told him that Numa was in a coma. Delgado returned immediately to the cabin and went to the side of his friend. Numa lay there with his eyes open, but he seemed unaware of Delgado's presence. His breathing was slow and labored. Delgado knelt beside him and began to say the rosary. As he prayed, the breathing stopped.

At midday the cushions were laid on the floor of the plane again. It had become a habit, because of the heat of the sun, to take a siesta. It depressed them all to lie impotently like this, but it was better than burning. They sat and talked or dozed off. Then, at about three in the afternoon, they began to file out again. On this particular afternoon, Javier Methol lay at the back of the plane. "Be careful," he said to Coche as he rose and stepped over Numa's body. "Be careful not to step on Numa."

"But Numa's dead," said Parrado.

Javier had not realized what had happened, and now that he understood his spirits dropped completely. He wept as he had wept at the death of Liliana, for he had grown to love the shy and simple Numa Turcatti as though he were his brother or son.

Turcatt's death achieved what argument and exhortation had failed to achieve; it persuaded Canessa that they could wait no longer. Roy Harley, Coche Inciarte, and Moncho Sabella were all weak and incipiently delirious. A day's delay could mean the difference between their death and their survival. It was therefore agreed by all that the final expedition should set off the next day due west to Chile.

That evening, before he went into the plane for the last time, Parrado drew the three Strauch cousins to one side and told them that if they ran short of food they should eat the bodies of his mother and sister. "Of course I'd rather you didn't," he said, "but if it's a matter of survival, then you must."

The cousins said nothing, but the expression on their faces betrayed how moved they were by what Parrado had said to them.

Annapurna

BY MAURICE HERZOG

In the first conquest of an 8,000-meter peak (26,493 feet) in 1950, French climber Maurice Herzog and his teammate Louis Lachenal wrote more than mountaineering history: They wrote a chronicle of human courage in the face of intense physical suffering and danger. With limbs horribly frozen in their climb to the summit, the two men barely escaped the mountain alive with the help of their companions.

Herzog lost his hands, but his prose later won the hearts of generations of readers who have shared his adventure through the pages of his classic book, which was republished by The Lyons Press in 1997. The two chapters presented here cover the successful summit bid of Herzog and Lachenal and the first stages of their retreat from the mountain.

In his typical self-effacing style, Herzog ended his book with these memorable words:

"One always talks of the ideal as a goal towards which one strives but which one never reaches. For every one of us, Annapura was an ideal that had been realized. In our youth we had not been misled by fantasies, nor by the bloody battles of modern warfare which feed the imagination of the young. For us the mountains had been a natural field of activity where, playing on the frontiers of life and death, we had found the freedom for which we were blindly groping and which was as necessary to us as bread. The mountains had bestowed on us their beauties, and we adored them with a child's simplicity and revered them with a monk's veneration of the divine.

"Annapurna, to which we had gone emptyhanded, was a treasure on which we should live the rest of our days. With this realization we turn the page: a new life begins.

"There are other Annapurnas in the lives of men."

*　　*　　*　　*　　*

Chapter XIII
The Third of June

On the third of June, 1950, the first light of dawn found us still clinging to the tent poles at Camp V. Gradually the wind abated, and with daylight, died away altogether. I made desperate attempts to push back the soft, icy stuff which stifled me, but every movement became an act of heroism. My mental powers were numbed: thinking was an effort, and we did not exchange a single word.

What a repellent place it was! To everyone who reached it, Camp V became one of the worst memories of their lives. We had only one thought— to get away. We should have waited for the first rays of the sun, but at half-past five we felt we couldn't stick it any longer.

"Let's go, Biscante," I muttered. "Can't stay here a minute longer."

"Yes, let's go," repeated Lachenal.

Which of us would have the energy to make tea? Although our minds worked slowly we were quite able to envisage all the movements that would be necessary—and neither of us could face up to it. It couldn't be helped—we would just have to go without. It was quite hard enough work to get ourselves and our boots out of our sleeping-bags—and the boots were frozen stiff so that we got them on only with the greatest difficulty. Every movement made us terribly breathless. We felt as if we were being stifled. Our gaiters were stiff as a board, and I succeeded in lacing mine up; Lahenal couldn't manage his.

"No need for the rope, eh, Biscante?"

"No need," replied Lachenal laconically.

That was two pounds saved. I pushed a tube of condensed milk, some nougat and a pair of socks into my sack; one never knew, the socks might come in useful—they might even do as Balaclavas. For the time being I stuffed them with first-aid equipment. The camera was loaded with a black and white film; I had a color film in reserve. I pulled the movie-camera out from the bottom of my sleeping-bag, wound it up and tried letting it run without film. There was a little click, then it stopped and jammed.

"Bad luck after bringing it so far," said Lachenal.

In spite of our photographer, Ichac's, precautions taken to lubricate it with special grease, the intense cold, even inside the sleeping-bag, had frozen it. I left it at the camp rather sadly: I had looked forward to taking it to the top. I had used it up to 24,600 feet.

We went outside and put on our crampons, which we kept on all day. We wore as many clothes as possible; our sacks were very light. At six o'clock we started off. It was brilliantly fine, but also very cold. Our super-lightweight crampons bit deep into the steep slopes of ice and hard snow up which lay the first stage of our climb.

Later the slope became slightly less steep and more uniform. Sometimes the hard crust bore our weight, but at others we broke through and sank into soft powder snow which made progress exhausting. We took turns in making the track and often stopped without any word having passed between us. Each of us lived in a closed and private world of his own. I was suspicious of my mental processes; my mind was working very slowly and I was perfectly aware of the low state of my intelligence. It was easiest just to stick to one thought at a time—safest, too. The cold was penetrating; for all our special eiderdown clothing we felt as if we'd nothing on. Whenever we halted, we stamped our feet hard. Lachenal went as far as to take off one boot which was a bit tight; he was in terror of frostbite.

"I don't want to be like Lambert," he said. Raymond Lambert, a Geneva guide, had to have all his toes amputated after an eventful climb during which he got his feet frostbitten.[1] While Lachenal rubbed himself hard, I looked at the summits all around us; already we overtopped them all except the distant Dhaulagiri. The complicated structure of these mountains, with which our many laborious explorations had made us familiar, was now spread out plainly at our feet.

The going was incredibly exhausting, and every step was a struggle of mind over matter. We came out into the sunlight, and by way of marking the occasion made yet another halt. Lachenal continued to complain of his feet. "I can't feel anything. I think I'm beginning to get frostbite." And once again he undid his boot.

I began to be seriously worried. I realized very well the risk we were running; I knew from experience how insidiously and quickly frostbite can set in if one is not extremely careful. Nor was Lachenal under any illusions. "We're in danger of having frozen feet. Do you think it's worth it?"

This was most disturbing. It was my responsibility as leader to think of the others. There was no doubt about frostbite being a very real danger. Did Annapurna justify such risks? That was the question I asked myself; it continued to worry me.

Lachenal had laced his boots up again, and once more we continued to force our way through the exhausting snow. The whole of the Sickle glacier was now in view, bathed in light. We still had a long way to go to cross it, and then there was that rock band—would we find a gap in it?

My feet, like Lachenal's, were very cold and I continued to wriggle my toes, even when we were moving. I could not feel them, but that was nothing new in the mountains, and if I kept on moving them it would keep the circulation going.

Lachenal appeared to me as a sort of specter—he was alone in his world, I in mine. But—and this was odd enough—any effort was slightly *less* exhausting than lower down. Perhaps it was hope lending us wings. Even through dark glasses the snow was blinding—the sun beating straight down on the ice. We looked down upon precipitous ridges which dropped away into space, and upon tiny glaciers far, far below. Familiar peaks soared arrow-like into the sky. Suddenly Lachenal grabbed me:

"If I go back, what will you do?"

A whole sequence of pictures flashed through my head: the days of marching in sweltering heat, the hard pitches we had overcome, the tremendous efforts we had all made to lay siege to the mountain, the daily heroism of all my friends in establishing the camps. Now we were nearing our goal. In an hour or two, perhaps, victory would be ours. Must we give up? Impossible! My whole being revolted against the idea. I had made up my mind, irrevocably. Today we were consecrating an ideal, and no sacrifice was too great. I heard my voice clearly:

"I should go on by myself."

I would go alone. If he wished to go down it was not for me to stop him. He must make his own choice freely.

"Then I'll follow you."

The die was cast. I was no longer anxious. Nothing could stop us now from getting to the top. The psychological atmosphere changed with these few words, and we went forward now as brothers.

I felt as though I were plunging into something new and quite abnormal. I had the strangest and most vivid impressions, such as I had never before known in the mountains. There was something unnatural in the way I saw Lechenal and everything around us. I smiled to myself at the paltriness of our efforts, for I could stand apart and watch myself making these efforts. But all sense of exertion was gone, as though there were no longer any gravity. This diaphanous landscape, this quintessence of purity—these were not the mountains I knew: they were the mountains of my dreams.

The snow, sprinkled over every rock and gleaming in the sun, was of a radiant beauty that touched me to the heart. I had never seen such complete transparency, and I was living in a world of crystal. Sounds were indistinct, the atmosphere like cotton wool.

An astonishing happiness welled up in me, but I could not define it. Everything was so new, so utterly unprecedented. It was not in the least like anything I had known in the Alps, where one feels buoyed up by the presence of others—by people of whom one is vaguely aware, or even by the dwellings one can see in the far distance.

This was quite different. An enormous gulf was between me and the world. This was a different universe—withered, desert, lifeless; a fantastic universe where the presence of man was not foreseen, perhaps not desired. We were braving an interdict, overstepping a boundary, and yet we had no fear as we continued upward. I thought of the famous ladder of St. Theresa of Avila. Something clutched at my heart.

Did Lachenal share these feelings? The summit ridge drew nearer, and we reached the foot of the ultimate rock band. The slope was very steep and the snow interspersed with rocks.

"Couloir!"

A finger pointed. The whispered word from one to another indicated the key to the rocks—the last line of defense.

"What luck!"

The couloir up the rocks though steep was feasible.

The sky was a deep sapphire blue. With a great effort we edged over the right, avoiding th rocks; we preferred to keep to the snow on account of our crampons and it was not long before we set foot in the couloir. It was fairly steep, and we had a minute's hesitation. Should we have enough strength left to overcome this final obstacle?

Fortunately the snow was hard, and by kicking steps we were able to manage, thanks to our crampons. A false move would have been fatal. There was no need to make handholds—our axes, driven in as far as possible, served us for an anchor.

Lachenal went splendidly. What a wonderful contrast to the early days! It was a hard struggle here, but he kept going. Lifting our eyes occasionally from the slope, we saw the couloir opening out on to . . . well, we didn't quite know, probably a ridge. But where was the top—left or right? Stopping at every step, leaning on our axes we tried to recover our breath and to calm down our racing hearts, which were thumping as though they would burst. We knew we were there now—that nothing could stop us. No need to exchange looks—each of us would have read the same determination in the other's eyes. A slight détour to the left, a few more steps—the summit ridge came gradually nearer—a few rocks to avoid. We dragged ourselves up. Could we possibly be there?

Yes!

A fierce and savage wind tore at us.

We were on top of Annapurna! 8,075 meters, 26,493 feet.

Our hearts overflowed with an unspeakable happiness.

"If only the others could know . . ."

If only everyone could know!

The summit was a corniced crest of ice, and the precipices on the far side which plunged vertically down beneath us, were terrifying, unfathomable. There could be few other mountains in the world like this. Clouds floated halfway down, concealing the gentle, fertile valley of Pokhara, 23,000 feet below. Above us there was nothing!

Our mission was accomplished. But at the same time we had accomplished something infinitely greater. How wonderful life would now become! What an inconceivable experience it is to attain one's ideal and, at the very same moment, to fulfill oneself. I was stirred to the depths of my being. Never had I felt happiness like this—so intense and yet so pure. That brown rock, the highest of them all, that ridge of ice—were these the goals of a lifetime? Or were they, rather, the limits of man's pride?

"Well, what about going down?"

Lachenal shook me. What were his own feelings? Did he simply think he had finished another climb, as in the Alps? Did he think one could just go down again like that, with nothing more to it?

"One minute, I must take some photographs."

"Hurry up!"

I fumbled feverishly in my sack, pulled out the camera, took out the little French flag which was right at the bottom, and the pennants. Useless gestures, no doubt, but something more than symbols—eloquent tokens of affection and goodwill. I tied the strips of material—stained by sweat and by the food in the sacks—to the shaft of my ice-axe, the only flagstaff at hand. Then I focused my camera on Lachenal.

"Now, will you take me?"

"Hand it over—hurry up!" said Lachenal.

He took several pictures and then handed me back the camera. I loaded a color-film and we repeated the process to be certain of bringing back records to be cherished in the future.

"Are you mad?" asked Lachenal. "We haven't a minute to lose: we must go down at once."

And in fact a glance round showed me that the weather was no longer gloriously fine as it had been in the morning. Lachenal was becoming impatient.

"We must go down!"

He was right. His was the reaction of the mountaineer who knows his own domain. But I just could not accustom myself to the idea that we had won our victory. It seemed inconceivable that we should have trodden those summit snows.

It was impossible to build a cairn; there were no stones; everything was frozen. Lachenal stamped his feet; he felt them freezing. I felt mine freezing too, but paid little attention. The highest mountain to be climbed by man lay under our feet! The names of our predecessors on these heights raced through my mind: Mummery, Mallory and Irvine, Bauer, Welzenbach, Tilman, Shipton. How many of them were dead—how many had found on these mountains what, to them, was the finest end of all?

My joy was touched with humility. It was not just one party that had climbed Annapurna today, but a whole expedition. I thought of all the others in the camps perched on the slopes at our feet, and I knew it was because of their efforts and their sacrifices that we had succeeded. There are times when the most complicated actions are suddenly summed up, distilled, and strike you with illuminating clarity: so it was with this irresistible upward surge which had landed us two here.

Pictures passed through my mind—the Chamonix valley, where I had spent the most marvelous moments of my childhood; Mont Blanc, which so tremendously impressed me! I was a child when I first saw "the Mont Blanc people" coming home, and to me there was a queer look about them; a strange light shone in their eyes.

"Come on, straight down," called Lachenal.

He had already done up his sack and started going down. I took out my pocket aneroid: 8,500 meters. I smiled. I swallowed a little condensed milk and left the tube behind—the only trace of our passage. I did up my sack, put on my gloves and my glasses, seized my ice-axe; one look around and I, too, hurried down the slope. Before disappearing into the couloir I gave one last look at the summit which would henceforth be all our joy and all our consolation.

Lachenal was already far below; he had reached the foot of the couloir. I hurried down in his tracks. I went as fast as I could, but it was dangerous going. At every step one had to take care that the snow did not break away beneath one's weight. Lachenal, going faster than I thought he was capable of, was now on the long traverse. It was my turn to cross the area of mixed rock and snow. At last I reached the foot of the rock-band. I had hurried and I was out of breath. I undid my sack. What had I been going to do? I couldn't say.

"My gloves!"

Before I had time to bend over, I saw them slide and roll. They went further and further straight down the slope. I remained where I was, quite stunned. I watched them rolling down slowly, with no appearance of stopping. The movement of those gloves was engraved in my sight as something irredeemable, against which I was powerless. The consequences might be most serious. What was I to do?

"Quickly, down to Camp V."

Rébuffat and Terray would be there. My concern dissolved like magic. I now had a fixed objective again: to reach the camp. Never for a minute did it occur to me to use as gloves the socks which I always carry in reserve for just such a mishap as this.

On I went, trying to catch up with Lachenal. It had been two o'clock when we reached the summit; we had started out at six in the morning, but I had to admit that I had lost all sense of time. I felt as if I were running, whereas in actual fact I was walking normally, perhaps rather slowly, and I had to keep stopping to get my breath. The sky was now covered with clouds, everything had become gray and dirty-looking. An icy wind sprang up, boding no good. We must push on! But where was Lachenal? I spotted him a couple of hundred yards away, looking as if he was never going to stop. And I had thought he was in indifferent form!

The clouds grew thicker and came right down over us; the wind blew stronger, but I did not suffer from the cold. Perhaps the descent had restored my circulation. Should I be able to find the tents in the mist? I watched the rib ending in the beak-like point which overlooked the camp. It was gradually swallowed up by the clouds, but I was able to make out the spearhead rib lower down. If the mist should thicken I would make straight for that rib and follow it down, and in this way I should be bound to come upon the tent.

Lachenal disappeared from time to time, and then the mist was so thick that I lost sight of him altogether. I kept going at the same speed, as fast as my breathing would allow.

The slope was now steeper; a few patches of bare ice followed the smooth stretches of snow. A good sign—I was nearing the camp. How difficult to find one's way in thick mist! I kept the course which I had set by the steepest angle of the slope. The ground was broken; with my crampons I went straight down walls of bare ice. There were some patches ahead—a few more steps. It was the camp all right, but there were *two tents!*

So Rébuffat and Terray had come up. What a mercy! I should be able to tell them that we had been successful, that we were returning from the top. How thrilled they would be!

I got there, dropped down from above. The platform had been extended, and the two tents were facing each other. I tripped over one of the guy-ropes of the first tent; there was movement inside, they had heard me. Rébuffat and Terray put their heads out.

"We've made it. We're back from Annapurna!"

Chapter XIV
The Crevasse

Rébuffat and Terray received the news with great excitement.

"But what about Biscante?" asked Terray anxiously.

"He won't be long. He was just in front of me! What a day—started out at six this morning—didn't stop . . . got up at last."

Words failed me. I had so much to say. The sight of familiar faces dispelled the strange feeling that I had experienced since morning, and I became, once more, just a mountaineer.

Terray, who was speechless with delight, wrung my hands. Then the smile vanished from his face: "Maurice—your hands!" There was an uneasy silence. I had forgotten that I had lost my gloves: my fingers were violet and white and hard as wood. The other two stared at them in dismay—they realized the full seriousness of the injury. But, still blissfully floating on a sea of joy remote from reality, I leaned over towards Terray and said confidentially, "You're in such splendid form, and you've done so marvelously, it's absolutely tragic you didn't come up there with us!"

"What I did was for the Expedition, my dear Maurice, and anyway you've got up, and that's a victory for the whole lot of us."

I nearly burst with happiness. How could I tell him all that his answer meant to me? The rapture I had felt on the summit, which might have seemed a purely personal, egotistical emotion, had been transformed by his words into a complete and perfect joy with no shadow upon it. His answer proved that this victory was not just one man's achievement, a matter for personal pride; no—and Terray was the first to understand this—it was a victory for us all, a victory for mankind itself.

"Hi! Help! Help!"

"Biscante!" exclaimed the others.

Still have intoxicated and remote from reality I had heard nothing. Terray felt a chill at his heart, and his thoughts flew to his partner on so many unforgettable climbs; together they had so often skirted death, and won so many splendid victories. Putting his head out, and seeing Lachenal clinging to the slope a hundred yards lower down, he dressed in frantic haste.

Out he went. But the slope was bare now; Lachenal had disappeared. Terray was horribly frightened, and he could only utter unintelligible cries. It was a ghastly moment for him. A violent wind sent the mist tearing by. Under the stress of emotion Terray had not realized how it falsified distances.

"Biscante! Biscante!"

He had spotted him, through a rift in the mist, lying on the slope much lower down than he had thought. Terray set his teeth, and glissaded down like a madman. How would he be able to brake without crampons, on the wind-hardened snow? But Terray was a first-class skier, and with a jump turn he stopped beside Lachenal, who was suffering from concussion after his tremendous fall. In a state of collapse, with no ice-axe, balaclava, or gloves, and only one crampon, he gazed vacantly around him.

"My feet are frost-bitten. Take me down . . . take me down, so that Oudot can see to me."

"It can't be done," said Terray sorrowfully. "Can't you see we're in the middle of a storm . . . It'll be dark soon."

But Lachenal was obsessed by the fear of amputation. With a gesture of despair he tore the axe out of Terray's hands and tried to force his way down; but soon saw the futility of his action and resolved to climb up to the camp. While Terray cut steps without stopping, Lachenal, ravaged and exhausted as he was, dragged himself along on all fours.

Meanwhile I had gone into Rébuffat's tent. He was appalled at the sight of my hands and, as rather incoherently I told him what we had done, he took a piece of rope and began flicking my fingers. Then he took off my boots with great difficulty for my feet were swollen, and beat my feet and rubbed me. We soon heard Terray giving Lachenal the same treatment in the other tent.

For our comrades it was a tragic moment: Annapurna was conquered, and the first eight-thousander had been climbed. Every one of us had been ready to sacrifice everything for this. Yet, as they looked at our feet and hands, what can Terray and Rébuffat have felt?

Outside the storm howled and the snow was still falling. The mist grew thick and darkness came. As on the previous night we had to cling to the poles to prevent the tents being carried away by the wind. The only two air-mattresses were given to Lachenal and myself while Terray and Rébuffat both sat on ropes, rucksacks, and provisions to keep themselves off the snow. They rubbed, slapped and beat us with a rope. Sometimes the blows fell on the living flesh, and howls arose from both tents. Rébuffat persevered; it was essential to continue painful as it was. Gradually life returned to my feet as well as to my hands, and circulation started again. Lachenal, too, found that feeling was returning.

Now Terray summoned up the energy to prepare some hot drinks. He called to Rébuffat that he would pass him a mug, so two hands stretched out towards each other between the two tents and were instantly covered with snow. The liquid was boiling though scarcely more than 60° centigrade (140° Fahrenheit). I swallowed it greedily and felt infinitely better.

The night was absolute hell. Frightful onslaughts of wind battered us incessantly, while the never-ceasing snow piled up on the tents.

Now and again I heard voices from next door—it was Terray massaging Lachenal with admirable perseverance, only stopping to ply him with hot drinks. In our tent Rébuffat was quite worn out, but satisfied that warmth was returning to my limbs.

Lying half unconscious I was scarcely aware of the passage of time. There were moments when I was able to see our situation in its true dramatic light, but the rest of the time I was plunged in an inexplicable stupor with no thought for the consequences of our victory.

As the night wore on the snow lay heavier on the tent, and once again I had the frightful feeling of being slowly and silently asphyxiated. I tried, with all the strength of which I was capable, to push off with both forearms the mass that was crushing me. These fearful exertions left me gasping for breath and I fell back into the same exhausted state. It was much worse than the previous night.

"Rébuffat! Gaston! Gaston!"

I recognized Terray's voice.

"Time to be off!"

I heard the sounds without grasping their meaning. Was it light already? I was not in the least surprised that the other two had given up all thought of going to the top, and I did not at all grasp the measure of their sacrifice.

Outside the storm redoubled in violence. The tent shook and the fabric flapped alarmingly. It had usually been fine in the mornings: did this mean the monsoon was upon us? We knew it was not far off—could this be its first onslaught?

"Gaston! Are you ready?" Terray called again.

"One minute," answered Rébuffat. He did not have an easy job: he had to put my boots on and do everything to get me ready. I let myself be handled like a baby. In the other tent Terray finished dressing Lachenal whose feet were still swollen and would not fit into his boots. So Terray gave him his own, which were bigger. To get Lachenal's on to his own feet he had to make slits in them. As a precaution he put a sleeping-bag and some food into his sack and shouted to us to do the same. Were his words lost in the storm? Or were we too intent on leaving this hellish place to listen to his instructions?

Lachenal and Terray were already outside.

"We're going down!" they shouted.

Then Rébuffat tied me on the rope and we went out. There were only two ice-axes for the four of us, so Rébuffat and Terray took them as a matter of course. For a moment as we left the two tents of Camp V, I felt childishly ashamed at leaving all this good equipment behind.

Already the first rope seemed a long way down below us. We were blinded by the squalls of snow and we could not hear each other a yard away. We had both put on our *cagoules,* for it was very cold. The snow was apt to slide and the rope often came in useful.

Ahead of us the other two were losing no time. Lachenal went first and, safeguarded by Terray, he forced the pace in his anxiety to get down. There were no tracks to show us the way, but it was engraved on all our minds—straight down the slope for 400 yards then traverse to the left for 150 to 200 yards to get to Camp IV. The snow was thinning and the wind less violent. Was it going to clear? We hardly dared to hope so. A wall of seracs brought us up short.

"It's to the left," I said, "I remember perfectly."

Somebody else thought it was to the right. We started going down again. The wind had dropped completely, but the snow fell in big flakes. The mist was thick, and, not to lose each other, we walked in line: I was third and I could barely see Lachenal who was first. It was impossible to recognize any of the pitches. We were all experienced enough mountaineers to know that even on familiar ground it is easy to make mistakes in such weather. Distances are deceptive, one cannot tell whether one is going up or down. We kept colliding with hummocks which we had taken for hollows. The mist, the falling snow-flakes, the carpet of snow, all merged into the same whitish tone and confused our vision. The towering outlines of the seracs took on fantastic shapes and seemed to move slowly around us.

Our situation was not desperate, we were certainly not lost. We would have to go lower down; the traverse must begin further on—I remembered the serac which served as a milestone. The snow stuck to our *cagoules,* and turned us into white phantoms noiselessly flitting against a background equally white. We began to sink in dreadfully, and there is nothing worse for bodies already on the edge of exhaustion.

Were we too high or too low? No one could tell. Perhaps we had better try slanting over to the left! The snow was in a dangerous condition, but we
did not seem to realize it. We were forced to admit that we were not on the
right route, so we retraced our steps and climbed up above the serac which
overhung us. No doubt, we decided, we should be on the right level now. With
Rébuffat leading, we went back over the way which had cost us such an effort.
I followed him jerkily, saying nothing, and determined to go on to the end. If
Rébuffat had fallen I could never have held him.

We went doggedly on from one serac to another. Each time we
thought we had recognized the right route, and each time there was a fresh
disappointment. If only the mist would lift, if only the snow would stop for a
second! On the slope it seemed to be growing deeper every minute. Only Terray and Rébuffat were capable of breaking the trail and they relieved each
other at regular intervals, without a word and without a second's hesitation.

I admired this determination of Rébuffat's for which he is so justly
famed. He did not intend to die! With the strength of desperation and at the
price of super-human effort he forged ahead. The slowness of his progress
would have dismayed even the most obstinate climber, but he would not give
up, and in the end the mountain yielded in face of his perseverance.

Terray, when his turn came, charged madly ahead. He was like a force
of nature: at all costs he would break down these prison walls that penned us
in. His physical strength was exceptional, his will power no less remarkable.
Lachenal gave him considerable trouble. Perhaps he was not quite in his right
mind. He said it was no use going on; we must dig a hole in the snow and wait
for fine weather. He swore at Terray and called him a madman. Nobody but
Terray would have been capable of dealing with him—he just tugged sharply
on the rope and Lachenal was forced to follow.

We were well and truly lost.

The weather did not seem likely to improve. A minute ago we had still
had ideas about which way to go—now we had none. This way or that . . . We
went on at random to allow for the chance of a miracle which appeared increasingly unlikely. The instinct of self-preservation in the two fit members of
the party alternated with a hopelessness which made them completely irre-
sponsible. Each in turn did the maddest things: Terray traversed the steep and
avalanchy slopes with one crampon badly adjusted. He and Rébuffat performed incredible feats of balance without the least slip.

Camp IV was certainly on the left, on the edge of the Sickle. On that
point we were all agreed. But it was very hard to find. The wall of ice that gave
it such magnificent protection was now ironical, for it hid the tents from us. In

mist like this we should have to be right on top of them before we spotted them.

Perhaps if we called, someone would hear us? Lachenal gave the signal, but snow absorbs sound and his shout seemed to carry only a few yards. All four of us called out together: "One . . . two . . . three . . . Help!"

We got the impression that our united shout carried a long way, so we began again: "One . . . two . . . three . . . Help!" Not a sound in reply!

Now and again Terray took off his boots and rubbed his feet; the sight of our frost-bitten limbs had made him aware of the danger and he had the strength of mind to do something about it. Like Lachenal, he was haunted by the idea of amputation. For me, it was too late: my feet and hands, already affected from yesterday, were beginning to freeze up again.

We had eaten nothing since the day before, and we had been on the go the whole time, but men's resources of energy in face of death are inexhaustible. When the end seems imminent, there still remain reserves, though it needs tremendous will power to call them up.

Time passed, but we had no idea how long. Night was approaching, and we were terrified, though none of us made any complaint. Rébuffat and I found a way that we thought we remembered, but were brought to a halt by the extreme steepness of the slope—the mist turned it into a vertical wall. We were to find next day that at that moment we had been only thirty yards from the camp, and that the wall was the very one that sheltered the tent which would have been our salvation.

"We must find a crevasse."

"We can't stay here all night!"

"A hole—it's the only thing."

"We'll all die in it."

Night had suddenly fallen and it was essential to come to a decision without wasting another minute; if we remained on the slope, we should be dead before morning. We would have to bivouac. What the conditions would be like, we could guess, for we all knew what it meant to bivouac above 23,000 feet.

With his axe Terray began to dig a hole. Lachenal went over to a snow-filled crevasse a few yards further on, then suddenly let out a yell and disappeared before our eyes. We stood helpless: should we, or rather would Terray and Rébuffat, have enough strength for all the maneuvers with the rope that would be needed to get him out? The crevasse was completely blocked up save for the one little hole which Lachenal had fallen through.

"Lachenal!" called Terray.

A voice, muffled by many thicknesses of ice and snow, came up to us. It was impossible to make out what it was saying.

"Lachenal!"

Terray jerked the rope violently; this time we could hear.

"I'm here!"

"Anything broken?"

"No! It'll do for the night! Come along."

This shelter was heaven-sent. None of us would have had the strength to dig a hole big enough to protect the lot of us from the wind. Without hesitation Terray let himself drop into the crevasse, and a loud "Come on!" told us he had arrived safely. In my turn I let myself go: it was a regular toboggan-slide. I shot down a sort of twisting tunnel, very steep, and about thirty feet long. I came out at great speed into the opening beyond and was literally hurled to the bottom of the crevasse. We let Rébuffat know he could come by giving a tug on the rope.

The intense cold of this minute grotto shriveled us up, the enclosing walls of ice were damp and the floor a carpet of fresh snow; by huddling together there was just room for the four of us. Icicles hung from the ceiling and we broke some of them off to make more head room and kept little bits to suck—it was a long time since we had had anything to drink.

That was our shelter for the night. At least we should be protected from the wind, and the temperature would remain fairly even, though the damp was extremely unpleasant. We settled ourselves in the dark as best we could. As always in a bivouac we took off our boots; without this precaution the constriction would cause immediate frost-bite. Terray unrolled the sleeping-bag which he had had the foresight to bring, and settled himself in relative comfort. We put on everything warm that we had, and to avoid contact with the snow I sat on the movie camera. We huddled close up to each other, in our search for a hypothetical position in which the warmth of our bodies could be combined without loss, but we couldn't keep still for a second.

We did not open our mouths—signs were less of an effort than words. Every man withdrew into himself and took refuge in his own inner world. Terray massaged Lachenal's feet; Rébuffat felt his feet freezing too, but he had sufficient strength to rub them himself. I remained motionless, unseeing. My feet and hands went on freezing, but what could be done? I attempted to forget suffering by withdrawing into myself, trying to forget the passing of time, trying not to feel the devouring and numbing cold which insidiously gained upon us.

Terray shared his sleeping-bag with Lachenal, putting his feet and hands inside the precious eiderdown. At the same time he went on rubbing.

Anyhow the frost-bite won't spread further, he was thinking.

None of us could make any movement without upsetting the others, and the positions we had taken up with such care were continually being altered so that we had to start all over again. This kept us busy. Rébuffat persevered with his rubbing and complained of his feet; like Terray he was thinking: We mustn't look beyond tomorrow—afterwards we'll see. But he was not blind to the fact that "afterwards" was one big question-mark.

Terray generously tried to give me part of his sleeping-bag. He had understood the seriousness of my condition, and knew why it was that I said nothing and remained quite passive; he realized that I had abandoned all hope for myself. He massaged me for nearly two hours; his feet, too, might have frozen, but he didn't appear to give the matter a thought. I found new courage simply in contemplating his unselfishness; he was doing so much to help me that it would have been ungrateful of me not to go on struggling to live. Though my heart was like a lump of ice itself, I was astonished to feel no pain. Everything material about me seemed to have dropped away. I seemed to be quite clear in my thoughts and yet I floated in a kind of peaceful happiness. There was still a breath of life in me, but it dwindled steadily as the hours went by. Terray's massage no longer had any effect upon me. All was over, I thought. Wasn't this cavern the most beautiful grave I could hope for? Death caused me no grief, no regret—I smiled at the thought.

After hours of torpor a voice mumbled "Daylight!"

This made some impression on the others. I only felt surprised—I had not thought that daylight would penetrate so far down.

"Too early to start," said Rébuffat.

A ghastly light spread through our grotto and we could just vaguely make out the shapes of each other's heads. A queer noise from a long way off came down to us—a sort of prolonged hiss. The noise increased. Suddenly I was buried, blinded, smothered beneath an avalanche of new snow. The icy snow spread over the cavern, finding its way through every gap in our clothing. I ducked my head between my knees and covered myself with both arms. The snow flowed on and on. There was a terrible silence. We were not completely buried, but there was snow everywhere. We got up, taking care not to bang our heads against the ceiling of ice, and tried to shake ourselves. We were all in our stockinged feet in the snow. The first thing to do was to find our boots.

Rébuffat and Terray began to search, and realized at once that they were blind. Yesterday they had taken off their glasses to lead us down and now they were paying for it. Lachenal was the first to lay hands upon a pair of boots. He tried to put them on, but they were Rébuffat's. Rébuffat attempted to climb up the chute down which we had come yesterday, and which the avalanche had followed in its turn.

"Hi, Gaston! What's the weather like?" called up Terray.

"Can't see a thing. It's blowing hard."

We were still groping for our things. Terray found his boots and put them on awkwardly, unable to see what he was doing. Lachenal helped him, but he was all on edge and fearfully impatient, in striking contrast to my immobility. Terray then went up the icy channel, puffing and blowing, and at last reached the outer world. He was met by terrible gusts of wind that cut right through him and lashed his face.

Bad weather, he said to himself, this time it's the end. We're lost . . . we'll never come through.

At the bottom of the crevasse there were still two of us looking for our boots. Lachenal poked fiercely with an ice-axe. I was calmer and tried to proceed more rationally. We extracted crampons and an axe in turn from the snow, but still no boots.

Well—so this cavern was to be our last resting-place! There was very little room—we were bent double and got in each other's way. Lachenal decided to go out without his boots. He called frantically, hauled himself up on the rope, trying to get a hold or to wiggle his way up, digging his toes into the snow walls. Terray from outside pulled as hard as he could. I watched him go; he gathered speed and disappeared.

When he emerged from the opening he saw the sky was clear and blue, and he began to run like a madman, shrieking, "It's fine, it's fine!"

I set to work again to search the cave. The boots *had* to be found, or Lachenal and I were done for. On all fours, with nothing on my hands or feet I raked the snow, stirring it around this way and that, hoping every second to come upon something hard. I was no longer capable of thinking—I reacted like an animal fighting for its life.

I found one boot! The other was tied to it—a pair! Having ransacked the whole cave I at last found the other pair. But in spite of all my efforts I could not find the movie camera, and gave up in despair. There was no question of putting my boots on—my hands were like lumps of wood and I could hold nothing in my fingers; my feet were very swollen—I should never be able to get boots on them. I twisted the rope around the boots as well as I could and called up the chute:

"Lionel . . . Boots!"

There was no answer, but he must have heard for with a jerk the precious boots shot up. Soon after the rope came down again. My turn. I wound the rope around me. I could not pull it tight so I made a whole series of little knots. Their combined strength, I hoped, would be enough to hold me. I had no strength to shout again; I gave a great tug on the rope, and Terray understood.

At the first step I had to kick a notch in the hard snow for my toes. Further on I expected to be able to get up more easily by wedging myself across the runnel. I wriggled up a few yards like this and then I tried to dig my hands and my feet into the wall. My hands were stiff and hard right up to the wrists and my feet had no feeling up to the ankles, the joints were inflexible and this hampered me greatly.

Somehow or other I succeeded in working my way up, while Terray pulled so hard he nearly choked me. I began to see more distinctly and so knew that I must be nearing the opening. Often I fell back, but I clung on and wedged myself in again as best I could. My heart was bursting and I was forced to rest. A fresh wave of energy enabled me to crawl to the top. I pulled myself out by clutching Terray's legs; he was just about all in and I was in the last stages of exhaustion. Terray was close to me and I whispered:

"Lionel . . . I'm dying!"

He supported me and helped me away from the crevasse. Lachenal and Rébuffat were sitting in the snow a few yards away. The instant Lionel let go of me I sank down and dragged myself along on all fours.

The weather was perfect. Quantities of snow had fallen the day before and the mountains were resplendent. Never had I seen them look so beautiful—our last day would be magnificent.

Rébuffat and Terray were completely blind; as he came along with me Terray knocked into things and I had to direct him. Rébuffat, too, could not move a step without guidance. It was terrifying to be blind when there was danger all around. Lachenal's frozen feet affected his nervous system. His behavior was disquieting—he was possessed by the most fantastic ideas:

"I tell you we must go down . . . down there . . ."

"You've nothing on your feet!"

"Don't worry about that."

"You're off your head. The way's not there . . . it's to the left!"

He was already standing up; he wanted to go straight down to the bottom of the glacier. Terray held him back, made him sit down, and though he couldn't see, helped Lachenal put his boots on.

Behind them I was living in my own private dream. I knew the end was near, but it was the end that all mountaineers wish for—an end in keeping with their ruling passion. I was consciously grateful to the mountains for being so beautiful for me that day, and as awed by their silence as if I had been in church. I was in no pain, and had no worry. My utter calmness was alarming. Terray came staggering towards me, and I told him: "It's all over for me. Go on . . . you have a chance . . . you must take it . . . over to the left . . . that's the way."

I felt better after telling him that. But Terray would have none of it: "We'll help you. If we get away, so will you."

At this moment Lachenal shouted: "Help! Help!"

Obviously he didn't know what he was doing . . . Or did he? He was the only one of the four of us who could see Camp II down below. Perhaps his calls would be heard. They were shrieks of despair, reminding me tragically of some climbers lost in the Mont Blanc massif whom I had endeavored to save. Now it was our turn. The impression was vivid: we were lost.

I joined in with the others: "One . . . two . . . three . . . *Help!* One . . . two . . . three . . . *Help!*" We tried to shout together, but without much success; our voices could not have carried more than ten feet. The noise I made was more of a whisper than a shout. Terray insisted that I should put my boots on, but my hands were dead. Neither Rébuffat nor Terray, who were unable to see, could help much, so I said to Lachenal: "Come and help me to put my boots on."

"Don't be silly, we must go down!"

And off he went once again in the wrong direction, straight down. I was not in the least angry with him; he had been sorely tried by the altitude and by everything he had gone through.

Terray resolutely got out his knife, and with fumbling hands slit the uppers of my boots back and front. Split in two like this I could get them on, but it was not easy and I had to make several attempts. Soon I lost heart—what was the use of it all anyway since I was going to stay where I was? But Terray pulled violently and finally he succeeded. He laced up my now gigantic boots, missing half the hooks. I was ready now. But how was I going to walk with my stiff joints?

"To the left, Lionel!"

"You're crazy, Maurice," said Lachenal, "it's to the right, straight down."

Terray did not know what to think of these conflicting views. He had not given up like me, he was going to fight; but what, at the moment, could he do? The three of them discussed which way to go.

I remained sitting in the snow. Gradually my mind lost grip—why should I struggle? I would just let myself drift. I saw pictures of shady slopes, peaceful paths, there was a scent of resin. It was pleasant—I was going to die in my own mountains. My body had no feeling—everything was frozen.

"Aah . . . aah!"

Was it a groan or a call? I gathered my strength for one cry: "They're coming!" The others heard me and shouted for joy. What a miraculous apparition! "Schatz . . . it's Schatz!"

Barely two hundred yards away Marcel Schatz, waist-deep in snow, was coming slowly towards us like a boat on the surface of the slope. I found this vision of a strong and invincible deliverer inexpressibly moving. I expected everything of him. The shock was violent, and quite shattered me. Death clutched at me and I gave myself up.

When I came to again the wish to live returned and I experienced a violent revulsion of feeling. All was not lost! As Schatz came nearer my eyes never left him for a second—twenty yards—ten yards—he came straight towards me. Why? Without a word he leaned over me, held me close, hugged me, and his warm breath revived me.

I could not make the slightest movement—I was like marble. My heart was overwhelmed by such tremendous feelings and yet my eyes remained dry.

"It is wonderful—what you have done!"

Translator's Note: In May 1952 Lambert, with the Sherpa Ang-Tsering, reached 28,215 feet on Mount Everest, possibly the highest point yet attained up to that time.

The Boat Journey

BY SIR ERNEST SHACKLETON

E ven though he never achieved his goal of reaching the South Pole, the name Sir Ernest Shackleton ranks among the legends of Antarctic exploration. His courage and perseverance during his expedition of 1914–16 represents one of the greatest feats of endurance and survival against overwhelming odds ever recorded.

Shackleton had man-hauled a sledge to within ninety-seven miles of the Pole during his expedition of 1907–09, turning back at the farthest point south ever reached at that time. Before he could make another attempt, Norwegian Roald Amundsen and four others reached the South Pole on December 15, 1911, followed on January 17, 1912, by the British group led by Robert Scott. (The Scott party perished before making it back to civilization. Their bodies and records of their journey were found later.)

The purpose of Shackleton's 1914 expedition was to cross the frozen continent on a journey of both exploration and scientific research. Disaster struck when the expedition's ship, the *Endurance,* became locked in a sea of ice at the very edge of the Antarctic continent. After ten months of drifting with the ice, the ship was eventually crushed. The twenty-eight men of the party managed to camp on ice floes for five months until all hands eventually landed on uninhabited Elephant Island in the South Shetland Islands.

There have been several excellent books about Shackleton and his expedition, but one of the finest comes from the pen of Sir Ernest Shackleton himself. His book *South* is the complete story of the 1914–16 expedition and is a treasure of great reading. This excerpt is but a small section of this enduring story of heroism and is taken from the edition of *South* published by The Lyons Press in 1998 with an introduction by Tim Cahill.

As we pick up the action, we are with Shackleton and his men on Elephant Island and he has made a dramatic decision. He will set out with five others of the crew in the largest of their lifeboats to cross eight hundred miles

273

of ocean to seek assistance. The other men will have to survive on Elephant Island in the meantime. If Shackleton and his companions are lost at sea, the men on the island may never be found.

The seas the open boat must cross are considered by sea-faring men everywhere to be the most savage on earth.

★　　★　　★　　★　　★

The increasing sea made it necessary for us to drag the boats farther up the beach. This was a task for all hands, and after much labour we got the boats into safe positions among the rocks and made fast the painters to big boulders. Then I discussed with Wild and Worsley the chances of reaching South Georgia before the winter locked the seas against us. Some effort had to be made to secure relief. Privation and exposure had left their mark on the party, and the health and mental condition of several men were causing me serious anxiety. Blackborrow's feet, which had been frost-bitten during the boat journey, were in a bad way, and the two doctors feared that an operation would be necessary. They told me that the toes would have to be amputated unless animation could be restored within a short period. Then the food-supply was a vital consideration. We had left ten cases of provisions in the crevice of the rocks at our first camping-place on the island. An examination of our stores showed that we had full rations for the whole party for a period of five weeks. The rations could be spread over three months on a reduced allowance and probably would be supplemented by seals and sea-elephants to some extent. I did not dare to count with full confidence on supplies of meat and blubber, for the animals seemed to have deserted the beach and the winter was near. Our stocks included three seals and two and a half skins (with blubber attached). We were mainly dependent on the blubber for fuel, and, after making a preliminary survey of the situation, I decided that the party must be limited to one hot meal a day.

A boat journey in search of relief was necessary and must not be delayed. That conclusion was forced upon me. The nearest port where assistance could certainly be secured was Port Stanley, in the Falkland Islands, 540 miles away, but we could scarcely hope to beat up against the prevailing northwesterly wind in a frail and weakened boat with a small sail area. South Georgia was over 800 miles away, but lay in the area of the west winds, and I could count upon finding whalers at any of the whaling-stations on the east coast. A boat party might make the voyage and be back with relief within a month, provided that the sea was clear of ice and the boat survive the great seas. It was not difficult to decide that South Georgia must be the objective, and I proceeded to plan ways and means. The hazards of a boat journey across 800 miles of stormy sub-Antarctic ocean were obvious, but I calculated that at worst the venture would add nothing to the risks of the men left on the island. There would be fewer mouths to feed during the winter and the boat would not require to take more than one month's provisions for six men, for if we did not make South Georgia in that time we were sure to go under. A consideration that had weight with me was that there was no chance at all of any search being made for us on Elephant Island.

The case required to be argued in some detail, since all hands knew that the perils of the proposed journey were extreme. The risk was justified solely by our urgent need of assistance. The ocean south of Cape Horn in the middle of May is known to be the most tempestuous storm-swept area of water in the world. The weather then is unsettled, the skies are dull and overcast, and the gales are almost unceasing. We had to face these conditions in a small and weather-beaten boat, already strained by the work of the months that had passed. Worsley and Wild realized that the attempt must be made, and they both asked to be allowed to accompany me on the voyage. I told Wild at once that he would have to stay behind. I relied upon him to hold the party together while I was away and to make the best of his way to Deception Island with the men in the spring in the event of our failure to bring help. Worsley I would take with me, for I had a very high opinion of his accuracy and quickness as a navigator, and especially in the snapping and working out of positions in difficult circumstances—an opinion that was only enhanced during the actual journey. Four other men would be required, and I decided to call for volunteers, although, as a matter of fact, I pretty well knew which of the people I would select. Crean I proposed to leave on the island as a right-hand man for Wild, but he begged so hard to be allowed to come in the boat that, after consultation with Wild, I promised to take him. I called the men together, explained my plan, and asked for volunteers. Many came forward at once. Some were not fit enough for the work that would have to be done, and others would not have been much use in the boat since they were not seasoned sailors, though the experiences of recent months entitled them to some consideration as seafaring men. McIlroy and Macklin were both anxious to go but realized that their duty lay on the island with the sick men. They suggested that I should take Blackborrow in order that he might have shelter and warmth as quickly as possible, but I had to veto this idea. It would be hard enough for fit men to live in the boat. Indeed, I did not see how a sick man, lying helpless in the bottom of the boat, could possibly survive in the heavy weather we were sure to encounter. I finally selected McNeish, McCarthy, and Vincent in addition to Worsley and Crean. The crew seemed a strong one, and as I looked at the men I felt confidence increasing.

The decision made, I walked through the blizzard with Worsley and Wild to examine the *James Caird*. The 20-ft. boat had never looked big; she appeared to have shrunk in some mysterious way when I viewed her in the light of our new undertaking. She was an ordinary ship's whaler, fairly strong, but showing signs of the strains she had endured since the crushing of the *Endurance*. Where she was holed in leaving the pack was, fortunately, about the water-line and easily patched. Standing beside her, we glanced at the fringe of the storm-swept, tumultuous sea that formed our path. Clearly, our voyage would be a big adventure. I called the carpenter and asked him if he could do anything to make the boat more seaworthy. He first inquired if he was to go with me, and seemed quite pleased when I said "Yes." He was over fifty years of age and not altogether fit, but he had a good knowledge of sailing-boats and was very quick. McCarthy said that he could contrive some sort of covering for the *James Caird* if he might use the lids of the cases and the four sledge-runners that we had lashed inside the boat for use in the event of a landing on Graham Land at Wilhelmina Bay. This bay, at one time the goal of our desire, had been left behind in the course of our drift, but we had retained the runners. The carpenter proposed to complete the covering with some of our canvas, and he set about making his plans at once.

Noon had passed and the gale was more severe than ever. We could not proceed with our preparations that day. The tents were suffering in the wind and the sea was rising. We made our way to the snow-slope at the shoreward end of the spit, with the intention of digging a hole in the snow large enough to provide shelter for the party. I had an idea that Wild and his men might camp there during my absence, since it seemed impossible that the tents could hold together for many more days against the attacks of the wind; but an examination of the spot indicated that any hole we could dig probably would be filled quickly by the drift. At dark, about 5 p.m., we all turned in, after a supper consisting of a pannikin of hot milk, one of our precious biscuits, and a cold penguin leg each.

The gale was stronger than ever on the following morning (April 20). No work could be done. Blizzard and snow, snow and blizzard, sudden lulls and fierce returns. During the lulls we could see on the far horizon to the northeast bergs of all shapes and sizes driving along before the gale, and the sinister appearance of the swift-moving masses made us thankful indeed that, instead of battling with the storm amid the ice, we were required only to face the drift from the glaciers and the inland heights. The gusts might throw us off our feet, but at least we fell on solid ground and not on the rocking floes. Two seals came up on the beach that day, one of them within ten yards of my tent. So urgent was our need of food and blubber that I called all hands and organized a line of beaters instead of simply walking up to the seal and hitting it on the nose. We were prepared to fall upon this seal *en masse* if it attempted to escape. The kill was made with a pick-handle, and in a few minutes five days' food and six days' fuel were stowed in a place of safety among the boulders above high-water mark. During this day the cook, who had worked well on the floe and throughout the boat journey, suddenly collapsed. I happened to be at the galley at the moment and saw him fall. I pulled him down the slope to his tent and pushed him into its shelter with orders to his tent-mates to keep him in his sleeping-bag until I allowed him to come out or the doctors said he was fit enough. Then I took out to replace the cook one of the men who had expressed a desire to lie down and die. The task of keeping the galley fire alight was both difficult and strenuous, and it took his thoughts away from the chances of immediate dissolution. In fact, I found him a little later gravely concerned over the drying of a naturally not over-clean pair of socks which were hung up in close proximity to our evening milk. Occupation had brought his thoughts back to the ordinary cares of life.

There was a lull in the bad weather on April 21, and the carpenter started to collect material for the decking of the *James Caird*. He fitted the mast of the *Stancomb Wills* fore and aft inside the *James Caird* as a hog-back and thus strengthened the keel with the object of preventing our boat "hogging"—that is, buckling in heavy seas. He had not sufficient wood to provide a deck, but by using the sledge-runners and box-lids he made a framework extending from the forecastle aft to a well. It was a patched-up affair, but it provided a base for a canvas covering. We had a bolt of canvas frozen stiff, and this material had to be cut and then thawed out over the blubber-stove, foot by foot, in order that it might be sewn into the form of a cover. When it had been nailed and screwed into position it certainly gave an appearance of safety to the boat, though I had an uneasy feeling that it bore a strong likeness to stage scenery, which may look like a granite wall and is in fact nothing better than canvas and lath. As events proved, the covering served its purpose well. We certainly could not have lived through the voyage without it.

Another fierce gale was blowing on April 22, interfering with our preparations for the voyage. The cooker from No. 5 tent came adrift in a gust, and, although it was chased to the water's edge, it disappeared for good. Blackborrow's feet were giving him much pain, and McIlroy and Macklin thought it would be necessary for them to operate soon. They were under the impression then that they had no chloroform, but they found some subsequently in the medicine-chest after we had left. Some cases of stores left on a rock off the spit on the day of our arrival were retrieved during this day. We were setting aside stores for the boat journey and choosing the essential equipment from the scanty stock at our disposal. Two ten-gallon casks had to be filled with water melted down from ice collected at the foot of the glacier. This was a rather slow business. The blubber-stove was kept going all night, and the watchmen emptied the water into the casks from the pot in which the ice was melted. A working party started to dig a hole in the snow-slope about forty feet above sea-level with the object of providing a site for a camp. They made fairly good progress at first, but the snow drifted down unceasingly from the inland ice, and in the end the party had to give up the project.

The weather was fine on April 23, and we hurried forward our preparations. It was on this day I decided finally that the crew for the *James Caird* should consist of Worsley, Crean, McNeish, McCarthy, Vincent, and myself. A storm came on about noon, with driving snow and heavy squalls. Occasionally the air would clear for a few minutes, and we could see a line of pack-ice, five miles out, driving across from west to east. This sight increased my anxiety to get away quickly. Winter was advancing, and soon the pack might close completely round the island and stay our departure for days or even for weeks, I did not think that ice would remain around Elephant Island continuously during the winter, since the strong winds and fast currents would keep it in motion. We had noticed ice and bergs going past at the rate of four or five knots. A certain amount of ice was held up about the end of our spit, but the sea was clear where the boat would have to be launched.

Worsley, Wild, and I climbed to the summit of the seaward rocks and examined the ice from a better vantage-point than the beach offered. The belt of pack outside appeared to be sufficiently broken for our purposes, and I decided that, unless the conditions forbade it, we would make a start in the *James Caird* on the following morning. Obviously the pack might close at any time. This decision made, I spent the rest of the day looking over the boat, gear, and stores, and discussing plans with Worsley and Wild.

Our last night on the solid ground of Elephant Island was cold and uncomfortable. We turned out at dawn and had breakfast. Then we launched the *Stancomb Wills* and loaded her with stores, gear, and ballast, which would be transferred to the *James Caird* when the heavier boat had been launched. The ballast consisted of bags made from blankets and filled with sand, making a total weight of about 1000 lb. In addition we had gathered a number of round boulders and about 250 lb. of ice, which would supplement our two casks of water.

The stores taken in the *James Caird,* which would last six men for one month, were as follows:

30 boxes of matches.
6½ gallons paraffin.
1 tin methylated spirit.
10 boxes of flamers.
1 box of blue lights.
2 Primus stoves with spare parts and prickers.
1 Nansen aluminum cooker.
6 sleeping-bags.
A few spare socks.
A few candles and some blubber-oil in an oil-bag.
Food:
3 cases sledging rations = 300 rations.
2 cases nut food = 200 ".
2 cases biscuits = 600 biscuits.
1 case lump sugar.
30 packets of Trumilk.
1 tin of Bovril cubes.
1 tin of Cerebos salt.
36 gallons of water.
112 lb. of ice.
Instruments:

Sextant.	Sea-anchor.
Binoculars.	Charts.
Prismatic compass.	Aneroid.

The swell was slight when the *Stancomb Wills* was launched and the boat got under way without any difficulty; but half an hour later, when we were pulling down the *James Caird,* the swell increased suddenly. Apparently the movement of the ice outside had made an opening and allowed the sea to run in without being blanketed by the line of pack. The swell made things difficult. Many of us got wet to the waist while dragging the boat out—a serious matter in that climate. When the *James Caird* was afloat in the surf she nearly capsized among the rocks before we could get her clear, and Vincent and the carpenter, who were on the deck, were thrown into the water. This was really bad luck, for the two men would have small chance of drying their clothes after we had got under way. Hurley, who had the eye of the professional photographer for "incidents," secured a picture of the upset, and I firmly believe that he would have liked the two unfortunate men to remain in the water until he could get a "snap" at close quarters; but we hauled them out immediately, regardless of his feelings.

The *James Caird* was soon clear of the breakers. We used all the available ropes as a long painter to prevent her drifting away to the north-east, and then the *Stancomb Wills* came alongside, transferred her load, and went back to the shore for more. As she was being beached this time the sea took her stern and half filled her with water. She had to be turned over and emptied before the return journey could be made. Every member of the crew of the *Stancomb Wills* was wet to the skin. The water-casks were towed behind the *Stancomb Wills* on this second journey, and the swell, which was increasing rapidly, drove the boat on to the rocks, where one of the casks was slightly stove in. This accident proved later to be a serious one, since some sea-water had entered the cask and the contents were now brackish.

By midday the *James Caird* was ready for the voyage. Vincent and the carpenter had secured some dry clothes by exchange with members of the shore party (I heard afterwards that it was a full fortnight before the soaked garments were finally dried), and the boat's crew was standing by waiting for the order to cast off. A moderate westerly breeze was blowing. I went ashore in the *Stancomb Wills* and had a last word with Wild, who was remaining in full command, with directions as to his course of action in the event of our failure to bring relief, but I practically left the whole situation and scope of action and decision to his own judgment, secure in the knowledge that he would act wisely. I told him that I trusted the party to him and said good-bye to the men. Then we pushed off for the last time, and within a few minutes I was aboard the *James Caird*. The crew of the *Stancomb Wills* shook hands with us as the boats bumped together and offered us the last good wishes. Then, setting our jib, we cut the painter and moved away to the north-east. The men who were staying behind made a pathetic little group on the beach, with the grim heights of the island behind them and the sea seething at their feet, but they waved to us and gave three hearty cheers. There was hope in their hearts and they trusted us to bring the help that they needed.

I had all sails set, and the *James Caird* quickly dipped the beach and its line of dark figures. The westerly wind took us rapidly to the line of pack, and as we entered it I stood up with my arm around the mast, directing the steering, so as to avoid the great lumps of ice that were flung about in the heave of the sea. The pack thickened and we were forced to turn almost due east, running before the wind towards a gap I had seen in the morning from the high ground. I could not see the gap now, but we had come out on its bearing and I was prepared to find that it had been influenced by the easterly drift. At four o'clock in the afternoon we found the channel, much narrower than it had seemed in the morning but still navigable. Dropping sail, we rowed through without touching the ice anywhere, and by 5:30 p.m. we were clear of the pack with open water before us. We passed one more piece of ice in the darkness an hour later, but the pack lay behind, and with a fair wind swelling the sails we steered our little craft through the night, our hopes centred on our distant goal. The swell was very heavy now, and when the time came for our first evening meal we found great difficulty in keeping the Primus lamp alight and preventing the hoosh splashing out of the pot. Three men were needed to attend to the cooking, one man holding the lamp and two men guarding the aluminum cooking-pot, which had to be lifted clear of the Primus whenever the movement of the boat threatened to cause a disaster. Then the lamp had to be protected from water, for sprays were coming over the bows and our flimsy decking was by no means water-tight. All these operations were conducted in the confined space under the decking, where the men lay or knelt and adjusted themselves as best they could to the angles of our cases and ballast. It was uncomfortable, but we found consolation in the reflection that without the decking we could not have used the cooker at all.

The tale of the next sixteen days is one of supreme strife amid heaving waters. The sub-Antarctic Ocean lived up to its evil winter reputation. I decided to run north for at least two days while the wind held and so get into warmer weather before turning to the east and laying a course for South Georgia. We took two-hourly spells at the tiller. The men who were not on watch crawled into the sodden sleeping-bags and tried to forget their troubles for a period; but there was no comfort in the boat. The bags and cases seemed to be alive in the unfailing knack of presenting their most uncomfortable angles to our rest-seeking bodies. A man might imagine for a moment that he had found a position of ease, but always discovered quickly that some unyielding point was impinging on muscle or bone. The first night aboard the boat was one of acute discomfort for us all, and we were heartily glad when the dawn came and we could set about the preparation of a hot breakfast.

This record of the voyage to South Georgia is based upon scanty notes made day by day. The notes dealt usually with the bare facts of distances, positions, and weather, but our memories retained the incidents of the passing days in a period never to be forgotten. By running north for the first two days I hoped to get warmer weather and also to avoid lines of pack that might be extending beyond the main body. We needed all the advantage that we could obtain from the higher latitude for sailing on the great circle, but we had to be cautious regarding possible ice-streams. Cramped in our narrow quarters and continually wet by the spray, we suffered severely from cold throughout the journey. We fought the seas and the winds and at the same time had a daily struggle to keep ourselves alive. At times we were in dire peril. Generally we were upheld by the knowledge that we were making progress towards the land where we would be, but there were days and nights when we lay hove to, drifting across the storm-whitened seas and watching, with eyes interested rather than apprehensive, the uprearing masses of water, flung to and fro by Nature in the pride of her strength. Deep seemed the valleys when we lay between the reeling seas. High were the hills when we perched momentarily on the tops of giant combers. Nearly always there were gales. So small was our boat and so great were the seas that often our sail flapped idly in the calm between the crests of two waves. Then we would climb the next slope and catch the full fury of the gale where the wool-like whiteness of the breaking water surged around us. We had our moments of laughter—rare, it is true, but hearty enough. Even when cracked lips and swollen mouths checked the outward and visible signs of amusement we could see a joke of the primitive kind. Man's sense of humour is always most easily stirred by the petty misfortunes of his neighbours, and I shall never forget Worsley's efforts on one occasion to place the hot aluminium stand on top of the Primus stove after it had fallen off in an extra heavy roll. With his frost-bitten fingers he picked it up, dropped it, picked it up again, and toyed with it gingerly as though it were some fragile article of lady's wear. We laughed, or rather gurgled with laughter.

The wind came up strong and worked into a gale from the north-west on the third day out. We stood away to the east. The increasing seas discovered the weaknesses of our decking. The continuous blows shifted the box-lids and sledge-runners so that the canvas sagged down and accumulated water. Then icy trickles, distinct from the driving sprays, poured fore and aft into the boat. The nails that the carpenter had extracted from cases at Elephant Island and used to fasten down the battens were too short to make firm the decking. We did what we could to secure it, but our means were very limited, and the water continued to enter the boat at a dozen points. Much baling was necessary, and nothing that we could do prevented our gear from becoming sodden. The searching runnels from the canvas were really more unpleasant than the sudden definite douches of the sprays. Lying under the thwarts during watches below, we tried vainly to avoid them. There were no dry places in the boat, and at last we simply covered our heads with our Burberrys and endured the all-pervading water. The baling was work for the watch. Real rest we had none. The perpetual motion of the boat made repose impossible; we were cold, sore, and anxious. We moved on hands and knees in the semi-darkness of the day under the decking. The darkness was complete by 6 p.m. and not until 7 a.m. of the following day could we see one another under the thwarts. We had a few scraps of candle, and they were preserved carefully in order that we might have light at meal-times. There was one fairly dry spot in the boat, under the solid original decking at the bows, and we managed to protect some of our biscuit from the salt water; but I do not think any of us got the taste of salt out of our mouths during the voyage.

The difficulty of movement in the boat would have had its humorous side if it had not involved us in so many aches and pains. We had to crawl under the thwarts in order to move along the boat, and our knees suffered considerably. When a watch turned out it was necessary for me to direct each man by name when and where to move, since if all hands had crawled about at the same time the result would have been dire confusion and many bruises. Then there was the trim of the boat to be considered. The order of the watch was four hours on and four hours off, three men to the watch. One man had the tiller-ropes, the second man attended to the sail, and the third baled for all he was worth. Sometimes when the water in the boat had been reduced to reasonable proportions, our pump could be used. This pump, which Hurley had made from the Flinders bar case of our ship's standard compass, was quite effective, though its capacity was not large. The man who was attending the sail could pump into the big outer cooker, which was lifted and emptied overboard when filled. We had a device by which the water could go direct from the pump into the sea through a hole in the gunwale, but this hole had to be blocked at an early stage of the voyage, since we found that it admitted water when the boat rolled.

While a new watch was shivering in the wind and spray, the men who had been relieved groped hurriedly among the soaked sleeping-bags and tried to steal a little of the warmth created by the last occupants; but it was not always possible for us to find even this comfort when we went off watch. The boulders that we had taken aboard for ballast had to be shifted continually in order to trim the boat and give access to the pump, which became choked with hairs from the moulting sleeping-bags and finneskoe. The four reindeer-skin sleeping-bags shed their hair freely owing to the continuous wetting, and soon became quite bald in appearance. The moving of the boulders was weary and painful work. We came to know every one of the stones by sight and touch, and I have vivid memories of their angular peculiarities even to-day. They might have been of considerable interest as geological specimens to a scientific man under happier conditions. As ballast they were useful. As weights to be moved about in cramped quarters they were simply appalling. They spared no portion of our poor bodies. Another of our troubles, worth mention here, was the chafing of our legs by our wet clothes, which had not been changed now for seven months. The insides of our thighs were rubbed raw, and the one tube of Hazeline cream in our medicine-chest did not go far in alleviating our pain, which was increased by the bite of the salt water. We thought at the time that we never slept. The fact was that we would dose off uncomfortably, to be aroused quickly by some new ache or another call to effort. My own share of the general unpleasantness was accentuated by a finely developed bout of sciatica. I had become possessor of this originally on the floe several months earlier.

Our meals were regular in spite of the gales. Attention to this point was essential, since the conditions of the voyage made increasing calls upon our vitality. Breakfast, at 8 a.m., consisted of a pannikin of hot hoosh made from Bovril sledging ration, two biscuits, and some lumps of sugar. Lunch came at 1 p.m., and comprised Bovril sledging ration, eaten raw, and a pannikin of hot milk for each man. Tea, at 5 p.m., had the same menu. Then during the night we had a hot drink, generally of milk. The meals were the bright beacons in those cold and stormy days. The glow of warmth and comfort produced by the food and drink made optimists of us all. We had two tins of Virol, which we were keeping for an emergency; but, finding ourselves in need of an oil-lamp to eke out our supply of candles, we emptied one of the tins in the manner that most appealed to us, and fitted it with a wick made by shredding a bit of canvas. When this lamp was filled with oil it gave a certain amount of light, though it was easily blown out, and was of great assistance to us at night. We were fairly well off as regarded fuel, since we had 6½ gallons of petroleum.

A severe south-westerly gale on the fourth day out forced us to heave to. I would have liked to have run before the wind, but the sea was very high and the *James Caird* was in danger of broaching to and swamping. The delay was vexatious, since up to that time we had been making sixty or seventy miles a day; good going with our limited sail area. We hove to under double-reefed mainsail and our little jigger, and waited for the gale to blow itself out. During that afternoon we saw bits of wreckage, the remains probably of some unfortunate vessel that had failed to weather the strong gales south of Cape Horn. The weather conditions did not improve, and on the fifth day out the gale was so fierce that we were compelled to take in the double-reefed mainsail and hoist our small jib instead. We put out a sea-anchor to keep the *James Caird's* head up to the sea. This anchor consisted of a triangular canvas bag fastened to the end of the painter and allowed to stream out from the bows. The boat was high enough to catch the wind, and, as she drifted to leeward, the drag of the anchor kept her head to windward. Thus our boat took most of the seas more or less end on. Even then the crests of the waves often would curl right over us and we shipped a great deal of water, which necessitated unceasing baling and pumping. Looking out abeam, we would see a hollow like a tunnel formed as the crest of a big wave toppled over on to the swelling body of water. A thousand times it appeared as though the *James Caird* must be engulfed; but the boat lived. The south-westerly gale had its birthplace above the Antarctic Continent, and its freezing breath lowered the temperature far towards zero. The sprays froze upon the boat and gave bows, sides, and decking a heavy coat of mail. This accumulation of ice reduced the buoyancy of the boat, and to that extent was an added peril; but it possessed a notable advantage from one point of view. The water ceased to drop and trickle from the canvas, and the spray came in solely at the well in the after part of the boat. We could not allow the load of ice to grow beyond a certain point, and in turns we crawled about the decking forward, chipping and picking at it with the available tools.

When daylight came on the morning of the sixth day out we saw and felt that the *James Caird* had lost her resiliency. She was not rising to the oncoming seas. The weight of the ice that had formed in her and upon her during the night was having its effect, and she was becoming more like a log than a boat. The situation called for immediate action. We first broke away the spare oars, which were encased in ice and frozen to the sides of the boat, and threw them overboard. We retained two oars for use when we got inshore. Two of the fur sleeping-bags went over the side; they were thoroughly wet, weighing probably 40 lb. each, and they had frozen stiff during the night. Three men constituted the watch below, and when a man went down it was better to turn into the wet bag just vacated by another man than to thaw out a frozen bag with the heat of his unfortunate body. We now had four bags, three in use and one for emergency use in case a member of the party should break down permanently. The reduction of weight relieved the boat to some extent, and vigorous chipping and scraping did more. We had to be very careful not to put axe or knife through the frozen canvas of the decking as we crawled over it, but gradually we got rid of a lot of ice. The *James Caird* lifted to the endless waves as though she lived again.

About 11 a.m. the boat suddenly fell off into the trough of the sea. The painter had parted and the sea-anchor had gone. This was serious. The *James Caird* went away to leeward, and we had no chance at all of recovering the anchor and our valuable rope, which had been our only means of keeping the boat's head up to the seas without the risk of hoisting sail in a gale. Now we had to set the sail and trust to its holding. While the *James Caird* rolled heavily in the trough, we beat the frozen canvas until the bulk of the ice had cracked off it and then hoisted it. The frozen gear worked protestingly, but after a struggle our little craft came up to the wind again, and we breathed more freely. Skin frost-bites were troubling us, and we had developed large blisters on our fingers and hands. I shall always carry the scar of one of these frost-bites on my left hand, which became badly inflamed after the skin had burst and the cold had bitten deeply.

We held the boat up to the gale during that day, enduring as best we could discomforts that amounted to pain. The boat tossed interminably on the big waves under grey, threatening skies. Our thoughts did not embrace much more than the necessities of the hour. Every surge of the sea was an enemy to be watched and circumvented. We ate our scanty meals, treated our frost-bites, and hoped for the improved conditions that the morrow might bring. Night fell early, and in the lagging hours of darkness we were cheered by a change for the better in the weather. The wind dropped, the snow-squalls became less frequent, and the sea moderated. When the morning of the seventh day dawned there was not much wind. We shook the reef out of the sail and laid our course once more for South Georgia. The sun came out bright and clear, and presently Worsley got a snap for longitude. We hoped that the sky would remain clear until noon, so that we could get the latitude. We had been six days out without an observation, and our dead reckoning naturally was uncertain. The boat must have presented a strange appearance that morning. All hands basked in the sun. We hung our sleeping-bags to the mast and spread our socks and other gear all over the deck. Some of the ice had melted off the *James Caird* in the early morning after the gale began to slacken, and dry patches were appearing in the decking. Porpoises came blowing round the boat, and Cape pigeons wheeled and swooped within a few feet of us. These little black-and-white birds have an air of friendliness that is not possessed by the great circling albatross. They had looked grey against the swaying sea during the storm as they darted about over our heads and uttered their plaintive cries. The albatrosses, of the black or sooty variety, had watched with hard, bright eyes, and seemed to have a quite impersonal interest in our struggle to keep afloat amid the battering seas. In addition to the Cape pigeons an occasional stormy petrel flashed overhead. Then there was a small bird, unknown to me, that appeared always to be in a fussy, bustling state, quite out of keeping with the surroundings. It irritated me. It had practically no tail, and it flitted about vaguely as though in search of the lost member. I used to find myself wishing it would find its tail and have done with the silly fluttering.

We revelled in the warmth of the sun that day. Life was not so bad, after all. We felt we were well on our way. Our gear was drying, and we could have a hot meal in comparative comfort. The swell was still heavy, but it was not breaking and the boat rode easily. At noon Worsley balanced himself on the gunwale and clung with one hand to the stay of the mainmast while he got a snap of the sun. The result was more than encouraging. We had done over 380 miles and were getting on for half-way to South Georgia. It looked as though we were going to get through.

The wind freshened to a good stiff breeze during the afternoon, and the *James Caird* made satisfactory progress. I had not realized until the sunlight came how small our boat really was. There was some influence in the light and warmth, some hint of happier days, that made us revive memories of other voyages, when we had stout decks beneath our feet, unlimited food at our command, and pleasant cabins for our ease. Now we clung to a battered little boat, "alone, alone, all, all alone, alone on a wide, wide sea." So low in the water were we that each succeeding swell out off our view of the sky-line. We were a tiny speck in the vast vista of the sea—the ocean that is open to all and merciful to none, that threatens even when it seems to yield, and that is pitiless always to weakness. For a moment the consciousness of the forces arrayed against us would be almost overwhelming. Then hope and confidence would rise again as our boat rose to a wave and tossed aside the crest in a sparkling shower like the play of prismatic colours at the foot of a waterfall. My double-barrelled gun and some cartridges had been stowed aboard the boat as an emergency precaution against a shortage of food, but we were not disposed to destroy our little neighbours, the Cape pigeons, even for the sake of fresh meat. We might have shot an albatross, but the wandering king of the ocean aroused in us something of the feeling that inspired, too late, the Ancient Mariner. So the gun remained among the stores and sleeping-bags in the narrow quarters beneath our leaking deck, and the birds followed us unmolested.

The eighth, ninth, and tenth days of the voyage had few features worthy of special note. The wind blew hard during those days, and the strain of navigating the boat was unceasing, but always we made some advance towards our goal. No bergs showed on our horizon, and we knew that we were clear of the ice-fields. Each day brought its little round of troubles, but also compensation in the form of food and growing hope. We felt that we were going to succeed. The odds against us had been great, but we were winning through. We still suffered severely from the cold, for, though the temperature was rising, our vitality was declining owing to shortage of food, exposure, and the necessity of maintaining our cramped positions day and night. I found that it was now absolutely necessary to prepare hot milk for all hands during the night, in order to sustain life till dawn. This meant lighting the Primus lamp in the darkness and involved an increased drain on our small store of matches. It was the rule that one match must serve when the Primus was being lit. We had no lamp for the compass and during the early days of the voyage we would strike a match when the steersman wanted to see the course at night; but later the necessity for strict economy impressed itself upon us, and the practice of striking matches at night was stopped. We had one water-tight tin of matches. I had stowed away in a pocket, in readiness for a sunny day, a lens from one of the telescopes, but this was of no use during the voyage. The sun seldom shone upon us. The glass of the compass got broken one night, and we contrived to mend it with adhesive tape from the medicine-chest. One of the memories that comes to me from those days is of Crean singing at the tiller. He always sang while he was steering, and nobody ever discovered what the song was. It was devoid of tune and as monotonous as the chanting of a Buddhist monk at his prayers; yet somehow it was cheerful. In moments of inspiration Crean would attempt "The Wearing of the Green."

On the tenth night Worsley could not straighten his body after his spell at the tiller. He was thoroughly cramped, and we had to drag him beneath the decking and massage him before he could unbend himself and get into a sleeping-bag. A hard north-westerly gale came up on the eleventh day (May 5) and shifted to the south-west in the late afternoon. The sky was overcast and occasional snow-squalls added to the discomfort produced by a tremendous cross-sea—the worst, I thought, that we had experienced. At midnight I was at the tiller and suddenly noticed a line of clear sky between the south and south-west. I called to the other men that the sky was clearing, and then a moment later I realized that what I had seen was not a rift in the clouds but the white crest of an enormous wave. During twenty-six years' experience of the ocean in all its moods I had not encountered a wave so gigantic. It was a mighty up-heaval of the ocean, a thing quite apart from the big white-capped seas that had been our tireless enemies for many days. I shouted, "For God's sake, hold on! It's got us!" Then came a moment of suspense that seemed drawn out into hours. White surged the foam of the breaking sea around us. We felt our boat lifted and flung forward like a cork in breaking surf. We were in a seething chaos of tortured water; but somehow the boat lived through it, half-full of water, sagging to the dead weight and shuddering under the blow. We baled with the energy of men fighting for life, flinging the water over the sides with every receptacle that came to our hands, and after ten minutes of uncertainty we felt the boat renew her life beneath us. She floated again and ceased to lurch drunkenly as though dazed by the attack of the sea. Earnestly we hoped that never again would we encounter such a wave.

The conditions in the boat, uncomfortable before, had been made worse by the deluge of water. All our gear was thoroughly wet again. Our cooking-stove had been floating about in the bottom of the boat, and portions of our last hoosh seemed to have permeated everything. Not until 3 a.m., when we were all chilled almost to the limit of endurance, did we manage to get the stove alight and make ourselves hot drinks. The carpenter was suffering particularly, but he showed grit and spirit. Vincent had for the past week ceased to be an active member of the crew, and I could not easily account for his collapse. Physically he was one of the strongest men in the boat. He was a young man, he had served on North Sea trawlers, and he should have been able to bear hardships better than McCarthy, who, not so strong, was always happy.

The weather was better on the following day (May 6), and we got a glimpse of the sun. Worsley's observation showed that we were not more than a hundred miles from the northwest corner of South Georgia. Two more days with a favourable wind and we would sight the promised land. I hoped that there would be no delay, for our supply of water was running very low. The hot drink at night was essential, but I decided that the daily allowance of water must be cut down to half a pint per man. The lumps of ice we had taken aboard had gone long ago. We were dependent upon the water we had brought from Elephant Island, and our thirst was increased by the fact that we were now using the brackish water in the breaker that had been slightly stove in in the surf when the boat was being loaded. Some sea-water had entered at that time.

Thirst took possession of us. I dared not permit the allowance of water to be increased since an unfavourable wind might drive us away from the island and lengthen our voyage by many days. Lack of water is always the most severe privation that men can be condemned to endure, and we found, as during our earlier boat voyage, that the salt water in our clothing and the salt spray that lashed our faces made our thirst grow quickly to a burning pain. I had to be very firm in refusing to allow any one to anticipate the morrow's allowance, which I was sometimes begged to do. We did the necessary work dully and hoped for the land. I had altered the course to the east so as to make sure of our striking the island, which would have been impossible to regain if we had run past the northern end. The course was laid on our scrap of chart for a point some thirty miles down the coast. That day and the following day passed for us in a sort of nightmare. Our mouths were dry and our tongues were swollen. The wind was still strong and the heavy sea forced us to navigate carefully, but any thought of our peril from the waves was buried beneath the consciousness of our raging thirst. The bright moments were those when we each received our one mug of hot milk during the long, bitter watches of the night. Things were bad for us in those days, but the end was coming. The morning of May 8 broke thick and stormy, with squalls from the north-west. We searched the waters ahead for a sign of land, and though we could see nothing more than had met our eyes for many days, we were cheered by a sense that the goal was near at hand. About ten o'clock that morning we passed a little bit of kelp, a glad signal of the proximity of land. An hour later we saw two shags sitting on a big mass of kelp, and knew then that we must be within ten or fifteen miles of the shore. These birds are as sure an indication of the proximity of land as a lighthouse is, for they never venture far to sea. We gazed ahead with increasing eagerness, and at 12:30 p.m., through a rift in the clouds, McCarthy caught a glimpse of the black cliffs of South Georgia, just fourteen days after our departure from Elephant Island. It was a glad moment. Thirst-ridden, chilled, and weak as we were, happiness irradiated us. The job was nearly done.

We stood in towards the shore to look for a landing-place, and presently we could see the green tussock-grass on the ledges above the surf-beaten rocks. Ahead of us and to the south, blind rollers showed the presence of uncharted reefs along the coast. Here and there the hungry rocks were close to the surface, and over them the great waves broke, swirling viciously and spouting thirty and forty feet into the air. The rocky coast appeared to descend sheer to the sea. Our need of water and rest was wellnigh desperate, but to have attempted a landing at that time would have been suicidal. Night was drawing near, and the weather indications were not favourable. There was nothing for it but to haul off till the following morning, so we stood away on the starboard tack until we had made what appeared to be a safe offing. Then we hove to in the high westerly swell. The hours passed slowly as we waited the dawn, which would herald, we fondly hoped, the last stage of our journey. Our thirst was a torment and we could scarcely touch our food; the cold seemed to strike right through our weakened bodies. At 5 a.m. the wind shifted to the north-west and quickly increased to one of the worst hurricanes any of us had ever experienced. A great cross-sea was running, and the wind simply shrieked as it tore the tops off the waves and converted the whole seascape into a haze of driving spray. Down into valleys, up to tossing heights, straining until her seams opened, swung our little boat, brave still but labouring heavily. We knew that the wind and set of the sea was driving us ashore, but we could do nothing.

The dawn showed us a storm-torn ocean, and the morning passed without bringing us a sight of the land; but at 1 p.m., through a rift in the flying mists, we got a glimpse of the huge crags of the island and realized that our position had become desperate. We were on a dead lee shore, and we could gauge our approach to the unseen cliffs by the roar of the breakers against the sheer walls of rock. I ordered the double-reefed mainsail to be set in the hope that we might claw off, and this attempt increased the strain upon the boat. The *James Caird* was bumping heavily, and the water was pouring in everywhere. Our thirst was forgotten in the realization of our imminent danger, as we baled unceasingly, and adjusted our weights from time to time; occasional glimpses showed that the shore was nearer. I knew that Annewkow Island lay to the south of us, but our small and badly marked chart showed uncertain reefs in the passage between the island and the mainland, and I dared not trust it, though as a last resort we could try to lie under the lee of the island. The afternoon wore away as we edged down the coast, with the thunder of the breakers in our ears. The approach of evening found us still some distance from Annewkow Island, and, dimly in the twilight, we could see a snow-capped mountain looming above us. The chance of surviving the night, with the driving gale and the implacable sea forcing us on to the lee shore, seemed small. I think most of us had a feeling that the end was very near. Just after 6 p.m., in the dark, as the boat was in the yeasty backwash from the seas flung from this ironbound coast, then, just when things looked their worst, they changed for the best. I have marvelled often at the thin line that divides success from failure and the sudden turn that leads from apparently certain disaster to comparative safety. The wind suddenly shifted, and we were free once more to make an offing. Almost as soon as the gale eased, the pin that locked the mast to the thwart fell out. It must have been on the point of doing this throughout the hurricane, and if it had gone nothing could have saved us; the mast would have snapped like a carrot. Our backstays had carried away once before when iced up and were not too strongly fastened now. We were thankful indeed for the mercy that had held that pin in its place throughout the hurricane.

We stood off shore again, tired almost to the point of apathy. Our water had long been finished. The last was about a pint of hairy liquid, which we strained through a bit of gauze from the medicine-chest. The pangs of thirst attacked us with redoubled intensity, and I felt that we must make a landing on the following day at almost any hazard. The night wore on. We were very tired. We longed for day. When at last the dawn came on the morning of May 10 there was practically no wind, but a high cross-sea was running. We made slow progress towards the shore. About 8 a.m. the wind backed to the north-west and threatened another blow. We had sighted in the meantime a big indentation which I thought must be King Haakon Bay, and I decided that we must land there. We set the bows of the boat towards the bay and ran before the freshening gale. Soon we had angry reefs on either side. Great glaciers came down to the sea and offered no landing-place. The sea spouted on the reefs and thundered against the shore. About noon we sighted a line of jagged reef, like blackened teeth, that seemed to bar the entrance to the bay. Inside, comparatively smooth water stretched eight or nine miles to the head of the bay. A gap in the reef appeared, and we made for it. But the fates had another rebuff for us. The wind shifted and blew from the east right out of the bay. We could see the way through the reef, but we could not approach it directly. That afternoon we bore up, tacking five times in the strong wind. The last tack enabled us to get through, and at last we were in the wide mouth of the bay. Dusk was approaching. A small cove, with a boulder-strewn beach guarded by a reef, made a break in the cliffs on the south side of the bay, and we turned in that direction. I stood in the bows directing the steering as we ran through the kelp and made the passage of the reef. The entrance was so narrow that we had to take in the oars, and the swell was piling itself right over the reef into the cove; but in a minute or two we were inside, and in the gathering darkness the *James Caird* ran in on a swell and touched the beach. I sprang ashore with the short painter and held on when the boat went out with the backward surge. When the *James Caird* came in again three of the men got ashore, and they held the painter while I climbed some rocks with another line. A slip on the wet rocks twenty feet up nearly closed my part of the story just at the moment when we were achieving safety. A jagged piece of rock held me and at the same time bruised me sorely. However, I made fast the line, and in a few minutes we were all safe on the beach, with the boat floating in the surging water just off the shore. We heard a gurgling sound that was sweet music in our ears, and, peering around, found a stream of fresh water almost at our feet. A moment later we were down on our knees drinking the pure, ice-cold water in long draughts that put new life into us. It was a splendid moment.

The next thing was to get the stores and ballast out of the boat, in order that we might secure her for the night. We carried the stores and gear above high-water mark and threw out the bags of sand and the boulders that we knew so well. Then we attempted to pull the empty boat up the beach, and discovered by this effort how weak we had become. Our united strength was not sufficient to get the *James Caird* clear of the water. Time after time we pulled together, but without avail. I saw that it would be necessary to have food and rest before we beached the boat. We made fast a line to a heavy boulder and set a watch to fend the *James Caird* off the rocks of the beach. Then I sent Crean round to the left side of the cove, about thirty yards away, where I had noticed a little cave as we were running in. He could not see much in the darkness, but reported that the place certainly promised some shelter. We carried the sleeping-bags round and found a mere hollow in the rock-face, with a shingle floor sloping at a steep angle to the sea. There we prepared a hot meal, and when the food was finished I ordered the men to turn in. The time was now about 8 p.m., and I took the first watch beside the *James Caird,* which was still afloat in the tossing water just off the beach.

Fending the *James Caird* off the rocks in the darkness was awkward work. The boat would have bumped dangerously if allowed to ride in with the waves that drove into the cove. I found a flat rock for my feet, which were in a bad way owing to cold, wetness, and lack of exercise in the boat, and during the next few hours I laboured to keep the *James Caird* clear of the beach. Occasionally I had to rush into the seething water. Then, as a wave receded, I let the boat out on the alpine rope so as to avoid a sudden jerk. The heavy painter had been lost when the sea-anchor went adrift. The *James Caird* could be seen but dimly in the cove, where the high black cliffs made the darkness almost complete, and the strain upon one's attention was great. After several hours had passed I found that my desire for sleep was becoming irresistible, and at 1 a.m. I called Crean. I could hear him groaning as he stumbled over the sharp rocks on his way down the beach. While he was taking charge of the *James Caird* she got adrift, and we had some anxious moments. Fortunately, she went across towards the cave and we secured her unharmed. The loss or destruction of the boat at this stage would have been a very serious matter, since we probably would have found it impossible to leave the cove except by sea. The cliffs and glaciers around offered no practicable path towards the head of the bay. I arranged for one-hour watches during the remainder of the night and then took Crean's place among the sleeping men and got some sleep before the dawn came.

The sea went down in the early hours of the morning (May 11), and after sunrise we were able to set about getting the boat ashore, first bracing ourselves for the task with another meal. We were all weak still. We cut off the topsides and took out all the movable gear. Then we waited for Byron's "great ninth wave," and when it lifted the *James Caird* in we held her and, by dint of great exertion, worked her round broadside to the sea. Inch by inch we dragged her up until we reached the fringe of the tussock-grass and knew that the boat was above high-water mark. The rise of the tide was about five feet, and at spring tide the water must have reached almost to the edge of the tussock-grass. The completion of this job removed our immediate anxieties, and we were free to examine our surroundings and plan the next move. The day was bright and clear.

King Haakon Bay is an eight-mile sound penetrating the coast of South Georgia in an easterly direction. We had noticed that the northern and southern sides of the sound were formed by steep mountain-ranges, their flanks furrowed by mighty glaciers, the outlets of the great ice-sheet of the interior. It was obvious that these glaciers and the precipitous slopes of the mountains barred our way inland from the cove. We must sail to the head of the sound. Swirling clouds and mist-wreaths had obscured our view of the sound when we were entering, but glimpses of snow-slopes had given us hope that an overland journey could be begun from that point. A few patches of very rough, tussocky land, dotted with little tarns, lay between the glaciers along the foot of the mountains, which were heavily scarred with scree-slopes. Several magnificent peaks and crags gazed out across their snowy domains to the sparkling waters of the sound.

Our cove lay a little inside the southern headland of King Haakon Bay. A narrow break in the cliffs, which were about a hundred feet high at this point, formed the entrance to the cove. The cliffs continued inside the cove on each side and merged into a hill which descended at a steep slope to the boulder beach. The slope, which carried tussock-grass, was not continuous. It eased at two points into little peaty swamp-terraces dotted with frozen pools and drained by two small streams. Our cave was a recess in the cliff on the left-hand end of the beach. The rocky face of the cliff was undercut at this point, and the shingle thrown up by the waves formed a steep slope, which we reduced to about one in six by scraping the stones away from the inside. Later we strewed the rough floor with the dead, nearly dry underleaves of the tussock-grass, so as to form a slightly soft bed for our sleeping-bags. Water had trickled down the face of the cliff and formed long icicles, which hung down in front of the cave to the length of about fifteen feet. These icicles provided shelter, and when we had spread our sails below them, with the assistance of oars, we had quarters that, in the circumstances, had to be regarded as reasonably comfortable. The camp at least was dry, and we moved our gear there with confidence. We built a fireplace and arranged our sleeping-bags and blankets around it. The cave was about 8 ft. deep and 12 ft. wide at the entrance.

While the camp was being arranged Crean and I climbed the tussock slope behind the beach and reached the top of a headland overlooking the sound. There we found the nests of albatrosses, and, much to our delight, the nests contained young birds. The fledgelings were fat and lusty, and we had no hesitation about deciding that they were destined to die at an early age. Our most pressing anxiety at this stage was a shortage of fuel for the cooker. We had rations for ten more days, and we knew now that we could get birds for food; but if we were to have hot meals we must secure fuel. The store of petroleum carried in the boat was running very low, and it seemed necessary to keep some quantity for use on the overland journey that lay ahead of us. A sea-elephant or a seal would have provided fuel as well as food, but we could see none in the neighbourhood. During the morning we started a fire in the cave with wood from the top-sides of the boat, and though the dense smoke from the damp sticks inflamed our tired eyes, the warmth and the prospect of hot food were ample compensation. Crean was cook that day, and I suggested to him that he should wear his goggles, which he happened to have brought with him. The goggles helped him a great deal as he bent over the fire and tended the stew. And what a stew it was! The young albatrosses weighed about fourteen pounds each fresh killed, and we estimated that they weighed at least six pounds each when cleaned and dressed for the pot. Four birds went into the pot for six men, with a Bovril ration for thickening. The flesh was white and succulent, and the bones, not fully formed, almost melted in our mouths. That was a memorable meal. When we had eaten our fill, we dried our tobacco in the embers of the fire and smoked contentedly. We made an attempt to dry our clothes, which were soaked with salt water, but did not meet with much success. We could not afford to have a fire except for cooking purposes until blubber or driftwood had come our way.

The final stage of the journey had still to be attempted. I realized that the condition of the party generally, and particularly of McNeish and Vincent, would prevent us putting to sea again except under pressure of dire necessity. Our boat, moreover, had been weakened by the cutting away of the topsides, and I doubted if we could weather the island. We were still 150 miles away from Stromness whaling-station by sea. The alternative was to attempt the crossing of the island. If we could not get over, then we must try to secure enough food and fuel to keep us alive through the winter, but this possibility was scarcely thinkable. Over on Elephant Island twenty-two men were waiting for the relief that we alone could secure for them. Their plight was worse than ours. We must push on somehow. Several days must elapse before our strength would be sufficiently recovered to allow us to row or sail the last nine miles up to the head of the bay. In the meantime we could make what preparations were possible and dry our clothes by taking advantage of every scrap of heat from the fires we lit for the cooking of our meals. We turned in early that night, and I remember that I dreamed of the great wave and aroused my companions with a shout of warning as I saw with half-awakened eyes the towering cliff on the opposite side of the cove.

Shortly before midnight a gale sprang up suddenly from the north-east with rain and sleet showers. It brought quantities of glacier-ice into the cove, and by 2 a.m. (May 12) our little harbour was filled with ice, which surged to and fro in the swell and pushed its way on to the beach. We had solid rock beneath our feet and could watch without anxiety. When daylight came rain was falling heavily, and the temperature was the highest we had experienced for many months. The icicles overhanging our cave were melting down in streams and we had to move smartly when passing in and out lest we should be struck by falling lumps. A fragment weighing fifteen or twenty pounds crashed down while we were having breakfast. We found that a big hole had been burned in the bottom of Worsley's reindeer sleeping-bag during the night. Worsley had been awakened by a burning sensation in his feet, and had asked the men near him if his bag was all right; they looked and could see nothing wrong. We were all superficially frost-bitten about the feet, and this condition caused the extremities to burn painfully, while at the same time sensation was lost in the skin. Worsley thought that the uncomfortable heat of his feet was due to the frost-bites, and he stayed in his bag and presently went to sleep again. He discovered when he turned out in the morning that the tussock-grass which we had laid on the floor of the cave had smouldered outwards from the fire and had actually burned a large hole in the bag beneath his feet. Fortunately, his feet were not harmed.

Our party spent a quiet day, attending to clothing and gear, checking stores, eating and resting. Some more of the young albatrosses made a noble end in our pot. The birds were nesting on a small plateau above the right-hand end of our beach. We had previously discovered that when we were landing from the boat on the night of May 10 we had lost the rudder. The *James Caird* had been bumping heavily astern as we were scrambling ashore, and evidently the rudder was then knocked off. A careful search of the beach and the rocks within our reach failed to reveal the missing article. This was a serious loss, even if the voyage to the head of the sound could be made in good weather. At dusk the ice in the cove was rearing and crashing on the beach. It had forced up a ridge of stones close to where the *James Caird* lay at the edge of the tussock-grass. Some pieces of ice were driven right up to the canvas wall at the front of our cave. Fragments lodged within two feet of Vincent, who had the lowest sleeping-place, and within four feet of our fire. Crean and McCarthy had brought down six more of the young albatrosses in the afternoon, so we were well supplied with fresh food. The air temperature that night probably was not lower than 38° or 40° Fahr., and we were rendered uncomfortable in our cramped sleeping quarters by the unaccustomed warmth. Our feelings towards our neighbours underwent a change. When the temperature was below 20° Fahr. we could not get too close to one another—every man wanted to cuddle against his neighbour; but let the temperature rise a few degrees and the warmth of another man's body ceased to be a blessing. The ice and the waves had a voice of menace that night, but I heard it only in my dreams.

The bay was still filled with ice on the morning of Saturday, May 13, but the tide took it all away in the afternoon. Then a strange thing happened. The rudder, with all the broad Atlantic to sail in and the coasts of two continents to search for a resting-place, came bobbing back into our cove. With anxious eyes we watched it as it advanced, receded again, and then advanced once more under the capricious influence of wind and wave. Nearer and nearer it came as we waited on the shore, oars in hand, and at last we were able to seize it. Surely a remarkable salvage! The day was bright and clear; our clothes were drying and our strength was returning. Running water made a musical sound down the tussock slope and among the boulders. We carried our blankets up the hill and tried to dry them in the breeze 300 ft. above sea-level. In the afternoon we began to prepare the *James Caird* for the journey to the head of King Haakon Bay. A noon observation on this day gave our latitude as 54° 10' 47" S., but according to the German chart the position should have been 54° 12' S. Probably Worsley's observation was the more accurate. We were able to keep the fire alight until we went to sleep that night, for while climbing the rocks above the cove I had seen at the foot of a cliff a broken spar, which had been thrown up by the waves. We could reach this spar by climbing down the cliff, and with a reserve supply of fuel thus in sight we could afford to burn the fragments of the *James Caird's* topsides more freely.

During the morning of this day (May 13) Worsley and I tramped across the hills in a north-easterly direction with the object of getting a view of the sound and possibly gathering some information that would be useful to us in the next stage of our journey. It was exhausting work, but after covering about 2½ miles in two hours, we were able to look east, up the bay. We could not see very much of the country that we would have to cross in order to reach the whaling-station on the other side of the island. We had passed several brooks and frozen tarns, and at a point where we had to take to the beach on the shore of the sound we found some wreckage—an 18-ft. pine-spar (probably part of a ship's topmast), several pieces of timber, and a little model of a ship's hull, evidently a child's toy. We wondered what tragedy that pitiful little plaything indicated. We encountered also some gentoo penguins and a young sea-elephant, which Worsley killed.

When we got back to the cave at 3 p.m., tired, hungry, but rather pleased with ourselves, we found a splendid meal of stewed albatross chicken waiting for us. We had carried a quantity of blubber and the sea-elephant's liver in our blouses, and we produced our treasures as a surprise for the men. Rough climbing on the way back to camp had nearly persuaded us to throw the stuff away, but we had held on (regardless of the condition of our already sorely tried clothing), and had our reward at the camp. The long bay had been a magnificent sight, even to eyes that had dwelt on grandeur long enough and were hungry for the simple, familiar things of everyday life. Its green-blue waters were being beaten to fury by the north-westerly gale. The mountains, "stern peaks that dared the stars," peered through the mists, and between them huge glaciers poured down from the great ice-slopes and -fields that lay behind. We counted twelve glaciers and heard every few minutes the reverberating roar caused by masses of ice calving from the parent streams.

On May 14 we made our preparations for an early start on the following day if the weather held fair. We expected to be able to pick up the remains of the sea-elephant on our way up the sound. All hands were recovering from the chafing caused by our wet clothes during the boat journey. The insides of our legs had suffered severely, and for some time after landing in the cove we found movement extremely uncomfortable. We paid our last visit to the nests of the albatrosses, which were situated on a little undulating plateau above the cave amid tussocks, snow-patches, and little frozen tarns. Each nest consisted of a mound over a foot high of tussock-grass, roots, and a little earth. The albatross lays one egg and very rarely two. The chicks, which are hatched in January, are fed on the nest by the parent birds for almost seven months before they take to the sea and fend for themselves. Up to four months of age the chicks are beautiful white masses of downy fluff, but when we arrived on the scene their plumage was almost complete. Very often one of the parent birds was on guard near the nest. We did not enjoy attacking these birds, but our hunger knew no law. They tasted so very good and assisted our recuperation to such an extent that each time we killed one of them we felt a little less remorseful.

May 15 was a great day. We made our hoosh at 7:30 a.m. Then we loaded up the boat and gave her a flying launch down the steep beach into the surf. Heavy rain had fallen in the night and a gusty north-westerly wind was now blowing, with misty showers. The *James Caird* headed to the sea as if anxious to face the battle of the waves once more. We passed through the narrow mouth of the cove with the ugly rocks and waving kelp close on either side, turned to the east, and sailed merrily up the bay as the sun broke through the mists and made the tossing waters sparkle around us. We were a curious-looking party on that bright morning, but we were feeling happy. We even broke into song, and, but for our Robinson Crusoe appearance, a casual observer might have taken us for a picnic party sailing in a Norwegian fiord or one of the beautiful sounds of the west coast of New Zealand. The wind blew fresh and strong, and a small sea broke on the coast as we advanced. The surf was sufficient to have endangered the boat if we had attempted to land where the carcass of the sea-elephant was lying, so we decided to go on to the head of the bay without risking anything, particularly as we were likely to find sea-elephants on the upper beaches. The big creatures have a habit of seeking peaceful quarters protected from the waves. We had hopes, too, of finding penguins. Our expectation as far as the sea-elephants were concerned was not at fault. We heard the roar of the bulls as we neared the head of the bay, and soon afterwards saw the great unwieldy forms of the beasts lying on a shelving beach towards the bay-head. We rounded a high, glacier-worn bluff on the north side, and at 12.30 p.m. we ran the boat ashore on a low beach of sand and pebbles, with tussock growing above high-water mark. There were hundreds of sea-elephants lying about, and our anxieties with regard to food disappeared. Meat and blubber enough to feed our party for years was in sight. Our landing-place was about a mile and a half west of the north-east corner of the bay. Just east of us was a glacier-snout ending on the beach but giving a passage towards the head of the bay, except at high water or when a very heavy surf was running. A cold, drizzling rain had begun to fall, and we provided ourselves with shelter as quickly as possible. We hauled the *James Caird* up above high-water mark and turned her over just to the lee or east side of the bluff. The spot was separated from the mountain-side by a low morainic bank, rising twenty or thirty feet above sea-level. Soon we had converted the boat into a very comfortable cabin *à la* Peggotty, turfing it round with tussocks, which we dug up with knives. One side of the *James Caird* rested on stones so as to afford a low entrance, and when we had finished she looked as though she had grown there. McCarthy entered into this work with great spirit. A sea-elephant provided us with fuel and meat, and that evening found a well-fed and fairly contented party at rest in Peggotty Camp.

Our camp, as I have said, lay on the north side of King Haakon Bay near the head. Our path towards the whaling-stations led round the seaward end of the snouted glacier on the east side of the camp and up a snow-slope that appeared to lead to a pass in the great Allardyce Range, which runs northwest and south-east and forms the main backbone of South Georgia. The range dipped opposite the bay into a well-defined pass from east to west. An ice-sheet covered most of the interior, filling the valleys and disguising the configuration of the land, which, indeed, showed only in big rocky ridges, peaks, and nunataks. When we looked up the pass from Peggotty Camp the country to the left appeared to offer two easy paths through to the opposite coast, but we knew that the island was uninhabited at that point (Possession Bay). We had to turn our attention farther east, and it was impossible from the camp to learn much of the conditions that would confront us on the overland journey. I planned to climb to the pass and then be guided by the configuration of the country in the selection of a route eastward to Stromness Bay, where the whaling-stations were established in the minor bays, Leith, Husvik, and Stromness. A range of mountains with precipitous slopes, forbidding peaks, and large glaciers lay immediately to the south of King Haakon Bay and seemed to form a continuation of the main range. Between this secondary range and the pass above our camp a great snow-upland sloped up to the inland ice-sheet and reached a rocky ridge that stretched athwart our path and seemed to bar the way. This ridge was a right-angled offshoot from the main ridge. Its chief features were four rocky peaks with spaces between that looked from a distance as though they might prove to be passes.

The weather was bad on Tuesday, May 16, and we stayed under the boat nearly all day. The quarters were cramped but gave full protection from the weather, and we regarded our little cabin with a great deal of satisfaction. Abundant meals of sea-elephant steak and liver increased our contentment. McNeish reported during the day that he had seen rats feeding on the scraps, but this interesting statement was not verified. One would not expect to find rats at such a spot, but there was a bare possibility that they had landed from a wreck and managed to survive the very rigorous conditions.

A fresh west-south-westerly breeze was blowing on the following morning (Wednesday, May 17), with misty squalls, sleet, and rain. I took Worsley with me on a pioneer journey to the west with the object of examining the country to be traversed at the beginning of the overland journey. We went round the seaward end of the snouted glacier, and after tramping about a mile over stony ground and snow-coated debris, we crossed some big ridges of scree and moraines. We found that there was good going for a sledge as far as the north-east corner of the bay, but did not get much information regarding the conditions farther on owing to the view becoming obscured by a snow-squall. We waited a quarter of an hour for the weather to clear but were forced to turn back without having seen more of the country. I had satisfied myself, however, that we could reach a good snow-slope leading apparently to the in-

land ice. Worsley reckoned from the chart that the distance from our camp to
Husvik, on an east magnetic course, was seventeen geographical miles, but we
could not expect to follow a direct line. The carpenter started making a sledge
for use on the overland journey. The materials at his disposal were limited in
quantity and scarcely suitable in quality.

We overhauled our gear on Thursday, May 18, and hauled our sledge
to the lower edge of the snouted glacier. The vehicle proved heavy and cum-
brous. We had to lift it empty over bare patches of rock along the shore, and I
realized that it would be too heavy for three men to manage amid the snow-
plains, glaciers, and peaks of the interior. Worsley and Crean were coming with
me, and after consultation we decided to leave the sleeping-bags behind us and
make the journey in very light marching order. We would take three days' provisions for each man in the form of sledging ration and biscuit. The food was
to be packed in three socks, so that each member of the party could carry his
own supply. Then we were to take the Primus lamp filled with oil, the small
cooker, the carpenter's adze (for use as an ice-axe), and the alpine rope, which
made a total length of fifty feet when knotted. We might have to lower ourselves down steep slopes or cross crevassed glaciers. The filled lamp would provide six hot meals, which would consist of sledging ration boiled up with biscuit. There were two boxes of matches left, one full and the other partially
used. We left the full box with the men at the camp and took the second box,
which contained forty-eight matches. I was unfortunate as regarded footgear,
since I had given away my heavy Burberry boots on the floe, and had now a
comparatively light pair in poor condition. The carpenter assisted me by
putting several screws in the sole of each boot with the object of providing a
grip on the ice. The screws came out of the *James Caird*.

We turned in early that night, but sleep did not come to me. My mind
was busy with the task of the following day. The weather was clear and the outlook for an early start in the morning was good. We were going to leave a weak
party behind us in the camp. Vincent was still in the same condition, and he
could not march. McNeish was pretty well broken up. The two men were not
capable of managing for themselves and McCarthy must stay to look after
them. He might have a difficult task if we failed to reach the whaling-station.
The distance to Husvik, according to the chart, was no more than seventeen
geographical miles in a direct line, but we had very scanty knowledge of the
conditions of the interior. No man had ever penetrated a mile from the coast
of South Georgia at any point, and the whalers I knew regarded the country as
inaccessible. During that day, while we were walking to the snouted glacier, we
had seen three wild duck flying towards the head of the bay from the eastward.

I hoped that the presence of these birds indicated tussock-land and not snow-fields and glaciers in the interior, but the hope was not a very bright one.

We turned out at 2 a.m. on the Friday morning and had our hoosh ready an hour later. The full moon was shining in a practically cloudless sky, its rays reflected gloriously from the pinnacles and crevassed ice of the adjacent glaciers. The huge peaks of the mountains stood in bold relief against the sky and threw dark shadows on the waters of the sound. There was no need for delay, and we made a start as soon as we had eaten our meal. McNeish walked about 200 yds. with us; he could do no more. Then we said good-bye and he turned back to the camp. The first task was to get round the edge of the snouted glacier, which had points like fingers projecting towards the sea. The waves were reaching the points of these fingers, and we had to rush from one recess to another when the waters receded. We soon reached the east side of the glacier and noticed its great activity at this point. Changes had occurred within the preceding twenty-four hours. Some huge pieces had broken off, and the masses of mud and stone that were being driven before the advancing ice showed movement. The glacier was like a gigantic plough driving irresistibly towards the sea.

Lying on the beach beyond the glacier was wreckage that told of many ill-fated ships. We noticed stanchions of teak-wood, liberally carved, that must have come from ships of the older type; iron-bound timbers with the iron almost rusted through; battered barrels and all the usual debris of the ocean. We had difficulties and anxieties of our own, but as we passed that graveyard of the sea we thought of the many tragedies written in the wave-worn fragments of lost vessels. We did not pause, and soon we were ascending a snow-slope, heading due east on the last lap of our long trail.

The snow-surface was disappointing. Two days before we had been able to move rapidly on hard, packed snow; now we sank over our ankles at each step and progress was slow. After two hours' steady climbing we were 2500 ft. above sea-level. The weather continued fine and calm, and as the ridges drew nearer and the western coast of the island spread out below, the bright moonlight showed us that the interior was broken tremendously. High peaks, impassable cliffs, steep snow-slopes, and sharply descending glaciers were prominent features in all directions, with stretches of snow-plain overlaying the ice-sheet of the interior. The slope we were ascending mounted to a ridge and our course lay direct to the top. The moon, which proved a good friend during this journey, threw a long shadow at one point and told us that the surface was broken in our path. Warned in time, we avoided a huge hole capable of swallowing an army. The bay was now about three miles away, and the continued roaring of a big glacier at the head of the bay came to our ears. This glacier, which we had noticed during the stay at Peggotty Camp, seemed to be calving almost continuously.

I had hoped to get a view of the country ahead of us from the top of the slope, but as the surface became more level beneath our feet, a thick fog drifted down. The moon became obscured and produced a diffused light that was more trying than darkness, since it illuminated the fog without guiding our steps. We roped ourselves together as a precaution against holes, crevasses, and precipices, and I broke trail through the soft snow. With almost the full length of the rope between myself and the last man we were able to steer an approximately straight course, since, if I veered to the right or the left when marching into the blank wall of the fog, the last man on the rope could shout a direction. So, like a ship with its "port," "starboard," "steady," we tramped through the fog for the next two hours.

Then, as daylight came, the fog thinned and lifted, and from an elevation of about 3000 ft. we looked down on what seemed to be a huge frozen lake with its farther shores still obscured by the fog. We halted there to eat a bit of biscuit while we discussed whether we would go down and cross the flat surface of the lake, or keep on the ridge we had already reached. I decided to go down, since the lake lay on our course. After an hour of comparatively easy travel through the snow we noticed the thin beginnings of crevasses. Soon they were increasing in size and showing fractures, indicating that we were travelling on a glacier. As the daylight brightened the fog dissipated; the lake could be seen more clearly, but still we could not discover its east shore. A little later the fog lifted completely, an then we saw that our lake stretched to the horizon, and realized suddenly that we were looking down upon the open sea on the east coast of the island. The slight pulsation at the shore showed that the sea was not even frozen; it was the bad light that had deceived us. Evidently we were at the top of Possession Bay, and the island at that point could not be more than five miles across from the head of King Haakon Bay. Our rough chart was inaccurate. There was nothing for it but to start up the glacier again. That was about seven o'clock in the morning, and by nine o'clock we had more than recovered our lost ground. We regained the ridge and then struck south-east, for the chart showed that two more bays indented the coast before Stromness. It was comforting to realize that we would have the eastern water in sight during our journey, although we could see there was no way around the shoreline owing to steep cliffs and glaciers. Men lived in houses lit by electric light on the east coast. News of the outside world waited us there, and, above all, the east coast meant for us the means of rescuing the twenty-two men we had left on Elephant Island.

The Devil's Thumb

BY JON KRAKAUER

J on Krakauer's name has been more or less a permanent fixture on best-seller lists during the recent years, thanks to two remarkable books that deserve both the respect and the numbers of readers they have earned. *Into the Wild* is the story of a young man's odyssey to the wilds of Alaska turning into tragedy, and *Into Thin Air* is Krakauer's dramatic account of surviving the Everest expedition that claimed six lives in 1997.

Another book that takes the Krakauer flag to the summit of excellent prose is his collection of climbing adventures titled *Eiger Dreams,* published by The Lyons Press. These are mountaineering stories of hardships and victories on the world's most difficult peaks, all told with great skill and firsthand experience.

In this vivid selection, Krakauer sets out on an extremely dangerous solo climb of Alaska's notorious Devil's Thumb. He was twenty-three years old at the time, 1977, and today there is no doubt that he looks back on the experience as one he was fortunate to survive.

★　★　★　★　★

By the time I reached the interstate I was having trouble keeping my eyes open. I'd been okay on the twisting two-lane blacktop between Fort Collins and Laramie, but when the Pontiac eased onto the smooth, unswerving pavement of I-80, the soporific hiss of the tires began to gnaw at my wakefulness like ants in a dead tree.

That afternoon, after nine hours of humping 2 × 10s and pounding recalcitrant nails, I'd told my boss I was quitting: "No, not in a couple of weeks, Steve; right now was more like what I had in mind." It took me three more hours to clear my tools and other belongings out of the rust-stained construction trailer that had served as my home in Boulder. I loaded everything into the car, drove up Pearl Street to Tom's Tavern, and downed a ceremonial beer. Then I was gone.

At 1 a.m., thirty miles east of Rawlins, the strain of the day caught up to me. The euphoria that had flowed so freely in the wake of my quick escape gave way to overpowering fatigue; suddenly I felt tired to the bone. The highway stretched straight and empty to the horizon and beyond. Outside the car the night air was cold, and the stark Wyoming plains glowed in the moonlight like Rousseau's painting of the sleeping gypsy. I wanted very badly just then to be that gypsy, conked out of my back beneath the stars. I shut my eyes—just for a second, but it was a second of bliss. It seemed to revive me, if only briefly. The Pontiac, a sturdy behemoth from the Eisenhower years, floated down the road on its long-gone shocks like a raft on an ocean swell. The lights of an oil rig twinkled reassuringly in the distance. I closed my eyes a second time, and kept them closed a few moments longer. The sensation was sweeter than sex.

A few minutes later I let my eyelids fall again. I'm not sure how long I nodded off this time—it might have been for five seconds, it might have been for thirty—but when I awoke it was to the rude sensation of the Pontiac bucking violently along the dirt shoulder at seventy miles per hour. By all rights, the car should have sailed off into the rabbitbrush and rolled. The rear wheels fishtailed wildly six or seven times, but I eventually managed to guide the unruly machine back onto the pavement without so much as blowing a tire, and let it coast gradually to a stop. I loosened my death grip on the wheel, took several deep breaths to quiet the pounding in my chest, then slipped the shifter back into drive and continued down the highway.

Pulling over to sleep would have been the sensible thing to do, but I was on my way to Alaska to change my life, and patience was a concept well beyond my twenty-three-year-old ken.

Sixteen months earlier I'd graduated from college with little distinction and even less in the way of marketable skills. In the interim an off-again, on-again four-year relationship—the first serious romance of my life—had come to a messy, long-overdue end; nearly a year later, my love life and still zip. To support myself I worked on a house-framing crew, grunting under crippling loads of plywood, counting the minutes until the next coffee break, scratching in vain at the sawdust stuck *in perpetuum* to the sweat on the back of my neck. Somehow, blighting the Colorado landscape with condominiums and tract houses for three-fifty an hour wasn't the sort of career I'd dreamed of as a boy.

Late one evening I was mulling all this over on a barstool at Tom's, picking unhappily at my existential scabs, when an idea came to me, a scheme for righting what was wrong in my life. It was wonderfully uncomplicated, and the more I thought about it, the better the plan sounded. By the bottom of the pitcher its merits seemed unassailable. The plan consisted, in its entirety, of climbing a mountain in Alaska called the Devils Thumb.

The Devils Thumb is a prong of exfoliated diorite that presents an imposing profile from any point of the compass, but especially so from the north: its great north wall, which had never been climbed, rises sheer and clean for six thousand vertical feet from the glacier at its base. Twice the height of Yosemite's El Capitan, the north face of the Thumb is one of the biggest granitic walls on the continent; it may well be one of the biggest in the world. I would go to Alaska, ski across the Stikine Icecap to the Devils Thumb, and make the first ascent of its notorious nordwand. It seemed, midway through the second pitcher, like a particularly good idea to do all of this solo.

Writing these words more than a dozen years later, it's no longer entirely clear just *how* I thought soloing the Devils Thumb would transform my life. It had something to do with the fact that climbing was the first and only thing I'd ever been good at. My reasoning, such as it was, was fueled by the scattershot passions of youth, and a literary diet overly rich in the works of Nietzsche, Kerouac, and John Menlove Edwards—the latter a deeply troubled writer/psychiatrist who, before putting an end to his life with a cyanide capsule in 1958, had been one of the preeminent British rock climbers of the day.

Dr. Edwards regarded climbing as a "psycho-neurotic tendency" rather than sport; he climbed not for fun but to find refuge from the inner torment that characterized his existence. I remember, that spring of 1977, being especially taken by a passage from an Edwards short story titled "Letter From a Man":

So, as you would imagine, I grew up exuberant in body but with a nervy, craving mind. It was wanting something more, something tangible. It sought for reality intensely, always if it were not there . . .

But you see at once what I do. I climb.

To one enamored of this sort of prose, the Thumb beckoned like a beacon. My belief in the plan became unshakeable. I was dimly aware that I might be getting in over my head, but if I could somehow get to the top of the Devils Thumb, I was convinced, everything that followed would turn out all right. And thus did I push the accelerator a little closer to the floor and, buoyed by the jolt of adrenaline that followed the Pontiac's brush with destruction, speed west into the night.

You can't actually get very close to the Devils Thumb by car. The peak stands in the Boundary Ranges on the Alaska-British Columbia border, not far from the fishing village of Petersburg, a place accessible only by boat or plane. There is regular jet service to Petersburg, but the sum of my liquid assets amounted to the Pontiac and two hundred dollars in cash, not even enough for oneway airfare, so I took the car as far as Gig Harbor, Washington, then hitched a ride on a northbound seine boat that was short on crew. Five days out, when the Ocean Queen pulled into Petersburg to take on fuel and water, I jumped ship, shouldered my backpack, and walked down the dock in a steady Alaskan rain.

Back in Boulder, without exception, every person with whom I'd shared my plans about the Thumb had been blunt and to the point: I'd been smoking too much pot, they said; it was a monumentally bad idea. I was grossly overestimating my abilities as a climber, I'd never be able to hack a month completely by myself, I would fall into a crevasse and die.

The residents of Petersburg reacted differently. Being Alaskans, they were accustomed to people with screwball ideas; a sizeable percentage of the state's population, after all, was sitting on half-baked schemes to mine uranium in the Brooks Range, or sell icebergs to the Japanese, or market mail-order moose droppings. Most of the Alaskans I met, if they reacted at all, simply asked how much money there was in climbing a mountain like the Devils Thumb.

In any case, one of the appealing things about climbing the Thumb— and one of the appealing things about the sport of mountain climbing in general—was that it didn't matter a rat's ass what anyone else thought. Getting the scheme off the ground didn't hinge on winning the approval of some personnel director, admissions committee, licensing board, or panel of stern-faced judges; if I felt like taking a shot at some unclimbed alpine wall, all I had to do was get myself to the foot of the mountain and start swinging my ice axes.

Petersburg sits on an island, the Devils Thumb rises from the mainland. To get myself to the foot of the Thumb it was first necessary to cross twenty-five miles of salt water. For most of a day I walked the docks, trying without success to hire a boat to ferry me across Frederick Sound. Then I bumped into Bart and Benjamin.

Bart and Benjamin were ponytailed constituents of a Woodstock Nation tree-planting collective called the Hodads. We struck up a conversation. I mentioned that I, too, had once worked as a tree planter. The Hodads allowed that they had chartered a floatplane to fly them to their camp on the mainland the next morning. "It's your lucky day, kid," Bart told me. "For twenty bucks you can ride over with us. Get you to your fuckin' mountain in style." On May 3, a day and a half after arriving in Petersburg, I stepped off the Hodads' Cessna, waded onto the tidal flats at the head of Thomas Bay, and began the long trudge inland.

The Devils Thumb pokes up out of the Stikine Icecap, an immense, labyrinthine network of glaciers that hugs the crest of the Alaskan panhandle like an octopus, with myriad tentacles that snake down, down to the sea from the craggy uplands along the Canadian frontier. In putting ashore at Thomas Bay I was gambling that one of these frozen arms, the Baird Glacier, would lead me safely to the bottom of the Thumb, thirty miles distant.

An hour of gravel beach led to the tortured blue tongue of the Baird. A logger in Petersburg had suggested I keep an eye out for grizzlies along this stretch of shore. "Them bears over there is just waking up this time of year," he smiled. "Tend to be kinda cantankerous after not eatin' all winter. But you keep your gun handy, you shouldn't have no problem." Problem was, I didn't have a gun. As it turned out, my only encounter with hostile wildlife involved a flock of gulls who dive-bombed my head with Hitchockian fury. Between the avian assault and my ursine anxiety, it was with no small amount of relief that I turned my back to the beach, donned crampons, and scrambled up onto the glacier's broad, lifeless snout.

After three or four miles I came to the snow line, where I exchanged crampons for skis. Putting the boards on my feet cut fifteen pounds from the awful load on my back and made the going much faster besides. But now that the ice was covered with snow, many of the glacier's crevasses were hidden, making solitary travel extremely dangerous.

In Seattle, anticipating this hazard, I'd stopped at a hardware store and purchased a pair of stout aluminum curtain rods, each ten feet long. Upon reaching the snowline, I lashed the rods together at right angles, then strapped the arrangement to the hip belt on my backpack so the poles extended horizontally over the snow. Staggering slowly up the glacier with my overloaded backpack, bearing the queer tin cross, I felt like some kind of strange *Penitente*. Were I to break through the veneer of snow over a hidden crevasse, though, the curtain rods would—I hoped mightily—span the slot and keep me from dropping into the chilly bowels of the Baird.

The first climbers to venture onto the Stikine Icecap were Bestor Robinson and Fritz Wiessner, the legendary German-American alpinist, who spent a stormy month in the Boundary Ranges in 1937 but failed to reach any major summits. Wiessner returned in 1946 with Donald Brown and Fred Beckey to attempt the Devils Thumb, the nastiest looking peak in the Stikine. On that trip Fritz mangled a knee during a fall on the hike in and limped home in disgust, but Beckey went back that same summer with Bob Craig and Cliff Schmidtke. On August 25, after several aborted tries and some exceedingly hairy climbing on the peak's east ridge, Beckey and company sat on the

Thumb's wafer-thin summit tower in a tired, giddy daze. It was far and away the most technical ascent ever done in Alaska, an important milestone in the history of American mountaineering.

In the ensuing decades three other teams also made it to the top of the Thumb, but all steered clear of the big north face. Reading accounts of these expeditions, I had wondered why none of them had approached the peak by what appeared, from the map at least, to be the easiest and most logical route, the Baird. I wondered a little less after coming across an article by Beckey in which the distinguished mountaineer cautioned, "Long, steep icefalls block the route from the Baird Glacier to the icecap near Devils Thumb," but after studying aerial photographs I decided that Beckey was mistaken, that the ice-falls weren't so big or so bad. The Baird, I was certain, really was the best way to reach the mountain.

For two days I slogged steadily up the glacier without incident, congratulating myself for discovering such a clever path to the Thumb. On the third day, I arrived beneath the Stikine Icecap proper, where the long arm of the Baird joins the main body of ice. Here, the glacier spills abruptly over the edge of a high plateau, dropping seaward through the gap between two peaks in a phantasmagoria of shattered ice. Seeing the icefall in the flesh left a different impression than the photos had. As I stared at the tumult from a mile away, for the first time since leaving Colorado the thought crossed my mind that maybe this Devils Thumb trip wasn't the best idea I'd ever had.

The icefall was a maze of crevasses and teetering seracs. From afar it brought to mind a bad train wreck, as if scores of ghostly white boxcars had derailed at the lip of the icecap and tumbled down the slope willy-nilly. The closer I got, the more unpleasant it looked. My ten-foot curtain rods seemed a poor defense against crevasses that were forty feet across and two hundred fifty feet deep. Before I could finish figuring out a course through the icefall, the wind came up and snow began to slant hard out of the clouds, stinging my face and reducing visibility to almost nothing.

In my impetuosity, I decided to carry on anyway. For the better part of the day I groped blindly through the labyrinth in the whiteout, retracing my steps from one dead end to another. Time after time I'd think I'd found a way out, only to wind up in a deep blue cul de sac, or stranded atop a detached pil-lar of ice. My efforts were lent a sense of urgency by the noises emanating un-derfoot. A madrigal of creaks and sharp reports—the sort of protests a large fir limb makes when it's slowly bent to the breaking point—severed as a reminder that it is the nature of glaciers to move, the habit of seracs to topple.

As much as I feared being flattened by a wall of collapsing ice, I was even more afraid of falling into a crevasse, a fear that intensified when I put a foot through a snow bridge over a slot so deep I couldn't see the bottom of it. A little later I broke through another bridge to my waist; the poles kept me out of the hundred-foot hole, but after I extricated myself I was bent double with dry heaves thinking about what it would be like to be lying in a pile at the bottom of the crevasse, waiting for death to come, with nobody even aware of how or where I'd met my end.

Night had nearly fallen by the time I emerged from the top of the serac slope onto the empty, wind-scoured expanse of the high glacial plateau. In shock and chilled to the core, I skied far enough past the icefall to put its rumblings out of earshot, pitched the tent, crawled into my sleeping bag, and shivered myself to a fitful sleep.

Although my plan to climb the Devils Thumb wasn't fully hatched until the spring of 1977, the mountain had been lurking in the recesses of my mind for about fifteen years—since April 12, 1962, to be exact. The occasion was my eighth birthday. When it came time to open birthday presents, my parents announced that they were offering me a choice of gifts: According to my wishes, they would either escort me to the new Seattle World's Fair to ride the Monorail and see the Space Needle, or give me an introductory taste of mountain climbing by taking me up the third highest peak in Oregon, a long-dormant volcano called the South Sister that, on clear days, was visible from my bedroom window. It was a tough call. I thought the matter over at length, then settled on the climb.

To prepare me for the rigors of the ascent, my father handed over a copy of *Mountaineering: The Freedom of the Hills,* the leading how-to manual of the day, a thick tome that weighed only slightly less than a bowling ball. Thenceforth I spent most of my waking hours poring over its pages, memorizing the intricacies of pitoncraft and bolt placement, the shoulder stand and the tension traverse. None of which, as it happened, was of any use of my inaugural ascent, for the South Sister turned out to be a decidedly less than extreme climb that demanded nothing more in the way of technical skill than energetic walking, and was in fact ascended by hundreds of farmers, house pets, and small children every summer.

Which is not to suggest that my parents and I conquered the mighty volcano: From the pages and pages of perilous situations depicted in *Mountaineering: The Freedom of the Hills,* I had concluded that climbing was a life-and-death matter, always. Halfway up the South Sister I suddenly remembered this. In the middle of a twenty-degree snow slope that would be impossible to fall from if you tried, I decided that I was in mortal jeopardy and burst into tears, bring the ascent to a halt.

Perversely, after the South Sister debacle my interest in climbing only intensified. I resumed my obsessive studies of *Mountaineering*. There was something about the scariness of the activities portrayed in those pages that just wouldn't leave me alone. In addition to the scores of line drawings—most of them cartoons of a little man in a jaunty Tyrolean cap—employed to illustrate arcana like the bootaxe belay and the Bilgeri rescue, the book contained sixteen black-and-while plates of notable peaks in the Pacific Northwest and Alaska. All the photographs were striking, but the one on page 147 was much, much more than that: it made my skin crawl. An aerial photo by glaciologist Maynard Miller, it showed a singularly sinister tower of ice-plastered black rock. There wasn't a place on the entire mountain that looked safe or secure; I couldn't imagine anyone climbing it. At the bottom of the page the mountain was identified as the Devils Thumb.

From the first time I saw it, the picture—a portrait of the Thumb's north wall—held an almost pornographic fascination for me. On hundreds—no, make that thousands—of occasions over the decade and a half that followed I took my copy of *Mountaineering* down from the shelf, opened it to page 147, and quietly stared. How would it feel, I wondered over and over, to be on that thumbnail-thin summit ridge, worrying over the storm clouds building on the horizon, hunched against the wind and dunning cold, contemplating the horrible drop on either side? How could anyone keep it together? Would I, if I found myself high on the north wall, clinging to that frozen rock, even attempt to keep it together? Or would I simply decide to surrender to the inevitable straight away, and jump?

I had planned on spending between three weeks and a month on the Stikine Icecap. Not relishing the prospect of carrying a four-week load of food, heavy winter camping gear, and a small mountain of climbing hardware all the way up the Baird on my back, before leaving Petersburg I paid a bush pilot a hundred and fifty dollars—the last of my cash—to have six cardboard cartons of supplies dropped from an airplane when I reached the foot of the Thumb. I showed the pilot exactly where, on his map, I intended to be, and told him to give me three days to get there; he promised to fly over and make the drop as soon thereafter as the weather permitted.

On May 6 I set up a base camp on the Icecap just northeast of the Thumb and waited for the airdrop. For the next four days it snowed, nixing any chance for a flight. Too terrified of crevasses to wander far from camp, I occasionally went out for a short ski to kill time, but mostly I lay silently in the tent—the ceiling was too low to sit upright—with my thoughts, fighting a rising chorus of doubts.

As the days passed, I grew increasingly anxious. I had no radio, nor any other means of communicating with the outside world. It had been many years since anyone had visited this part of the Stikine Icecap, and many more would likely pass before anyone did so again. I was nearly out of stove fuel, and down to a single chunk of cheese, my last package of ramen noodles, and half a box of Cocoa Puffs. This, I figured, could sustain me for three or four more days if need be, but then what would I do? It would only take two days to ski back down the Baird to Thomas Bay, but then a week or more might easily pass before a fisherman happened by who could give me a lift back to Petersburg (the Hodads with whom I'd ridden over were camped fifteen miles down the impassable, headland-studded coast, and could be reached only by boat or plane).

When I went to bed on the evening of May 10 it was still snowing and blowing hard. I was going back and forth on whether to head for the coast in the morning or stick it out on the icecap, gambling that the pilot would show before I starved or died of thirst, when, just for a moment, I heard a faint whine, like a mosquito. I tore open the tent door. Most of the clouds had lifted, but there was no airplane in sight. The whine returned, louder this time. Then I saw it: a tiny red-and-white speck, high in the western sky, droning my way.

A few minutes later the plane passed directly overhead. The pilot, however, was unaccustomed to glacier flying and he'd badly misjudged the scale of the terrain. Worried about winding up too low and getting nailed by unexpected turbulence, he flew a good thousand feet above me—believing all the while he was just off the deck—and never saw my tent in the flat evening light. My waving and screaming were to no avail; from that altitude I was indistinguishable from a pile of rocks. For the next hour he circled the icecap, scanning its barren contours without success. But the pilot, to his credit, appreciated the gravity of my predicament and didn't give up. Frantic, I tied my sleeping bag to the end of one of the crevasse poles and waved it for all I was worth. When the plane banked sharply and began to fly straight at me, I felt tears of joy well in my eyes.

The pilot buzzed my tent three times in quick succession, dropping two boxes on each pass, then the airplane disappeared over a ridge and I was alone. As silence again settled over the glacier I felt abandoned, vulnerable, lost. I realized that I was sobbing. Embarrassed, I halted the blubbering by screaming obscenities until I grew hoarse.

I awoke early on May 11 to clear skies and the relatively warm temperature of twenty degrees Fahrenheit. Startled by the good weather, mentally unprepared to commence the actual climb, I hurriedly packed up a rucksack nonetheless, and began skiing toward the base of the Thumb. Two previous Alaskan expeditions had taught me that, ready or not, you simply can't afford to waste a day of perfect weather if you expect to get up anything.

A small hanging glacier extends out from the lip of the icecap, leading up and across the north face of the Thumb like a catwalk. My plan was to follow this catwalk to a prominent rock prow in the center of the wall, and thereby execute an end run around the ugly, avalanche-swept lower half of the face.

The catwalk turned out to be a series of fifty-degree ice fields blanketed with knee-deep powder snow and riddled with crevasses. The depth of the snow made the going slow and exhausting; by the time I front-pointed up the overhanging wall of the uppermost *bergschrund,* some three or four hours after leaving camp, I was whipped. And I hadn't even gotten to the "real" climbing yet. That would begin immediately above, where the hanging glacier gave way to vertical rock.

The rock, exhibiting a dearth of holds and coated with six inches of crumbly rime, did not look promising, but just left of the main prow was an inside corner—what climbers call an open book—glazed with frozen melt water. This ribbon of ice led straight up for two or three hundred feet, and if the ice proved substantial enough to support the picks of my ice axes, the line might go. I hacked out a small platform in the snow slope, the last flat ground I expected to feel underfoot for some time, and stopped to eat a candy bar and collect my thoughts. Fifteen minutes later I shouldered my pack and inched over to the bottom of the corner. Gingerly, I swung my right axe into the two-inch-thick ice. It was solid, plastic—a little thinner than I would have liked but otherwise perfect. I was on my way.

The climbing was steep and spectacular, so exposed it made my head spin. Beneath my boot soles, the wall fell away for three thousand feet to the dirty, avalanche-scarred cirque of the Witches Cauldron Glacier. Above, the prow soared with authority toward the summit ridge, a vertical half-mile above. Each time I planted one of my ice axes, that distance shrank by another twenty inches.

The higher I climbed, the more comfortable I became. All that held me to the mountainside, all that held me to the world, were six thin spikes of chrome-molybdenum stuck half an inch into a smear of frozen water, yet I began to feel invincible, weightless, like those lizards that live on the ceilings of cheap Mexican hotels. Early on a difficult climb, especially a difficult solo climb, you're hyperaware of the abyss pulling at your back. You constantly feel its call, its immense hunger. To resist takes a tremendous conscious effort; you don't dare let your guard down for an instant. The siren song of the void puts you on edge, it makes your movements tentative, clumsy, herky-jerky. But as the climb goes on, you grow accustomed to the exposure, you get used to rubbing shoulders with doom, you come to believe in the reliability of your hands and feet and head. You learn to trust your self-control.

By and by, your attention becomes so intensely focused that you no longer notice the raw knuckles, the cramping thighs, the strain of maintaining nonstop concentration. A trance-like state settles over your efforts, the climb becomes a clear-eyed dream. Hours slide by like minutes. The accrued guilt and clutter of day-to-day existence—the lapses of conscience, the unpaid bills, the bungled opportunities, the dust under the couch, the festering familial sores, the inescapable prison of your genes—all of it is temporarily forgotten, crowded from your thoughts by an overpowering clarity of purpose, and by the seriousness of the task at hand.

At such moments, something like happiness actually stirs in your chest, but it isn't the sort of emotion you want to lean on very hard. In solo climbing, the whole enterprise is held together with little more than chutzpa, not the most reliable adhesive. Late in the day on the north face of the Thumb, I felt the glue disintegrate with a single swing of an ice axe.

I'd gained nearly seven hundred feet of altitude since stepping off the hanging glacier, all of it on crampon front-points and the picks of my axes. The ribbon of frozen melt water had ended three hundred feet up, and was followed by a crumbly armor of frost feathers. Though just barely substantial enough to support body weight, the rime was plastered over the rock to a thickness of two or three feet, so I kept plugging upward. The wall, however, had been growing imperceptibly steeper, and as it did so the frost feathers became thinner. I'd fallen into a slow, hypnotic rhythm—swing, swing; kick, kick; swing, swing; kick, kick—when my left ice axe slammed into a slab of diorite a few inches beneath the rime.

I tried left, then right, but kept striking rock. The frost feathers holding me up, it became apparent, were maybe five inches thick and had the structural integrity of stale cornbread. Below was thirty-seven hundred feet of air, and I was balanced atop a house of cards. Waves of panic rose in my throat. My eyesight blurred, I began to hyperventilate, my calves started to vibrate. I shuffled a few feet farther to the right, hoping to find thicker ice, but managed only to bend an ice axe on the rock.

Awkwardly, stiff with fear, I started working my way back down. The rime gradually thickened, and after descending about eighty feet I got back on reasonably solid ground. I stopped for a long time to let my nerves settle, then leaned back from my tools and stared up at the face above, searching for a hint of solid ice, for some variation in the underlying rock strata, for anything that would allow passage over the frosted slabs. I looked until my neck ached, but nothing appeared. The climb was over. The only place to go was down.

Heavy snow and incessant winds kept me inside the tent for most of the next three days. The hours passed slowly. In the attempt to hurry them along I chain-smoked for as long as my supply of cigarettes held out, and read. I'd made a number of bad decisions on the trip, there was no getting around it, and one of them concerned the reading matter I'd chosen to pack along: three back issues of the *Village Voice,* and Joan Didion's latest novel, *A Book of Common Prayer.* The *Voice* was amusing enough—there on the icecap, the subject matter took on an edge, a certain sense of the absurd, from which the paper (through no fault of its own) benefited greatly—but in that tent, under those circumstances, Didion's necrotic take on the world hit a little too close to home.

Near the end of *Common Prayer,* one of Didion's characters says to another, "You don't get any real points for staying here, Charlotte." Charlotte replies, "I can't seem to tell what you do get real points for, so I guess I'll stick around here for awhile."

When I ran out of things to read, I was reduced to studying the ripstop pattern woven into the tent ceiling. This I did for hours on end, flat on my back, while engaging in an extended and very heated self-debate: Should I leave for the coast as soon as the wether broke, or stay put long enough to make another attempt on the mountain? In truth, my little escapade on the north face had left me badly shaken, and I didn't want to go up on the Thumb again at all. On the other hand, the thought of returning to Boulder in defeat—of parking the Pontiac behind the trailer, buckling on my tool belt, and going back to the same brain-dead drill I'd so triumphantly walked away from just a month before—that wasn't very appealing, either. Most of all, I couldn't stomach the thought of having to endure the smug expressions of condolence from all the chumps and nimrods who were certain I'd fail right from the get-go.

By the third afternoon of the storm I couldn't stand it any longer: the lumps of frozen snow poking me in the back, the clammy nylon walls brushing against my face, the incredible smell drifting up from the depths of my sleeping bag. I pawed through the mess at my feet until I located a small green stuff sack, in which there was a metal film can containing the makings of what I'd hoped would be a sort of victory cigar. I'd intended to save it for my return from the summit, but what the hey, it wasn't looking like I'd be visiting the top any time soon. I poured most of the can's contents onto a leaf of cigarette paper, rolled it into a crooked, sorry looking joint, and promptly smoked it down to the roach.

The reefer, of course, only made the tent seem even more cramped, more suffocating, more impossible to bear. It also made me terribly hungry. I decided a little oatmeal would put things right. Making it, however, was a long, ridiculously involved process: a potful of snow had to be gathered outside in the tempest, and stove assembled and lit, the oatmeal and sugar located, the remnants of yesterday's dinner scraped from my bowl. I'd gotten the stove going and was melting the snow when I smelled something burning. A thorough check of the stove and its environs revealed nothing. Mystified, I was ready to chalk it up to my chemically enhanced imagination when I heard something crackle directly behind me.

I whirled around in time to see a bag of garbage, into which I'd tossed the match I'd used to light the stove, flare up into a conflagration. Beating on the fire with my hands, I had it out in a few seconds, but not before a large section of the tent's inner wall vaporized before my eyes. The tent's built-in rain-fly escaped the flames, so the shelter was still more or less weatherproof; now, however, it was approximately thirty degrees cooler inside. My left palm began to sting. Examining it, I noticed the pink welt of a burn. What troubled me most, though, was that the tent wasn't even mine—I'd borrowed the shelter from my father. An expensive Early Winters OmnipoTent, it had been brand new before my trip—the hang-tags were still attached—and had been loaned reluctantly. For several minutes I sat dumbstruck, staring at the wreckage of the shelter's once-graceful form amid the acrid scent of singed hair and melted nylon. You had to hand it to me, I thought: I had a real knack for living up to the old man's worst expectations.

The fire sent me into a funk that no drug known to man could have alleviated. By the time I'd finished cooking the oatmeal my mind was made up: the moment the storm was over, I was breaking camp and booking for Thomas Bay.

Twenty-four hours later, I was huddled inside a bivouac sack under the lip of the *bergschrund* on the Thumb's north face. The weather was as bad as I'd seen it. It was snowing hard, probably an inch every hour. Spindrift avalanches hissed down from the wall above and washed over me like surf, completely burying the sack every twenty minutes.

The day had begun well enough. When I emerged from the tent, clouds still clung to the ridge tops but the wind was down and the icecap was speckled with sunbreaks. A patch of sunlight, almost blinding in its brilliance, slid lazily over the camp. I put down a foam sleeping mat and sprawled on the glacier in my long johns. Wallowing in the radiant heat, I felt the gratitude of a prisoner whose sentence has just been commuted.

As I lay there, a narrow chimney that curved up the east half of the Thumb's north face, well to the left of the route I'd tried before the storm, caught my eye. I twisted a telephoto lens onto my camera. Through it I could make out a smear of shiny grey ice—solid, trustworthy, hard-frozen ice—plastered to the back of the cleft. The alignment of the chimney made it impossible to discern if the ice continued in an unbroken line from top to bottom. If it did, the chimney might well provide passage over the rime-covered slabs that had foiled my first attempt. Lying there in the sun, I began to think about how much I'd hate myself a month hence if I threw in the towel after a single try, if I scrapped the whole expedition on account of a little bad weather. Within the hour I had assembled my gear and was skiing toward the base of the wall.

The ice in the chimney did in fact prove to be continuous, but it was very, very thin—just a gossamer film of verglas. Additionally, the cleft was a natural funnel for any debris that happened to slough off the wall; as I scratched my way up the chimney I was hosed by a continuous stream of powder snow, ice chips, and small stones. One hundred twenty feet up the groove the last remnants of my composure flaked away like old plaster, and I turned around.

Instead of descending all the way to base camp, I decided to spend the night in the 'schrund beneath the chimney, on the off chance that my head would be more together the next morning. The fair skies that had ushered in the day, however, turned out to be but a momentary lull in a five-day gale. By midafternoon the storm was back in all its glory, and my bivouac site became a less than pleasant place to hang around. The ledge on which I crouched was continually swept by small spindrift avalanches. Five times my bivvy sack—a thin nylon envelope, shaped exactly like a Baggies brand sandwich bag, only bigger—was buried up to the level of the breathing slit. After digging myself out the fifth time, I decided I'd had enough. I threw all my gear in my pack and made a break for base camp.

The descent was terrifying. Between the clouds, the ground blizzard, and the flat, fading light, I couldn't tell snow from sky, nor whether a slope went up or down. I worried, with ample reason, that I might step blindly off the top of a serac and end up at the bottom of the Witches Cauldron, a half-mile below. When I finally arrived on the frozen plain of the icecap, I found that my tracks had long since drifted over. I didn't have a clue how to locate the tent on the featureless glacial plateau. I skied in circles for an hour or so, hoping I'd get lucky and stumble across camp, until I put a foot into a small crevasse and realized I was acting like an idiot—that I should hunker down right where I was and wait out the storm.

I dug a shallow hole, wrapped myself in the bivvy bag, and sat on my pack in the swirling snow. Drifts piled up around me. My feet became numb. A damp chill crept down my chest from the base of my neck, where spindrift had gotten inside my parka and soaked my shirt. If only I had a cigarette, I thought, a single cigarette, I could summon the strength of character to put a good face on this fucked-up situation, on the whole fucked-up trip. "If we had some ham, we could have ham and eggs, if we had some eggs." I remembered my friend Nate uttering that line in a similar storm, two years before, high on another Alaskan peak, the Mooses Tooth. It had struck me as hilarious at the time; I'd actually laughed out loud. Recalling the line now, it no longer seemed funny. I pulled the bivvy sack tighter around my shoulders. The wind ripped at my back. Beyond shame, I cradled my head in my arms and embarked on an orgy of self-pity.

I knew that people sometimes died climbing mountains. But at the age of twenty-three personal mortality—the idea of my own death—was still largely outside my conceptual grasp; it was as abstract a notion as non-Euclidian geometry or marriage. When I decamped from Boulder in April, 1977, my head swimming with visions of glory and redemption on the Devils Thumb, it didn't occur to me that I might be bound by the same cause-effect relationships that governed the actions of others. I'd never heard of hubris. Because I wanted to climb the mountain so badly, because I had thought about the Thumb so intensely for so long, it seemed beyond the realm of possibility that some minor obstacle like the weather or crevasses or rime-covered rock might ultimately thwart my will.

At sunset the wind died and the ceiling lifted 150 feet off the glacier, enabling me to locate base camp. I made it back to the tent intact, but it was no longer possible to ignore the fact that the Thumb had made hash of my plans. I was forced to acknowledge that volition alone, however powerful, was not going to get me up the north wall. I saw, finally, that nothing was.

There still existed an opportunity for salvaging the expedition, however. A week earlier I'd skied over to the southeast side of the mountain to take a look at the route Fred Beckey had pioneered in 1946—the route by which I'd intended to descend the peak after climbing the north wall. During that reconnaissance I'd noticed an obvious unclimbed line to the left of the Beckey route—a patchy network of ice angling across the southeast face—that struck me as a relatively easy way to achieve the summit. At the time, I'd considered this route unworthy of my attentions. Now, on the rebound from my calamitous entanglement with the nordwand, I was prepared to lower my sights.

On the afternoon of May 15, when the blizzard finally petered out, I returned to the southeast face and climbed to the top of a slender ridge that abutted the upper peak like a flying buttress on a gothic cathedral. I decided to spend the night there, on the airy, knife-edged ridge crest, sixteen hundred feet below the summit. The evening sky was cold and cloudless. I could see all the way to tidewater and beyond. At dusk I watched, transfixed, as the house lights of Petersburg blinked on in the west. The closest thing I'd had to human contact since the airdrop, the distant lights set off a flood of emotion that caught me completely off guard. I imagined people watching the Red Sox on the tube, eating fried chicken in brightly lit kitchens, drinking beer, making love. When I lay down to sleep I was overcome by a soul-wrenching loneliness. I'd never felt so alone, ever.

That night I had troubled dreams, of cops and vampires and a gangland-style execution. I heard someone whisper, "He's in there. As soon as he comes out, waste him." I sat bolt upright and opened my eyes. The sun was about to rise. The entire sky was scarlet. It was still clear, but wisps of high cirrus were streaming in from the southwest, and a dark line was visible just above the horizon. I pulled on my boots and hurriedly strapped on my crampons. Five minutes after waking up, I was front-pointing away from the bivouac.

I carried no rope, no tent or bivouac gear, no hardware save my ice axes. My plan was to go ultralight and ultrafast, to hit the summit and make it back down before the weather turned. Pushing myself, continually out of breath, I scurried up and to the left across small snowfields linked by narrow runnels of verglas and short rock bands. The climbing was almost fun—the rock was covered with large, in-cut holds, and the ice, though thin, never got steep enough to feel extreme—but I was anxious about the bands of clouds racing in from the Pacific, covering the sky.

In what seemed like no time (I didn't have a watch on the trip) I was on the distinctive final ice field. By now the sky was completely overcast. It looked easier to keep angling to the left, but quicker to go straight for the top. Paranoid about being caught by a storm high on the peak without any kind of shelter, I opted for the direct route. The ice steepened, then steepened some more, and as it did so it grew thin. I swung my left ice axe and struck rock. I aimed for another spot, and once again it glanced off unyielding diorite with a dull, sickening clank. And again, and again: It was a reprise of my first attempt on the north face. Looking between my legs, I stole a glance at the glacier, more than two thousand feet below. My stomach churned. I felt my poise slipping away like smoke in the wind.

Forty-five feet above the wall eased back onto the sloping summit shoulder. Forty-five more feet, half the distance between third base and home plate, and the mountain would be mine. I clung stiffly to my axes, unmoving, paralyzed with fear and indecision. I looked down at the dizzying drop to the glacier again, then up, then scraped away the film of ice above my head. I hooked the pick of my left axe on a nickel-thin lip of rock, and weighted it. It held. I pulled my right axe from the ice, reached up, and twisted the pick into a crooked half-inch crack until it jammed. Barely breathing now, I moved my feet up, scrabbling my crampon points across the verglas. Reaching as high as I could with my left arm, I swung the axe gently at the shiny, opaque surface, not knowing what I'd hit beneath it. The pick went in with a heartening *THUNK!* A few minutes later I was standing on a broad, rounded ledge. The summit proper, a series of slender fins sprouting a grotesque meringue of atmospheric ice, stood twenty feet directly above.

The insubstantial frost feathers ensured that those last twenty feet remained hard, scary, onerous. But then, suddenly, there was no place higher to go. It wasn't possible, I couldn't believe it. I felt my cracked lips stretch into a huge, painful grin. I was on top of the Devils Thumb.

Fittingly, the summit was a surreal, malevolent place, an improbably slender fan of rock and rime no wider than a filing cabinet. It did not encourage loitering. As I straddled the highest point, the north face fell away beneath my left boot for six thousand feet beneath my right boot the south face dropped off for twenty-five hundred. I took some pictures to prove I'd been there, and spent a few minutes trying to straighten a bent pick. Then I stood up, carefully turned around, and headed for home.

Five days later I was camped in the rain beside the sea, marveling at the sight of moss, willows, mosquitoes. Two days after that, a small skiff motored into Thomas Bay and pulled up on the beach not far from my tent. The man driving the boat introduced himself as Jim Freeman, a timber faller from Petersburg. It was his day off, he said, and he'd made the trip to show his family the glacier, and to look for bears. He asked me if I'd "been huntin', or what?"

"No," I replied sheepishly. "Actually, I just climbed the Devils Thumb. I've been over here for twenty days."

Freeman kept fiddling with a cleat on the boat, and didn't say anything for a while. Then he looked at me real hard and spat, "You wouldn't be givin' me double talk now, wouldja, friend?" Taken aback, I stammered out a denial. Freeman, it was obvious, didn't believe me for a minute. Nor did he seem wild about my snarled shoulder-length hair or the way I smelled. When I asked if he could give me a lift back to town, however, he offered a grudging, "I don't see why not."

The water was choppy, and the ride across Frederick Sound took two hours. The more we talked, the more Freeman warmed up. He still didn't believe I'd climbed the Thumb, but by the time he steered the skiff into Wrangell Narrows he pretended to. When we got off the boat, he insisted on buying me a cheeseburger. That night he even let me sleep in a derelict step-van parked in his backyard.

I lay down in the rear of the old truck for a while but couldn't sleep, so I got up and walked to a bar called Kito's Kave. The euphoria, the overwhelming sense of relief, that had initially accompanied my return to Petersburg faded, and an unexpected melancholy took its place. The people I chatted with in Kito's didn't seem to doubt that I'd been to the top of the Thumb, they just didn't much care. As the night wore on the place emptied except for me and an Indian at a back table. I drank alone, putting quarters in the jukebox, playing the same five songs over and over, until the barmaid yelled angrily, "Hey! Give it a fucking rest, kid! If I hear 'Fifty Ways to Lose Your Lover' one more time, *I'm* gonna be the one who loses it." I mumbled an apology, quickly headed for the door, and lurched back to Freeman's step-van. There, surrounded by the sweet scent of old motor oil, I lay down on the floorboards next to a gutted transmission and passed out.

It is easy, when you are young, to believe that what you desire is no less than what you deserve, to assume that if you want something badly enough it is your God-given right to have it. Less than a month after sitting on the summit of the Thumb I was back in Boulder, nailing up siding on the Spruce Street Townhouses, the same condos I'd been framing when I left for Alaska. I got a raise, to four dollars an hour, and at the end of the summer moved out of the job-site trailer to a studio apartment on West Pearl, but little else in my life seemed to change. Somehow, it didn't add up to the glorious transformation I'd imagined in April.

Climbing the Devils Thumb, however, had nudged me a little further away from the obdurate innocence of childhood. It taught me something about what mountains can and can't do, about the limits of dreams. I didn't recognize that at the time, of course, but I'm grateful for it now.

About the Editor

Lamar Underwood is a former editor-in-chief of *Sports Afield* and *Outdoor Life* and is presently editorial director of the Outdoor Magazine Group of Harris Publications in New York.

Lamar edited *The Bass Almanac,* published by Nick Lyons and Doubleday in 1978, and is the author of the novel *On Dangerous Ground,* published by Doubleday in 1989 and later in paperback by Berkley. Lamar's novel draws considerably on his experiences as a magazine editor in New York, and his outdoor experiences in Alaska, where he was graduated from Fairbanks High School in 1954, when Alaska was still a territory. Son of a career Army officer who was stationed in Alaska during the Korean War, Lamar has maintained his affection for the Alaska outdoors, visiting there every chance he gets.

Lamar has edited several books for Amwell Press and four published in 2000 by The Lyons Press. They were *The Quotable Soldier, The Greatest Hunting Stories Ever Told, The Greatest Fishing Stories Ever Told,* and *Man Eaters.* This year, in addition to THE GREATEST SURVIVAL STORIES EVER TOLD, The Lyons Press is publishing another anthology edited by Lamar, *The Greatest War Stories Ever Told.*

Permissions Acknowledgments

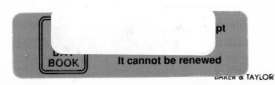